Historic Linwood Cemetery

of

Columbus, Muscogee Co., Georgia

Volume 1

Sections A & B

by

Dolores Autry

Updated and edited by

Lea Lewis Dowd and Carol Johnson

i

CONTENTS

DEDICATION

To Dolores Autry for all of your blood, sweat and tears, without her this never would have been possible. To Carol Johnson who worked until the week before her death to keep filling in the blanks that we had. You were an inspiration to us all and are deeply missed. To my mother and father, Robert Magruder Lewis Jr. and Laura Jeanne Anderson, for their love and support. Lastly, to my sister Laura Lewis Rutland, who started this obcession for me.

Thank you to Kimberly Martz for her wonderful assistance in getting this all typed and put together. Without her assistance, this would have probably taken another five years.

Dear Ancestor
Author Unknown

Your tombstone stands among the rest;
Neglected and alone,
The name and date are chiseled out
On polished marbled stone.
It reaches out to all who care
It is too late to mourn.
You did not know that I exist.
You died and I was born.
Yet each of us are cells of you
In flesh, in blood, in bone.
Our blood contracts and beats a pulse
Entirely not our own
Dear Ancestor, the place you filled
One hundred years ago
Spreads out among the ones you left
Who would have loved you so.
I wonder if you lived and loved,
I wonder if you knew
That someday I would find this spot,
And come to visit you.

INTRODUCTION

This volume is the first to begin reprinting Dolores Autry's original Linwood Cemetery of Columbus, Muscogee Co., Georgia tombstone transcription. We have used the original transcriptions and added to the materials that were presented in the original work. Some references were originally given to Ms. Autry, now deceased. The information has been retained in these volumes because of the genealogical value; however, I cannot provide citations for many of these. The additional information was taken from legal records (i.e. Census, Wills, Deeds, Obituaries and Military Records) as well as original genealogical research. The original transcription book did not always have sources named and some of the material is now unreadable and had to be omitted. The additional material and information added contain citations when available.

In reading this book, you will find numerous spelling errors of the names. We have left original misspellings as written. Due to the additions and subsequent increased length of the new book, we have had to split her original compilation into several volumes. This volume contains the Sections A and B as designated by the original transcriptions.

ABBREVIATIONS USED

- B   born or birth date
- Bur.   Buried
- c/o   child of
- D   Death or death date
- d/o   Daughter of
- Dau(s)   daughter(s)
- Dght(s)   daughter(s)
- DIL   Daughter-in-law
- Exr(s)   Executer(s)
- (f)   female
- Inf   infant
- (m)   male
- M   Married or marriage date
- M1   Marriage 1
- M2   Marriage 2
- MIL   Mother-in-law
- s/o   Son of
- SIL   Son-in-law
- (sic)   printed exactly as shown and is not a transcription error.
- SR   Sexton records
- WB   Will Book
- w/o   wife of
- ww   will written
- wp   will proved

DOLORES HILL AUTRY
1936-1997

Born and raised in Columbus, GA, Dolores was a 1954 graduate of Jordan Vocational High School. Dolores Hill Autry was a loving, devoted wife and mother of three. She was the first uniformed female law enforcement officer in Columbus, GA and served in all three branches of law enforcement prior to her retirement.

She had learned early in life of the murders of her grandmother and great-grandmother and found a passion for genealogy as she researched both of these events. Family history was high in her pursuits of this event and later broadened to other genealogical events. She researched and proved lineal heritage to seventeen Confederate soldiers. It was through this research that she developed a love for Linwood Cemetery. Seeing the neglected condition and understanding the historical importance of Linwood, she organized and became a founding member of the Friends of Linwood Cemetery. This organization evolved into the current Historic Linwood Foundation.

Her Linwood Cemetery book is a great example of her attention to detail, patience and tenacity. Over a period of approximately five years, she mapped the entire cemetery and subdivided it into sections. She walked each section writing down each grave location and all headstone inscriptions. She took that large list of names and researched through microfilmed newspapers, microfiche copies of historical documents, old family bibles when available and any other possible sources of information. All collected information was hand written on index cards and then organized by last names. Additionally, she purposefully included the names of family members listed in obituaries of those interred as an additional resource for those that would be using her index in the future. Of particular interest in her index is her map of the "Old Section" of Linwood. This is the original section of Linwood and had never been documented on previous maps. Burials were not recorded at all in Linwood's Old Cemetery. It wasn't until 1845 that lots were systematically plotted outside the Old Cemetery.

After publication, her book quickly became the definitive source for researching Linwood Cemetery. Copies of her Linwood Cemetery book were given to friends, including Murray Craig who was a friend and major benefactor. The book is also available at Columbus University Library, Columbus Memorial Library, the Russell County Historical Commission and both the Georgia and Alabama archives.

Her other Cemetery reference books included the Girard and Pine Grove cemeteries in Phenix City, AL.

She died in 1997 from a brain aneurysm after three months in intensive care. Her family and many friends still love and miss her very much.

HISTORIC LINWOOD FOUNDATION

Historic Linwood Foundation, Inc. was founded in 1997. It was the result of an effort by the Lizzie Rutherford Chapter of the United Daughters of the Confederacy to form a Friends of Linwood Cemetery in order to focus attention on the care of the historic cemetery, long neglected by the city. The sitting president, Mrs. Donna Stubbs, appointed a committee consisting of Linda Kennedy, Dolores Autry, and Ailene Craig. This committee sent letters to people in the community who was thought to be interested in preserving Linwood Cemetry, inviting them to attend a meeting.

The first public meeting drew so many enthusiastic, concerned citizens that a full blown private, non-profit corporation was established, with eighteen members on its Board of Directors. An Executive Director was hired and work was systematically begun to survey the lots, to restore and repair some sites, and to fulfill its mission. Linwood Cemetery is owned by the city of Columbus, Georgia. The Board quickly developed a Memorandum of Understanding with the city defining the responsibilities of each group, so that the Foundation could restore and maintain the cemetery in cooperation with the City, the Sexton and staff.

The Foundation has continuously expanded its restoration efforts each year, last year being the first time that Stone Faces and Sacred Spaces, a restoration and conservation group, came and repaired monuments. Plans are underway for them to come again and work both on monuments and fences.

HISTORY OF LINWOOD CEMETERY

by Mary Jane Galer

Linwood Cemetery is a place where the past jumps to life among the many unique marble and granite markers that yield the names of those from various cultures who came to this frontier town to stay or intended to pass through to new vistas, only to remain at rest permanently in the cemetery.

Columbus City government began "functioning" four months before the creation of the town. The Georgia General Assembly called for the establishment of a "trading town at the Falls of the Chattahoochee" River. Five appointed Commissioners hired surveyor Edward Lloyd Thomas. Thomas' son, Truman, who was assisting his father, became ill during the survey and died on March 26, 1828. Thomas buried him in the area, which was designated as the town cemetery. The location of Truman's grave is not known.

The earliest marked graves in Linwood are dated 1833, five years after the cemetery was established. This location was called the City Cemetery until 1894 when it was officially designated as Linwood Cemetery. A fashionable suburb known as Linwood, named from a popular novel, Ernest Linwood, by Caroline Lee Hentz, who briefly lived in Columbus, was nearby and the cemetery took on that name. The cemetery reflects the development of Columbus. The simple headstones randomly placed and family plots enclosed by locally crafted iron fences or brick walls containing modest slabs or elaborately carved monuments let visitors read the economic and social history of Columbus in stone.

Burials were not recorded at all in Linwood's Old Cemetery, which was on top of the hill, guarded by the large oak trees. It was not until 1845 that lots were systematically plotted outside the Old Cemetery and a record of sales was first recorded. Cemetery records of burials were not kept in ledgers until 1866. Before that time, the Sexton provided separate lists of burials monthly or quarterly to the Columbus Council. These reports are lost to historians today. Throughout the cemetery, there are many unmarked graves. It will never be known who lies there, or what contribution they made to the community.

Thomas designated a location for a second cemetery, for "slaves and free Negroes", which today has only an iron marker to indicate the site. Later, Porterdale Cemetery was developed for Black burials.

The City of Columbus has four major cemeteries. They are Porterdale and Linwood, which are on the National Historic Register, East Porterdale, and Riverdale. All City Cemetery Records are kept at the City Sexton's Office located at Riverdale Cemetery.

Records of all cemeteries were last microfilmed in 2000. Microfilmed records are available in Columbus, Georgia, in Atlanta at the Georgia State Archives, and the LDS Family History Library throughout the world.

You are invited to tour Linwood Cemetery.

Historic Linwood Foundation Inc.,
P.O. Box 1057 •721 Linwood Blvd.
Columbus, GA 31902
Phone: 706.321.8285

http://www.historiclinwood.org
E-mail: hlfinfo@knology.net

CEMETERY MAP

LINWOOD CEMETERY
OLD CEMETERY
A
B
D
E
F
G
H
I
J
K
L

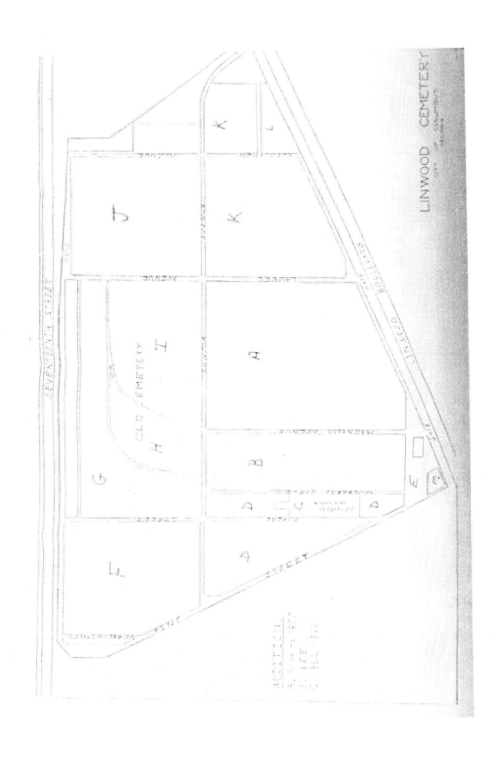

SECTION A

We have not been able to locate a copy of the individual map of Section A.

Lot 1, T. I. Pearce on wall

Isaac F. Pearce	Feb. 27, 1867	June 28, 1924

- 1910 Muscogee Census: Isaac F. Pearce 42 AL GA GA, wife Effie C. 30 L AL AL (mar. 14 yrs; 3 children/2living), dau Lila M. 7 GA, son Theodore E. 4 GA, and mother-in-law Francis E. Willis 66 AL GA GA (m1 40 yrs, 6 children/4living).

Mollie Cox Pearce	Nov. 30, 1883	Apr. 5, 1983
Tillman I. Pearce	Jan. 29, 1826	July 24, 1893

- 1860 Muscogee Census: Tillman Pierce 33 GA, Nancy 32 GA, Eliza G. 12 GA, Mary L. 14 GA, Augustus 6 GA, Ida 1 GA, William 4 GA and John S. 10 GA.

- 1880 Muscogee Census: Tillman Pearce 54 GA GA GA, wife Nancy 53 GA GA GA, dau Mary 28 GA, son William 21 GA, son Isaac 12 GA and son Alvah 6 GA.

Lila Pearce	Mar. 15, 1846	Oct. 6, 1923	w/o Alford James Renfroe

- Obit. - Widow of late Alfred James Renfroe, eldest child of Nancy Thomason & Tillman Pearce, born Harris Co., GA, 7 children, Wellborn J., of Dothan, AL, Josiah of Bainbridge, GA, Broussals A., Misses Bennie, Gussie, Annie May & Bessie Lou, all of Columbus, GA, 2 sisters, Mrs. R.O. Cresap, of Lakeland, FL, Mrs. Ida Thomason of Guntersville, AL, 2 brothers, Geo A. & Isaac F. Pearce, both of Columbus.

- Obit -Lila Pearce born Putnam Co., GA, children; G. A., J. T., T. C., I.F., & A, all of Columbus, GA, W. J. of Birmingham, AL, Mrs. W. L. Thomason of Guntersville, AL, Mrs. R. O. Cresap of Lakeland, AL, Mrs. A. J. Renfroe of this city.

Aylmer Pearce Collins	July 12, 1889	Sept 27, 1952	d/o Ida Embry & George A. Pearce
Alvah Pearce	June 1, 1874	Dec 7, 1917	

- Atlanta Constitution, 10/14/1906, Society in Columbus: Last Sunday at Tuskegee, AL; Miss Mollie Mae Cox of that place and Mr. Alvah Pearce of Columbus; were happily married. The marriage was set for later in the winter, but decided last Sunday to be married immediately. The marriage was performed at the home of the Bride's parents, Mr. & Mrs. George E. Cox.

Roy Deignam Pearce	Mar. 18, 1896	June 13, 1897	s/o I. F. & E. C. Pearce

William J. Pearce	Mar. 14, 1859	Dec. 11, 1899	Our brother
Geo Augustus Pearce	Aug. 8, 1853	Aug. 11, 1933	

- George Augustus Pearce owned the City Mills. He married Ida Embry, d/o J. N. Embry.

- George A. Pearce was born in Harris Co., GA August 8, 1854 (sic), the son of Tillman I. Pearce and Nancy Thomasson (sic). Tillman and Nancy had 9 children. He was married 11/15/1878 to Miss Ida Embry, the d/o J. N. Embry and had 5 daughters: Odelle, Effie May, Kate Mitchell, George Alma and Mabel Clare.[1]

- 1920 Muscogee Census: George A. Pearce 69 AL AL AL, SIL Tom Andrews Jr. 26 GA GA GA, dau Mabel P. 27 GA and gdau Augusta P. 8 GA.

Ida E. Embry	July 1, 1869	Sept 27, 1952	w/o George A. Pearce

- 1870 Muscogee Census: Jasper Embry 44 GA, Lucy 39 GA, Rose 18 GA, Antoinette 13 GA, Ida 11 GA and Effie 7 GA.

Elsie Mae Pearce	Aug. 24, 1903	Dec. 18, 1903	d/o Fannie & Alvah Pearce
Alfred James Renfroe	Nov. 19, 1847	Oct. 23, 1915	

- Obit. – Born Russell Co., AL, leaves wife & 7 children, Misses Bennie, Gussie, Annie Mae, Bessie Lou Renfroe, Bruce A., all of Columbus, W.J. of Dothan, AL, Josiah of Bainbridge, GA, 1 sister, Mrs. John B. Day of Columbus.

- 1880 Muscogee Census: Alfred Renfroe 24 AL GA GA, Lila 24 GA GA GA, son Wellborn 10 Al, dau Ida 9 AL, dau Gussie 4 AL, son Joe 3 GA.

Forest Auburn Duncan	Feb. 23, 1907	Aug. 24, 1980	
Tillman C. Pearce	Mar. 31, 1861	Feb. 26, 1911	Our brother

- 1880 Muscogee Census: Tillman Pearce 54 GA GA GA, wife Nancy 53 GA GA GA, dau Mary 28 GA, son William 21, son Phil 12 GA and son Alver 6 GA.

Nancy Pearce		Aug. 31, 1884	w/o Tillman I. Pearce, age 56 years

- Obit: d/o late Jack Thomason of Harris Co., GA., where she was born.

Geo Augustus Pearce, Jr.	Dec. 27, 1901	Nov. 11, 1931	
Infant		no date	Inf. d/o Geo & Ida A. Pearce. SR: bur. 5/3/88.
Fannie Walton	Nov. 6, 1876	Oct. 26, 1903	w/o Alvah Pearce

Lot 2, J. N. Embry on wall

Odelle Pearce Hunt	Dec. 20, 1879	June 16, 1958	w/o Charles D. Hunt, Jr.

- 1930 Muscogee Census: Odelle P. Hunt 50 GA GA GA (married at age 19)

- 1920 Muscogee Census: Charles D. Hunt 42 GA GA GA, wife Odella P. 40 GA AL GA and dau Odella Embry 21 GA GA GA (single).

- 1880 Muscogee Census: George Pearce 26 GA GA GA, wife Ida 19 GA GA GA and dau Odelle 5/12/GA.

J. N. Embry	Sept. 12, 1826	Aug. 31, 1893

- Obit: born Oglethorpe Co, GA, reared Harris Co., GA, 4 daus, Mrs. J.T. Pearce, Mrs. Geo A Pearce, both of Columbus, Mrs. B.T. Lynch, of LaPlasse, AL, Mrs. A.A. Stivender of Leesburg, FL.

- Jasper Embry married Lucinda A. Philips 10/1/1847 in Harris Co., GA.[2] Lucinda was the d/o Ambrose Philips (1803-1854) and Lydia Strozier (1810-1882) who married 11/21/1828 in Wilkes Co., GA.[3]

- 1850 Harris Co., GA Census: Ambrose Philips 47 GA, Lydia 40 GA, Reuben 14 GA and William 15 GA.

- 1870 Muscogee Census: Jasper Embry 44 GA, Lucy 39 GA, Rose 18 GA, Antoinette 13 GA, Ida 11 GA and Effie 7 GA.

- 1880 Muscogee Census: Jasper N. (Newton) Embry 54 GA GA GA, wife Lucy 48 GA GA GA, dau Rosebella 28 GA, dau Effie 17 GA.

Mabel Pearce Andrews	Aug. 17, 1929	Dec. 11, 1943	d/o Mabel Pearce & Tom Andrews
Annie E. Pearce	Jan. 16, 1857	Feb. 5, 1931	w/o John T. Pearce

- Obit: widow of John T., born Harris Co., GA, d/o Mr. & Mrs. J.N. Embry, member of D.A.R., King's Daughters, U.D.C., 3 sons, Herbert E., J. Embry Pearce, & John T., 2 daus., Mrs. R.H. French (nee Miss Annie Will Pearce), 6 g/ch.

Effie E. Lott	Dec. 11, 1862	May 16, 1892	w/o Wm. L. Lott, d/o J.N. & Lucy Embry
Lucy A. Embry	Dec. 29, 1831	July 7, 1893	w/o J.N. Embry

- Obit: leaves husband & 4 children, Mrs. John T. Pearce, Mrs. Geo A. Pearce of Columbus, Mrs. A. Stivender of Leesburg, FL, Mrs. S.C. Lynch of LaPlace, AL, 1 sister, Mrs. Fannie Ligon of Atlanta, GA, 1 brother, Reuben Phillips of East Point, GA.

John T. Pearce	Feb. 6, 1850	Dec. 6, 1914

- Obit: eldest s/o late Tillman I. Pearce, reared in Russell Co., AL, married Miss Annie Embry, Nov. 15, 1877, d/o J.N. Embry, leaves wife, 3 sons, Herbert J. & J.T., Jr., 1 dau. Miss Annie Will Pearce, 3 brothers, Geo A., I.F. & Alvah, 3 sisters Mrs. A.J. Renfroe of Columbus, Mrs. R.O. Cresap of Lakeland, FL, Mrs. Ida Thomason of Guntersville, AL.

Ernest Pearce	Oct. 28, 1870	Sept. 2, 1901	s/o John T. & Annie Pearce
Odelle Embry Hunt	Aug. 30, 1898	Jan. 3, 1967	w/o Wm. P. Holmes
Katharine Pearce Jones	Oct. 24, 1884	Nov. 3, 1960	d/o Ida Embry & Geo Pearce
Lucy Belle	June 28, 1890	Sept. 13, 1890	inf. d/o Jas. T. & Annie Pearce

Lot 3, no name on wall

Alexander C. Kirven   Dec. 2, 1832   Feb. 17, 1874   b. Columbus, GA, d. Vicksburg, MS., father

- Obit: funeral notice mentions Mrs. Thirza B. Estes.

- Alexander Columbus Kirven was the s/o James Henry Kirven (1804-1855) and Thirza Ann Bevers Gray (1812 Morgan Co., GA -1892). Thirza was the daughter of Richard Gray and his wife Margaret. Richard was born c1779 in Hanover Co., NC. Thirza married secondly to a Mr. Estes. Alexander married Susan E. Andrews, the d/o Samuel A. R. Andrews (c1794-1862) and his second wife, Elizabeth Day (1809-1872). After Alexander's death, Susan married Willis Massey.

- Muscogee Co., GA WB A p. 118 Richard Gray ww 5/4/1848 – wp 3/26/1851 Legatees: wife Margaret,
  sons: William C. Gray and his heirs, Francis M. Gray and his heirs, Richard M. Gray and his heirs, James T. Gray and his heirs. Mentions James H. Kirven and his heirs and Henson S. Estes. Ex: son William C. Gray. Wit: W. A. Bedell, D. R. Stone, and James D. Johnson.

- 1850 Floyd Co., GA Census: Jas. W. Kirvan (sic) 46 NC, Thurza 39 GA, Alexander C. 18 GA, Margaret A. W. 16 GA, William H. 14 GA, Martha J. 12 GA and Albert W. 1 GA.

- 1860 Muscogee Census: Mrs. T. B. Kirvin (sic) 48 GA (Boarding House), Wm H. 22 GA, Joseph A. 11 GA, Richard M. 9 GA and Alexander 6 GA.

- 1860 Muscogee Census: Alex C. Kirvin 30 AL, Susan 25 GA and Noble 6/12 GA.

Susan E. Massey   Dec. 20, 1839   Sept. 6, 1882   mother
                         Columbus, GA   Columbus, GA

- Obit: Mrs. Willie W. Massey, d/o late Samuel R. Andrews, sister of J.C. Andrews, Davis A. Andrews, Mrs. William Ragland, all of Columbus, several years ago, she married A.C. Kirven, had 2 children, Noble & Clarence Kirven.

- 1880 Muscogee Census shows Willis Massey 30 GA GA AL, wife Susan 40 GA GA AL and son Clarence 9 MS. (Note: Clarence is really a Kirven). Noble Kirven 20 GA is a boarder in Wallace Acee's household in Muscogee.

Inf. d/o G & I.M. Pearce   no dates

Lot 4, partial brick wall, no name

P.T. Giddings   1886   Feb 3, 1917

- 1930 Muscogee Census: Perry T. Giddens 49 FL FL FL married @32, wife Susie 45 GA GA GA married @28.

- 1910 Colquitt Co., GA Census: Perry G. Giddens 29 FL GA GA, mother Mary J. 52 GA GA GA (widow, 10 children/ 9 living), brother Frank 17 GA, sister Bettie 17 GA, sister Mollie 13 GA and brother John D. 9 GA.

Annie Baker Giddings   Mar. 8, 1880   Oct. 20, 1962
Martin

Lot 5, no name on wall

Ben Autry   Jan. 18, 1870   Aug. 25, 1943

- Obit: 2 g/daus. Mrs. Mary Allen, Mrs. Frances Owens, both of Atlanta, GA, 2 brothers, Marion & Tom, both of Tuscan, AZ, 1 sister, Mrs. O.E. Moore of Columbus.
- 1880 Muscogee Census: William Autry 38 GA NC GA, wife Clara 34 GA GA GA and children; Marion 13 GA, Ben 11 GA, Youla 9 GA, Rebecca 7 GA, Alonzo 6 GA, Anna 3 GA and Reese 7 GA.
- The GA Death Index gives his middle initial as "D."

Lot 6, fenced lot, no name

1 child's slab, n/m

Lot 7, open lot

Carrie Elizabeth (no last name)		Jul. 23, 1874	
Ellen K. Robinson	Jan. 3, 1879	Mar. 27, 1928	
Cecil Edw. Robinson	Jan. 3, 1904	May 12, 1968	
Edward B. Robinson	Nov. 23, 1878	Apr. 28, 1928	
William T. Robinson		Apr. 19, 1895	b. St. Joseph, FL, d. Columbus, GA

- Obit - lived several years in New Orleans, LA, Mariner Engineer, leaves wife, 1 son, Edw. Robinson of Columbus, GA.
- 1880 Muscogee Census shows William T. Robinson (retail grocer) 41 FL Mass Mass, wife Virginia 41 AL AL AL and son Edward 2 GA.

Lot 8, James Smith on wall

Walter Collins Smith	May 1, 1894	Aug. 18, 1894	s/o Hugh Ritchie & Beulah Cranford Smith
Lynnette Elise Smith	Oct. 20, 1895	Aug. 15, 1899	d/o Hugh Ritchie & Beulah Cranford Smith
Albert Drummond Smith	Mar. 11, 1880	May 14, 1881	s/o Jas. E.C. Smith
Archie G. Smith	Mar. 11, 1880	July 21, 1962	
Bernard Smith	Apr. 15, 1886	Apr. 24, 1888	s/o Jas. E. & E.C. Smith

- 1880 Muscogee Census: Jas. Smith 40 VA VA VA, wife Bettie 33 VA VA VA, son George 12 GA, son Hugh 11 GA, son Jas. 9 GA, son Walter 8 GA, son Chas? 4 GA, dau Maggie 2 GA and sons Albert & Archie 3/12 GA.

Lot 9, no name on wall

James Smith   Dec. 25, 1839   May 3, 1913   Capt. Co. E, 41st Va. Inf. C.S.A.

- Obit: leaves wife, Mrs. Elizabeth Smith, nee Miss Elizabeth Davis of Richmond, VA, 6 sons, 1 dau., Geo H., Walter D., Archie G., all of Columbus, GA, Hugh H., of Hamlet, NC, Charles S. of Norfolk, VA, James Jr. of Atlanta, GA, Mrs. W.D. Britt, Mrs. J.L. White, both of Columbus, 1 brother, Archie G. of Petersburg, VA, 3 sisters, Mrs. James V. Glass of Shelbyville, KY, Mrs. Ann R. Smith, Mrs. Jane Harrison both of Petersburg, VA, borned & reared in Petersburg, VA.

- 1850 Petersburg, Dinwiddie Co., VA Census shows: James Smith 37 Scotland, Ann 34 Scotland, William 13, James 11, Hugh 9, John 7, Jannet 5, Jane 2 and Archibald Gray 23.

- 1880 Muscogee Census: Jas Smith 40 VA VA VA, wife Bettie 33 VA VA VA, children Geo 13 GA, Hugh 11 GA, Jas 9 GA, Walter 8 GA, Chas 4 GA, Maggie 2 GA, Albert 3/12 GA and Archie 3/12 sons.

- Smith, James: enl. 8/9/61 Petersburg; Co. D; b. 1840; in Petersburg 1860, lived with father, corner S. Pine St. and Smith's Alley; brother of Hugh Ritchie Smith and William Crawford Smith; medical discharge 12/6/61. (Henderson, William D., 12th Virginia Infantry, 1984)

Elizabeth Davis   July 17, 1846   Mar. 12, 1931   w/o James Smith

- Obit: born Virginia, widow of late James Smith, 2 daus., Mrs. W.D. Britt of Birmingham, AL, Mrs. J.L. White of Columbus, 4 sons, Hugh R. of Hamlet, NC, Charles S. of Norfolk, VA, Archie G. & Walter D., both of Columbus, GA, 1 sister, Mrs. Maggie Payne of Richmond, VA, 2 brothers, Sam Davis of Danville, VA, Geo Davis of Spokane, WA, 19 g/ch., 5 g/g/ch.

- 1930 Muscogee Census: Elizabeth Smith 73 VA, son Walter D. 47 GA, son Archie G. 39 GA, d-l-l Nellie P. 21 GA and granddaughter Nellie P. 1 4/12(?) GA.

Lot 10, Smith on wall

James Smith, Jr.	July 24, 1870	June 2, 1925	
Walter Davis Smith	May 29, 1872	Mar. 22, 1957	
Ida White	July 7, 1873	Mar. 6, 1944	w/o James Smith, Jr.

Lot 11, no name on wall

Francis Boykin   July 31, 1825   Aug. 11, 1863

- 1860 Census Barbour Co., AL: Francis Boykin 35 GA, L. A. (f) 28 GA, Sallie 8 GA.

- Francis Boykin was born in Milledgeville, Baldwin Co., GA, the son of Dr. Samuel

Boykin (1786-1848) and his second wife Narcissa Cooper (1803-1859), the d/o Thomas and Margaret Cooper.[4] Samuel and Narcissa were married 7/31/1822 in Putnam Co., GA.[5] Francis married Laura A. Nuchols (sic) 11/24/1849 and were the parents of Sallie Boykin. Francis died in Barbour Co., AL. Dr. Samuel and Narcissa Boykin are also buried in Linwood Cemetery.

- Muscogee Co., GA Will Book A:94-96.
  Samuel Boykin, 4/28/1848:5/20/1848. Legatees: wife: Narcissa. Sons: Francis, Samuel, Thomas, Leroy. Daus. mentioned but not named. Exrs: wife, Narcissa Boykin, Francis Boykin, Samuel Boykin, Mark A. Cooper. Wits: Leroy Holt, Frank A. Nisbet, James N. Owens, John E. Bacon.

Leanora Bradley	July 10, 1927	July 11, 1927	d/o Eleanor Armstrong & Frank B. Bradley
Alice B. Wilson	Mar. 14, 1886	Aug. 17, 1953	

- Atlanta Constitution, 5 Nov 1905 and 12/3/1905: Mrs. & Mrs. Forbes Bradley of Ft. Mitchell, AL have issued invitations to the wedding of their daughter Alice Geraldine Bradley to Benjamin Carl Hatcher on the evening of 12 December, at their home in Ft. Mitchell. Names as her uncle, Mr. W. C. Bradley. Mr. Hatcher is the son of Mr. & Mrs. R. T. Hatcher of "Bonnie Castle" in Oswitchee, Al.

- 1910 Jefferson Co., AL Census: Martha H. Hartwell 61 AL GA GA, dau Willie V. 37 AL, son Charles W. 36 AL, roomer Ben C. Hatcher 30 GA GA GA (m. 4 yrs.), roomer Allie (sic) B. Hatcher 24 AL AL AL.

- 1920 Russell Co., AL Census: Forbes Bradley 68 AL, dau Willie 38 Al and dau Alice B. Hatcher 32 AL widowed.

Frank B. Bradley	Apr. 4, 1898	May 21, 1983

- 1930 Muscogee Census: Frank B. Bradley 32 AL AL AL (married @28), wife Eleanor B. 30 GA GA GA (married @26) and son Frank B. Jr. 1 GA.

James M. Morgan	Dec. 16, 1885	Mar. 24, 1963

- 1930 Muscogee Census: James M. Morgan 31 single GA GA GA roomer with Laverna A. Sims.

Sallie B. Bradley	Sept. 5, 1884	Aug. 7, 1885
Forbes Bradley	Jan. 16, 1852	June 27, 1921

- 1860 Russell Co., AL Census: Forbes Bradley 51 CT, Terace? 32 GA, Emma 14 AL, Alice 12 AL, Edmon 10 AL, Forbes 8 AL, Daniel 4 AL and Harriett 2 AL.

- 1880 Russell Co., AL Census: Forbes Bradley 28 AL, Sallie F. 27 AL, Lula H. 8/12 (Sept.)

- 1920 Russell Co., AL Census: Forbes Bradley 68 AL, dau Willie 38 Al and dau Alice B. Hatcher 32 AL widowed.

- Forbes Bradley was the son of Forbes Bradley, I of CT (1809-1890) and his wife Theresa Ann Clark (1827-1871), who were married 5/29/1845 in Muscogee Co., GA.[6] Forbes, II married Sallie F. Boykin the daughter of Francis Boykin.

- Forbes Bradley, I (1809-1890) was the s/o Dan Bradley (1784-1827) and Ann Forbes (1782-1824).[7] He married Theressa A. M. Clark (1827-1881), the d/o William Clark and Rebecca Peddy, on 5/29/1845 in Muscogee Co., GA.[8, 9]

Frank B. Bradley, Jr.	Oct. 2, 1928	Mar. 17, 1971

Willie Bradley Morgan	July 19, 1891	Sept. 16, 1989	
Edmond Bradley	August 9, 1889	July 10, 1927	
Sallie F. Boykin	June 30, 1853	Nov. 3, 1917	w/o Forbes Bradley

- 1860 Census Barbour Co., AL Census: Francis Boykin 35 GA, L. A. 28 GA and Sallie 8 GA.

- According to Family Bible records[5], Francis Boykin married Laura A. Nuckolls 11/24/1849.

| Eleanor Armstrong | Oct. 4, 1899 | Aug. 9, 1960 | w/o Frank B. Bradley |

Lot 12, open lot

| James M. Broadnax | Jan. 1, 1829 | Oct. 1, 1880 |

- Obit: leaves wife and 5 children, s/o Dr. Broadnax, sister, Mrs. Stockton. Member of "City of Light Guards".

- James M. Broadnax was born in Waynesboro, GA, the son of Dr. Robert Emmett Broadnax (1787-1842) and his wife, Mary Elizabeth (c1812-1852).

- 1850 Muscogee Census: Mrs. Elizabeth Broadnax 38 GA, James 21 GA, Mariah 15 GA and Victoria 12 GA. (Note: Rev. James E. Broadnax, son of John Travis Broadnax is also enumerated in the 1850 Muscogee Census.)

- 1860 Muscogee Census: James Broadnax 30 GA, Mary 27 GA, Victoria 5 GA and Jane 3 GA. Also in household: Henrietta Roper 16 GA, Joel Roper 21 GA and Alexander Roper 19. The 1850 Muscogee Census shows the Roper's to be the wife and children of Wiley Roper 43 SC and Henrietta 43 SC. A daughter Mary Roper age 17 is also listed with them in 1850.

- 1880 Muscogee Census: James Bradanax (sic) 50 GA GA GA, Mary 42 GA GA GA, Victoria 24 GA, James 23 GA, Emma 19 GA, Hennie (f) 17 GA and Emmett 12 GA.

| 1 adult slab | | bad condition, broken. SR: Mrs. James Broadnax bur. 7/18/1885, 51 yrs. |

Lot 13, J. W. Wright on wall

| Madison Dancer | Mar. 2, 1812 | Aug. 3, 1880 | 68 yrs. 5 mo 1 dy |

- Obit-early settler of Columbus, leaves wife. Thrown from buggy.

- 1860 Muscogee Census: Madison Dancer 48 SC timber cutter, Zephna 41 SC, Zephanna 16 GA, and Sarah M. 14 GA.

- 1870 Muscogee Census: Madison Dancer 58 SC, Zilpha 51 SC, and Savannah Dobson 23 GA.

- 1880 Muscogee Census: Madison Dancer 68 SC SC SC and Zilpha 60 SC SC SC.

- Muscogee Co., GA WB A:91-92.
  Lewis J. Clark, 1/3/1848:3/14/1848. Legatees: mother - Harriet Clark, father - James Clark of Clayton, Barbour Co., Ala, sisters Elizabeth Clark and Zilphia Dancer. Exr: Dozier Thornton. Wits: Sterling F. Grimes, William P. Yonge, J. R. Jones.

Evidence of 2 graves; small granite markers at head & feet, "M.K." & "M.E."

Lot 14, Gautier on wall

| Julia Dowdell Gautier | Aug. 2, 1855 | Jan. 12, 1918 | |

- William Thomas Gautier (1854-1925) was the son of Dr. William Jones Gautier (1854-1925) and Mary Eliza Jane Hora, who were married 11/25/1853 in NYC, NY. William was a druggist in Tuskegee, AL before moving to Columbus in 1882. William married Julia Caroline Dowdell 12/23/1879 in Macon Co., AL.

- Julia was the d/o Rev. Lewis F. Dowdell and his wife Arcadia Mitchell, who are both buried in the City Cemetery in Tuskegee, AL.

| Katie May Gautier | Feb. 24, 1881 | Nov. 21, 1882 | d/o Wm. T. & Julia C. Gautier |

| Lucy B. Gautier | Aug. 14, 1892 | Jan. 11, 1901 | |

Lot 15, no name on wall

| C.A. Lovelace | Oct. 9, 1849 | May 25, 1929 | |

- Obit: Charles A. Lovelace, born Troup Co., GA (sic), died LaFayette, AL, leaves wife, 1 daughter, Miss Kate Cleghorn, 4 brothers, Frank of LaGrange, GA, George & Sid of Marietta, GA, John of Selma, AL, 1 sister, Miss Maggie Lovelace of Miami, FL.

- Charles married Mary Eugenia Nance, the widow of Samuel B. Cleghorn, 6/1/1882 in Muscogee Co., GA.

- 1870 Troup Co., GA Census: William Lovelace 44 NC, Josephine 42 TN, Charles 20 TN, Margaret 16 TN, John 11 GA, Josephine 7 GA, William F. 5 GA, Albert S. 3 GA and George 1/12 GA.

| Hugh H. Parkyn | | May 31, 1861 Pensacola, FL. | s/o Hugh Parkyn of England |

- Hugh H. Parkyn married Isabella R. Mann June 28, 1859 in Muscogee Co., GA.

- 1860 Richmond Co., GA Census: Hugh H. Parkyn 35 England. Isabella 25 Mass., Charles M. 12 GA.

- CSA - Enlisted as a Musician on 11 May 1861 Co. A., 5th Inf. Regt., "Clinch Rifles", died on 31 May 1861 in Pensacola, FL

| Charles Cleghorn | May 10, 1805 Georgia | Mar. 9, 1863 Columbus, GA | |

- Charles Cleghorn married Katherine Henry 12/30/1828 (d/o William Henry & Sarah Pickens) in Coweta Co., GA. Katherine is the d/o William Henry (1777-1856) and Sarah D. Pickens (c1779-1863). Charles married secondly Elizabeth Ross 8/24/1843 Muscogee.

- 1850 Muscogee Census: Robert L. Bass 31 GA, John H. Bass 29 GA, Charles Cleghorn 45 GA Hotel Keeper, Elizabeth 38 CT, Sarah 13 GA, Samuel 11 GA and numerous boarders, including Charles A. Lovelace 27.

- In 1828, Coweta County Surveyor Charles Cleghorn laid out the site for the Coweta county court square and the streets.

Mary Eugenia Lovelace   Oct. 3, 1849   Aug. 16, 1930

- Obit: widow of C.A. Lovelace, nee Miss Eugenia Nance, born Muscogee Co., GA, 1 dght, Miss Kate Cleghorn, married Samuel B. Cleghorn in 1867, married Mr. Lovelace in 1882, 1 sister, Mrs. D.S. Gregory of New York.

- 1850 Muscogee Census: H. W. Nance 35 SC, Elizabeth 25 GA, Laura L. 6 GA, Emma A. 4 GA and Eugenia 2 GA.

- 1860 Muscogee Census: Harvey W. Nance 45 SC, Elizabeth 34 GA, Laura 16 GA, Emma 12 GA, Eugenia 11 GA, Clara 9 GA and Jane 6 GA.

- Harvey Nance married Elizabeth Blackman 10/29/1840 in Muscogee Co., GA.

1 adult slab	no dates	An unknown Confederate Soldier
Elizabeth Ross Cleghorn	Feb 11, 1811 Boston, MA	Aug. 12, 1866 Columbus, GA
Lucy B. Gautier	Aug. 14, 1892	Jan. 11, 1901
Isabella Ross Parkyn		Dec. 10, 1866 d/o I. & S.H. Mann of Boston, w/o Hugh Parkyn of England.
Kate Cleghorn	Oct. 30, 1869	Feb 22, 1946
Samuel B. Cleghorn	June 21, 1839	Apr. 19, 1881

- Obit - member of Columbus Guards, 20th Regt. Inf. Co. G., "Ivey Guards", 2nd Lt., wounded in battle of Wilderness, Mayor of Columbus twice.

- Atlanta Constitution 12/17/1873
  Mayor Elect of Columbus – Samuel B. Cleghorn, one of the most gallant wearers of the gray, has been elected Mayor of Columbus. The Sun says – Our new Mayor elect is only thirty-four years old. He was, antedating 1862, the wealthiest young man in Columbus. Freeing the slaves cost him, like thousands of others, their fortunes. He was Mayor for one term a year ago. He is a true gentleman and one of the most gallant Confederate soldiers. The loss of a leg and some fingers of both hands at the Battle of the Wilderness, in Virginia, and his actions ever since, attest his fidelity to the Lost Cause. He is the youngest Mayor Columbus has ever had. He is possessed of a cool, clear brain and will ably fill the position.

- CSA Co. G., 20th Regt. - Cleghorn, Samuel B.-Jr. 2nd Lieutenant July 15 1861. Elected 2nd Lieutenant Jan 31 1863; 1st Lieutenant Sept 19 1863. Wounded at Wilderness Va May 6 1864. Left leg amputated May 1864. In Columbus Ga hospital Mar 27 1865.

Sarah E. Cleghorn   Oct. 18, 1915   My Auntie

- Obit: from family of old and most prominent family, died as the result of being burned. 1 niece, Miss Kate Cleghorn.

Lot 17, J. Benton on wall

Jonathan Benton   Nov. 24, 1858   May 20, 1888

- 1880 Muscogee Census: John C. Benton 22 GA GA GA (single) and Joe A. Benton 20 GA GA GA (single).

John B. Newsome   May 7, 1838   Apr. 16, 1895   Co. K, 12th GA Inf.

C.S.A.

- 1880 Lee Co., AL Census: John Newsom 42 GA GA GA, wife Elizabeth 46 GA GA GA, children; Mary E. 24 GA, Sarah L. 22 GA, Ada C. 12 GA, William T. 10 GA, James K. 8 GA, and Samuel J. 5 GA.

- John B. Newsome resided in Marion Co., GA, enlisted as a Private on 15 June 1861 in Co. K, 12th Inf. Regt. On rolls present on 31 August 1864 (No further record).

- 1850 Marion Co., GA Census: Thomas H. Newsom (sic) 38 GA, Amanda 38 GA, John 12 GA, Francis (f) 10 GA, Kinchen 7 GA, William 5 GA, Nancy 4 GA, Hesekiah 2 GA and Mary 1 GA.

Sarah L. Newsome	Jan. 4, 1859	Sept. 25, 1916

1 baby slab, n/m

Lot 18, open lot

James H. Ware	Apr. 5, 1857	Oct. 24, 1858
Henry N. Ware	Sept. 25, 1859	Aug. 19, 1860
Henry Ware	Nov. 2, 1817	May 24, 1879

- 1870 Russell Co., AL Census: Henry Ware 52 GA, Elizabeth 43 GA Evans D. Long 19 AL, Molly Ware 15 AL, Robert A. Ware 9 AL, Elizabeth A. Ware 6 AL and Lewis C. J. Ware 2 AL.

Archie Ware	no dates	
Mary L. Ware	no dates	SR: Bur. 7/10/1890

2 adult slabs, n/m   2 baby brick slabs, n/m

Sexton Records indicate buried in this lot:

R. A. Ware		*bur. 12/19/1912, 61 yrs.*
Henry Ware		*bur. 9/4/1897, 13 yrs.*

Lot 19, Whatley on wall

John T. Whatley, Sr.	Sept 12, 1887	Feb. 16, 1979

- John Thomas Whatley (1887-1979) married Mattie T. Willis 10/21/1912. John was the son of John Thomas Whatley (1858-1930) and his wife, Lilla Ora Land (1862-1932) who were married 1/3/1884 in Muscogee. The elder John Whatley was the son of Gibson Flournoy Whatley (1833-1918 Troup Co., GA) and his wife, Elizabeth Anne Hand (1838-1915 Troup Co., GA) who were married 2/25/1855. Gibson F. Whatley served in Co. H. 21st GA Infantry.

- 1920 Muscogee Census: John T. Whatley Jr. 32 GA AL GA, wife Mattie T. 30 GA GA GA, son Jack W. 6 GA, son John T. 2 7/12 GA, and aunt Janie Johnson 63 widowed. Next door Judson C. Willis 62 GA GA GA and wife Susie E. 44 GA GA GA.

Mattie Willis	Mar. 3, 1890	Oct. 5, 1973	w/o John T. Whatley,

Sr.

- Mattie is the d/o Judson Carey Willis and his first wife Emma Eliza Watt, d/o James Watt and Theresa McCrary who were married 1/16/1838 in Muscogee Co., GA.

- 1870 Muscogee Census: Theresa Watt 48 GA, Robert L. 26 AL, James A. 24 AL, Martha T. 21 AL, Virginia P. 20 GA, Emma E. 17 AL, Ida G. 15 AL, Claddie J. (f) 13 GA and Matilda L. 14 AL.

- 1880 Muscogee Census: Theresa Watt 57 GA SC SC, Martha 31 AL, SC GA, Jinsey 29 AL SC GA, Claude (f) 22 AL SC GA and Emma 27 AL, GA SC.

Jack Willis Whatley	June 6, 1913	Mar. 1, 1970	Ret. employee of Seaboard Coastline R.R.

Lot 20, no name on wall

John J. Edmundson	1847	1880	
Leo Allen	1907	1917	SR: bur. 10/22/1917
2 adult brick slabs, n/m		1 child slab, n/m	

Lot 21, Cowdery on wall

Sarah Perry Cowdery	Jan. 4, 1850	June 18, 1873
Lucile Dunn Slade	Jan. 4, 1882	May 7, 1966
Eugene Cowdery	May 4, 1923	July 1, 1939
Lester L. Cowdery	July 11, 1807 Hartford, CT	Oct. 17, 1889 Columbus, GA

- Lester Leander Cowdery married 1) Harriet Dunham in Hartford CT 10/29/1834 and 2) Eveline Giddings 3/10/1846. Lester was the s/o Ambrose Cowdery & Dency Coe. Eveline was the d/o Erastus Giddings and his first wife.

- 1870 Muscogee Census: Lester Cowdery 63 CT, Eveline 40 SC, Almarine 20 GA, Lester 15 AL, Mattie 14 AL, Louis 11 GA, Eveline 10 GA, Katie 9 GA, Lucy 7 GA and Walter 4 GA.

Margaret Young Cowdery		Jan. 29, 1965	only date
Mattie J. Cowdery	June 22, 1852	Feb 8, 1908	
Jefferson Cowdery	Sept. 22, 1887	Feb. 12, 1889	s/o B.C. & Lucile Farmer
Eveline Cowdery	May 30, 1858	Nov. 27, 1909	
Eveline Giddings Cowdery	Sept. 25, 1825	June 26, 1901	

- Obit: born Union District, SC, came to Columbus 1832, children, Mrs. Thomas H. Slade, Mrs. L.W. Fitts, both of Carrollton,, GA, Mrs. E.G. Farmer of Dothan, AL, Misses Mattie & Evelyn L. Cowdery, L.L. & Walter, all of Columbus, GA, L.W. of Lakeland, FL.

George H. Kimbell	Nov. 27, 1862	July 16, 1959
Lester Cowdery Slade	Sept. 27, 1874	June 17, 1938
"Ocie" our baby boy		no other data
Lester Leander Cowdery	Mar. 8, 1854	Apr. 9, 1907
Lyman Walter Cowdery	Apr. 3, 1866	Jan. 8, 1939
James E. Young	Nov. 22, 1848	Mar. 8, 1930

- Obit: last surviving s/o late William H. Young, a Columbus pioneer, leaves wife and 1 dght, Mrs. L. Walter Cowdery of Columbus, GA.

Lewis Well Cowdery	May 19, 1856	Jan. 16, 1916

- The National Society of the Daughters of the American Revolution Volume 95, page 186 Miss Almarine Slade. DAR ID Number: 94609. Born in Columbus, Ga. Descendant of Lieut. William Slade, Col. Benjamin Blount, Edmund Blount, and Ambrose Cowdrey, as follows:
  1. Thomas Bog Slade, Jr. (b. 1834), m. 1871 Almarine Cowdrey (b. 1848).
  2. Thomas Bog Slade (1800-82) m. 1824 Ann Jacqueline Blount (1805-91); Lester Leander Cowdrey (1807-89) m. 1846 Eveline Giddings (1825-1901).
  3. Jeremiah Slade (1775-1824) m. 1798 Janet Bog (1774-1831); James Blount (1780-1820) m. 1803 Elizabeth de Roulhac (1786-1824); Ambrose Cowdrey (1784-1862) m. 1805 Dency Coe (1788-1868).
  4. William Slade m. Anne Gainor; Edmund Blount m. 1777 Judith Rhodes; Ambrose Cowdrey m. 1st Mary Reed.
  5. Benjamin Blount m. Affie Smithwick.
  William Slade (1750-91) was ensign and lieutenant, 1777. He served to the close of the war and became a member of the Cincinnati. He was born and died in Martin County, N. C.

- 1860 Muscogee Census: Thomas B. Slade 60 NC, Ann G. 55 NC, Tammett E. 30 GA, Mary L. 28 GA, Stella B. 20 GA, Hellen 18 GA and John H. ___ GA.

- 1870 Muscogee Census: Lester Cowdery 63 CT, Evaline 40 SC, Almarine 20 GA, Lester 15 AL, Mattie 14 AL, Louis 11 GA, Evaline 10 GA, Katie 9 GA, Lucy 7 GA, Walter 4 GA.

1 adult slab, n/m

Lot 22, no name on wall

Mrs. Maggie B. Lakey	Apr. 26, 1876	Apr. 20, 1962	
C.H. Buchannon	Aug. 12, 1848	Mar. 8, 1926	
Susie R. Buchannon	Nov. 12, 1852	Feb. 8, 1926	
1 baby slab, n/m			SR: c/o C.H. Buchannon

Lot 23, no name on wall

Arabell McDaniel		Sept. 13, 1872	19 yrs, 9 mo 20 dys
3 adult slabs, n/m	1 baby brick slab,		

n/m

Elizabeth Tillman		Oct. 28, 1883 age 69 years	w/o W.W. McDaniel d/o Richard & Pennie Tillman
Susan K. McDaniel		no dates	SR: bur. 9/4/1916, 79 yrs.
Nancy L. McDaniel		no dates	SR: bur. 3/10/1924, 62 yrs.

- 1850 Muscogee Census: William McDaniel 41 NC, Elizabeth 36 NC, Martha A. 19 GA, John H. 12 GA, Julia A. 11 GA, Elizabeth A. 9 GA, Lesa M. 7 GA, Susan W. 5 GA and Nancy L 2 GA.

- 1860 Muscogee Census: William W. McDaniel 51 NC, Elizabeth 50 NC, Martha A. 28 GA, Juliet 19 GA, Elizabeth 17 GA, Minerva 15 GA, Susan 13 GA, Nancy 11 GA and Arabella 8 GA. Sophia Langford 13 GA was also enumerated in this household.

- Elizabeth Tillman married William W. McDaniel 10/7/1830 in Jones Co., GA. She was the d/o Richard Tillman and Pennie Mullins. Richard Tillman was born ca 1794 in Brunswick Co., GA and died in Jones Co., GA. He was the son of Roger Tillman/Tillghman (c1752-1792) and Martha Lumpkin.

- (personal correspondence from Trish Kashima)
  William W. was the son of Benjamin Watts McDaniel who was b ca 1785, Chatham Co NC, married Nancy Brantley (d/o of John Brantley and Sarah Minter), died 1818, Jones Co GA. Children: Kirk; William W.; Evaline b ca 1805, married Anderson C. Smith 1821 Jones Go, died aft 1880 TX; Benjamin; Martha; Yancy; Elinor; Lexi; Brantley who was in 1827 land lottery with grandfather and 2 uncles Samuel and Jacob Jr.

Sexton Records indicate buried in this lot:

W. W. McDaniel   *Bur. 10/10/1888, 71 yrs.*

Lot 24, no name on wall

John Diffley	June 24, 1854	May 3, 1901

- Obit: leaves wife, 8 children, his mother, Mrs. L.J. Diffey of Montgomery, AL, 3 brothers, P.F., of Montgomery, AL, Henry of Tallasse, AL, W.M. of Nashville, TN, 3 sisters; Mrs. Sarah Pike of Birmingham, AL, Mrs. Martha Hane of Montgomery, AL and Mrs. Ellen Schoolcraft of Columbus.

- John May Diffley was the son of Peter F. Diffley and Jane Wade who were married 2/5/1846 in Muscogee. His father was born in Ireland ca 1818. John married Ada M. Smith 6/24/1875 in Harris Co., GA. Ada M. Smith was born 4/4/1859 was the d/o William T. and Amanda Smith of Harris Co., GA.

Lot 25, no name on wall

Jerry L. Mullin	June 21, 1870	Aug. 2, 1945

- Obit: born Lee Co., AL, 1 dght, Mrs. Ralph Miller of Phenix City, AL, 1 son, Joseph, of Phenix City, AL, 2 brothers, Homer Summerline of Dallas, TX, & Al Summerline of

Columbus, GA, 2 g/dghts., 1 g/son.

- Jerry Lee Mullin married Birdie Lorena White 5/16/1897 in Lee Co., AL.   Giles Summerlin married Amelia Mullin 5/22/1879 in Lee Co., AL.

- 1880 Lee Co., Al Census shows: Giles Summerlin(e) 44 AL AL AL, wife Amelia 38 GA GA GA, son Henry L. 13 AL, son Archie A. 11 AL, son Raiford G. 6 AL, son Homer F. 3/12 AL and step-son Walton L. Mullin 9 AL.

- 1920 Lee Co., AL Census: Jerry L. Mullin 49 GA GA GA, Birdie L. AL IL AL, Joe 21 AL, Winney 13 AL and Annie F 10 AL.

J.A. Allen	C.S.A. SR: bur. 11/16/1894

- 1880 Lee Co., Al Census: James A. Allen 32 GA GA SC, wife Eugenia 28 GA GA SC, dau May 3 AL and son LaFayette 1 AL.

1 adult slab, n/m

Sexton Records indicate buried in this lot:

Annie Allen	*bur. 12/24/1909, 46 yrs.*
Eugenia Allen	*bur. 5/17/1884, 34 yrs.*

Lot 26, no name on wall

Fred Jackson Buchanan	May 9, 1884	Feb. 7, 1920	
Lilian B. Buchanan	May 6, 1885	Oct. 1, 1925	w/o F.J. Buchanan
Leonard H. Jones	1886	1917	SR: bur. 6/15/1917, 32 yrs

Lot 27, no name in wall

1 baby brick slab, n/m			SR: c/o Robt. Gregory 4/12/1880, 4 mo
Mollie Lee Gregory	June 16, 1852	Dec. 21, 1887	
Robert T. Gregory	Feb. 23, 1847	Jan. 6, 1930	G/M Co. I, GA Cav. C.S.A.

- Obit: born Stewart Co., GA, C.S.A. vet. in Cav. under Gen. Wheeler, leaves wife, nee Mrs. Lula Moshall, 3 dghts., Mrs. John K. Hinds of Atlanta, GA, Mrs. B.Y. Hill of Columbus, GA, Mrs. J.G. Derrick of El Paso, TX, 2 sons, Robert T., Jr. of New York, Herbert H. of Columbus, GA.

- 1850 Stewart Co., GA Census: Ivy Gregory 41 NC, Lucinda 38 GA, Seney 15 Ga, William 12 GA, P. H. (male) 10 GA, Julia 8 GA, Ann 5 GA, Robert 3 GA, John (?) ___ GA. Ivey William Gregory and his wife Lucinda Turner are buried in Whit Wiggins Cemetery in Stewart Co., GA. Ivey was born 12/21/1808 in Onslow Co., NC and died 11/14/1856. Lucinda was born 1/8/1813 and died 4/23/1857.

- 1870 Stewart Co., GA Census: Dr. W. A. Gregory 32 GA, Allie 32 GA, Robert T. Gregory 23 GA, Bartow 9 GA and Catherine Powell(?) 75 GA.

- 1880 Muscogee Census: R. T. Gregory (male) 31 GA GA GA, Robt. Gregory 36 GA GA GA, wife M. L. 28 GA GA GA, dau Grace 6 GA, brother-in-law A.L. Williams 22 GA GA GA, sister Delilah White 19 GA GA GA.

- 1920 Muscogee Census: Robert T. Gregory 72 GA NC SC, wife Lula 58 GA NY GA, son Henry H. 21 GA and sister Mary Mozkell (sic) 64 GA GA GA.

- Robert Taylor Gregory served in CSA in Co. I, 10th Confederate Calvary. His Civil War pension is in Muscogee County. He states that he has resided in GA since Feb. 23, 1847. Copy of ML included. Robert married Lula M. Putnam 7/29/1891 in Muscogee Co.

- GA Death Index shows Lula M. Gregory died 11/12/1935 in Muscogee Co., GA. The 1880 Census of Russell Co., Al shows Lula Moshell 18 GA NY GA as a daughter of Henry Moshell 57 NY NY NY.

Lot 28, Layfield on wall

| Indeanna Dobbs Layfield | Mar. 23, 1837 | Nov. 6, 1922 | w/o C.C. Layfield |

- Obit: born Muscogee Co., GA, 3 sons, deputy sheriff, C.C. Layfield, J.B., both of Columbus, GA., J.C. of Richland, GA., 5 dghts, Mrs. Millie Land, Mrs. Allie Griffin, Mrs. G.W. Lamb, all of Columbus, GA, Mrs. Abbie McBride of Thomasville, GA.

| Christopher Columbus Layfield | Mar. 23, 1832 | Feb. 25, 1899 | G/M Co. H, 17th GA Inf. C.S.A. |

- Obit: born Taylor Co., GA, lived in Harris & Chattahoochee counties, C.S.A. vet., Benning's Brig.

- Christopher Columbus Layfield filed as a Pensioner in Muscogee County in 1897. He enlisted 4/11/1862 in Co. H. 17th GA Regt. Of GA Volunteers, Benning's Brigade. While serving in Virginia on 8/31/1862 he was shot in the back over left scapular with a minnie ball. He suffers much pain from this wound and has only partial use of his left arm. He was captured at Ft. Harrison, VA on 9/29/1864 and held prisoner until paroled at the end of the war.

- Christopher married Indiana Fletcher Dobbs 12/18/1854 in Harris Co., GA. Christopher was the son of James Henderson Layfield (c1774-1877) and Sallie Lee (1809-1899). Indiana was the daughter of Samuel Dobbs and Luraney Harrington (aka Dr. Rainey Dobbs).

- 1850 Talbot Co., GA Census: James Layfield 51 GA, Sarah 41 GA, Columbus 17 GA, Cynthia (?) 17 GA, Malchesian 11 GA, Nancy 10 GA, Henderson 9 GA, Missouri (?) 8 GA, Sarah 5 GA and Martha 2 GA.

- 1880 Harris Co., GA Census: James Layfield Sr. 97 NC MD MD and Sarah 73 SC SC SC.

- 1880 Harris Co., GA Census: C. C. Layfield 48 GA GA GA, wife I. F. (female) 43 GA GA GA, dau Ella May 13 GA, dau Adeline (?) J. 12 GA, dau Abbie Lee 9 GA, son Christopher C. 8 GA, dau Sallie F. 3 GA and dau Willie M. 1 GA.

Lot 29, H. G. on wall

Henry Grader   Oct. 9, 1864   Feb. 2, 1929

- 1920 Muscogee Census: Henry G. Grader 55 Germany and wife Alice 59 Ohio.

- 1930 Muscogee Census: Alice Grader 69 OH OH PA.

- The Atlanta Constitution of 10/8/1911 states that Mr. & Mrs. Henry Grader and Miss Pearl Grader have just returned from a European trip.

Lot 30, no name on wall

Edwin Huson Sims, M.D.   Jan. 10, 1859   Nov. 27, 1919   SR: bur. 9/27/1926, 63 yrs.

- The Directory of Deceased American Physicians 1804-1929 shows Edwin Sims (1862-11/28/1919) Emory University School of Medicine, Atlanta: Atlanta Medical College, 1883; practicing Columbus 1883. Journal of the American Medical Association citation: 73:1953. He died of heart disease.

- 1900 Muscogee Census: Edwin H. Sims Jan 1859 GA SC SC, wife Annie B. June 1870 SC SC SC, son Edwin H. Jr. June 1898 GA and M-I-L Allice B. Bessellian Aug 1844 SC SC SC widow 5 children/1 living.

- Atlanta Constitution

    o 2/1/1903 "Society in Columbus": Miss Annie Lou Russell, of Macon, arrived in the city Tuesday and is the guest of Dr. & Mrs. Edwin H. Sims.

    o 5/7/1911 "Society in Columbus": Mrs. Edwin H. Sims entertained at bridge luncheon in honor of Mrs. J. T. Johnson, of Savannah.

    o 6/11/1911 "Society in Columbus": Miss Dorothy Hamilton of Savannah, is the guest of Mrs. Edwin H. Sims.

- 1930 Muscogee Census: Annie B. Sims 58 SC SC SC.

1 adult slab, n/m

Lot 31, J. H. Brady on wall

J.H. Brady   1863   1926   SR: bur. 9/27/1926, 63 yrs.

- 1870 Muscogee Census: Charles Brady 37 Ireland, Rose 36 Ireland, Michael 11 GA, Mary A. 9 GA and John 6 GA.

- 1880 Muscogee Census: Rosa Brady 50 Ireland Ireland Ireland widowed, dau M. A. 19 GA, son Michael 21 GA and son John 17 GA.

- 1920 Muscogee Census: John Brady 54 GA Ireland Ireland, wife Hattie 50 AL CT CT and son Curtis 16 GA.

2 adult slabs, n/m   2 baby slabs, n/m

Sexton Records indicate buried in this lot:

Carrie Brady   *bur. 11/7/1901, 31 yrs.*

Hattie F. Brady   *bur. 12/14/1922, 55 yrs.*

Lot 32, no name on wall

3 adult slabs, n/m

Lot 33, no name on wall

2 adult brick slabs, n/m

Lot 34, P.M. Morehead on wall

W.E. Morehead   May 16, 1868   Nov. 1, 1908

- 1870 Lee Co., AL Census: T. Morehead 28 SC, P. (f) 28 AL, C. (f) 8 AL, and W. (m) 2 AL.

- 1880 Lee Co., AL Census: Thomas Morehead 38 SC SC SC, wife Martha 38 AL GA GA, son William 12 SC, son-in-law Charles Faulkner 20 SC SC SC and dau Callie 17 Al GA AL.

- 1920 Lee Co., AL Census: H. John Robinson 34 AL AL AL, wife Mary 35 VA GA AL, son E. William 2 6/12 AL and grandmother M. Patsie Morehead widowed 73 AL GA GA.

Patsy M. Morehead   Sept. 28, 1841   Feb. 22, 1930   in memory of our grandmother

- Obit: died in Phenix City, AL, 5 g/dghts, Mrs. J.F. Robinson of Phenix City, AL, Mrs. W.R. Adams, Mrs. S.R. Shaw, both of Birmingham, AL, Mrs. J.W. Thompson of Pisgah, AL, Mrs. W.V. Guerard of Meridian, MS, 1 niece, Mrs. Emma Lovelace of Phenix City, AL.

Lot 35, no name

Emma Reese Mason   Oct. 12, 1851   Sept. 23, 1912   w/o John W. Walton Drake

- Emma C. Mason married John W. W. Drake April 28, 1863 in Macon Co., AL.[10]

Catherine B. Mason   Jan. 10, 1832   Mar. 9, 1877   w/o J.J. Mason

John James Mason   July 24, 1826   Jan. 13, 1902

- Obit: Dr. John James Mason was 76 years of age. He was born near Wetumpka and moved to Columbus shortly after the close of the Civil War. He attended colleges in New Orleans and Charleston. It also mentions the hospital in Auburn. He leaves 7 children, (named, but unreadable.)

- John James Mason married Catherine B. Rogers Jan. 25, 1849 in Sumter Co., AL.[11]

- 1860 Auburn, Macon Co., AL Census: J. J. Mason 34 GA, Catherine 24 GA, Martha J. 9 AL, Emma R. 7 AL, Catherine Jr. 5 AL, William Y. 2 AL and Harriett 1/3 AL.

- 1880 Muscogee Census: John Mason (Doctor) 52 GA GA GA, dau Mattie 25 AL GA GA, dau Katie 22 AL, son Willie 21 AL, dau Hattie 18 AL, dau Annie 16 AL, son George 10 GA and dau Addie 7 GA. Also in the same household listed as boarders: Walton Drake (Dentist) 30 AL and Emma 24 AL.

Lot 36, no name on wall

Effie Melton Smith	Apr. 16, 1881	Nov. 7, 1954
Harry S. Smith	Aug. 5, 1883	Feb. 5, 1948

- 1930 Muscogee Census: Harry Smith 40 NY Europe Europe, Effie 35 GA GA GA and mother-in-law Ella A. Melton (widow) 68 GA SC SC.

Ella Greene Melton	Aug. 3, 1862	Mar. 3, 1944	w/o Wm. T. Melton

- 1910 Harris Co., GA Census: John W. Camp 32 GA GA GA (mar. 9 yrs), wife Effie 28 GA GA GA and MIL Ella A. Melton 48 GA GA GA (wd).

- 1920 Muscogee Census: Ella A. Melton (widowed) 58 GA SC SC and dau Effie Melton (widowed) 29 GA GA GA

Lot 37, open lot

Sarah Hoffman	Jan. 1, 1833 b. SC	Apr. 19, 1904 d. Phenix City, AL

- 1870 Muscogee Census: Eliza Pitman 41 SC, Drucilla 19 AL and Sarah Huffman (sic) 38 SC.

- 1880 Muscogee Census: Sarah Hoffman 45 SC SC SC, sister Eliza Pitman 50 SC SC SC, niece Lucille Cassy (sic) 29 AL AL AL, nephew Daniel Cassy 29 AL AL AL and nephew Oscar Cassy 9 GA GA GA.

10 adult brick slabs, n/m   1 baby brick slab, n/m

Sexton Records indicate buried in this lot:

Eliza Shirley	*bur. 12/4/1899, 71 yrs.*
Mary Stephens	*bur. 4/21/1908, 81 yrs.*

- Obit: Mary Stephens leaves 1 daughter-in-law Mrs. Abbie Stephens, 1 g/dght Mrs. G.M. Sayers, 1 niece, Mrs. Drucilla Casey, all of Phenix City, AL.

Ellen Shirley	Aug. 8, 1838 b. SC	Apr. 8, 1865 d. Columbus, GA
Phireby Shirley	July 16, 1801 b. SC	Nov. 13, 1862 d. Columbus, GA our dear Mother

- 1860 Muscogee Census: Pheriby Sherly (sic) 61 GA, Eliza 23 SC, Catherine 16 SC,

Rosetta 10 AL and Jacob 4 AL.

Robert E. Stephens	Dec. 15, 1841 b. SC	Nov. 25, 1861 d. Columbus, GA	
Benjamin Stephens	May 4, 1821 b. SC	Dec. 5, 1863 d. Columbus, GA	

- 1860 Muscogee Census: Benjamin Stevens 38 SC, Mary 35 SC, Robert E. 19 SC and Wade H. 14 SC. Next door is Mary Sherley 28 SC and Jacob 8 AL.

Wade H. Stephens	Apr. 2, 1844 b. SC	Oct. 5, 1880 d. Columbus, GA	

Lot 38, no name on wall

J. J. Smith		1918	SR: born 1855 bur. 5/6/1918, 52 yrs
Warnie Pittman Smith		Sept. 5, 1949	76 yrs old

- 1880 Russell Co., AL Census: James Pittman 40 GA -- --, Elizabeth 34 AL GA SC, and dau Warnie 8 AL.

1 baby brick slab, n/m

Lot 39, no name on wall

Esprea A. Martin	May 3, 1842	Apr. 27, 1878	d/o Wm. B. & G.A. Martin
Maggie L. Martin	Nov. 4, 1872	June 12, 1942	
Augustus A. Martin	Jan. 11, 1882	June 11, 1935	
Margaret Martin	Jan. 15, 1915	Jan. 2, 1936	
Mrs. Willie McKenzie	1879	1924	SR: bur. 6/11/1924, 45
Ulysses L. Martin	Sept. 8, 1838	Mar. 2, 1892	Masonic emblem

- Obit: died Girard, AL, leaves wife & 4 children, Mrs. Bettie Jones of Shady Grove, PA, J.R. Martin, Misses Nellie & Lizzie, Mr. Martin was the last of 3 brothers, all of whom lived & died in the same community.

- Ulysses Lewis Martin enlisted 4/1/1862, into Co. "I" 34th Alabama. The enlistment data shows him to be 24 years old, 5 feet 10 inches tall, born in Russell County Ala., fair complexion, blue eyes, light hair, a laborer by occupation. Hospitalized on Nov. 18, 1862 and discharged at Tullahoma TN the next day suffering from myopia.

- 1860 Russell Co., AL Census: William B. Martin 59 VA, Gracella A. 36 NC, Ulysses L. Martin 21 AL, Esprea 17 AL, William A. 16, Martha H. 14, Mary 12 and Joseph 9.

- 1870 Russell Co., AL Census: U.L. Martin 31 AL, S.E. (f) 24 GA and Jane Carter 40 GA domestic servant.

- 1880 Russell Co., AL Census (Ulysses was the Census taker): Ulysses L. Martin 41 AL VA NC, wife Sophronia 36 GA GA GA, dau Bettie 10 AL, son James R. 7 AL, dau Nellie

5 GA, dau Lissie 3 AL, and 2 Edmundson boarders.

- Bible records show that Ulysses married Sophronia Kendrick.

- 1850 Pike County, GA Census: Richmond R. Kindrick 47 M GA, Penelope 36 GA, Cincinatus B. 15 GA, Zebulon R. 13 GA, Eugenius C. 11 GA, Alonzo P. 8 GA, Sophronia E. Kendrick 7 GA, Alphonso S. 6 GA and Leonadus N. 2 GA.

- 1860 Russell County, AL Census: Richard R. Kendrick 58 GA, Penelope 46 GA, Zebulon R. 22 GA, Eugene C. 20 GA, Alonzo P. 18 GA, Sophronia E. 16 GA, Alphonzo C. 14 GA, Lenidus N. 12 GA, Hezakiah Kendrick 10 GA and Henry C. 7 AL.

- Richmond R. Kendrick married Penelope Edmundson 11/21/1833 in Troup Co., GA.

Mrs. Amanda Martin	1852	1930	SR: bur. 3/21/1930, 79 yrs.

Lot 40, no name on wall

Laurens Cargill	May 20, 1870	May 20, 1870	s/o J.W. & M.L. Cargill
Maria Louisa Cargill	Mar. 16, 1839	Oct. 6, 1923	d/o Wm. & Martha A. Holland, w/o John W. Cargill

- Obit: born Fredonia, AL, 2 dghts, Mrs. Ed F. Cook of Nashville, TN, Mrs. James J. Gilbert of Columbus, GA, 2 sons, Walter Hurt of Columbus, GA, John Ralston of Americus, GA, 1 brother, W.H. Holland of Seale, AL.

- William Holland, son of Isaac Holland (c1770 Sussex Co., DE-c1832 Monroe Co., G) and Amelia Brewington (1772 Worchester Co., MD-c1864 Monroe Co., GA) married Martha Ann Bilbro ca 1831. William Holland is a brother to James Cayle Holland who is also buried in Linwood Cemetery. Amelia B. Holland is listed as Permelia Holland living with daughter Permelia/Amelia Askin in the 1850 and 1860 Morgan Co., GA Censuses.

- 1850 Russell Co., AL Census: William Holland 47 GA, Martha 39 GA, Mary 16 GA, Julia 13 GA, Mariah 10 AL, Ann 8 AL and William 5 AL.

Malcolm MacDonell Cook, M.D.	June 15, 1906	Feb. 20, 1955	
Walter Hurt Cargill	Nov. 30, 1878	Mar. 29, 1941	
Mamie Love Burts Cargill	Mar. 28, 1895	Nov. 30, 1967	
Annie Pridgen	Jan. 26, 1842	Feb. 24, 1920	d/o Wm. and Martha Ann Holland, w/o Thos C. Pridgen

- Obit: widow of late Thomas Pridgen, lived with Mr. & Mrs. James Gilbert, 1 sister Mrs. John W. Cargill, of Columbus, GA, 1 brother, Wm. H. Holland, Seale, AL.

- 1870 Muscogee Census: Thomas C. Pridgeon 48 GA and Annie 28 AL.

- 1880 Muscogee Census (next door to John Cargill) Thomas Pridget 58 GA GA GA and wife Annie 38 AL GA GA.

John Wesley Cargill	Nov. 19, 1833 b. Laurens Dist., SC	July 15, 1899 d. Columbus, GA	

- Obit: C.S.A. under Col. Hardaway, leaves wife, 2 dghts Mrs. Ed F. Cook of Savannah, GA, Mrs. James J. Gilbert of Columbus, GA, 2 sons, J. Ralston Cargill of Savannah, GA, Walter Hart Cargill of Columbus, GA.

- 1880 Muscogee Census: John Cargill 46 SC SC SC, wife Maria 40 AL GA GA, dau Annie 12 AL, dau Evelyn 7 GA, son Roylston 4 GA and son Walter 2 GA.

- John Wesley Cargill (1833-1899) was the son of Dr. John Wesley Cargill (1798-1876) and Rebecca Long (1800-1867). Rebecca Long was named in her father, Robert Long's will in Laurens District, SC. [12]

Edmund Francis Cook, D.D.   Jan. 24, 1867   Apr. 10, 1957

- GA Death Index shows Edmund F. Cook died 4/10/1957 in Bibb Co., GA age 90 years.

- 1920 Jackson Co., MO Census shows Edmond Cook 52 GA GA GA, wife Annie 47 AL SC AL, son Malcolm 13 GA.

Annie Cargill Cook   June 2, 1868   June 15, 1967

Lot 41, no name on wall

John M. Frazer   Feb. 19, 1829   Oct. 28, 1910

- Obit: born Charleston, SC, engaged in railroad business, died in New York City, married twice, 1st to Miss Reaves, a relative of Mrs. C. Lary of this City, 2nd wife, Miss Annie Johnson, d/o George L. Johnson of this City, leaves 2 children, Ethel, 14 & John, 10.

- 1880 Muscogee Census: George Johnson, machinist 46 GA GA GA listed as other in household of Randall and Louse Ramsey.

- 1910 Talbot Co., GA Census: Elizabeth Dougherty 69 AL GA GA, brother-in-law John M. Frazer 80 GA NC NC and sister Mary A. Frazer 76 GA GA GA.

Mrs. G.L. Johnson   Feb 9, 1839   Jan. 23, 1922

- Obit: died in New York City from burns, leaves husband, 1 daughter, Mrs. J.M. Frazer of New York, 1 son, G. Wilfrid of Mexico City, Mexico.

Lot 42, no name on wall

Major Wiley Williams   Feb. 5, 1871   68 yrs.

- Obit: attorney of Russell Co., AL, formerly of Marion Co., GA, former Mayor of Columbus, former editor and owner of "The Columbus Enquirer", died at residence of son, John W. Williams.

- 1850 Muscogee Census: Wiley Williams 45 GA, Mrs. W. 30 SC, William F. 21 GA, John W. 18 GA, Wilhelmina 5 GA. Also in household Augustus Nagel 28 SC, Elizabeth 21 SC and Ella G. 3 SC.

- 1870 Russell Co., AL Census: Wiley Williams 66 GA, Willa 50 SC and Willa 28 GA.

Willa Nagel Williams   April 30, 1896   76 yrs.

- Obit: died at Ridge Springs, SC, one of the oldest and highly respected ladies in this community and was returning from a visit to relatives in Columbia, SC when taken ill, widow of Maj. Wiley Williams, 1 step-son, John Williams, of Opelika, AL, step grandchildren, among whom is Chief Wiley Williams of Columbus, GA.

- Major Augustus G. Nagel was born in Anhalt, Germany, and died in Macon, Ga., Dec. 26th 1866, aged about 80 years. His father and two brothers were ministers of the gospel in the Presbyterian Church... In early manhood he made a tour of the United States, and having married a lady in Edgefield Dist., S. C., settled permanently there, where he raised a large family. He was the last surviving member of the old Savannah Guards of 1812.[13]

Lot 43, no name on wall

Felix J. Jenkins	Aug. 17, 1841	May 4, 1914	C.S.A.

- Obit: leaves 1 son B. Crawford Jenkins of Midland, GA, 3 brothers, W.W. & A.I. both of Midland, GA, 2 sisters, Mrs. H.L. Dudley of Russell Co., AL & Mrs. T.H. Kimbrough of Cataula, GA.
- 1870 Muscogee Census: William Jenkins 27 GA, Felix Jenkins 25 GA and Stephen McClendon 19 GA
- 1900 Muscogee Census: Felix J. Jenkins Mar 1846 GA GA GA, wife Ella Apr 1849 GA GA GA and son Crawford Aug 1881 GA.

Clara Carr Jenkins	1886	1964	SR: bur. 8/3/1964
Ella Crawford Jenkins	June 29, 1858	Aug. 27, 1932	w/o Felix J. Jenkins

- 1870 Muscogee Census: Bennett H. Crawford 35 GA, Mary L. 30 GA, Ellen 11 GA, Bennetta 8 GA, Andrew L. 4 GA, Mary 1 GA and others in household.

W. F. Scott	Sept. 16, 1837	Aug. 6, 1855	19 yrs

- Obit: only son of Thomas R. & Elizabeth Scott.

Bennett Crawford Jenkins	May 13, 1885	May 6, 1928	s/o Felix & Ella C. Jenkins

Lot 44, H.S. Estes on wall

William Gray Estes	Aug. 6, 1860	Nov. 28, 1921	
Clara Blanche Hatcher			inf. d/o B.T. & M.J. Hatcher age 5 months
Martha J. Estes		Aug. 31, 1822	b. Muscogee Co., GA

- Obit: nee Gray, w/o Henson Estes, 8 children, Dr. C.E. Estes, Mrs. B.T. Hatcher, both of Columbus, GA, George H. & W.G. of Birmingham, AL, Joe & Richard, both of Dallas, TX, died in Talbotton, GA at residence of her daughter Mrs. A.R. Wilkinson.

Albert Ausbon Estes	Dec. 8, 1864	Dec. 17, 1870	s/o H.S. & M.J. Estes
Inf. s/o J.D. & R.R. Estes		no dates	
Jimmie Gardner	Sept. 16, 1864	Apr. 28, 1950	w/o Wm. G. Estes

Martha J. Estes	Oct. 21, 1851	May 2, 1912	w/o Benj. T. Hatcher, Mother
Marion Scott Estes	Mar 15, 1862 Wynnton, Muscogee Co., GA	Jan. 10, 1880 Dallas, TX	
John Estes	July 3, 1881	Aug. 30, 1881	s/o Geo H. & Annie G. Estes
Benjamin T. Hatcher	Oct. 30, 1847	Jan. 26, 1911	Father

- Obit: born Columbus, s/o Samuel J. & Elizabeth McGehee Hatcher, C.S.A. vet., married Oct. 1870 to Martha Jane Estes, d/o Henson S. Estes, leaves wife & 4 children, Mrs. Lottie H. Estes, Mrs. G. Everett Strupper, both of Columbus, Mrs. C.C. McGehee, Jr., of Atlanta, GA, B. Carl Hatcher of Louisville, KY, 1 brother, Hon. Samuel B. Hatcher, 1 sister, Mrs. W.P. Hunt, both of Columbus.

| Henson S. Estes | June 2, 1811 Greenville Dist., SC | Dec. 20, 1888 Columbus, GA | |

- Obit: s/o Joel D. Estes, married Martha J. Gray, 18th Feb. 1841, in Muscogee Co, GA, born Greenville Dist., SC was brother of J. Marion Estes, children, Dr. C.E. Estes, R.H. Estes, both of Columbus, George of Talbotton, GA, Wm. G. of Birmingham, AL, Scott & Joel D., both of Texas, Mrs. W.W. Bussey, Mrs. Ben T. Hatcher, both of Macon, GA., Mrs. A.R. Wilkinson of Talbotton, GA

- Mr. Henson S. Estes died yesterday morning at the residence of his son-in-law, Mr. W.W. Bussey on Fourth Avenue. He was a prominent and highly esteemed citizen of Columbus and was always noted for his gentleness of disposition, his kindness of heart and his true Christian charity. Mr. Estes was a deacon of the First Baptist Church for over thirty years, and at the time of his death he was the senior deacon of that church. He was in his seventy-eighth year, being born in Greenville District on June 2, 1811. He came to Columbus in 1884, and has resided here since. He was a brother of Mr. J. Marion Estes, and father of Dr. O.B. Estes and Mr. R.H. Estes of this city; Mr. George Estes of Talbotton; Mr. William G. Estes of Birmingham; Scott and Joel D. Estes of Texas; Mrs. W.W. Bussey; Mrs. Ben T. Hatcher of Macon; and Mrs. A.R. Wilkinson of Talbotton.

Inf. Kendrick		1940	s/o Martha Dimon & Kendrick, Jr.
Joseph Homer Dimon			SR: died 12 Jan 1951, 81 yrs.
Nellie Dimon Acree			SR: bur. 13 Jun 1961. Born 6 July 1895, d/o Joseph Homer Dimon Sr. & Martha Estes Dimon.

Lot 45, no name on wall

| Wilson Emery Estes | Dec. 2, 1859 Cumming, GA | Jan. 15, 1908 Savannah, GA | |

- 1880 Census Fulton Co., GA: Joshua Estes 40 GA GA GA, wife Mary 38 GA GA GA, son Wilson 19 GA, dau. Cora 18 GA, dau Mattie 13 GA, son Eddie 8 GA and son Bobby 2 GA.

35

George Jasper Golden	Aug. 28, 1888	Feb. 28, 1974	
	Girard, AL	Atlanta, GA	
Charlotte T. Hatcher	1871	1948	w/o Wilson E. Estes

- Charlotte, "Lottie", was the d/o Benjamin T. Hatcher and Martha Estes. She married 1st about 1889, William Bendell Swift. She married 2nd March 20, 1905 Wilson Estes.

Inf. s/o Geo J. & Lyre Swift Golden	May 26, 1923	May 27, 1923	
Lyra Swift Golden	Aug. 31, 1896	Feb. 28, 1974	
	b. Columbus, GA	d. Atlanta, GA	

- d/o William Bendell Swift and Lottie Hatcher. She married George Golden April 26, 1915.

| Benjamin Carl Hatcher | Nov. 13, 1879 | Dec. 25, 1927 | s/o Benj. Thomas & Martha Estes Hatcher |

- Atlanta Constitution, 12/3/1905: Mrs. & Mrs. Forbes Bradley of Ft. Mitchell, AL have issued invitations to the wedding of their daughter Alice Geraldine Bradley to Benjamin Carl Hatcher on the evening of 12 December, at their home in Ft. Mitchell.

- 1910 Jefferson Co., AL Census: Martha H. Hartwell 61 AL GA GA, dau Willie V. 37 AL, son Charles W. 36 AL, roomer Ben C. Hatcher 30 GA GA GA (m. 4 yrs.), roomer Allie (sic) B. Hatcher 24 AL AL AL.

- 1920 Russell Co., AL Census: Forbes Bradley 68 AL, dau Willie 38 Al and dau Alice B. Hatcher 32 AL widowed.

Lot 46, no name on wall

| Peirre Emmett Griffith | Mar. 23, 1860 | Aug. 15, 1918 | |
| Frankie McGehee Griffith | Mar. 2, 1862 | Feb. 3, 1919 | one slab |

- 1900 Muscogee Census: P. E. Griffith Mar 1860 AL GA GA, wife Frankie Mar 1862 GA GA GA (married 15 yrs, 4/4 children), dau Mary Dec 1890 GA, dau Lucy Dec 1892 GA, son Lewis Dec 1893 GA, son P. E. Jr. Nov 1896 GA and mother (sic) M. J. McGehee Nov 1839 GA NC GA, wd (5/3 child).

- 1870 Dale Co., AL Census: E. W. Griffith 43 SC, S.W. (f) GA, P.E. (m) 10 AL, O. E. (f) 5 AL, W. O. (m) 3 AL and F. W. (f) 1 AL.

- Pierre Emmett is the son of Elmore Wyatt Griffith 1827 Barnwell Co., SC-1916 Dale Co., AL and Sally W. Gawley (1836 GA-after 1800). The Gawley's were from Stewart Co., GA.

| Mrs. Tyna Adams Greer | Jan. 17, 1882 | Jan. 24, 1961 |
| G. Mason Adams | Oct. 22, 1879 | Apr. 5, 1932 |

- 1930 Muscogee Census: Mason Adams 51 GA GA GA (m@30 yrs), wife Lucy 36 GA GA GA m@15, son Cullen 19 GA, son Mason 15 GA and son William 7/12 GA.

- 1880 Muscogee Census: Columbus Adams 23 GA GA GA, wife Julia 22 GA GA GA and son Mason 2 GA.

- Columbus Adams married Julia Elder 9 Dec 1877 in Muscogee Co., GA.

Lucy Griffith	Sept. 1, 1892	Sept. 4, 1947	w/o Mason Adams
R.W. Denton	Apr. 1821	June 22, 1862	

- 1860 Muscogee Census: R. Watson Denton 36 PA, Fany J. 28 GA, Richard L. 4 GA and Letetia N. Walker 16 GA.

F.C. Weisiger	Dec. 23, 1834	Nov. 9, 1912	one slab
Sue B. Weisiger	June 26, 1835	June 10, 1915	

- Obit: F.C. Weisiger borned and reared in Manchester, VA, leaves wife & 3 sons, J.B., W.P., & S.C., loved ones attending his funeral, Mr. & Mrs. J.B. Weisiger of Norfolk, VA.

- Sue B. Weisiger died at home of son in Newport, VA, 3 sons, James of Richmond, VA, William of Atlanta, GA, & Clarence of Newport News, VA.

- 1860 Chesterfield Co., VA Census: W. W. Weisiger 54 VA, Sarah 44 VA, Wm B. 22 VA, Saml 15 VA, David 10 VA, Irvine 8 VA, Bernard 6 VA, Addison 2 VA, Fredrick 25 VA, Susan 25 VA James 6/12 VA and Wm A Royale 25 VA

- Frederick Clarke Weisiger was CSA treasurer who signed Confederate currency. He married Susan Boisseau Bott 10 Feb 1859 in Chesterfield Co., VA. She was the d/o James Bott (1796-ca1866 and Susan Boisseau Hatcher.

- Richmond (VA) Enquirer, Saturday, March 1831, p 3, col 6:. Married on Tuesday the 15th instant, by the Rev. Phillip Courtney, Mr James Bott of Amelia, to Miss Susan B Hatcher, daughter of Mrs Susan Hatcher of Chesterfield."

Lot 47, T.J. Grier on wall

P.H. Kelly	Oct. 12, 1856	Apr. 18, 1928	
Thomas J. Grier		Apr. 17, 1885	age 64 years

- 1870 Muscogee Census: Thomas Grier 49 Ire, Maria 39 Ire, Mary 18 VT, Lizzie 16 VT, Katie 4 GA and Tillie 2 GA.

- Thomas Grier was a marble cutter and carved several Linwood tombstones..

Maria Clark Grier	Mar. 11, 1827	Feb. 3, 1910

- 1900 Muscogee Census: Mariah Greir (sic) Mar 1827 Ire Ire Ire (wd, 5/- children), dau Mary E. Davis Mar 1852 VT Ire Ire, SIL R. A. Mar 1851 AL GA GA (mar. 24 yrs), gdau Emma M. Oct 1877 GA, gson Jimmie July 1881 GA, gson Thomas J. Dec 1884 GA, gson Leo B. Dec 1888 GA and gdau Mariah L. Oct 1891 GA.

Lot 48, no name on wall

Mary A.H. Smith	Mar. 2, 1856	Nov. 19, 1893 d. St. Paul Parsonage	w/o Rev. W. C. Lovett

- Obit: wife of Rev. W. C. Lovett, pastor of St. Paul church, died last Sunday at 1:30 PM. She was a daughter of Rev. J. Blakely Smith of sainted memory in GA, whose wife the mother of Mrs. Lovett, had died only a week or two before. Her father was pastor and presiding elder here, the family residing in Greenville in 1865 through 1867.

- Atlanta Constitution 1 Nov 1893: Death of Mrs. J. Blakely Smith, formerly of Macon,.

Mrs. Smith was the mother of Rev. W. T. Smith, of Savannah and Mrs. W. C. Lovett, of Columbus.

Inf of Rev. & Mrs. J.G. Harrison	Aug. 12, 1893		
Little Ruth	Apr. 12, 1900	Apr. 15, 1900	inf. d/o Rev. & Mrs. C.T. Clark
Warren Chandler Copeland	Dec. 21, 1901	Jan. 1, 1904	

Lot 49, L.F. Humber on wall

Mrs. Salatha F. Humber	Oct. 5, 1849	Mar. 25, 1883 d. Columbus	w/o Lucius F. Humber

- Chattahoochee Co., GA WB 1853-1885. 12 Mar 1860. Parham D. Redding was appointed guardian of is minor children: James D., Julia E., William K., Selitha, Charles A., minor ch, entitled to seperate estate in Chattahoochee Co. James A. Redding, sec.
  - Parham Redding's wife, Amy Goodwin Jackson died 1852.
- 1860 Stewart Co., GA Census: Thomas R. Scott 43 GA, Elizabeth 36 GA and Salatha F. Redding 11 GA.
  - Thomas R. Scott married Elizabeth Speights 18 December 1837 in Hancock Co., GA.
- 1870 Stewart Co., GA Census shows Elizabeth Scott 45 GA, a widow boarding in household of J. S. Wimberly.
- Obit: Atlanta Constitution 5 May 1905. Columbus, GA May 4. Mrs. T. R. Scott of Columbus aged 82 died this afternoon at the home of Lucius Humber on Third Avenue.

Lucius Flowers Humber	1848	1922	Co. E, 27th Bn. GA Inf., C.S.A. SR: d. 5/19/1922 bur.5/20/1922

- Obit: murdered by wife, Leila C., brother & sisters, R.L. & J.T. Humber, both of Lumpkin, GA, C.N. Hunter of Fort Mitchell, AL, Mrs. Matte Little of Carrollton, GA, Mrs. M.D. Goode of Lumpkin, GA, his children, Mrs. F.D. Patterson of Cuthbert, GA, Mrs. Hugh Oversby of Richland, GA, W.T. of Russell Co., AL, C.R., Mary Owsley Humber, & Roberth Henry Humber, all of Columbus, GA.
- 1880 Stewart Co., GA Census: Lucius Humber 32 GA GA GA, wife Salatha 30 GA GA GA, dau Mary 10 GA, dau Elizabeth 8 GA, dau Clara 7 GA, dau Lucia 4 GA, son Thomas 1 GA and Elizabeth Scott 56 GA GA GA.
- Atlanta Constitution 18 April 1898: (April 16) Humber-Overton Marriage. Miss Lucia Humber and Mr. Hugh Overby were married this morning at the beautiful home of Mr. Lycius Humber. She is the youngest daughter of Mr. Lucius Humber or the firm of Humber & Blanchard. Mr. Overby is one of the leading planters of Stewart County.
- 1920 Russell Co., AL Census: Lucious Humber 71 GA GA GA, wife Leila 50 AL GA AL, dau Mary 8 GA, son Robert 5 AL, SIL Clay King 30 AL AL AL, dau Mary Elizabeth 27 AL, GD Roberta 4 AL and GD Frances 2 AL.
- Lucius, married 1) 22 Oct 1868 Salatha Flewellen Redding the d/o Parham Redding (1799-1882) and Amy Goodwin Jackson (c1806-1852) and 2)Leila (Jones) King.

- 1850 Troup Co., GA Census: Charles C. Humber 23 GA, Mary J. 18 GA, Lucius F. 2 GA, Robert T. 3/12 GA and Robert Bickerstaff 9 AL. (Martha Christian Humber, Lucius' aunt, married Capt. William Jefferson Bickerstaff 12 Sept 1839 in Butts Co., GA.)

- 1900 Lee Co., AL Census: Lela King Oct 1869 AL AL AL (wd 6/5 child.), son Clay Feb 1890 AL, son Willie Apr 1893 AL, son Mark Apr 1894, dau Marie Jun 1896 AL, son Cullen Nov 1898 AL and aunt Emma Forman 1839 AL AL AL (single). (Note: Lela C. Jones married George W. King 6 Dec 1888 in Lee Co., AL)

Mamie Louise	Aug. 8, 1869	Oct. 3, 1896	w/o C.P. Mooty, d/o Lucius F. & Salatha F. Humber
Elizabeth Scott	Jan 26, 1871	Sept. 29, 1902	d/o Lucius & Salatha Humber w/o J.L. Brooks

Lot 50, no name on wall

Francis Xavier Profumo	Jan. 28, 1837 Genoa, Italy	Oct. 25, 1910 Columbus, GA	C.S.A.

- Obit: children, F.X., Jr., Misses Angela, Eva & Mary, all of Columbus, member 46th GA Reg., C.S.A.

- Old-timers still talk about Profumo's ice cream as the best they ever ate. And it had cost as little (or as much) as $.05 for a bowlful! Francis Xavier Profumo had been born in Genoa, Italy in 1837, immigrating to the United States at the age of twelve (or thirteen) and coming to Columbus. He was the proper age to see service during the War Between the States and did so in the Confederate Army. In 1867, he married Columbusite Henrietta Hoffman and, in 1872, opened his own confectionary store at 1214 Tenth Street. In business until his death in 1910, Profumo's most celebrated dish was that flavorsome sweet which, in an early form of take-out-service, was available in pint and quart containers that were returned when empty (probably to be filled nup again!). He is seen in the accompanying photo with his daughter Mary, who apparently did not inherit his blue eyes. The firm closed upon his death, and the recipe for the delicious cold dessert remains a closely-guarded family secret to this day.

- 1870 Muscogee Census: Francis X. Profumo 33 Italy, Henrietta 28 GA, Angelo 1 GA, Sebastian J. Huffman (sic) 22 GA, and Victoria Huffman 19 GA.

- 1880 Muscogee Census: F. X. Profumo 41 IT IT IT, wife Henretta 39 GA __ Bavaria, dau Angela 11 GA, dau Eva 8 GA, son Frank 4 GA and dau Mary 2 GA.

Eva Profumo		Oct. 19, 1933	62 years
Mary T. Profumo	1878	1919	*SR: b. 5/15/1878 bur. 9/10/1919*
Henrietta Profumo	1841	1928	*SR: bur. 6/20/1928, 87 yrs.*

- Obit: widow of late Francis E. Profumo, 1 son, F.X., 2 daughters, Misses Angela & Eva Profumo, all of Columbus, GA.

- 1850 Muscogee Census: Sebastin Hoffman 34 Ger, Anna E. 31 Bavaria, Ragenia 11 GA, Barbara H. S. 9 GA, Mary L__ 7 GA, John J. 5 GA, Sebastian J. 2 GA and Victoria M. 1/12 GA.

- 1860 Muscogee Census: Sabastian Hohhman 50 Germany, Sarah 26 GA, John 15 GA,

Sabastian 13 GA, Victoria 10 GA, Rujena 21 GA, and Henrietta 19 GA.

Angela Profumo	Mar. 21, 1869	Mar. 24, 1956
Francis Xavier Profumo	Feb. 4, 1876	Oct. 23, 1948

Lot 51, Jackson on wall

William Jackson	Mar. 26, 1862	Oct. 14, 1896
	Barbour Co., AL	

- 1880 Muscogee Census: William Jackson 55 GA SC SC, wife Mary 47 GA GA GA, dau Lola 22 GA, dau Ida 20 NC, son William 18 AL, dau Clara 16 AL, dau Alice 14 AL, dau Mary 12 AL, dau Annie 10 GA and son Stephen 6 GA.

1 adult slab, n/m

SR: indicate buried in this lot.

Mary Jackson	*Bur. 4/20/1879, 20 yrs.*

Lot 52, Whitsitt on wall

Jeremiah L. Whitsitt	May 5, 1844	Apr. 8, 1902
	Graham, NC	Columbus, GA

- Obit: leaves wife, 1 daughter, Miss Nell Whitsitt, & mother in Graham, NC, 3 sisters, Mrs. Joe Hold, Mrs. Jerry Holt, Mrs. Wood, all of Burlington, NC, 5 brothers, Dr. George, John W., Henry, Joseph & Alfred.
- 1900 Chatham Co., GA Census: Jeremiah L. Whitsitt May 1844 NC NC NC, wife June 1844 Eng Eng Sco, and dau Barbara N. Mar 1882 NC.

Mary Allen Lamb	June 23, 1844	May 14, 1916 w/o J.L. Whitsitt

- Obit: widow of late Jerry L. Whitsitt, 1 daughter, Mrs. H.L. Abbot, nieces, Misses Mamie, Nellie Webster of Columbus, Mrs. Barbara Dibbell of Montgomery, AL, 1 nephew, W.O. Webster of Columbus, GA.

Louie Webster		May 10, 1897 Infant s/o Wm. O & Irene Webster. 9 mo 23 dys
Frank Huff Doughtie	Aug. 16, 1873	Jan. 4, 1955

- 1920 Muscogee Census: Frank H. Doughtie 45 KY AL KY, wife Barbara 47 NC NC Eng, son Frank H. Jr. 12 GA and son Jerry W. 10 GA.

Nell Whitsitt Doughtie	Mar. 19, 1882	Oct. 19, 1975

1 adult brick slab, n/m   1 baby grave, no data

Lot 53, open lot

Dr. J. L. Cheney	Sept. 4, 1811	May 25, 1877

- Obit: born Monroe Co., GA, leaves wife, 1 son Bobbie, who died 7 Feb. 1857, 6 children, moved to Upson Co., GA before coming to Columbus, druggist, 1 brother Judge Isaac Cheney.

- 1870 Muscogee Census: John Cheney 56 GA, Espie 53 GA, Mary 23 GA and John 17 GA.

- Dr. John Lisbon Cheney was a son of Aquilla J. Cheney Jr., grandson of Aquilla J. Sr. and great-grandson of Levi Cheney of Walpole, Mass. He was born in Monroe Co., GA and married Miss Epsie Brockman Needham 12 Jan. 1834. They moved to Columbus in 1855. He served the latter part of the War as a surgeon. Dr. & Mrs. Cheney were the parents of three sons and four daughters; William Monroe (b. Dec. 4, 1834 and m. Sarah Elizabeth Robinson 1865), Ann Eliza, Mattie Estelle (b. June 9, 1842 and m. 1860 James A. Roquemore), Mittie Louise (b. July 30, 1844 and m. 1861 James Thomas Ogletree), Mary Francena (b. Jan. 18, 1848 and m. 1870 W. J. Perryman), Isaac Perkins (b. April 5, 1850 and m. 1870 Mattie S. Humber) and John Calvin Cheney (b. Oct. 10, 1853 and m. 1875 Emma Parramore). Dr. J. L. Cheney died of a spider bite.[14]

E. B. Cheney — May 28, 1818 — Apr. 21, 1892 — w/o Dr. J.L. Cheney

- 1880 Muscogee Census: John Cheney 27 GA GA GA, wife 25 GA GA GA, son Frederick 5 GA, son Willie 1/12 (May) and mother Essie Cheney 63 GA NC NC.

Judge Isaac Cheney — Mar. 1812 — Dec. 6, 1872 — of Talbot Co., GA

- Obit: born Talbot Co., GA, died at residence of brother, Dr. John Cheney.

- 1850 Talbot Co., GA Isaac Cheney 42 GA, Matilda 49 GA, Alfred Patrick 21 GA, Thomas Patrick 16 GA, Georgianna Patrick 13 GA and Missouri Davis 13 GA.

- 1870 Talbot Co., GA Census: Isaac Cheney 58 GA, Matilda 65 GA, Louisiana Love 58 GA, Mittie Love 25 GA, Isaac Thompson 15 GA and Isaac McCrory 15 GA.

evidence of 1 child's grave, 1 small marker

Lot 54, no name on wall

no visible graves

Lot 55 Bramhall on wall

Joseph Bramhall — Oct. 11, 1863 — Oct. 3, 1880 — s/o J. H. & L.J. Bramhall

- 1880 Muscogee Census: Joseph H. Bramhall 53 NY NY NY, wife Lucinda J. 37 GA GA GA, son Joseph E. 16 GA, dau. Lucinda E. 14 GA, son Charles H. 13 GA and dau. Laura 10 GA.

Arthur Kendrick — — Apr. 24, 1873 — inf. c/o C.A. & L. M. M. Kendrick 20 mos, 22 days

Lot 56, no name on wall

Mary E. Cargill — Feb. 11, 1854 — July 12, 1871

James E. Cargill, Sr.	Sept. 11, 1838	Feb. 2, 1925

- Obit: wife was Mrs. Mollie S. Battle, d/o Dr. T.W. Battle, she died 14 yrs ago, 3 children, Thomas B., James E., Jr., both of Columbus, Mrs. S.D. Zuber, Jr., of Lakeland, FL, 1 brother, E.B. of Columbus, GA, member of C.S.A. City Light Guards.

- 1880 Muscogee Census: James Cargill 39 AL AL AL, wife Mollie 28 GA GA GA, son Thomas 4 GA, son James 8/12 (Sept) GA.

Mrs. E.B. Cargill		Jan 5, 1882

- 1880 Muscogee Census: Edwin B. Cargill 33 GA SC GA, wife Mary A. 34 AL GA GA, day Mary 1 AL and son George 6/12 GA.

Elizabeth Cargill	May 19, 1814	Mar. 21, 1899

- Obit: wife of late Edwin F. Cargill, he died 1887, children, J.E. Cargill of Atlanta, GA, John S. Cargill of Athens, GA, D.F. Cargill of Winder, GA, George W. Cargill of Russell Co, AL, & E.B. Cargill.

- Family records indicate her last name as Garnett, possibly of Wilkes Co., GA.

Mary Battle Cargill	Aug. 8, 1850	Dec. 5, 1910

- Mary "Mollie" Battle d/o Dr. Thomas W. Battle (1816-1889) and Ann Cherry Ball (1833-1904). Mary Sophia Battle married James Efford Cargill 6/8/1875 in Muscogee Co., GA.

Edwin Cargill	Feb. 26, 1804	Nov. 28, 1886

- 1880 Russell Co., AL Census: Edwin F. Cargill 76 SC VA VA, wife Elizabeth 66 GA GA GA, sister Mary A. 91 VA VA VA, son Jno S. 39 GA, DIL Julia 39 GA, gs James A. 12 GA and gs Frank L. 10 GA.

Sexton Records indicate buried in this lot:

James E. Cargill		*bur. 11/9/1932, 53 yrs.*

- James Efford Cargill, Jr., s/o James Efford and Mary Battle Cargill.

Lot 57, wrought iron fence, no name

Daniel Williams		no dates	child
Thomas Chaffin	June 20, 1830	Feb. 20, 1911	SR: bur. 2/21/1911, 81 yrs.

- Obit: born Crawfordsville, GA, June 20, 1830, s/o Thomas & Sarah G. Chaffin, Columbus Guards, member of Paul J. Semmes's Brig, surrendered at Appomattox, never married, last of a family of 5 boys and 3 girls.

- 1870 Muscogee Census: Thomas P. Chaffin (physician) 42 GA, Fannie C. 37 GA, Cassie I. 17 GA, Thomas M. 15 GA, Edward B. 12 AL and John B. 7 AL.

- 1880 Muscogee Census: In household of Wm Fogle; 42 (Dentist) GA NC GA, wife Sarah 33 GA GA GA, Thomas Chaffin (Doctor) 50 GA GA GA, wife Janie 20 GA GA GA, dau Brodie 20 GA, son Tom 23 GA, son John 17 AL.

Elizabeth Chaffin		no dates	w/o W. J. Chaffin

- Obit: died in Atlanta, GA, widow of W. J. Chaffin, sister-in-law of Capt. Thomas Chaffin & Mrs. Josephine L. Peabody of Columbus, GA, 1 son, Jeptha Chaffin of Atlanta, GA.

| Sarah Taylor Chaffin | no dates | SR: b.2/13/1809 bur. 10/5/1910, 71 yrs. |

- Thomas Chafin (sic) married Sarah G. Taylor 12/27/1824 in Greene Co., GA.

| Thomas B. Chaffin | | SR: |

- 1850 Muscogee Census: Thomas Chaffin 52 GA, Mrs. S. G. 46 GA, James A. 24 GA, William 22 GA, Thomas 20 GA, Miles H. 18 GA, Laura P. 16 GA, Mary F. 14 GA, George R. 10 GA and Sarah E. 3 GA.

- 1870 Muscogee Census: Thomas Chaffin, Sr. 70 GA enumerated in the household of William Williams.

| W.J. Chaffin | no dates | SR: bur. 2/13/1880, 52 |

| Martha Hornsburger | no dates | |

| Miles Chaffin | no dates | |

| George Chaffin | no dates | SR: bur. 7/3/1906, 63 yrs. |

- Obit: Died at Rankin House, resident of Atlanta, GA, 1 brother, Capt. Thomas Chaffin, 1 sister, Mrs. John Peabody, 1 daughter, a resident of Florida.

Lot 58, Mott on wall

| Charles B. Woodruff | Aug. 27, 1861 | Oct. 23, 1924 | |

- 1860 Muscogee Census: L. T. Woodruff (Steamboat Capt.) 47 NJ, Aurora E. 35 VA, Harry 7 GA and Frank 3 GA.

- 1870 Muscogee Census: Emeline Woodruff 40 GA, Harry 15 GA, Frank 13 GA and Charles 7 GA.

- 1880 Muscogee Census: Frank Woodruff 23 GA GA GA, brother Charles 20 GA GA GA.

- 1910 Muscogee Census: Charles Woodruff Aug 1860 GA NJ VA (m. 10 yrs.), wife Mary Lou Mar 1867 GA GA GA (2ch/2liv.), son Randolph 1893 GA, son Frank Dec. 1896 GA, mother Annie E. Mott May 1843 GA GA GA, boarder Jess P. Turner April 1863 GA and boarder Mildred Turner Dec. 1866.

| Annie Battle | Jan. 10, 1869 | Mar. 30, 1947 | w/o J.R. Mott |

- Annie Lucile Battle was the w/o James Randolph Mott and the d/o Dr. Thomas William Battle (1816-1889) and Ann Cherry Ball (1833-1904). Her sister, Mary Sophia Battle married James Efford Cargill.[15]

| Louis F. Woodruff | Dec. 6, 1896 | Feb. 24, 1962 | |

| Mary Louise Mott | Mar. 12, 1867 | Aug. 1, 1947 | w/o Charles B. Woodruff |

| John R. Mott | Sept. 2, 1841 | Jan. 19, 1874 | |

- John Randolph Mott is the s/o Randolph L. Mott and Mary Ann Jeter, who were married 9/30/1821 in Baldwin Co., GA.

- 1860 Muscogee Census: Randolph Mott 60 VA, Mary A. 50 GA, John R. 19 GA and Frank G. 17 GA.

- 1870 Muscogee Census: John Mott 29 GA, Anna 26 GA, Randolph 6 GA and Mary L. 3 GA.

Randolph Mott Woodruff	Oct. 2, 1893	Aug. 2, 1968
J. Randolph Mott	Sept. 28, 1864	Apr. 29, 1945
Anna E. Mott	May 30, 1842	w/o John R. Mott

- Obit: widow of John R. Mott, d/o late James E. & Elmina Shivers Chapman, 1 dght, Mrs. Mary L. Woodruff of Columbus, GA, 1 son, J. Randolph Mott of Albany, GA, 2 grandsons.

- SR: buried September 29, 1929.

3 baby slabs, n/m

Sexton Records indicate buried in this lot:

Frank Mott   *bur. 3/7/1871, 2 yrs.*

Lot 59, open lot

1 adult slab, n/m

Lot 60, no name on wall

1 adult slab, unable to read

Lot 61, R.M. Adams on wall

Annie Theara Jones	Dec. 18, 1883	Dec. 4, 1939
John R. Jones	June 24, 1861	May 13, 1943

- 1920 Muscogee Census: John R. Jones 59 AL AL AL wd, dau Annie 35 AL.

Leila E. Jones	July 11, 1909 Columbus, GA	w/o John R. Jones, age 42

2 adult slabs, n/m

Sexton Records indicate buried in this lot:

R. M. Adams   *bur. 10/15/1896, 49 yrs. Policeman, shot to death.*

Lot 62, no name on wall

Rev. Jessie H. Campbell D.D	Feb. 10, 1807 McIntosh Co., GA	Apr. 16, 1888 Columbus, GA	

- Jesse H. Campbell married Frances Stanley 6/24/1830 in Putnam Co., GA. He married Mrs. Emily S. Moore 3/27/1873 in Houston Co., GA.

- 1850 Stewart Co., GA Census: Jesse H. Campbell 43 GA, Francis 49 GA, Martha 18 GA, Jesse 16 GA, Sherwood 14 GA, Cooper 12 GA, Alva 10 GA and Charles 8 GA.

William Cooper Campbell	July 28, 1881	May 23, 1951	daddy
Woodie Schley Campbell	Dec. 10, 1883	Apr. 25, 1973	mother
Frances Lillian Campbell	Mar. 22, 1914	Oct. 5, 1915	d/o W.C. & Woodie S. Campbell

Lot 63, Henry Ingram on wall

Henry Ingram	Feb. 10, 1858	June 4, 1897

- 1880 Muscogee Census: Henry Ingram 22 AL.

Corinne Evans	Sept. 29, 1870	Jan. 10, 1944

1 adult slab, n/m

Sexton Records indicate buried in this lot:

Norman Ingram   *bur. 8/22/1913*

Lot 64, C.J. Roberts on wall

Jane Florence Fullerton	Nov. 11, 1855	Mar. 26, 1924	w/o Chas. J. Roberts
W.R. Roberts	July 28, 1878	Aug. 21, 1939	
J.T. Roberts	Aug. 28, 1874	Sept. 25, 1912	
Charles Jenkins Roberts	Nov. 7, 1853	Oct. 14, 1896	Badge emblem City of Columbus, died in the discharge of his duty.

- 1880 Lee Co., AL Census: Charles Roberts 27 AL AL AL, wife Florence 24 AL AL AL, son Jim 5 AL, son Robert 3 AL, brother James 25 AL.

1 child grave, n/m

Lot 65, no name on wall

Martha Ann Brannon   Feb. 5, 1837   Apr. 23, 1908   w/o James Alvin Bolin

- Obit: mother of Mrs. E.F. Roberts, W.S. Bolin of Birmingham, AL, J.A. of San Francisco, CA, Mrs. W.E. Weathers of Frederick, OH, Mrs. J.W. Head of Opelika, AL.

Lot 66, no name on wall

Edward F. Roberts   1858   1915   SR: bur. 11/8/1915

- 1880 Lee Co., AL Census: Edwin (sic) Roberts

- 1900 Muscogee Census: Ed F Roberts Mar 1858 AL GA GA, wife May 1871 ? At Sea SC and son Fredrick? June 1878 AL.

May Roberts   May 31, 1871   Feb. 25, 1941

- 1920 Muscogee Census: May Roberts 49 IN? unk. TN?

Lot 67, Preer on wall

Achsah Preer   Apr. 21, 1866   Sept. 29, 1917   w/o Eugene Francis Colzey

- Achial (sic) Preer married E Frank Colsey (sic) 12/17/1884. The bride is the d/o Peter Preer. [16]

- 1860 Macon Co., GA Census: Eugene F. Colzey 28 SC physician.

- 1870 Muscogee Census: Eugene F. Colzie 38 GA, Annie E. 30 GA, Mary M. 14 GA, Frank E. 8 GA and Louisa C. 1 GA. (He is dead by the 1880 Census and his widow, Ann Cody is in Atlanta, GA.)

- 1900 Muscogee Census: Martha A. Preer Mar 1835 GA SC SC, son William Nov. 1860 AL, dau Achsah P. Colzy April 1866 AL (m. 15 yrs. 3ch/0 liv.) and SIL Eugene F. Colzy Oct 1862 GA SC (m. 15 yrs.) GA.

Mary Preer Walton   Dec. 18, 1876   Dec. 9, 1913

Florence Augusta Preer   no dates   SR: bur. 11/18/1926, 61

Thomas S. Preer   1862   1923   SR: bur. 7/26/1923

Peter Preer   Feb. 17, 1829   Jan. 19, 1889

- Obit: married Mattie A. Jones, born Athens, GA, C.S.A., Clayton's Reg, AL troops, a Mason, several children (not named).

- 1850 Muscogee Census: Peter Preer is a 21 year old clerk living in the household of William H. Jackson aged 23, also a clerk.

- 1860 Russell Co., AL Census: Peter Preer 31 GA, Mary A. Preer 35 SC and Mary Preer 65 New York.

- 1880 Muscogee Census: Peter Preer 51 GA VA VT, wife Martha A. 45 GA SC SC, dau Sarah P. 18 AL, son Charles D. 16 AL, dau Aehsah 14 AL, son William 12 AL, dau Martha J. 10 GA, son Peter 5 GA and dau Mary Grimes 3 GA GA GA

Jack Walton	Mar. 25, 1903	May 20, 1946	
Sarah Perry Preer	Jan. 17, 1862	Apr. 26, 1919	w/o Early H. Epping
Peter Preer	Sept. 15, 1874	Mar. 23, 1907	s/o Peter & Martha A. Preer
Aleck Young	Feb. 6, 1891	Oct. 7, 1896	s/o E.F. & Achsah Colzey
Frank Colzey	May 26, 1888	May 28, 1888	s/o E.F. & Achsah Colzey
Charles E. Walton, Jr.	Oct. 21, 1896	Apr. 16, 1942	
Mary Ann Walton	Apr. 3, 1921	Aug. 2, 1931	
Herman Preer	June 30, 1886	Jan. 7, 1890	s/o E.H. & S.P. Epping
William Preer	no dates		SR: bur. 11/27/1923, 55
Tabitha Perkins	June 9, 1815	Oct. 4, 1895	
Eugene Francis Colzey	May 20, 1861	Dec. 11, 1911	
Peter Preer	Apr. 29, 1889	Aug. 31, 1890	s/o E.F. & Achsah Colzey
Charles Esington Walton	Feb. 16, 1875	Sept. 6, 1932	one slab with Louise Crawford Walton

- 1910 Muscogee Census: Charles E. Walton 35 VA Can VA (m. 15 yrs), wife Mary P. 33 GA GA GA (m. 15, 3ch/3liv), son Charles E. Jr. 13 GA, son Peter P. 10 GA and son Jack 7 GA.

- 1920 Muscogee Census: Charles E. Walton 44 VA Can VA wd, son Charles E. Jr. 23 GA, son Peer 20 GA and son Jack 16 GA. Also listed several boarders.

Louise Crawford Walton	Nov. 6, 1902	Nov. 3, 1916	w/o Charles E. Walton, Jr.
Martha Ann Jones	Feb 26, 1835	Oct. 24, 1905	w/o Peter Preer

- Obit: born Muscogee Co., GA, five of her seven children survive her, Mrs. H. H. Epping, Mrs. Frank Colzey, Mrs. Charles Walton, William Preer & Peter Preer.

- 1850 Muscogee Census: Andrew P. Jones 47 SC, Mrs. W. H. Jones 42 SC, James B. Jones 21 SC, Martha A. Jones 15 GA and other boarders.

- 25 May 1886 – (Winnefred Ann Prince) Died-Mrs W.A. Jones died at the residence of her son, Mr James Giddings in Talbotton on May 20 after several days illness. She was born in Union District S.C. April 1807. She married Mr (Erastus) Giddings (c1800-1838) early in life and they moved to Columbus Ga in 1828, where her husband died. She married Judge Andrew P. Jones in Columbus who died some years ago. She lived in Columbus until about 8 years ago when she came to live with her only child, Mr James Giddings in Talbotton. She leaves two sets of step-children and several grandchildren here and in Columbus to mourn her loss. She was buried in Columbus on Friday.

Early Hurt Epping	May 23, 1862	Dec. 16, 1909	s/o Henry Herman & Isabel Epping

- 1880 Muscogee Census: Henry Epping 59 Ger Ger Ger, wife Isabella 54 Sco Sco Sco, son Early 18 Al, dau 15 AL, and boarders; Henry Epping Jr. 23 AL, Dora? 23 Al, John Flournoy 32 GA GA GA, Frank 9 GA and Beca 6 GA. (John Flournoy married Rebecca Epping (1852-1873), d/o Henry & Isabella. John married 2nd Sept. 1881 Mary Welch Reynolds and had 7 more children.

| Pattie Preer | Jan. 7, 1870 | Aug. 10, 1898 | d/o Peter & Martha A. Preer |

1 baby brick slab, n/m   3 adult brick slabs, n/m

Sexton Records indicate buried in this lot:

| *Charles D. Preer* | | | *bur. 1/22/1899* |
| *Mrs. Preer & son* | | | *bur. 2/23/1870* |

Lot 68, no name on wall

| T.J. DeVore | no dates on slab | | G/M City Lights C.S.A. 1861-1865. SR: bur. 8/28/1878, 45 yrs. |

- Obit: born Union Springs, AL, married a daughter of J. Ennis, dry goods business, a Mason.

| Sarah W. DeVore | | no dates | SR: bur. 1/16/1915, d. Memphis, TN. |

- Obit: died Memphis, TN.

- 1870 Muscogee Census: James Ennis 56 SC, Martha 47 GA, Henry 20 GA, William 18 GA, Lyman 16 GA, Lily 8 GA, Thomas DeVore 34 GA and Sarah 27 GA.

- 1880 Muscogee Census: Martha Ennis 55 GA GA GA, son Henry 30 GA, son William 28 GA, son Lyman 26 GA, dau Lily 18 GA, dau Sallie Devore 32 GA, gd Lula 4 GA, gs James 2 GA.

| Thomas Lyman Ennis | July 15, 1853 | Aug. 13, 1924 | G/M. R.A. Ennis C.S.A. 1861-65 |

Sexton Records indicate buried in this lot:

| *J. William Ennis* | | | *bur. 12/9/1910* |

- Obit: died Raston, LA, 2 brothers, Henry Ennis of Columbus, Ga, Lyman of Raston, LA, 2 sisters, Miss Lillie Ennis of Raston, LA, Mrs. S.W. DeVore of Memphis, TN.

Lot 69, open lot

1 baby brick slab, unable to read headstone

Lot 70, open lot

no evidence of graves

Lot 71, Averett on wall

Eula Averett Chapman	Feb. 7, 1870	May 10, 1957	w/o Joseph E. Chapman
Lydia Amelia Cole	Oct. 8, 1849	Feb. 13, 1941	w/o Eli M. Averett

- Obit: widow of E. M. Averett, 1 son, Cliff Averett, 2 dghts, Mrs. S.W. Lyden of Richland, GA, Mrs. J.E. Chapman of Columbus, GA, Mrs. Joe Taylor of Daytona Beach, FL.

Martha Jane Averett	Oct. 16, 1846	Dec. 7, 1929	w/o J.W. McCrary

- Obit: only surviving sister of late E.M. Averett, 1 niece Mrs. J.E. Chapman, with whom she resided, other relatives, Mrs. E.M. Averett, Richland, GA, Mrs. S.W. Lide of Richland, GA, Curtis Stevens of Renfoe, GA, Mrs. Gertrude Wallace of Harris, Co., GA, Cliff Averett, C.C. Averett & Herbert Snider, all of Columbus, GA.

Joseph Edgar Chapman	Nov. 13, 1865	May 13, 1947

- 1920 Muscogee Census: Joseph E. Chapman 55 GA GA GA, wife Eula 49 GA GA GA, dau Irene 26 GA, dau Lucy 23 GA, dau Eula 19 GA, son Joseph E. Jr. 17 GA and dau Lydia B. 13 GA.

Eva Mae Averett Taylor	Oct. 20, 1882	June 25, 1949	
Charles Harold Averett	Dec. 25, 1899	Dec. 8, 1900	s/o Charlie & Gertrude Averett
Mary Irene Chapman	Mar. 14, 1893	Aug. 16, 1978	
Eli Monroe Averett	Oct. 26, 1841	Oct. 2, 1920	

- Obit: born Stewart Co., GA, leaves wife, 3 dghts, Mrs. E. Chapman, Miss Bell Averett, Mrs. S. Taylor, all of Columbus, GA, 2 sons, C.C. & C.M. both of Columbus, GA, 15 g/ch.

- 1880 Stewart Co., GA Census: E. M. Everett 38 GA GA GA, wife L. A. 30 GA GA GA, dau Eulalia 10 GA, son Charles 7 GA, dau Irene 5 GA, dau Belle 2 GA, John B. Cole 63 GA NC NC and son A. L. Cole 17 GA.

- 1900 Muscogee Census: Eli M. Averett Oct. 1841 GA GA GA, wife Lidia A. Oct. 1849 GA GA GA, dau Lillie B. Oct. 1878 GA, dau Eva M. Oct. 1882 GA and son Clifford M. Nov. 1886 GA.

- 1920 Muscogee Census: Eli M. 77 GA GA GA, wife Lydia A. 70 GA GA GA, sister Martha McCrary 73 GA GA GA, dau Julie Belle Averett 40 GA, gs Eli Averett 16 GA

Belle Averett Lide	Oct. 2, 1877	May 21, 1964	w/o Samuel W. Lide

- 1920 Stewart Co., GA Census: Samuel W. Lyde (sic) 54 SC SC SC, wife Charlotte E. 51 AL GA AL, dau Mildred 22 FA, MIL Martha Beall 75 AL,

Irene Averett Snider	June 1, 1875	Nov. 11, 1900	w/o H. B. Snider

Lot 73, open lot

no evidence of graves

Lot 74, Butts-Kelly on wall

T. Jeff Kelly	Aug. 20, 1889	Dec. 17, 1957	
T.U. Butts	Nov. 4, 1854 Hancock Co., GA	Mar. 22, 1916 Columbus, GA	

- 1910 Muscogee Census: Thomas Butts 54 GA GA GA (m^1 22), wife Mattie 44 (m^1, 2/2) TX AL GA, dau Oline 20 GA, son Tom 13 GA and 2 lodgers.

Oline Butts	May 12, 1889	Mar. 1, 1959	w/o T. Jeff Kelly
Mattie L. Beall	Jan. 26, 1866 Gregg Co., TX	Nov. 10, 1938 Columbus, GA	w/o T.U. Butts
Thomas J. Kelly, Jr.	Mar. 27, 1920	Aug. 2, 1988	PFC U.S. Army WWII
T.U. Butts, Jr.	Feb. 20, 1897	Feb. 21, 1957	
Ada Veasey	Sept. 16, 1904	Feb 7, 1961	w/o T.U. Butts, Jr.

Lot 75, no name on wall

Clara Glenn Perry	b. Feb 5, 1863 Auburn, AL		w/o Wm. M. Perry SR: bur. 9/10/1915
Catherine M. Perry	1814	1890	w/o Wm. Perry
Sarah C. Perry	1825	1863	w/o Wm. Perry
Andrew P. Jones	no dates		SR: bur. 3/28/73, 70 yrs.

- 1860 Muscogee Census: Andrew P. Jones 55 SC, Mrs. W. A. 52 SC, Wm B. Giddings 28 GA, Clara Prurylin 5 GA and Andrew P. Jones 13 SC.

- 1870 Muscogee Census: Anderson (sic) P. Jones 67 SC, Winnefred A. 63 SC.

- 25 May 1886 – (Winnefred Ann Prince) Died-Mrs W.A. Jones died at the residence of her son, Mr James Giddings in Talbotton on May 20 after several days illness. She was born in Union District S.C. April 1807. She married Mr (Erastus) Giddings (c1800-1838) early in life and they moved to Columbus Ga in 1828, where her husband died. She married Judge Andrew P. Jones in Columbus who died some years ago. She lived in Columbus until about 8 years ago when she came to live with her only child, Mr James Giddings in Talbotton. She leaves two sets of step-children and several grandchildren here and in Columbus to mourn her loss. She was buried in Columbus on Friday.

William M. Perry	Mar. 17, 1856	Nov. 4, 1883	s/o Wm. & Sarah C. Perry
James Jones	no dates		s/o Andrew P. & Ann Jones
Mrs. Andrew P. Jones	no dates		SR: bur. 9/28/1868
James Perry			C.S.A. 1861-1865
William Perry	1808	1890	SR: bur. 7/18/1890

- William Perry married Sarah C. Jones 6/1/1841 Muscogee Co., GA.

- 1850 Muscogee Census: William Perry 33 GA, Sarah C. 26 SC, James M. 6 GA, Andrew P. Jones 47 SC, Mrs. W. H. Jones 42 SC, James B. Jones 21 SC, Martha A. Jones 15 GA and other boarders.

- 1870 Muscogee Census: William Perry 58 GA, Catherine 45 GA and William 14 GA.

- 1880 Muscogee Census: William Perry 66 GA SC GA, wife Catherine 55 GA GA GA, son William M. 24 GA.

Mrs. Ann Jones	Nov. 30, 1801	May 13, 1843	w/o Andrew P. Jones
Marina Catherine	May 22, 1832	Aug. 12, 1838	
Joseph West	June 1, 1840	Sept 22, 1840	
Ann	Dec. 14, 1842	Nov. 24, 1844	

Lot 76, Stewart on wall

Sarah Elizabeth Stewart			d/o John D. Stewart of Columbus, GA, w/o Wm. Letford of Fernandina, FL.
Cephalie Stewart	Aug. 15, 1884	Apr. 14, 1980	
Olivia C. Stewart	July 31, 1812 Norfolk, VA	June 27, 1853 Columbus, GA	consort of Jno D. Stewart, d/o Emily DeLaunay

- 1850 Muscogee Census: John D. Stewart 42 GA, Mrs. O. C. 37 VA, James A. 16 GA, Sarah E. 12 GA, E. G. (m) 11 AL, Virginia E. 10 AL, Emily A. 9 AL, Hampton S. 6 AL, Frances M. 3 AL, John B. 1 AL and St. John Delaunay 8 GA.

Emily Del. Stewart	Jan. 25, 1842	Jan. 29, 1919

2 adult slabs, n/m

Sexton Records indicate buried in this lot:

J. D. Stewart	*bur. 2/28/1883*

- 2/27/1883 Columbus: Mr. John D. Stewart died yesterday morning at his plantation near Eufaula, after a brief illness of typhoid fever. For many years a resident of Columbus. Several children survive him, among who are Mr. Baker Stewart, who lived with him, and Mrs. Ulysses Lewis, of Atlanta.

Lot 77, no name on wall

Wm. Godwin Cotton	Nov. 21, 1870	Nov. 4, 1930

- 1920 Muscogee Census: W. G. Cotton 46 GA GA GA, wife Mamie 46 GA GA GA, son Ralph 19 GA, dau Mary 8 GA, sil Alonzo Truett 21 GA GA GA and dau Dorothy Truett 17 GA.

- 1880 Harris Co., GA Census: William Cotton 38 GA GA GA, wife Mary Elizabeth 35 GA GA GA, son Walter Lee 14 GA, dau Ermine Claire 11 GA, son William G. 9 GA, dau Mattie Ugenia 7 GA, son James Wiley 5 GA, dau Susan Elizabeth 3 GA, and dau Louise Herie 1 GA.

Mary Louis Ivey	May 2, 1880	Mar. 11, 1928	w/o W.G. Cotton
Barbara Ann	June 11, 1926	June 12, 1926	d/o W.G. & Mary Louise Ivey Cotton

Lot 78, Cox-Binn on wall

A. Brainard Binns	Nov. 22, 1868	Apr. 6, 1935	
Volicia Smith Cox	Feb. 5, 1847	Aug. 8, 1935	SR: bur. 8/9/1935, 88 yrs.

- Obit: born Harris Co., GA, d/o late William T. & Amanda I. Moore Smith, widow of late John J. Cox, 1 dght, Miss Minnie Cox of Columbus, GA.

Minnie E. Cox		Jan. 5, 1949	d/o John J. & Volicia S. Cox
Justina Jackson Binns	Oct. 8, 1877	Oct. 30, 1952	
John Sterling Jenkins	Nov. 23, 1877	Apr. 20, 1960	

- 1920 Muscogee Census: John S. Jenkins 43 GA GA GA, wife Eddie Belle 40 GA GA GA, son James Harris 17 GA and dau Louise Frances 9 GA.

Lucia A. Cox		Aug. 1901	d/o John J. & Volicia Smith Cox
John J. Cox	Aug. 23, 1848	Oct. 1, 1912	G/M Capt. Pemberton Co., GA Cav. C.S.A.

- Obit: born Harris Co., GA, C.S.A., leaves wife, 1 dght, Miss Minnie Cox, 2 brothers V.A. & W.J. of Columbus, GA., 2 sisters, Mrs. Carrie Martin, Crawford, AL, Mrs. Tom Cunningham of Stovall, AL.

- 1880 Harris Co., GA: John Cox 32 GA GA GA, wife Volicia 29 GA GA GA, dau Minnie 11 GA, dau Lucy 9 GA and son Jesse 6 GA.

Eddie Belle Jackson Jenkins	Aug. 21, 1879	July 6, 1963	

Lot 79, open lot

Mrs. R.A. McGraw	1840	1918	SR: bur. 10/16/1918, 78
Mary S. Matthews	1829	1916	SR: bur. 2/10/1916, 87

- Obit: died at residence of son J.E. Mathews.

3 adult slabs, n/m

Lot 80, no name on wall

Jessie	1874	1961	SR: born 6/12/1874, bur. 4/21/1961
Tulula Clark	1863	1962	SR: bur. 8/6/1942

Lot 81, wrought iron fence, no name

Samuel Francis Boykin	June 15, 1874 Dallas Co., AL	July 26, 1953 Wilmington, DE	h/o Anne Alexander

- 1880 Dallas Co., AL Census: S. F. Boykin 34 AL SC GA, wife Margaret A. 31 SC SC SC, son Douglas A. 10 AL, son S. Frank 6 AL, dau Mattie R. 4 AL, son W. A____ 3 AL, son L. Deas 1 AL and father William W. 67 SC SC SC.

- 1900 Fulton Co., GA Census: Samuel F. Boykin June 1874 AL AL SC, wife Anna A. Mar. 1879 and dau Martha C. Jan 1900 GA.

- 1920 Fulton Co., GA Census: Samuel F. Boykin 45 AL AL SC, wife Annie U. 41 AL AL AL, grandniece (sic) Martha C. 20 GA AL AL and grandniece Frances H. 7 GA GA GA.

Richard H. Bennett, Jr.	Aug. 16, 1896 Norfolk, VA	Mar. 20, 1972 Jacksonville, FL	
Peyton Colquett	Jan. 29, 1864	July 1, 1864	s/o J.A. & E.F. Shingleur
Inf. of Wm. L. & Mary C. Chambers	no dates		
Robert Bruce Alexander	June 29, 1884 Rome, GA	Mar. 23, 1939 Mobile, AL	
James M. Chambers	July 13, 1801	Mar. 11, 1869	

- Obit: colonel, died in Wynnton.

- 1850 Muscogee Census: James M. Chambers 49 Burke? GA, Martha I. 44 Hancock GA, Eveline A. 19 Putnam GA, James M. 15 Putnam GA, Martha S. 13 Putnam GA, Robert A. 11 Muscogee GA, John S. 8 Muscogee GA and Mary E. 6 Muscogee GA.

- James M. Chambers married Martha J. Alexander 11/10/1825 in Putnam Co., GA.[17]

Robert Alexander Chambers	Feb. 1839	June 8, 1864	

- Obit: on roll of dead, "City Light Guards", died in service.

Thomas T. Chambers	May 3, 1860	Sept. 5, 1861	double headstone.
James M. Chambers	Mar. 27, 1862	Nov. 25, 1862	s/o James M. & M.F. Chambers
Hugh B. Dawson	Aug. 14, 1833 Columbia Co., GA	Sept. 29, 1862	

- Obit: C.S.A., Lt. in Capt. Flewellen Co., s/o Dr. Thomas H. Dawson of Russell Co., AL

- 1850 Russell Co., AL: Dr. Thomas Dawson 41 GA and Amelia 22 GA.

George Hurt	1861	1863	
Abner H. F.		Sept. 14, 1851 age 1 yr 2 days	one slab
James M. Chambers	Aug. 26, 1870	Jan. 9, 1936	one slab, husband & wife
Florence Nisbet Chambers	July 8, 1872	July 5, 1958	

- James McCoy Chambers married Florence Bloom Nisbet, d/o Robert A. & Florence Bloom Nisbet, 10/14/1896 in Russell Co., AL.

- Obit: died Savannah, GA, 1 dght, Mrs. Alexander S. Cassels of Savannah, GA, 1 son, James M. Chambers of Savannah, GA, 2 brothers, Henry Nesbit of San Jose, CA, Frank Nesbit of Dallas, TX.

Anne Flewellen Alexander	Nov. 20, 1878 Seale, AL	June 4, 1975 Jacksonville, FL	
William H. Chambers	Oct. 17, 1826	July 4, 1881	father

- Obit: wife Ann Flewellen, colonel, professor of Agriculture.

- William Henry Chambers married Anne Lane Flewellen 5/19/1847 in Muscogee Co.

Inf. d/o J.A. & E.F. Shingleur		Sept.? (unable to read)	
Charlie Chambers	Sept. 12, 1874	Sept. 4, 1875	children of J.H. & M.F. Chambers
Mary Chambers	Oct. 27, 1878	Sept. 16, 1879	
W. Henry Alexander	July 17, 1846 Oswichee, AL	Dec. 3, 1896 Atlanta, GA	

- Obit: died in Atlanta, GA, leaves wife & dght, 1 sister, Mrs. Merritt of Marion, FL, 5 brothers, Samuel, Chambers, Johhn, James & Charles.

Martha J. Chambers		Aug. 13, 1859	w/o James M. Chambers, age 53 yrs 9 m0 3 dys
Gordon Flewellen Chambers		no dates	SR: bur. 8/4/1934, 53 yrs
Col. Wm. T. Harris		no dates	
Frederick A. Shingleur	June 18, 1866	Feb. 19, 1885	

- 1880 Muscogee Census: Gus Shingleur 42 SC SC SC, wife Elvira 40 GA GA GA, son Fred 14 AL, son Flewellen 11 GA, dau Annie 9 GA, dau Lizzie 6 GA and mother Elizabeth Thomas 61 SC SC SC.

William Alexander		June 27, 1840	s/o Dr. A.H. Flewellen, age 16 yrs
Mary F. Clorton	Jan. 5, 1835 Warrenton, GA	Feb. 25, 1888 Montgomery, AL	w/o David Clorton, d/o T.P. & Ann W. Threewits
Mary Gordon Chambers	Mar. 23, 1852	Oct. 18, 1918	one slab

Andrew Galbraith Gordon	Mar. 4, 1856	May 6, 1895	
Martha Chambers Boykin	Jan. 31, 1900 Atlanta, GA	May 10, 1987 Jacksonville, FL	w/o Richard H. Bennett, Jr.
Anne L. Chambers	May 2, 1829	Aug. 16, 1871	

- Obit: married Wm. H. Chambers, 19th May, 1847, d/o late Dr. Abner H. Flewellen, sister of A.C. Flewellen of Columbus, GA, died in Oswachee, Russell Co., AL.

James H. Chambers	May 31, 1848	Jan. 27, 1917	
Flournoy Chambers	Feb. 7, 1877	May 24, 1905	one slab
Mary Alexander	Sept. 26, 1851	July 2, 1927	

- Obit: James H. Chambers died in Atlanta, GA, b. Eufaula, AL, married Mrs. Mary Abercrombie who survives him, s/o Judge Wm. Chambers, 4 sons, J.M., of Macon, GA, Dr. Will of U.S. Army, Dr. Gordon of Columbus, GA, J.S. of Atlanta, GA, 3 brothers Judge W.L. Chambers formerly Chief Justice of the Supreme Court of the Samoa Island, Dr. E.F., & J.B., both of New York, 1 sister, Mrs. Wm. H. Alexander of Atlanta, GA.

- Mary Alexander is the wife of James H. Chambers.

- 1880 Russell Co., AL Census: J. H. Chambers 32 GA GA GA, wife Mary F. 39 AL GA GA, son James McC. 10 AL, son William H. 7 AL, son Gordon F. 5 AL and son Josiah F. 3 AL.

Martha Chambers	Mar. 29, 1857 Eufaula, AL	Oct. 16, 1918 Sellman, MD	w/o Wm. Henry Alexander
John Flewellen	May 9, 1841	Nov. 25, 1856	s/o James M. & Martha J. Chambers
James M. Chambers	Jan 7, 1835	June 22, 1862	

- Obit: C.S.A., "Shorter Guards", died in Columbus, MS.

Lizzie Flewellen	Nov. 8, 1859	Oct. 1, 1860	d/o H.B. & L.F. Dawson
Lizzie Dawson	Nov. 2, 1836	Mar. 23, 1861	w/o Hugh B. Dawson, d/o Dr. A.H. & Elvira Flewellen

- Obit: Eliza, d/o late Dr. A.H. & Mrs. Elvira Flewellen, w/o Hugh B. Dawson.

Alexander Holloway		no dates	s/o Dr. A.H. & Elvira Flewellen
Elvira A. Flewellen	Nov. 24, 1807	June 13, 1859	w/o Dr. A.H. Flewellen

- Obit: drowned in river.

- 1850 Muscogee Census: Elvira Flewellen 41 Putnam GA, Abner E. 24 Jones Cty, Nancy J. 19, Eliza 14, Martha Elvira 11 and Alexander H. 7.

- Muscogee Co. WB A:257-258 Elvire Flewellen. 19 May 1859/1 Aug 1859. Legatees: sons Hugh B. Dawson & Abner C. Flewellen; daus. Eliza Dawson and Martha E. Flewellen; niece Eliza Flewellen Nisbet. Extrs. Abner C. Flewellen & Hugh B. Dawson. Wit: John J. Burwell, S. A. Billing & William H. Chambers.

Dr. Abner H. Flewellen		Dec. 28, 1849	age 49 yrs 7 mo 10 dy

- Obit: Dr. Abner H. Flewellen was born in Warren Co., Ga., on 19 May 1800, and died in Wynnton 28 Dec 1849, being 49 years and 7 months of age.
- Dr. Abner Flewellen, born was the s/o Abner Flewellen (1760-1815 and Ann Lane (1766-1846). He married 1) Nancy C. Jones and 2) Elvira Alexander.

Inf. d/o J.A. & E.F. Shingleur		April 28, 1879	May 7, 1879

Lot 82, wrought iron fence

Sarah A. Smith		May 2, 1806	Sept. 22, 1850	consort of Hampton S. Smith, 44 yrs 4 mo 20 dys

- Hampton and Sarah Antoinette Redd were married 10/19/1829 in Putnam Co., GA.

Minnie Farmey Smith	Apr. 28, 1860 Clark Co., MS	Sept. 2, 1897 Atlanta, GA	w/o J.F. Smenner
Sarah Eliza	Oct. 3, 1849	Jan. 10, 1854	inf. d/o W.T. & L.O. Smith
Bessie Hemphill Smith	Mar. 12, 1858 Clark Co., MS	July 13, 1879 Columbus, GA	d/o W.T. & L.O. Smith
Cornelius Bascom			s/o H.S. & S.A. Smith, age 3 yr, 5 mo, 24 dy
Hampton Sidney Smith	Dec. 29, 1800	Oct. 8, 1876	

- Obit: This gentleman aged about 80 years died Friday in Rome, GA, of an affliction of the heart. Rev. Dr. Joseph Key preached the funeral at St. Paul church. The remains were carried to the cemetery accompanied by__ Carter, J.A. Urquhart, R.A. Ware, Dr. J. Kyle, F.G. Wilkins and T.W. Grimes, Sr. and followed by friends and acquaintances. The deceased was one of the oldest _____ and once the most prominent cotton merchants of Columbus. He was superintendent of a branch of the Bank of the State of Georgia at this place before the war. In 1852 he moved to Mobile, AL, and at the time of his death, he had been a resident of Rome about one year. He died a pious consistent Christian, which he had been from his youth.
- 1850 Muscogee Census: Hampton S. Smith 49 SC, Mrs. S. A. 44 GA, Hampton S. 17 GA, Frances E. 12 GA, Sarah A. 10 GA, John M. 8, James R. 5 and John B. 3 GA.
- Hampton married 2) in October 1851, Mrs. Eliza Early (Cunningham) Grimes, the widow of Dr. Joseph W. Grimes. She was the d/o James Grimes, born 7/13/1807 in Greensboro, GA, the d/o James Cunningham. She died 8/22/1868 in Enterprise, MS.

Louisana O. Hopkins	Oct. 3, 1831 Columbus, GA	Mar. 18, 1905	nee Smith, d/o Dr. Hudson A. Thornton

- Obit: relict of late Major Hopkins, 1 daughter, Mrs. W.W. Whitfield of Miss.

- She was first married to Capt. Wm. T. Smith and then married Major Hopkins.

- 1870 Clarke Co., MS: Lou Hopkins 39 GA, Luella T. 18 GA, Nellie 17 GA, Bessa H. 12 MS and Minnie T. 11 MS.

- 1880 Muscogee Census: Mother Lou Hopkins 48 GA GA GA, dau Minnie Smith 16 MS GA GA, dau Antoinette Whitfield 25 MS, son (sic) William Whitfield 29 MS NC NC and numerous boarders.

Capt. Wm. T. Smith	Aug. 9, 1826 Clark Co., MS	May 29, 1862	s/o H.S. & S.A. Smith, C.S.A.

- Mrs. Nettie Smith Whitfield, DAR ID Number 124222.
  Born in Columbus, GA. Wife of W. W. Whitfield
  Descendant of Ensign John Daniel and of Capt. Aaron Smith, as follows:
  1. William Thomas Smith (1826-1862) m. 1848 Louisiana Olivia Thornton (1830-1905)
  2. Hampton Sidney Smith (1800-76) m. 1825 Sarah Antoinette Redd (1806-50).
  3. William Redd (1775-1839) m. Elizabeth Ann Daniel (1780-1855); Thomas Keeling Smith (1753-1827) m. 1777 Eleanor (d. 1816)
  4. John Daniel m. 1779 Sarah Cunningham; Aaron Smith m. 1741 Elizabeth Carraway (d. 1776).
  John Daniel served as ensign in Col. Henry Skipwith's regiment around Malvern Hill, 1779. He was born in Virginia, died 1830 in Prince Edward Co., VA
  Also No. 117168
  Aaron Smith served as captain in the 3d company, Col. Williamson's regiment, in Camp '96, South Carolina. He was massacred in South Carolina.

Marion Thornton Seals	July 7, 1898 Clayton, AL	Oct. 1, 1910	died in serv. of U.S. Navy on North River, N.Y.
Daniel Morgan Seals	Sept. 22, 1875	Aug. 20, 1918	
Luella Seals	Feb. 3, 1852 Columbus, GA	Jan. 5, 1900	

- 1880 Barbour Co., AL Census: W. A. Seals 28 AL GA AL, wife Luella T. 27 GA GA GA, son Smith 7 AL, son Dan 5 AL and dau Louis 2 AL.

James R. Smith	Nov. 1, 1845	July 25, 1864

Lot 83, wrought iron fence

Capt. John K. Redd	Mar. 28, 1810	July 30, 1861	Capt. C.S.A.
Inf. s/o J. Frank & J. Willie Redd	July 15, 1876	July 16, 1876	
Willard Redd Estes	Mar. 4, 1909	Dec. 30, 1965	
Capt. Joseph Riddick Estes	July 11, 1899	Apr. 29, 1926	s/o Joseph Riddick Estes, Sr. & Willie F. Redd.
William A. Redd	Mar. 24, 1803	Oct. 9, 1866	

- Obit: native of Greene Co., GA

- s/o William Anderson Redd (1775-1839) married Eliza C. Kendrick 10/31/1826 Jasper Co., GA.

- 1850 Muscogee Census: William A. Redd 47 Greene Co. GA, Eliza C. 32 Putnam Co. GA, Charles 19 Troup Co. GA, William 14 Troup Co. GA, John 10 Musc. and Frank 5 Musc.

Willie Edw. Redd	Jan. 27, 1849 LaGrange, GA	Sept. 30, 1919 Birmingham, AL	w/o James F. Redd
Willie Franc Redd Estes	Jan. 3, 1879	Jan. 5, 1942	w/o Joseph Riddick Estes
Francis Redd Estes	Dec. 19, 1897	Sept. 19, 1907	c/o Jos. & Willie Estes, g/child of Frank & Willie E. Redd
Mrs. Elizabeth C. Redd	Dec. 27, 1807 Putnam Co., GA	May 31, 1887 Columbus, GA	w/o William A. Redd

- Obit: died at residence of g/son Wm. A. Redd, b. Putnam Co., GA., widow of W.A. Redd, 3 children, Capt. C.A. Redd, William Redd, of Columbus, GA., J. Frank Redd of Atlanta, GA.

- Elizabeth Caroline Kendrick was the d/o Martin and Jane Kendrick.

- Putnam Co., GA WB B:99. Jane Kendrick, Will Proved 8/2/1890 Legatees: son John Kendrick, dau Sarah Clapton and dau Eliza C. Read (sic). SIL William Read. Wit: Amy Branham.

James Francis Redd	Feb. 5, 1845 Columbus, GA	Sept. 28, 1892 Atlanta, GA	

- Obit: d. Atlanta, GA, dght, Miss Willie Frank Redd, other relatives mentioned, Gen. Edwards & his wife, James Carter, Mr. & Mrs. Charles Handy & dght, Capt. Ed Cox, Dr. James Beasly, Ed Crow & Mrs. Redd of Atlanta, GA.

Joseph Riddick Estes	Aug. 2, 1868	July 16, 1944	

- 1910 Jefferson Co., AL Census: Joseph R. Estes 42 NC VA VA, wife Willie F.R. 31 GA GA GA (m. 15 yrs. 3 child/2 liv.), son J. Riddick 10 AL, son Willard R. 1 2/12 AL and MIL J. Willie Redd 56 GA GA GA (2 child/1 liv.).

Martin J. Kendrick	July 12, 1829	Mar. 9, 1851	Here lieth the last of a … 21 yrs 7 mos 27 dy

- Obit: died at home of uncle William A. Redd.

- 1850 Houston Co., GA Census; Martin Kendrick 26? GA, Eliza 24 NC and Francis 2 GA.

- Son of Ephraim Jones Kendrick of Houston Co., GA.

1 adult slab, n/m

Lot 84, open lot

4 children slabs, n/m

Lot 85, wrought iron fence

Little George	Sept. 14, 1851	Mar. 24, 1854	s/o Jos. W. Woolfolk & Lucy M. Winters
John Woolfolk	Apr. 12, 1781 Burke Co., GA	May 13, 1861 near this City	

- 1850 Muscogee Census: John Woolfolk 69 – and Margaret R. T 60 --.

- Muscogee Co., GA WB 1832-1862 P. 294. John Woolfolk will. April 29, 1861/May 17, 1861. Legatees: Sons: Joseph W. and William G. Daus: Mrs. Cornelia M. Walker, Mrs. Eliza W. Moore of Augusta. Trustee Dr. James B. Walker for Mrs. Eliza W. Moore. Exrs: Joseph W. Woolfolk, William G. Woolfolk. Wits: Joel E. Hurt, William K. Schley, Thomas Sloan.

- John A. Woolfolk married Margaret Taylor Collier 23 Feb 1809, the d/o Edmond L. Collier and Ann Washington.

Emily Meigs Woolfolk	Apr. 6, 1854	Mar. 4, 1920	
Maria Byrd Nelson Woolfolk	Nov. 29, 1827	July 10, 1904	

- Obit: born Clark Co., VA, married Col. Wm. G. Woolfolk, Jan. 16, 1846, in VA, 9 children, T.N. of Albany, GA, J.W. of New York, A.S. & Robert of Montgomery, AL, A.R. of Atlanta, GA, Mrs. Robert Ober of Baltimore, MD, W.E., H.B. & C.M. of Columbus, GA, 1 sister, Mrs. Rosa N. Ticknor of Albany, GA.

- Maria Byrd Nelson married Col. William Gray Woolfolk in Virginia 16 Jan 1846. She was the d/o Thomas Mauditt Nelson (1782-1853) and Sarah Walker Page (1790-1834).

John Collier Woolfolk	May 29, 1851	Jan. 22, 1891	s/o Wm. G & M.B. Woolfolk
William W. Walker	May 27, 1839	Sept. 18, 1839	s/o John A. & Cornelia A. Walker
Joseph Washington Woolfolk	Aug. 20, 1819	Sept. 5, 1864	

- 1850 Muscogee Census: Joseph Woolfolk 27 Augusta GA, Lucy 24 Augusta GA, John 5 Columbus, Joseph 6 Columbus and Lucy 1 AL.

Joseph Washington Woolfolk	July 15, 1853	Oct. 31, 1915	
William E. Woolfolk	Mar. 29, 1849	Oct. 3, 1919	
Wm. Gray Woolfolk	July 11, 1822	Oct. 2, 1903	

- Obit: born Edgefield Dist. SC, children, T.N., of Albany, GA, W.E., H.H., C.M. of Columbus, GA, J.W. of New York, Mrs. Robert Ober of Baltimore, MD, A.R. of Atlanta, GA, Robert of Montgomery, AL.
- 1870 Muscogee Census: William Woolfolk 46 SC, Maria 42 VA, William 21 GA, John 19 GA, Joseph 16 GA, Rosa 14 GA, Arthur 12 GA, Henry 10 GA, Albert 8 GA, Robert 6 GA and Charles 2 GA.

John Edward Walker	Mar. 4, 1845	Sept. 26, 1886	City Light Guards 2nd Ga. Bat. C.S.A. 1861-1865

- Obit: died at residence of sister, Mrs. D'Antigner in Wynnton, GA.

Margaret Taylor Woolfolk	Nov. 13, 1789	Jan. 31, 1853	w/o John Woolfolk, d/o Edmund L. Collier & Ann Washington of Virginia
Margaret Walker Dozier	Apr. 1, 1850	Nov. 10, 1930	

- Obit: died Decatur, GA, leaves husband, Homer W. Dozier, 1 dght. Mrs. John Ridley of Decatur, GA, 1 son, Walker of Carolina.

Josie Wilkins Woolfolk	Oct. 11, 1859	May 18, 1917	w/o J.W. Woolfolk
John Collier Woolfolk	May 29, 1851	Jan. 22, 1891	s/o Wm. G. & M.B. Woolfolk
Cornelia Margaret Woolfolk		Nov. 1, 1816	w/o John A. Walker d/o Jno. & Margaret C. Woolfolk

- Died at residence of son-in-law, H.W. Dozier, in Atlanta, GA, d/o Col. John Woolfolk (one of the first settlers of Columbus), 5 children, Woolfolk Walker, Mrs. L.B. D'Antigner, J.E. Woolfolk, J.H. Woolfolk, Mrs. H.W. Dozier, 1 dead son J.E. She was 71 years of age.
- 1850 Muscogee Census: Cornelia Walker 38 Augusta GA, Walker 12 Augusta GA, Louisa 8 Burke Co. GA, Edward 5 Burke Co. GA, Herbert 3 Burke Co. GA and Margarett 9/12 Musc.

John Auerbridge Walker	Oct. 12, 1813	Aug. 10, 1850	s/o ? & A.C. Walker
Samuel Dawser Walker	Apr. 20, 1842	Nov. 6, 1849	s/o John A. Walker & Cornelia M. Walker

2 adult brick slabs, n/m

Sexton Records indicate buried in this lot:

J. Hub Walker   *bur. 10/25/1898, 52.*

Lot 86, W.G. Woolfolk on wall

Elizabeth S. M. Carter	June 27, 1870	June 23, 1952	
Charles Marion Woolfolk	Feb 3, 1905 Columbus, GA	Feb 5, 1972 Columbus, GA	
Mary Agnes Carter	May 15, 1870	July 1, 1890	d/o Wm. A & Agnes L. Carter

Curtis Braxton Carter	Oct. 15, 1867	Oct. 6, 1953	
Henry Barry Woolfolk, Jr.	Aug. 31, 1909	Nov. 3, 1909	
Charles Marion Woolfolk	Feb. 11, 1868	May 1, 1926	
Agnes L. Carter	Feb. 14, 1843	Apr. 29, 1921	w/o Wm. Arthur Carter

- Obit: w/o Rev. William A. Carter, nee Miss Agnes Law Quigley of Columbia, SC, leaves husband, sons, W.A. of Tampa, FL, Dr. C.B. of Columbus, 1 dght. Mrs. C.M. Woolfolk of Columbus, GA.

Elizabeth Miller Carter	Jan. 18, 1897	Nov. 29, 1971	
Edith Lee Carter	July 18, 1872	Nov. 8, 1946	w/o Chas. M. Woolfolk
William Arthur Carter	May 13, 1836	Feb. 26, 1922	

- Obit: died Tampa, FL, Presbyterian minister, C.S.A. vet., 31st AL Reg. Woodruff Rifles, later Chaplain. Born Mobile, AL, s/o Dr. Jesse & Mary Louise Carter, married Miss Agnes Law Quigley of Columbia, SC, 1 brother, Jesse Carter of New York, 1 sister, Miss Mary Carter of Mobile, AL, 3 children, Judge W.A. Carter, Jr. of Tampa, FL, Dr. C.B. Carter & Mrs. C.M. Woolfolk of Columbus, GA, 4 grandchildren.

- 1870 Escambia Co., FL Census: William Carter 34 AL, Agnes 25 SC, Alonzo 5 SC, Adger 4 AL, Curtis 2 AL and Agnes 1/12 FL.

Lot 87, Boatrite on wall

Sue Hall Boatrite	1849	1928	w/o A.V. Boatrite SR:bur.8/26/1928

Obit: member of pioneer family, died the 24th, in Chattanooga, TN, widow of A.V. Boatrite, sister of Rev. Dr. Hall, 1 son, J.E. of Philadelphia, 1 niece, Mrs. John Bright of Chattanooga, TN.

1920 Hamilton Co., TN Census: John Bright 38 Mass., wife Elizabeth H. 32 GA, son Neal 13 TN, son John Jr. 11 TN and aunt Sue W. Boatright 70 AL NC CT.

A.V. Boatrite	1832	1899	SR: bur. 5/21/1899, 66
Mrs. Mary J. Boatrite		no dates	SR: bur. 9/?/1874

- 1850 Muscogee Census: Alex. F. Boatrite 38 VA, Mary J. 29 GA and James E. 11 GA.

Lot 88, wrought iron fence, no name

Wm. Harris Crawford	Oct. 22, 1886	Mar. 24, 1975	s/o Martine J. & Sarah A. Crawford
Martin J. Crawford	Mar. 17, 1820	July 22, 1883	

- Obit: Judge Martin J. Crawford died at the home of Mr. A. R. Redd, victim of yellow fever. s/o Hardy Crawford of Pike Co. and was born in Zebulon in 1820. He was married twice. First to (Mary Craig) a d/o Osborn Cook (his stepfather) who was only 18. She lived only a year after her marriage and died childless. She was a d/o Mrs. D. P. Hill of Atlanta. Secondly, he married Miss Amanda Reese, d/o Judge Augusta Reese of Madison. She survives him. Of this union was 4 children; one dau. now dec'd, Reese,

Matthew and Toombs Crawford. brother Bennett Crawford of Columbus.

- Martin Jenkins Crawford, s/o Hardy Crawford and Elizabeth Jenkins, married his step-father's (Osborn Crook) daughter, Mary Craig Crook January 28, 1840 in Harris Co., GA.

- 1870 Muscogee Census: Martin J. Crawford 50 GA, Amanda R. 44 GA, Reese 23 GA, Martin 16 GA and Toombs 8 GA.

- 1880 Muscogee Census: Martin Crawford 58 GA NC NC, wife Amanda 40 GA VA NC, son Toombs 18 GA, son Mart 24 GA and dil Sallie 22 GA AL AL.

Reese Crawford	Oct. 29, 1846	May 7, 1912	s/o M. J. & Amanda R. Crawford C.S.A. Vet. 1861-1865

- Obit: Judge, leaves wife, 1 son, Henry B. of Brazil, 1 bro, Toombs Crawford, of New Orleans, LA

Henrietta Budd Crawford	Monticella, FL	Oct. 31, 1923	d/o Joseph & Eliz Budd w/o Henry Benning Crawford

- Obit: w/o Henry Benning Crawford, d/o Josiah T. Budd, of Monticello, Fl, leaves husband, 1 dght, Mrs. Henry Peter Burgard, II of Albany, NY.

Martin J. Crawford	May 4, 1881	June 23, 1910	s/o M.J. & S.A. Crawford
Martin J. Crawford	July 28, 1853	July 28, 1907	s/o M.J. & A.R. Crawford
Augusta Benning Crawford	June 21, 1848	Mar. 7, 1928	d/o Gen. Henry L. & Mary Howard Benning w/o Reese Crawford
Sallie Allen Crawford		May 21, 1921	w/o M.J. Crawford

- Obit: 1 son, W.H. Crawford, 3 sisters, Mrs. A.H. McNeal, Mrs. Annie Laurie Bandy, Mrs. Belle Allen Ross, all of Montgomery, AL, 1 bro. Robert Lee Allen, San Antonio, TX, member of U.D.C. & D.A.R.

Amanda Reese Crawford	July 16, 1825	Oct. 13, 1906	w/o Martin J. Crawford
Clara Crawford		July 8, 1862	age 17
Heny Benning Crawford	Dec. 4, 1874	Jan. 22, 1956	s/o Augusta Benning & Reese Crawford

Lot 89, walled lot, no name

Lt. Samuel McClary			Co. GA, 5th GA C.S.A. 1861-1865
Bennett H. Crawford	May 26, 1835	Aug. 22, 1894	

- Obit: b. Harris Co., GA, s/o Mr. & Mrs. Hardy Crawford, wife, Mary Lowe, d/o B.T. Lowe of Harris Co, GA, Capt. in C.S.A., 4 yrs State Senator, 1 bro, Judge Martin Crawford, children who survive, Mrs. Ella Jenkins, Mrs. Bennetta Murphy, & Andrew Crawford

- 1880 Muscogee Census: Bennett H. Crawford 45 GA NC GA, wife Mary 40 GA GA GA, dau Ella 20 GA, dau Bennetta 18 GA and son Andrew 14 GA.

Name	Birth	Death	Notes
Rosa Perry	July 19, 1872	June 15, 1940	w/o Andrew Lowe Crawford
Alice Crawford Parkman	Dec. 26, 1893	May 8, 1921	
Mary L. Crawford	Apr. 11, 1840	July 26, 1900	

- Obit: widow of Bennett H. Crawford, 3 children survive, Mrs. F.J. Jenkins, & Andrew L. Crawford, both of Columbus, Mrs. D. C.E. Murphy of Atlanta, GA, nee Mary L. Lowe.

Name	Birth	Death	Notes
Mary Crawford		Nov. 3, 1878	age 9 years
Terrell Lee Crawford		Sept. 14, 1866	age 2 years
Andrew Lowe Crawford	Feb. 13, 1866	Oct. 15, 1930	
2 childrens slabs, n/m		3 adult slabs, n/m	

Lot 90, wrought iron fence, no name

Name	Birth	Death	Notes
John E. Dawson D.D.		1860	10 yrs pastor 1st Bapt. Ch. of Columbus, age 59 yrs.

- 1850 Muscogee Census: John E. Dawson 45 GA, Mary 34 GA, John W. 23 GA, Mrs. Georgia 20 GA and Alexander 17 GA.

Name	Birth	Death	Notes
Ellie W. West	July 13, 1860	Oct. 13, 1907	w/o Thomas B. West d/o Austin M. Walker & Mary V. Fannin
Mary E. Dawson		1862	w/o John E. Dawson SR: b.9/22/1862
Mary Fears Walker	Jan. 5, 1826	Sept. 4, 1868	
Mary Fannie Walker	Mar. 2, 1858	Nov. 11, 1884	
Dr. Austin Martin Walker	Aug. 5, 1808	June 3, 1878	s/o Wm. & Mary Walker

- Obit: died in Macon, GA, born Eatonton, GA lived here 45 yrs. moved to Macon, leaves 3 wives & 9 children.

- Austin M. Walker married (Martha) Angeline Marshall 10/24/1838 Putnam Co., GA. She was the d/o Rev. Jabez Marshall and Martha Flournoy.

- 1850 Muscogee Census: Austin Walker 41 GA.

- 1860 Harris Co., GA: A. M. Walker 57 GA,.

Name	Birth	Death	Notes
Wm. Marshall Walker	Feb. 17, 1845	July 30, 1863 Mt. Jackson, VA	s/o Austin M. & Martha Marshall Walker

Benoni Porte Walker   Aug. 20, 1868   Apr. 25, 1886   s/o Austin M. & Mary
                                                                           F. Walker

Sacred to the memory of
Martha Angelina
wife of
A. M. Walker M. D.
and daughter of
Rev. J. P. Marshall
who was born Nov. 12, 1818
baptized Sept. __ 1838
and died Mar. 2nd 1845

Lot 91, partial brick wall, no name

Fannie Virginia Pierce   Oct. 16, 1846   May 21, 1873   w/o Marcellus A.
                                                                             Pierce d/o Walton B.
                                                                             & Jane F. Harris

- Obit: d/o Hon. W.B. Harris, State Senator from Russell Co., AL, died Girard, AL, leaves husband, 2 inf. children.

Walton B. Harris   Feb. 10, 1804   Sept. 22, 1880

- Walton B. Harris married Jane F. Herring 3/22/1825 in Clarke Co., GA. He was the s/o Walton Harris, Jr. (1775-1820) and his wife Virginia Billups.

- 1850 Russell Co., AL Census: Walton B. Harris 46 GA, Jane F. 46 GA, Walton K. 24 GA, Sarah I. 21 VA, Robert B. 22 GA, Alexander W. 19 GA, Beverly H. 17 GA, Stapleton 11 GA, Thomas B. 8 AL, Jeptha A. 5 AL and Frances V. 3 AL.

3 adult brick slabs, n/m

Lot 92, open lot

James Randall Jones   Oct. 13, 1803   Aug. 1, 1871

- Obit: thrown from horse and killed, born middle GA, former State Legislator from Jones Co., GA.

- 1850 Muscogee Census: James Randal Jones 45 Warren Co., Ann C. 33 Baldwin, Clara 14 Musc., William 12 Musc., Boykin 11 Musc., Wiley 9 Musc., Frank 7 Musc., Ann C. 5 Musc., Howard 3 and Mary 1.

- 1870 Russell Co., AL Census: J. R. Jones 66 AL, Ann C. 62 GA, Billy 32 GA, Kate 24 GA, Molly 20 GA, Lena 18 GA, R. S. (m) 16 GA and Clifton 11 AL.

Clifton Jones   July 19, 1859   June 9, 1903

Willis S. Holstead   1848   1890

- 1850 Muscogee Census: Willis S. Holstead 41 NC, Mary A. 26 GA, William H. H. 8 GA, Willis S. 6 GA and Alberta 2 GA.

Katie Holstead Clark	1884	1929	w/o Joseph B. Tyrrell Clark SR:bur.9/10/1929
Ann C. Boykins	Mar. 2, 1817	May 1, 1886	w/o James Randall Jones

- Ann Catherine Boykin was the d/o James William Boykin and Clarissa Ann Owens. She married James Randall Jones 5/20/1835 in Muscogee Co.

| Nina Jones Holstead | Mar. 31, 1852 | Jan. 13, 1941 | |
| Ann Catherine Jones | Dec. 13, 1844 | Nov. 23, 1926 | |

- Obit: d/o James Randall & Ann Boykins Jones, sister of late Frank Jones, Wiley Jones Boykins, late of Pensacola, Clifton, late of Columbus, William, late of Tampa, 1 brother survives, Russell Flewellen Jones of Albany, GA, 2 sisters, Mrs. Nina Holstead, Mrs. Mary Jones both of Columbus, Mrs. William Clifton, dec. of Camden, SC.

| Willis S. Holstead | Jan. 3, 1883 | Oct. 12, 1910 in Panama | |

5 baby brick slabs, n/m   5 adult brick slabs, n/m

Sexton Records indicate buried in this lot:

Mrs. W. A. Jones   *bur. 5/21/1886, 79 yrs.*

Lot 93, brick wall, no name

no evidence of graves

Lot 94, Mitchell on wall

Henry Bradford Thompson	no dates		

- Obit: tribute from Columbia Lodge #7, 20 Nov. 1868.

Susan W. Flewellen	Dec. 20, 1812	July 3, 1877	
Mary A. Flewellen	June 18, 1845	Oct. 1, 1904	
Patrick Henry Carnes	July 28, 1846 Muscogee, Co., GA	Jan. 3, 1912 Little Rock, AR	one slab

- Mary A. Flewellen w/o P.H. Carnes, d/o E.R. & S.W. Flewellen.

| Juntus Jefferson | Aug. 15, 1834 | Apr. 5, 1854 LaGrange, GA | top of monument toppled s/o E.R. & S.W. Flewellen |
| Antionette Virginia Johnson | Sept. 17, 1830 | Apr. 7, 1882 | d/o Capt. E. Flewellen consort of Dr. E.B. Johnson |

- Obit: died Eufaula, AL, w/o Dr. Egbert Johnson d/o Russell Flewellen, 1st husband was Col. Henry H. Thompson

Jule C. Mitchell	Oct. 8, 1868	Jan. 27, 1916	
Josiah Law Mitchell		Oct. 26, 1924	Gov't marker GA Yeoman, 1st Cl. U.S. Navy
Charles A. Flewellen	Sept. 26, 1838	Aug. 1866	headstone toppled s/o E.R. Flewellen
Enos Russell Flewellen	May 13, 1810	Sept. 1, 1884	our father

- Obit: Russell, Capt. died at residence of daughter Mrs. Julius Mitchell, Capt. in Indian War.

- 1860 Barbour Co., AL Census: E. R. Flewellen 50 GA, Susan W. 45 GA, Martha E. 19 GA, James R. 17 GA, Mary A. 15 AL, Georgia E. 12 AL and Susan Z. 11 AL.

- 1870 Barbour Co., AL: Eos (sic) Flewellen 60 GA, Susan W. 57 GA, Martha E. 29 GA, Mary A. 25 AL and Zuleike 20 AL.

- Enos Flewellen married Susan Jones 10/15/1829 in Jones Co., GA. In 1830, they were in Upson Co., GA. He was the s/o Archelaus Flewellen and Nancy Pace. The Flewellen file at the Upson Archives in Thomaston note that Archelaus was born 4/2/1774 and died 9/9/1823.

Mattie Elizabeth Flewellen	June 20, 1841	Aug. 18, 1912	d/o E.R. & S.W. Flewellen

- Obit: died at home of nephew J.C. Mitchell, sister Mrs. Georgia Mitchell of Columbus 1 brother in TX.

Ellen Hardin	Mar. 29, 1871	Apr. 14, 1944	w/o Jule C. Mitchell
Zuleika Flewellen	Mar. 10, 1850	July 8, 1882	w/o S.D. Reid d/o E.R. & S.W. Flewellen

- Obit: Mrs. Samuel Reed of FL, died at res. of father Capt. E.R. Flewellen, leaves 2 children.

Sexton Records indicate buried in this lot:

Georgia Flewellen Mitchell	*bur. 4/16/1919, mother of late Julius C. Mitchell*
J. C. Mitchell	*inf. bur. 1/25/1893*

Lot 95, J.C. Knowles on wall

Samuel Pasco Moore, Jr.	Jan. 24, 1909	Nov. 23, 1969
J. Cliff Knowles	Oct. 27, 1883	Mar. 7, 1954
Odelle Voight Knowles	Oct. 31, 1890	Aug. 4, 1979

Lot 96, walled lot, no name

Oscar Dallas Smith	1886	1986	SR:b.3/18/1886 bur.8/9/1986 2nd wife Corrine W. Watson
Marie Bething Smith	1887	1936	w/o Oscar D. Smith

Lot 97, no name on wall

Robert Endeman			C.S.A. 1861-1865

- Obit: born Florida, wounded in battle, buried 30, Sept. 1863.

Adona Coleman	Sept. 11, 1845	Sept. 7, 1921	d/o James David & A.A. Williford of Columbus w/o Thomas G. Coleman

- Obit: widow of late Thomas Coleman, 3 sons, Thomas G., Dana B., both of Columbus, Ralph of Jacksonville, FL, 5 dghts, Mrs. A.C. Nix, Misses Carrie, Helen, Mable, all of Columbus, Mrs. S.E. Young of Midland, GA, 1 sister, Amores? Willford.

- 1850 Muscogee Census: James D. Williford 27 GA, Mrs. A. V. 23 GA, Adona 5 GA, Amores 3 GA Infant (m) 1 GA and Josephine M. Brooks 17 GA.

Catherine Coleman	Jan. 12, 1814	Dec. 21, 1885	d/o Samuel & Mary Maultsby of Waynesville, NC w/o Benj. F. Coleman
Dana B. Coleman	June 22, 1889		(only date)
Cornelia Patterson	Feb. 21, 1891	Dec. 5, 1944	
Carrie S. Coleman	1873	1935	SR:bur.4/2/1935, 62
Thomas Goulding Coleman	May 7, 1838	Sept. 25, 1902	s/o Benj. F. & Catherine Coleman

- Obit: born Columbus, GA, oldest son of Benj. f. & Catherine Coleman, wife Adona Coleman, 9 children, B.F., T.G. Jr., Ralph, Dana R., Misses Amoret, Carrie, Helen, Mable all of Columbus, Mrs. S.E. Young of Midland, GA.

- 1880 Muscogee Census: T. G. Coleman 42 GA NY NC, wife Adona 32 GA GA GA, son B. F. Jr. 19 GA, dau C. W. 12 GA, dau A. 10 GA, dau C. S. 8 GA, son T. G. Jr. __ GA, son Ralph 6/12 GA and SIL Amores Williford 25 GA.

Benjamin Franklin Coleman	Nov. 14, 1804	Mar. 16, 1888	s/o Elijah & Dorothy Coleman of Orange Co, New York

- 1850 Muscogee Census: Benjamin F. Coleman 41 NY, Catherine 35 NC, Thomas G. 12 GA, John M. 10 GA, Charles 8 GA, Benjamin 1 GA, Mrs. Fedora Endeman 33 NC, John R. Endeman 14 FL, Mary A. Endeman 12 FL and Catherine C. Endeman 8 FL.

- Marriage Bond: Benjamin F. Coleman & Catherine Maultsby 10/9/1832 Cumberland Co., NC.

Charles Coleman	Sept. 7, 1842	Jan. 10, 1883	s/o Benj. F. & Catherine Coleman

- Obit: died Orlando, FL, leaves wife, 3 children, s/o Judge B.F. Coleman, and member of Columbus Guards.

Mabel Parrott	Feb. 28, 1928	Apr. 23, 1928	d/o Thomas G. & Adona Coleman w/o James M. Parrott
Mary Louisa	Aug. 28, 1833	Oct. 31, 1833	
Josephus	Apr. 10, 1836	June 25, 1836	one slab, children of B.F. & Catherine Coleman
Ruth	May 13, 1846	July 24, 1847	
Benj Franklin	July 1, 1850	Sept. 6, 1853	
Catharine Shepherd	Oct. 3, 1852	Nov. 10, 1854	

2 adult brick slabs, n/m   3 baby b/s, n/m

Sexton Records indicate buried in this lot:

Mrs. Annie F. Coleman		*bur. 9/13/1896*
ch/o Thos. G. Coleman		*bur. 1/1/1872*
B. F. Coleman		

Lot 98, no name on wall

Mrs. E.A. Shingleur	Sept. 19, 1818	May 13, 1882	w/o Grigsby E.Thomas, Sr.
Grigsby Thomas, Jr.			C.S.A. 1861-1865 SR:b.9/7/1842, bur.4/30/1903, 61

- 1880 Muscogee Census: Grigsby E. Thomas 38 GA GA GA, wife Fannie W. 35 GA GA GA, son Wellborn W. 12 GA and Grace A. Ray 20 GA GA GA.

- Grigsby Thomas married Frances Wellborn Davie 1/21/1864 in Talbot Co., GA. Frances was the d/o Wellborn G. Davie and Nancy Loflin.

James L.Sibley	1883	1929	one headstone, sons of Sallie Chandler & John A. Sibley
Eugene Sibley	1885	1969	
Frank C. Sibley	1888	1977	
Grigsby E. Thomas, Sr.	Jan. 10, 1796 Hancock Co., GA	July 3, 1865 Columbus, GA	s/o Frederick G. & Rebecca Thomas

- Married Mary A. Shivers 10/16/1821 in Hancock Co., GA.

Annie Cornelia Chandler	May 5, 1865	May 7, 1947	
Sarah Chandler Sibley	1859	1905	
Mary E. Thomas		May 1, 1847	w/o Lemuell Downing, age 22 yrs

Mary A. Thomas	Sept. 30, 1806	May 22, 1845	w/o Grigsby E. Thomas, Sr, s/o Banaby Shivers
Fannie Wellborn Thomas	Aug. 1, 1844	Sept. 26, 1884	w/o Grigsby E. Thomas d/o W.G. & N.J. Davie
Mattie E. Davie		Oct. 1, 1877	d/o Wm. G. & N.J. Davie
Sarah M. Chandler	Oct. 2, 1826	Apr. 21, 1895	one monument
Isaac C. Chandler	May 4, 1823	July 3, 1896	

- Married Sarah M. Thomas 10/16/1850 in Muscogee Co., GA.

- 1850 Muscogee Census: Isaac C. Chandler 26 NJ.

- 1880 Talbot Co., GA Census: Isaac Chandler 56 NJ NJ NJ, wife Sarah 52 GA GA GA, dau Sallie 21 GA, son Grigsby 18 GA, dau Annie 15 GA and son Isaac 14 GA.

1 adult brick slab, n/m   1 small obelisk, unable to read

Lot 99, no name on wall

Lock Weems	Apr. 19, 1835	July 10, 1862

- Obit: Capt., killed in battle at Richmond, VA

- Lock Weems was Adjutant of the 15th Alabama Regeiment and then elected Captain of Company A., Stonewall Jackson's Corps. He fell mortally wounded at the head of his men at the Battle of Malvern Hill and died July 10, 1862 just after his wife reached his bedside. Married Eugenia Blackmon and had 1 daughter who died just before her wedding day.[18]

A.H. Shepherd			C.S.A 1861-1865
Nicholas Ware		Oct. 27, 1865	s/o Dr. R.A. & M.C. Ware, age 20 yrs.
Margaret Caldwell Ellison	July 22, 1814	Jan. 30, 1894	d/o James S. & Jane Ellison w/o Dr. Robert A. Ware

- Obit: nee Ellison, married Dr. Robert Alexander Ware, 29 Mar. 1831, born Fairfield Dist., SC, 4 children, Mrs. Jane Martin, Mrs. W.R. Bedell, both of Columbus, GA, Mrs. G.M. Willis & R.A. Ware of Macon, GA, 1 brother, Col. William H. Ellison, 1 sister, Miss S.E. Ellison.

- Margaret E. Elison married Robert A. Wear (sic) 3/29/1831 in Talbot Co., GA.

- Margaret was the d/o James Ellison (1788 SC-1869 GA) and Jane A. Patterson (1795 Ire-1874). James Ellison of Fairfield District, SC was the s/o Capt. Robert Ellison and his first wife Elizabeth Potts.[19]

Little Charley		July 1, 1863	age 1 yr 2mo 6 d, s/o C. & E.W. Redd

- Charles Andrew Redd married Eugenia Almira Weems 12/14/1853.

Mary S. Park	Nov. 27, 1836	Aug. 19, 1882	d/o Lock & Felixina Weems w/o H.S. Park

- 1870 Muscogee Census: Hampton S. Park 33 GA, Mary W. 31 GA, Eugenia R. 3 GA and Lottie W. Weems 29 GA.

- Hampton Park was the s/o Dr. Ezekiel E. Park and Frances A. Redd.

Maria Weems		May 18,1850	w/o Lock Weems, 37 yrs.

- Obit: leaves husband, sons & daughter.

- Charlston, SC Observer: Married at Washington, Ga., on the 15th July by the Rev. N. Hoyt, Mr. Lock Weems, to Miss W. F. Shepard. In Laurens county, on the 24th ult.[20]

- Lock Weems, born 7/25/1804 in Port Tobasco, MD was the 7th son of Rev. John Weems and Elizabeth Smoot. He first married 1) Eugenia A. Long of Marianna, FL 3/20/1827 (d/o Col. Nicholas Long) and 2) Mariah Felixsia Shepherd 7/15/1830, d/o Andrew and Mary Millhouse Shepherd in Wilkes Co., GA. Lock died 8/25/1853. Lock had one son by Eugenia, William Junius Weems. He and Maria had: Edward Mortimer 2/5/1832, Eugenia Almira 6/18/1833, Lock Jr. 4/10/1835, Mary Shepherd 11/27/1836, Charlotte Woodville 1/5/1839, John Andrew 6/22/1845 and Felix Shepherd 5/12/1850. Mary Hillhouse Shepherd was the d/o David Hillhouse born at Montville, CT 5/11/1756 and died Wilkes Co., GA 3/24/1803 and his second wife, Sarah Porter of Mass.[21]

- Muscogee Co., GA WB 1838-1862: 145-146. Lock Weems, ww 1/23/1851 and wp 10/3/1853. Legatees: sons: Edward M., Lock, John A., Felix S., William J and daughters: Eugenia A., Mary S., Charlotte W. Exrs: Edward T. Shepherd, A. H. Shepherd. Wits: Robert B. Kyle, Aaron Ferguson, Samuel R. Andrews.

James Ware			35th GA Legion C.S.A. 1861-1865

- Obit: Adjutant, 35th GA Regt., killed in battle at Richmond, VA, s/o Dr. R.A. Ware, born & raised in Columbus, Ga.

Dr. Robt. Alex Ware	May 10, 1807 Augusta, GA	July 19, 1893	s/o Hon. Nicholas & Susan Ware

- 1850 Muscogee Census: Robert A. Ware 42 GA, Mrs. M. C. 36 SC, Jane E. 18 GA, Nicholas 16 GA, Susan C. 14 GA, James H. 12 GA, Mary V. 10 GA, Margaret E. 7 GA and Sarah Ellison 16 GA.

- Nov 1, 1825. Executor's Sale - On Thurs, Dec 15, at plantation of late Col. Nicholas Ware on Little River, Columbia County, the corn, fodder, farming utensils, stock of horses and mules...the stock of cattle, hogs and the plantation;--there are about 1500acres...enough cleared and in cultivation to give employment to 25 or 30 hands...Also, at the same time and place will be sold the Grist and Saw mills on Little River...known as Ware's, with about 40 acres attached thereto, and on Thursday, the 22d December, there will be sold at the plantation on Savannah River, Columbia Cty, at the mouth of the Kiokee Creek, the corn, fodder, farming utensils and stock belonging to that place, and also the plantation itself, containing about 600 acres of land...and on Thurs, Dec 29 will be sold at the market house, in the city of Augusta, about 40 likely negroes... Susan B. Ware, Ex's, William w. Holt, Ex'or.[22]

- Dr. Ware was the s/o Senator Nicholas B. Ware and his (second) wife Susan Brooks Carr. Hon. Nicholas Ware was born in Virginia, about 1776. While young, his father settled in South Carolina. Having finished his Academic course, he studied medicine with Dr. Murray of Augusta. He afterwards studied law in the office of the late Col. Seaborn Jones, and subsequently attended lectures of Judge Reeves in Litchfield, Conn. He sustained a high rank as a lawyer. Mr. Ware was a friend of science; he was one of the active trustees of Richmond Academy, the President of the Board when he died. He represented Richmond County, and in the Legislature opposed, with much ability, the celebrated, but little commended "Alleviating Law". He was for some time the Mayor of Augusta, and Judge of the City Court, but he resigned these offices when elected to the United States Senate. He died at New York, in 1824, in the 49th year of his age. He departed this life with the lively hope of blessed immortality.[23]

- 1880 Muscogee Census: Robert Ware 73 GA GA GA, wife Margaret 64 SC SC Ire, son Willie 22 GA and several boarders.

Terressa E. Weems	Nov. 23, 1833	June 5, 1896	d/o Theophius & Narcissa F. Sapp w/o Edw. M. Weems, mother

- Obit: died Cottage Mills, Chattahoochee Co., GA, 62 years old, relict of E. Martinere Weems, 1 dght., Mrs. T.M. Adams, 2 sons, Lock & Will Weems.

- d/o Theophilus Sapp (1808-1877) and Narcissa Frances Clark (1813-1862).

Addie C. Ware		Nov. 7, 1876	age 1y 8d
Jane E. Martin	1832	1920	SR:b.1/9/1832 bur. 5/6/1920

- Obit: d/o late Dr. R.A. Ware & Margaret Caldwell Ellison Ware, w/o Peter Marshall Martin, son-in-law, Joseph S. Harrison, 4 g/ch Maggie & Agnes Harrison, Mrs. Henry Clay, of San Francisco, CA, Mrs. Edward Fleetwood of Pensacola, FL, charter member of D.A.R., U.D.C.

- 1880 Muscogee Census: Jane Martin 48 GA GA SC and Sally Martin 20 GA GA GA were boarders in the household of Robert Ware age 73.

Mrs. Mary Shepherd		Apr. 22, 1876	age 72 yrs.
Mary F. Weems	Mar. 8, 1855	Dec. 10, 1881	sister
Little Janie	no dates		inf. d/o J.M. & S.J. Ware
Lottie Weems Johnston	Jan. 5, 1839	May 14, 1907	d/o Lock & Felixina Weems w/o M.P. Johnston
Edw. Mortimer Weems	Feb. 5, 1832	Nov. 11, 1871	father

- Obit: died in Chattahoochee Co., GA, raised in Columbus.

- 1870 Chattahoochee Co., GA Census: Edward Weems 38 GA, Teressa 36 GA, Lock 17 GA, Mary 14 GA, William 12 GA and Charlotte 10 GA.

Genie Park	Oct. 9, 1866	Aug. 1, 1890	d/o H.S. & Mary W. Park

- Obit: funeral notice mentions Mr. & Mrs. C.A. Redd, 22 years old, an orphan, resided with family of W.A. Redd at "Flora".

- 1870 Muscogee Census: Hampton S. Park 33 GA, Mary W. 31 GA and Eugenia R. 3 GA.

John & Emmie		no dates	infant sons of W.R. & Margaret Ware

3 baby brick slabs, n/m

Lot 100, J.C. Blain on wrought iron fence

1 adult brick slab, n/m

Sexton Records indicate buried in this lot:

J. C. Blain   *bur. 3/13/1886, 76 yrs.*

- 1870 Muscogee Census: Jesse C. Blain 60 PA boat builder.

Lot 101, no name on wall

Mrs. Salina Hearn   Nov. 16, 1854   June 13, 1928

- Obit: died at residence of daughter, Mrs. G.D. Glass.

R.G. Hearn   May 15, 1857   Nov. 1, 1940

- Raliegh Green Hearn married Salina Jane Ledbetter.

- 1870 Troup Co., GA Census: Benjamin Hearn 38 GA, Mary 44 GA, George 6 GA, Green 14 GA and Minnie 4 GA.

- 1880 Troup Co., GA Census: Raleigh Hearne 24 GA GA GA, wife Salina 20 GA GA GA and son Archie 1 GA.

- 1900 Muscogee Census: Salina Hearn Nov. 1857 GA NC GA (m. 24 yrs. 4 child/4 liv) husband Rolly May 1853 GA GA GA, son Archie 21 GA, daughter Florence Glass July 1880 (m. 3 yrs. 1child/1 liv.), dau (sic) Rubie Jan 1900 GA, husband-SIL Oska Aug 1889 GA GA GA and son Clarence Aug. 1887.

- 1920 Muscogee Census: Rollin (sic) G. Hearn 64 GA US GA, wife Salina A. 78 GA GA GA and son Clarence 34 GA.

2 adult slabs, n/m

Lot 102, open lot

Nicholas Howard   Feb. 22, 1787   Nov. 1, 1849
                                     Virginia   Columbus, GA

- The 1850 GA Mortality Schedule shows Nichols M. Howard age 55 died in Muscogee.

- The National Society of the Daughters of the American Revolution Volume 114, page 238
Mrs. Mary Eugenia Campbell Edwards.
DAR ID Number: 113717
Born in Meriwether County, GA   Wife of Theodore H. Edwards.
Descendant of William Howard and of Lieut. John Harris, as follows:
1. Nicholas Charles Campbell (1839-95) m. 1864 Mary Eliza Howard (b. 1842).
2. Callett Campbell (1797-1862) m. 1820 Susan P. Harris (1798-1858); John Theophilus Howard (1813-52) m. 1836 Martha Birch (1818-68).
3. Nicholas Howard (1787-1849) m. 1812 Judith Campbell (1791-1843); John Harris m. 1794 Rebecca Britain (1778-1848).
4. William Howard m. 1774 Mary Thorpe (1754-86).

William Howard (1750-81) served in the VA militia as a private, 1777, when he furnished a substitute. He reenlisted, 1781, and lost his life in the army. He was born in Caroline County, Va.

| Sarah Howard | 1856 | 1932 | SR:bur.5/27/1932, 76 yrs old |

| Judith Howard | July 7, 1793 | Jan. 12, 1865 | |

- Judith Campbell married Nicholas Howard 7/6/1812 in Clarke Co., GA.

| Julia Howard | Apr. 18, 1852 | Feb. 11, 1901 | w/o Rev. W.D. McGreggor |

| Nicholas L. Howard | Feb. 24, 1815 | July 22, 1877 | |

- Obit: born Greene Co., GA, s/o Gen. Nicholus Howard, Judge of Inferior Ct. several terms, Judge of County Court.

- Married Elizabeth Abercrombie, d/o Anderson Abercrombie (1786-1867) & Sidney Grimes, 8/5/1841 in Russell Co., AL.

- 1870 Muscogee Census: Nicholas Howard 55 GA, Elizabeth 49 AL, Anna 23 GA, John 22 GA, Anderson 20 GA, Julia 17 GA, Sallie 14 GA, Josephine 12 GA, Augustus 16 GA and Florida 11 GA.

| Elizabeth Abercrombie | Nov. 30, 1819 | Nov. 20, 1892 | w/o N.L. Howard, our mother |

- Obit: died at residence of M.J. Pollard, d/o Gen. Andrew Abercrombe, & the widow of Nicholus L. Howard, 7 children, Sallie of Columbus, Mrs. Mary Newman of Macon, GA, Mrs. Anna Snelson of Greenville, GA, Mrs. Wm. M. McGregor of Sprindell, GA, Anderson Howard of Atlanta, GA, John L. Howard of Jacksonville, FL, W.S. Howard of Thomasville, GA.

- Elizabeth is the d/o Gen. Anderson Abercrombie and Sydney Grimes.

3 adult brick slabs, n/m

Lot 103, no name on wall

Douglas Franklin Smith	Dec. 11, 1895	May 15, 1914	
Thomas Franklin Smith	Nov. 18, 1854	Apr. 20, 1913	
Carrie Douglas Smith		Nov. 3, 1919	w/o Thos. Franklin Smith

1 adult brick slab, n/m

Lot 104, no name on wall

| Sgt. Benjamin W. Knowles | Aug. 22, 1877 | Apr. 23, 1919 |
| John Wesley Knowles | Aug. 1. 1851 | Aug. 30, 1932 |

- 1880 Lee Co., AL Census: John W. Knowles 28 GA GA GA, wife Sarah L. 24 AL SC GA, son William 4 GA and son Benjamin 3 TX.

- 1910 Muscogee Census: John W. Knowles 60 AL AL AL, wife Mattie 49 AL AL GA (m. 27 yrs. 7ch/7 liv.), son Clifford 27 AL, dau Emmie 23 Al, son Carter C. 21 AL, son Thomas L. 18 AL, son Spencer 13 AL dau Ruby M. 11 AL and son James W. 7 AL.

Harry H. Byrd	Mar. 11, 1898	Sept. 21, 1936	
James W. Knowles	Nov. 4, 1902	Dec. 15, 1972	AL Pvt. U.S/. Army WWII
William E. Knowles	Aug. 22, 1876	Jan. 9, 1938	
Martha Roberts	Aug. 29, 1860	July 6, 1935	w/o John Wesley Knowles
Carter C. Knowles	May 4, 1884	May 30, 1946	
Robert Wesley Knowles	Jan. 24, 1927	Jan. 4, 1929	s/o Mr. & Mrs. E.S. Knowles
Mrs. Ruby Knowles Byrd	Oct. 29, 1900	Mar. 27, 1935	
Miss Emmie T. Knowles	Feb. 12, 1886	Sept. 6, 1970	
6 adult slabs, n/m		1 child slab, n/m	

Lot 105, no name on wall

J. D. Odom	no dates	
Mary V. Odom		SR:6/6/1898
		one slab
Elizabeth Odom		

- Obit: Mary V. Odom known as "Miss Pop Odom", born near Bethel, Muscogee Co., GA, 1 brother, John Odom, 3 sisters, Miss Bettie Odom, Mrs. George R. Clark, both of Columbus, GA, 1 sister in LA.

- Obit: Elizabeth Odom – bur. 3/1/1910, 64, died at residence of J.M. Johnson, 1 brother, Jack Odom of New York, 1 sister Mrs. Emmie Craw of LA.

Sexton Records indicate buried in this lot:

Charley Odom   *bur. 8/11/1879*

Lot 106, no name on wall

Sam'l J. Hatcher	Sept. 19, 1812 Chesterfield Co., VA	Apr. 10, 1861	removed to this City 1836, where he resided until his death, 48 y 7 mo 21 d

- Obit: born Chesterfield Co., VA, moved to Columbus 1836.

- Samuel married Elizabeth McGehee 11/26/1843 in Harris Co., GA as Elizabeth McGehee.

- 1850 Muscogee Census: Samuel J. Hatcher 37 VA, Elizabeth 30, Marshall 4, Benjamin

3, Susan 1.

- 1860 Muscogee Census: Saml. J. Hatcher 46 VA, Elizabeth 41 GA, Marshall 14 GA, Ben 12 GA, Susan 10 GA, John 8 GA and Peytonia 6 GA. Also in household Sarah Jefferson 14 GA, Emory? (f) Jefferson 12 GA and Hatcher McGehee no age GA. (The 1850 Muscogee Census shows Sarah C. Jefferson 6 GA and Emory (m) Jefferson 4 GA in the household of Benjamin Jefferson 40 and Harriet 28 GA. Benjamin Jefferson married Harriet McGhee 12/14/1843 in Harris Co., GA.)

- Muscogee Co., GA WB A pages 291-292. Samuel J. Hatcher, 4/2/1861:5/6/1861. Legatees: wife Elizabeth, extrx. Daus: Susan A., Peytona E. Other ch. Wits: Gustavus DeLauney, Bennett H. Crawford, Pleasant J. Philips.

- 1870 Marion Co., GA Census: Elizabeth Hatcher 82 GA and Benjamin T. 22 GA.

Little Seab		Sept. 14, 1883	14 months
Samuel B. Hatcher, Jr.	Aug. 6, 1887	Oct. 17, 1968	
Inf/o S.W. & S.A. McMichael		no dates	
Samuel B. Hatcher	Aug. 27, 1850 Columbus, GA	Oct. 12, 1937 Columbus, GA	

- Obit: retired attorney, former State Senator, born Columbus, GA, s/o Samuel J. & Elizabeth McGehee Hatcher, his father was a pioneer of Columbus, married Mary L. Taylor, in Macon, GA, Oct. 14, 1873, 3 dghts, 1 son, the one surviving dght. married Reynolds Flournoy, son, Samuel B., 1st wife died Aug. 26, 1887, 2nd wife Susie M. Madden in Brunswick, GA, Feb. 23, 1889, children by this marriage, Mrs. W.H. Clark of Jacksonville, FL, Mrs. Susie Boykin of Atlanta, GA, J. Madden Hatcher of Columbus, GA.

Mary Louise	Sept. 12, 1876	July 16, 1883	d/o Sam'l & Mary Lou Hatcher
Sweet Louisa		June 1, 1881	age 2 yrs
Ramona Elizabeth		June 27, 1872	inf/ S.W. & S.A. McMichael 1y 8 mo 16 d
Seaborn W. McMichael	Mar. 5, 1841	Oct. 8, 1844	
Susie H. Boykin	Jan. 16, 1894	Aug. 2, 1977	
Fleurine Hatcher Clark	May 4, 1890	Dec. 22, 1975	
Mary Lou Taylor	Oct. 11, 1856	Aug. 26, 1887	w/o Sam'l B. Hatcher
Inf. /o S.W. & S.A. McMichael		no dates	
no name		no dates	our mother SR: Mrs. S. Hatcher bur.9/15/1878, 60 yrs.

- Obit: died Sept. 13, 1878, w/o Samuel J. Hatcher, d/o Abner McGehee (sic), 5 children, R.T., S.B., Mrs. S.J. McMichael, Mrs. T.J. Hunt, Marshall J. Hatcher, sister of A.C. & Henry McGehee, 66 yrs. old.

Samuel Hatcher		no dates	inf/o S.W. & S.A. McMichael

Susie A. Hatcher	July 8, 1849	Dec. 22, 1888	w/o S.W. McMichael
Susie Morris Madden	Feb. 23, 1869	Aug. 15, 1949	w/o Samuel B. Hatcher
Sallie E. Hatcher	Dec. 3, 1879	Jan. 13, 1881	d/o Sam'l & Mary Lou Hatcher

Lot 107, J.M. Estes on wall

Margaret Estes	Nov. 5, 1888	Aug. 26, 1889	Inf. d/o E.C. & Addie L. Estes
Joel Marion Estes	Aug. 10, 1828	Jan. 31, 1891	

- Obit: died at residence of son Edwin C. Estes, born in Gwinnett Co., GA hardware business, sons, Edwin C of Columbus, J.D. of Atlanta, GA., J.C. of Chattanooga, TN, Herman C. of Tuskaloosa, AL

- 1870 Muscogee Census: Joel M. Estes 42 GA, Margaret 36 GA, Edwin C. 15 GA, Joel M. L. 14 GA, James 8 GA and Herman M. 9/12. Also in household Ella R. Kirvin 16 GA.

Edwin Clarence Estes	Jan. 8, 1885	Mar 10, 1891	
Mary Estes	Jan. 3, 1807 Morgan Co., GA	Apr. 2, 1865 Columbus, GA	2nd w/o Joel D. Estes
Margaret A. Estes	Nov. 7, 1834	Dec. 10, 1910	

- Obit: died in Chattanooga, TN, w/o late J. Marion Estes, brothers, J.A., R.M. Kirven, sisters, Mrs. Ella R. Cocke of Hollis, CA, Mrs. M.J. Acree of Anniston, AL, children, Herman Estes of Chattanooga, TN, J.L.M. of Atlanta.

- Margaret was the d/o James Kirven (1804-1855) also buried in Linwood Cemetery.

Joel D. Estes	Apr. 15, 1788 Greenville Dist., SC	Apr. 9, 1870 Columbus, GA	our father

- Obit: in Gwinnett Co., GA, 1827, in Benton Co., AL 1833, Lauderdale Co., AL in 1842, also lived in Marion Co., GA Chambers Co., AL, at time of death living in Opelika, AL, at the home of his son, M.M. Estes, another son is Henson Estes.

- Atlanta Constitution 4/12/1870: The Columbus Sun announces the death of Mr. Joel Estes, at the residence of his son M. J. Estes. He was born in Greenville, SC on Sept. 15, 1786 (sic) and hence was nearly 82 years old. For many years he resided in Russell Co., AL.

Charlotte Estes	Oct. 10, 1788 Wilmington, DE	June 3, 1831 Gwinnett Co., GA	our mother 1st wife of Joel D. Estes

- The National Society of the Daughters of the American Revolution Volume 67 page 195. Mrs. Charlotte Estes Bussey. DAR ID Number: 66520. Born in Columbus, Ga. Wife of William Wallace Bussey. Descendant of Brig.-Gen. Charles Scott. Daughter of Henson Scott Estes and Martha Jane Gray, his wife. Granddaughter of Joel Dodson Estes and Charlotte Scott, his wife. Gr-granddaughter of Charles Scott and Frances Howard Sweeney, his wife. Charles Scott (1733-1813) commanded Virginia troops at Trenton, and, in 1777, was made brigadier general, Continental Army. He was at Valley Forge, Princeton, Monmouth, captured at Charleston and on parole to the close of the war. He was born in Cumberland County, Va.; died in Woodford County, Ky.

1 adult slab, n/m   2 inf. slabs: Little Martha & Inf. d/o J.M. & M.A. Estes

Lot 108, E.T. Davis on wall

lot completely covered with concrete, no evidence of graves

Lot 109, J.A. Beard on wall

Jessie Frances Beard	Apr. 6, 1889	Oct. 25, 1975	
Nellie Beard		June 4, 1894	Inf. d/o Pauline & J. Beard
Jesse A. Beard	Apr. 8, 1850	Aug. 20, 1930	

- Obit: Former Sheriff Jesse A. Beard, 81 years of age, died at his home at ???? Peacock Avenue Wednesday morning at 4:4? o'clock (unable to read rest of lengthly obit).

- Jesse Beard married Pauline Dunaway 2/23/1887 in Columbus. Not only Mr. Beard did he serve as Chief of Police for Columbus, he also served several years as Sexton for Linwood Cemetery.

- 1910 Muscogee Census: Jesse A. Beard 60 GA GA GA, wife Pauline 48 GA GA GA (8 children/3 living), dau Jessie F. 19 GA, dau Alice 21 GA and son Paul E. 15 GA.

- 1920 Muscogee Census: Jesse A. Beard 69 GA GA GA, wife Pauline 58 GA GA GA and dau Jessie Jr. 30 GA.

J.A., inf. s/o Pauline & J. Beard		Apr. 28, 1888	
Pauline Dunaway	Dec. 8, 1861	Apr. 18, 1949	w/o Jesse A. Beard

1 adult brick slab, n/m

Lot 110, Gray on wall & Tyler on wall

Rosa S. Tyler		Jan. 20, 1911	Aunt Rosa

- Obit: funeral notice mentions Mrs. W.E. Gray, Miss Rose Tyler, died at home of sister, Mrs. W.E. Gray.

John A. Tyler	Mar. 15, 1796 Orangberg Dist., SC	Sept. 28, 1875 Columbus, GA	father

- Obit: John Alonzo Tyler was born in Orangeburg, S. C., and died in Columbus, Ga., September 28th 1875, aged sixty-nine years and six months. A. M. Wynn.

- 1850 Murray Co., GA Census: Jno A. Tyler 44 SC, Elizabeth M. 38 SC, Ann A. 17 SC, Alonzo K. 15 SC, Cornelia J. 13 SC, Emma J. 11 SC, Mary C. 9 SC, Clarence O.? 7 SC and Sarah R. 5 SC.

- 1860 Muscogee Census: John A. Tyler 53 SC, Elizabeth M. 46 SC, Anna E. 18 SC, Emma J. 23 SC, Mary 21 SC, Rosa 15 GA, Alice 9 GA, John 5 GA and Cornelia 23 SC.

- 1870 Muscogee Census: John A. Tyler 63 SC, Elizabeth M. 58 SC, Anna A. 30 SC,

Rosa S. 20 SC and Alice L. 16 GA.

Ludie Lamar	Jan. 25, 1879	Nov. 18, 1917	w/o Clarence E. Gray
Marion Edgar Gray	Sept. 24, 1849	July 19, 1909	

- Obit: born Columbus, s/o late Frances Marion Gray, worked for railway, leaves wife, 2 sons, Clarence Edgar, Rev. Elmer E. Gray, 3 g/ch., 1 sister Mrs. Alice Daniel of Atlanta, GA, his mother died last week.

- 1880 Muscogee Census: Edgar Gray 30 GA GA GA, Alice 25 GA GA GA, Clarence 6 GA and Elmer 2 GA.

Emma J. Tyler	July 5, 1837	Apr. 22, 1914	w/o N.F. Bynum
Elizabeth M. Tyler	Orangeburg, SC	Columbus, GA	w/o J.A. Tyler d/o Dr. V.D.V. Jamison, age 57, mother

- Obit: Elizabeth M. Tyler: w/o John Tyler, funeral notice mentions J.A. Tyler, leaves a large family. died Aug. 1, 1871

Adjt. Henry Alonzo Tyler		Oct. 5, 1895	a Confederate Soldier he was in the Battle of Ft. Sumpter & in 1861 w/Gen L. Johnston in 1865
Clarence E. Gray	Sept. 3, 1873	June 7, 1931	oldest s/o M.E. & A.L. Gray
Elmer Wynn Gray	Dec. 17, 1877	Sept. 17, 1935	
M.E. Gray, Jr.	July 25, 1908	Sept. 19, 1908	s/o E.W. & B.G. Gray
Marion Lamar	Nov. 10, 1902	July 29, 1915	d/o C.E. & L.P. Gray
Anna E. Tyler		Oct. 16, 1891	sister

- Obit: funeral notice mentions Mr. & Mrs. M.E. Gray, Misses Rosa & Anna Tyler

Wm. Clarence		Jan. 7, 1906	s/o C.E. & L.P. Gray (baby)
Harry E. Knight, Sr.	Dec. 25, 1906	Apr. 13, 1961	
Bessie Giddis Gray	Sept. 15, 1878	July 30, 1948	
Alice Laura Tyler	Mar. 29, 1851	Dec. 27, 1932	w/o M.E. Gray
Cornelia J. Tyler	Oct. 1, 1835	Apr. 20, 1913	

- Obit: sister, Mrs. M.E. Gray

1 child slab, n/m

Lot 111, Springer on wall

Johanna F. Gittinger		June 20, 1855	age 72 yrs

- Obit: Johanna Frederike, died near Columbus.

Philip A. Gittinger	Sept. 23, 1809 Germany	June 26, 1890 Columbus, GA

- Obit: Mr. Gettinger was born in Germany 23 Feb 1809 in Germany and came to this country when he was only 21 years of age. He remained in New York a few years when he moved to Detroit, MI. It was there that he married and remained until moving to Columbus.

- 1850 Muscogee Census: Phillip Gittenbuger 41 Ger., Adelaid 39 France, Phillip 12 Muscogee, Emily 13 Muscogee, Mrs. Bonough 65 France and Felix Bonough 28 France.

Capt. P.W. Gittinger   Oct. 17, 1863   24 yr 11 mo 15 dy

- Obit: Co. F, 17th GA Reg. mortally wounded Sept. 19, at Battle of Chickamauga.

Francis Joseph Springer   Mar. 7, 1834   Nov. 17, 1882

- Obit: h/o Emily Gittinger, 6 children, 3 sons, 3 dghts, born Marlenhein, France, lived awhile in Columbus, OH.

- 1880 Muscogee Census: F. J. Springer 46 France France France, wife Emily GA Wartemberg Kramen, dau Adella 20 GA, son Charlie 19 GA, dau Allice 17 GA, son Philip 15 GA, dau Anna 12 GA and son Frank 7 GA.

- 1900 Muscogee Census: Adela L. Foley Nov. 1859 GA France GA (wd, 4 children/4 living), son Joseph G. Nov. 1883 GA Iowa GA, son Theo___ M. Apr. 1886 GA, son Frank S. Aug 1888 GA, son Charlie B. June 1891 GA, mother Emlie Springer June 1837 GA Germany France(wd, 6 children/6 living) and brother Frank H. Springer Mar 1870 GA.

Catherina F. Burrus   Sept. 16, 1856   age 67 years, native
                                                                                   of Marlheim, France

Charles Burrus   May 1825   Oct. 26, 1878
                                  Marlheim, France   Columbus, GA

- 1860 Barbour Co., AL Census: Charles Burrus 34 France and Henry Hubner 22 Hanover Germany.

Philip G. Springer   Oct. 10, 1865   Jan. 8, 1912

Mrs. A.M. Gittinger   May 27, 1812   May 2, 1870
                                  Marlhein, France   Columbus, GA

- Obit: resident of Columbus since 1836; mentions husband & Mr. & Mrs. F.J. Springer.

Frank H. Springer   Mar. 1, 1870   May 31, 1927

Emelie G. Springer   June 26, 1837   July 6, 1916

- Obit: d/o Philip A. & Adelia Gittinger, in 1858, married F.G. Springer, 6 children, 5 of whom survive, Mrs. Alice Kinkaid of Griffin, GA, Mrs. Adele Foley, Mrs. R.E. Bize, Frank G. & Charles all of Columbus, GA.

Lot 112, open lot

1 child's brick slab, n/m

Lot 113, Meyer on wall

Helen G. Meyer   1881   1954

Charles Mason Meyer	Mar. 20, 18??	Dec. 23, 1911	
Ralph J. Meyer	1888	1949	
Charles Wm. Meyer	1853	1906	SR:but.3/25/1906, age 53 yrs.
Mrs. Frances H. Meyer	Feb. 6, 1850	Mar. 5, 1922	

- Obit: leaves 2 sons, Ralph of Columbus, GA, George of Atlanta, GA, 2 dghts, Mrs. Frank Hargrove, Miss Helen Meyer, both of Columbus, GA, 2 sisters, Mrs. H.W. Garrett of Columbus, Mrs. J.L. Clyatt of Tuscaloosa, AL, 2 g/ch.

Frederick Ed. Meyer	1819	1874	SR:bur.12/24/1874

- 1870 Muscogee Census: Frederick Meyer 52 Hamburg, William 27 Hanover, Frederick 19 GA, Charles 16 GA, Harry 10 GA, Louisa 19 GA, Mary 14 GA, Caroline Roland 30 NY, George Roland 14 GA and Jacob Roland 13 GA.

Ida Day	Dec. 21, 1866	Mar. 9, 1900	w/o A.J. Day
S.T. Roper	June 19, 1840	May 29, 1913	

- Obit: S.T. Roper, retired steamboat captain, died last night at his home on Eleventh Avenue in Columbus, after an illness of several months of Bright's disease. Captain Roper was 73 years old and was captain of a on the Chattahoochee River, which brought the material to build the Georgia Home Insurance Company building. He was a prominent member of the I.O.O.F. Girard Lodge No 172. The deceased was the son of the late Dr. James Roper of Iowa and is survived by his wife and three daughters Mrs. T.L. Ingram of Atlanta, Mrs. John Barfield and Mrs. Henry Gant of Columbus. The funeral will be conducted this afternoon at 2 o'clock from the residence and the services will be held by the Rev. F. M. Lowrey. The pallbearers have been chosen from members of the Girard Lodge of the I.O.O. F. and are: Henry Fuller, Jr., James Averett, J.B. Marchant, ? Skinner, H.W. Williams and O.H. Hagan? (The Interment will be in Linwood cemetery.)

- 1880 Muscogee Census: S. T. Roper 41 GA GA GA, wife Julie 34 GA GA GA, dau Ida 13 GA, dau Carrie 11 GA, dau Allene 9 GA, dau Julia 7 GA and dau Katie 4.

2 adult brick slabs, n/m   1 inf. brick slab, n/m

Sexton Records indicate buried in this lot:

Mrs. Carrie Roland   *bur. 5/3/1901*

- Obit: A noble woman passed away when Mrs. Carrie Roland breathed her last breath at her home at No. 704 First Avenue yesterday morning after an illness of pneumonia. She was 65 years of age and born in NY, being the d/o Mr. Frederick Meyer. When a young girl, she removed to Talbot Co., GA and afterwards to Columbus. One of the old members of St. Luke Church and was a consecrated Christian woman. Survved by 3 brothers; Mr. Fred Meyer of Montgomery, and Messrs. Charles and Henry Meyer of this city and one sister Mrs. J. C. Albright. The late Julia Roper and Mrs. J. E. Deaton were her sisters. She is survived by one son Mr. J. A. Roland and quite a few nieces and nephews.

- 1880 Muscogee Census: Carrie Rolan 41 NY NY NY, son George ? GA, son Jake 22 GA.

Lot 114, no name on wall

Helen Waynman Swift	May 24, 1844 Waymanville, Upson Co., GA	July 16, 1915 Ashville, NC	w/o S. G. Murphy

- Obit: eldest dght of Col. & Mrs. George P. Swift, leaves husband & 2 dghts, Mrs. Jho. M. Biddle, of Washington, D.C., Mrs. Jno C. Breckenridge of Paris, France 2 sisters, Mrs. James H. Shorter of Macon, GA, Mrs. James P. Kyle of Columbus, GA, 2 brothers, Ed W. Swift & Charles J. Swift, both of Columbus.

- 1880 Muscogee Census: enumerated with George Swift; dau Helen Murphy 36 GA MA MA, Ethel Murphy 6 GA and Adlade Murphy 1 GA.

S. G. Murphy	Nov. 6, 1837 Greensboro, NC	Mar. 18, 1926

- 1870 Muscogee Census: Living in the household of George Swift Sr.; Samuel G. Murphy 35 NC and Ellen W. 26 GA.

Lot 115, no name on wall

Frances L. Bambush	Sept. 17, 1859	Mar. 11, 1920
Joseph F. Bambush	Oct. 18, 1861	May 1, 1916

- 1870 Russell Co., AL Census: Joseph Bambush 35 Baden, Margaret 30 GA, Virginia 10 SC, Joseph 8 GA, Charles 5 GA, Martha 3 GA and Laura 10/12 GA.

- Joseph Bambush married Fannie Olillis 11/2/1882 in Muscogee Co., GA

- 1910 Muscogee Census: Joseph F. Bambush 48 GA Germany SC (married 21 yrs.), wife Frances L. 48 AL SC GA (5 ch/3 liv), and dau Thelma 14 GA.

SR indicate Marcus Bambush bur. 4/18/1885 is buried in this lot.

Lot 116, Boyce Baird on wall

Isabelle Baird Woodward	Feb. 27, 1899	Mar. 11, 1956	w/o Nicholas Dodge Woodward
Frank Benj. Boyce	Dec. 29, 1865	June 29, 1945	

- 1910 Muscogee Census: Frank Boyce 43 AL Eng AL, wife Alice 40 AL GA AL (m. 17 yrs. 4 ch/3 liv.), dau Nellie 15 GA, son Frank 12 GA and son Harry 2 GA.

- 1920 Muscogee Census: Frank B. Boyce 53 AL Eng AL, wife Alice 51 AL GA GA, son Henry F. 11 GA, son Frank J. 12? GA, sil Frank C. Baird 25 GA GA GA, dau Nella 24 GA and gdau Nella 1 1/12 GA.

Little Ralph	Feb. 21, 1903	June 8, 1906	s/o Frank B. & Alice Boyce
Hugh Baird	July 12, 1868 Russell Co., AL	Mar. 31, 1934 Columbus, GA	

- 1870 Russell Co., AL Census: John Baird 35 Scotland, Issabella 25 AL, Marion 8 AL, Jane 5 Al and Hugh 2 AL.

- 1880 Lee Co., AL Census: John Baird 45 Sco Sco Sco, wife Isabella M. 35 AL Sco Sco, son Hugh 11 Al, dau Isabella 6 Al and son John 2 AL.

- Hugh Baird married Leigh Davidson 7/6/1892 in Lee Co., AL.

- 1900 Russell Co., AL Census: Hugh Baird July 1868 AL Sco AL, wife ___ L. Nov 1869 (m. 8 yrs. 5ch/3 liv), son Morton W. May 1893 AL, dau Mary ___ 1896, dau Isabel W. Feb ____ and boarder Bess Davidson Apr 1878.

- 1920 Muscogee Census: Hugh Baird 51 AL Sco Al, wife Leigh 50 AL GA AL, dau Isabella 20 AL, dau Mildred 17 GA, SIL James W. Wilkerson 29 Al, dau Mary 23 Al and grandson James W. Jr. 4 GA.

Hugh Baird, Jr.	Apr. 4, 1904	Apr. 23, 1919	s/o Hugh & Leigh D. Baird
Leigh Davidson Baird	Nov. 22, 1869 Russell Co., AL	Feb. 25, 1960 Atlanta, GA	
Alice Leigh Enson	Oct. 27, 1868	Nov. 4, 1938	w/o Frank B. Boyce

2 inf slabs, n/m

Sexton Records indicate buried in this lot:

Ralph H. Boyce			*bur. 6/9/1906, 3 yrs.*
Harry Boyce			*inf.*

Lot 117, open lot

B.P. ?? unable to read			17th GA Legion killed Aug. 30, 1862 C.S.A. 1861-1865

Lot 118, Hamilton-Jefferson, lot 297-300 on wall

Dr. Hamilton Jefferson	Dec. 26, 1885	June 26, 1920	
Rollin Jefferson		Aug. 26, 1875	2nd s/o Rollin & M.V. Jefferson, 9 mo 3 days
Hamilton Jefferson		Nov. 2, 1878	3rd s/o Rollin & M.V. Jefferson, 2 yr 7 mo 24 dys
Morris J. Burts	May 14, 1875	July 2, 1931	

- Morris J. Burts died in Baldwin Co., GA.[24]

John Hamilton	Nov. 3, 1796	Nov. 8, 1856	

- Obit: b. Lamark, Scotland, died Harris Co., GA.

Rollin Jefferson	Feb. 9, 1849	April 6, 1912	

- Obit: leaves 4 sons, Dr. Ben Jefferson of Colorado, Rollins, Jr. of FL, Albert of Columbus, Hamilton of Baltimore, MD, 1 dght, Mrs. J.D. McPhail of Richmond, VA, 2 brothers, Wesley Jefferson of Buena Vista, GA, Emory, Sr. of Columbus, GA

- 1880 Muscogee Census: Rollin Jefferson 30 GA MD MD, wife Marietta 35 GA GA GA, son Benjamin 8 GA and son Rollin 2 GA.

- 1900 Muscogee Census: Rollin Jefferson Feb 1849 GA GA GA, wife Mary E. Feb 1853 GA GA GA, son Rollin Jr. Feb. 1898, son Albert Aug. 1880 GA, dau Metta V. Aug. 1883 and son Hamilton Aug. 1885.

- 1910 Muscogee Census: Rollin Jefferson 61GA MD AL, wife Merietta V. 57 GA GA GA (m. 40 yrs. 10 ch/5 liv), and son Albert 28 GA.

Melta V. Jefferson	1853	1928	w/o Rollin Jefferson, SR: bur. 6/18/1928

- Rollin Jefferson married Marietta V. Harp 12/20/1870 in Chattahoochee Co., GA. She was born 2/28/1853, the d/o Lafayette Harp and Callie King.

James McLester Jefferson	Feb. 12, 1874	Apr. 12, 1931	
Ann M. Hamilton	Aug. 3, 1807	Oct. 7, 1857	w/o John Hamilton
Harriett McGehee	Oct. 13, 1820	Oct. 27, 1854	w/o Benj. Jefferson

- Benjamin Jefferson married Harriet McGehee 12/14/1843 in Harris Co., GA.

- 1850 Muscogee Census: Benjamin Jefferson 40 MD, Harriet 28 Jones Co., GA, Sarah C. 6 Musc., Emory 4 Musc. and Rollin 2 Musc.

Emory Jefferson	Oct. 19, 1846	Mar. 30, 1926

- Obit: born Columbus, GA, s/o Benj. Jefferson & Harriet McGehee, whose home was the old Munro place in Wynnton, parents died when only a few yrs old, reared by guardian, the late Samuel B. Hatcher, C.S.A. vet., May 6, 1869, married Miss Carrie McLester of Chattahoochee Co., GA, leaves wife & children, Thomas & G.B. of Columbus, Emery R. of Montgomery, AL, Mrs. M.E. Rushin of Vienna, GA, Mrs. Homer Hardin of Dyas, GA, Mrs. John A. Porter of Macon, GA, Mrs. Louise Jefferson of Columbus, brothers, the late Rollin Jefferson, Dr. Wesley Jefferson, of Buena Vista, GA, sister, the late Mrs. Sarah Burts.

Caroline L. McLester	Sept. 8, 1851	Dec. 29, 1927	w/o Emory Jefferson

- Obit: widow of Emory Jefferson, d/o late Dr. James McLester of Chattanooga, sister of late Loonidere McLester, born Chattahoochee Co., GA, 2 sisters, Mrs. M.F. Shipp of Columbus, Mrs. C.B. Wooten, Macon, GA, children surviving, Mrs. Louis Jefferson, Thomas Jefferson, both of Columbus, Mrs. Homer Hardin, Dyas, GA, Mrs. John E. Porter, Macon, GA, Emory R. Jefferson of Montgomery, AL.

Duncan Burts	May 13, 1833	Aug. 7, 1881

- Obit: C.S.A. vet., lawyer, GA Legislature from Chattahoochee Co., GA, born Muscogee Co., GA.

- Duncan Hartsfield Burts married 1) Addie Cobb on 3/6/1864 and 2) Sarah Caroline Burts on 12/14/1869 both in Chattahoochee Co., GA.

- 1880 Muscogee Census: Duncan H. Burts 47 GA, Sarah C. 35 GA, Edgar 7 GA and Maurice 5 GA.

Sarah C. Burts	Jan. 15, 1845	Mar. 19, 1908	w/o Duncan Burts SR: bur. 3/21/1908

- Obit: born Columbus, nee Sarah Caroline Jefferson, d/o Benj. Jefferson & Harriet McGehee, widow of Duncan Burts, brothers, Emory, Rollin, both of Columbus, Dr. Wesley of Buena Vista, GA, 1 son, Morris Burts, 1 deceased son Edgar D. Burts (d. 3 yrs ago).

Lot 119, open lot

1 adult brick slab, n/m

Lot 120, open lot

no evidence of graves

Lot 121, J.L. Biggers on wall

James Clements Woolridge, M.D.　　　May 13, 1877　　　Sept. 7, 1962

- 1920 Muscogee Census: James C. Wooldridge 42 GA GA GA and wife Kate B. 40 GA GA GA.

Joseph Lawson Biggers　　　July 29, 1839　　　June 7, 1922

- Obit: leaves wife, 1 son, L.M., 2 dghts, Mrs. J.W. Blackmon, Mrs. J.C. Wooldrige, 5 sisters, Mrs. Gussies Davis of Tallahassee, FL, Mrs. J.D. Anthony of DeSoto, GA, Mrs. M. J. Wade, Miss Sallie Biggers, both of Smith Station, Al, Mrs. N.J. Crane of Columbus, GA.
- 1850 Muscogee Census: Lorenzo M. Biggers 40 SC, Elizabeth A. 35 Wilkes Co. GA, Francis L. (f) 14 Musc., Sarah E. 12 Musc., Joseph L. 10 Musc., Margarett J. 8 Musc., Marianna 6 Musc., Josephine 4 Musc., Lorenzo J. 3 Musc. and Richard J. M. 1 Musc.

Katherine Biggers Woolridge　　　Dec. 27, 1878　　　June 17, 1965

Lorenzo Marion Biggers　　　Feb 24, 1865　　　June 16, 1944

Minerva Cox Biggers　　　Jan. 19, 1848　　　Sept. 21, 1922　　　mother

- Obit: w/o late J.L. Biggers, who died about 2 mos ago, 74 yrs. b. Harris Co., GA, 2 dghts, Mrs. J.W. Blackmon, Mrs. J.C. Woolridge, 1 son, L.M. Biggers, 2 sisters, Mrs. K.M. Thomas of Montgomery, AL, Mrs. Mattie E. Copeland of Troy, AL, 1 bro. James M. Cox of Mounteagle, TN.
- d/o James Cox and Exa Robinson of Harris Co., GA.[25]
- 1880 Muscogee Census: Joseph Biggers 40 GA SC SC, wife Minerva 30 GA GA GA, son Lorenzo 15 GA, dau Lula 10 GA, dau Jesse 4 GA and dau Katie 2 GA.

Lot 122, Blackmon on steps of wall

Joseph Walter Blackmon　　　Dec. 14, 1901　　　Aug. 14, 1987

Jessie Biggers Blackmon	Dec. 6, 1876	Dec. 15, 1966	mother

- d/o Joseph L. and Minerva Cox Biggers.

James Walter Blackmon	Nov. 11, 1872	Apr. 1, 1923

- 1900 Muscogee Census: James Blackmon Nov. 1872 GA GA GA (m. 4 yrs.), wife Jessie Dec. 1875 GA GA GAand daughter Myrtle June 1879 GA.

- 1920 Muscogee Census: James W. Blackmon 47 GA GA GA, wife Jesie 42 GA GA GA, dau Myrtle 20 GA and son Joseph W. 18 GA.

Bright Bickerstaff Blackmon	Apr. 13, 1905	July 29, 1976

Lot 123, open lot

R.G. Huckaba	Mar. 31, 1824	Mar. 28, 1880

- Obit: 55 years old, Police Officer, unmarried, leaves mother, sisters & brother, lived several miles above City.

Harris	drummer of the Columbus Guards, C.S.A. 1861-1865 SR:bur. 10/3/1871

- Obit: Huey B. Harris, 80 years old, shoemaker, served in War of 1812, Mexican War 1847, and late War with the Columbus Guards as a Drummer.

Lot 124, wrought iron fence, partially down

Mary Andrews	Dec. 25, 1853 Russell County, AL	w/o Green Andrews born NC, died in Russell County, AL at the residence of her daughter Mary R. Rose, age 72 years

- 1850 Russell Co., AL Census: Columbus Rose 23 GA, Mary 40 GA, Mary 18 GA and Mary Andrews 80 NC.

- Mary Andrews married David C. Rose 3/25/1823 in Hancock Co., GA.

Juveria	July 19, 1856	Apr. 3, 1859	child of Mary & G.A ? (unable to read)

Lot 125, no name on wall

J. Lawrence Hunt	June 6, 1878	Oct. 21, 1945
John Kettle Harris	Sept. 30, 1854	Apr. 12, 1928

Martha Rebecca	Apr. 27, 1831	July 21, 1885	
Lyra Myrtis Harris	Apr. 24, 1885	Dec. 20, 1971	w/o J. Lawrence Hunt
Mattie Middleton	Jan. 11, 1882	Sept. 20, 1892	d/o J.K. & M.J. Harris
Mary Justina Jackson	Mar. 12, 1856	June 11, 1921	
Jeptha Crawford Harris	Feb. 3, 1814	Jan. 12, 1883	

- Obit: born Watkinsville, Clarke Co., GA, lived in Girard, AL, dentist.

- The National Society of the Daughters of the American Revolution Volume 112 page 315. Mrs. Lyra Harris Hunt. DAR ID Number: 111987. Born in Columbus, Ga. Wife of J. Lawrence Hunt.
  Descendant of Walton Harris, as follows:
  1. John Keeble Harris (b. 1854) m. 1878 Mary Justina Jackson (b. 1856).
  2. Jeptha Crawford Harris (1814-83) m. 1847 Martha Rebecca Upshaw (1831-85).
  3. Walton Harris, Jr. (1775-1820), m. 1802 Virginia Beverly Billups (1787-1877)
  4. Walton Harris m. 1760 Rebecca Lanier (b. 1744).
  Walton Harris (1739-1809) received land grant in Wilkes County Ga., for service as private in the Revolution. He was born in Brunswick County, Va.; died in Greene County, Ga.

1 child slab & marker
(unable to read)

Lot 126, wrought iron fence, no name

Michael Kenny	May 23, 1861	aged 92 yrs. native of County Carlow, Ireland

- 1860 Muscogee Census: Catherine London 37 Ire, Henry 14 Ire, Mary 12 Ire, Anna 10 Ire, Michael Kenney 90 Ire, Frederick Tomlin 36 Eng and Emily 26 SC.

- His son, Thomas Kenny was a stone carver and has tombstones in Linwood. This family emigrated from Ireland to Canada, then down to GA. The marriage record of his son John Kenney states that his mother was Honora Madden.[26]

Patrick Adams	14 Feb. 1855	age 46 yrs. native of county Mayo Ireland

- One of the earliest stone carvers in Muscogee Co.

- 1850 Muscogee Census: Patrick Adams 40 Ire, Ann 28 Ire, John 13 NY, Mary 9 GA and Francis 6/12 GA.

- Muscogee Co., GA WB A p. 177-178. Patrick Adams. 10 Feb 1855/5 Mar 1855. Legatees: Wife Anne who is believed to now be pregnant; dau Mary Teresa Adams and son Francis Adams. Extrx. Anne Adams. Wit: Thomas Kenney, James T. Brown & William Perry.

1 adult brick slab, n/m

1 large marker: erected by Ann Adams in memory of her 6 children whom the Lord has taken to himself (no names or dates).

Lot 127, Ryckeley on wall

George Joseph Ryckeley	Mar. 01, 1050	Aug. 24, 1928	d/o (sio) Laura McKnight
Texas Adler	Jan. 19, 1855 Montgomery, AL	Dec. 29, 1927 Columbus, GA	w/o Charles Edw. Ryckeley d/o Joseph M. Heard & Margaret Eliz. Updegraff D.A.R #184464

- Obit: 1 dght., Mrs. Mary H.R. Pepperman of Montgomery, AL, 2 sons, Henry M. of Wayne, MI, J.C. of Columbus, GA, 1 sister, Mrs. Dr. Epatha R.H. Krentner of Montgomery, AL

- Mrs. Texas A. Ryckeley, widow of Lieutenant Charles E. Ryckeley, died at the city hospital at 2/45 o'clock yesterday afternoon. Mrs. Ryckeley was well known in Columbus where she lived many years and her friends learn of her death with much regret. She was a member of the church of the Holy Family and was also a member of the Daughters of the American Revolution. Her father was a grandson of Major Barnard Heard, of Revolution fame, who played a prominent part in the victory at Kettle Creek, Wilkes County, GA. The ancestors of Mrs. Ryckeley's mother, who was Mrs. Margaret Elizabeth Updegraff, came to this country with William Penn. Surviving Mrs. Ryckeley are a daughter, Mrs. Mary H. R. Pepperman of Montgomery, AL, 2 sons Henry M. of Watne, MI, J. C. of Columbus, GA, 1 sister Mrs. Dr. Epatha R. H. Krentner of Montgomery, AL, a number of grandchildren and great grandchildren and David D. Updegraff uncle of Mrs. Ryckeley.

R.W. Ryckeley	1888	1913	SR:born 1/31/1888 bur. 9/15/1913
L.E. Ryckeley	May 16, 1880	Aug. 16, 1918	
George E. Ryckeley	Aug. 21, 1848	Jan. 22, 1856	s/o John E. & Mary Ann Ryckeley
Little Patie	June 1875	Oct. 1879	
Charles E. Ryckeley	May 21, 1846 Apalachicole, FL	Aug. 25, 1920 Columbus, GA	eldest s/o John E. & Mary A. (Colgan) Ryckeley Co. C, Naval Bat. Mar. 1864-Apr. 1865 C.S.A.

- Obit:Lt. Columbus Police Dept., leaves wife, Mrs. Texas Heard Ryckeley, 4 children, Mrs. Mary R. Pepperman of Montgomery, AL, C.J., Henry M. & John C., 2 brothers, Louis T. & G. Joseph, all of Columbus, GA, G.B. of Apalachicola, FL

John Emile Ryckeley	1861	1865	
Mary A.T. Ryckeley	1825	1890	SR: bur. 6/8/1890 one slab
E. Adel Ryckeley	1867	1917	bur. 8/27/1917
1 adult brick slab, n/m		1 baby brick slab, n/m	

- John E. Ryckeley married Mary Ann T. Colgan 6/20/1844 NYC, NY.
- 1860 Muscogee Census: John A. Ryckeley 41 France stone carver, Mary A. 33 NY, Charles 14 FL, Louisa 11 GA, Louise? 6 GA and Joseph 3 GA.

Sexton Records indicate buried in this lot:

Inf./o C. J. Ryckeley	*bur. 6/28/1900*
A. E. Ryckeley	*bur. 3/4/1894*

Lot 128, open lot, no name

Whit Smith	C.S.A. 1861-1865, SR: bur. 11/30/1877, 37 yrs. old

Lot 129, no name on wall

Lula Barnett	no dates		
Lucy A. Barnett	Apr. 28, 1828	Oct. 28, 1875	w/o J.N. Barnett

- Obit: Mrs. Lucy A. Barnett was born in Houston County, Ga., April 11, 1828; married Mr. John N. Barnett, September 18, 1845; and died in Columbus, Ga., October 28, 1875. Jas. O. Branch.

William Barnett	no dates	
John N. Barnett	May 10, 1818	July 10, 1889

- Obit: 1 daughter Louella died 14 Oct. 1856, son John died 4 July 1854, son William H. died 2 Aug. 1847, wife Lucy, nee Lucy A. Pitts.
- 1850 Muscogee Census: John N or W. Barnett 33 NC, Lucy 21 GA and Frances P. 2 GA.
- 1870 Muscogee Census: John Barnett 50 AL, Lucy 42 AL, James 15 GA, Mary 13 GA, Lucy 10 GA, Julia 7 GA and Lavenia 4 GA.

Lot 130, no name on wall

Corine DeLaunay	Mar. 6, 1851	Mar. 12, 1920	d/o Gustavus & Lucy A. DeLaunay
Alfred A. Wellborn	Jan 15, 1874	Oct. 13, 1913	
Lucy C. Jones	Dec. 30, 1820	Oct. 20, 1892	

- Obit: died Leesburg, VA, widow of late Judge Gustavus DeLauney, nee Lucy A. Jones, resided in Leesburg several years with several of her daughters.

Pauline DeLaunay		Aug. 16, 1900	our dear & eldest sister, Mignonne
Lavinia Leboudais	Feb. 29, 1840	Sept. 11, 1912	d/o Gustavus & Lucy A. DeLauney

- Obit: oldest of 4 sisters, Mrs. C. DeL. Hines, Mrs. F. Worsley, Miss Corine DeLauney.

Thomas J. Hines   Sept. 26, 1845   May 22, 1884

- Obit: son of T. Jeff Hines of Stewart Co., GA, b. Randolph Co., GA at 16 volunteered for C.S.A. served 31st GA Regt., 1 brother Randolph Hines, 1 sister, Mrs. Wm. Cade
- s/o Thomas Jefferson Hines who is buried in Green Hill Methodist Church Cemetery in Stewart Co., GA.

Gustavus DeLaunary   May 1, 1811   June 4, 1877

- Obit: born Norfolk, VA, his father was a refugee from St. Domingo and removed to Jones Co, GA, lived in Milledgeville, then to Lumpkin, GA, soldier in Indian War, moved here about 1856, Justice of the Inferior Court for awhile, his son died in Civil War, several daughters survive.
- s/o James A. Delaunay (c1761-1831 Jones Co., GA) and Emilie LeBourdais.
- 1870 Muscogee Census: Gustavus DeLaunay 59 VA, Lucy 49 GA, Lavinia 30 GA, Clotilde 23 GA, Corinne 19 GA and Moselle 16 GA.

LaMartin DeLaunay		Jan. 29, 1855	d/o Gustavus & Lucy DeLaunay, 6 yr, 2 mo, 20 dys
Harrison Jones		Aug. 27, 1862	only s/o Gustavus & Lucy DeLaunay d. in Conf. Army, 20 yrs 7 mos 10 dy
Moselle DeLauney	May 6, 1854	Feb. 12, 1921	w/o Thomas Lee Worsley

- 1880 Leesburg, Loundon Co., VA Census:Thomas Worsley 38 VA VA VA, wife Moselle 25 GA VA France, dau Corine 2 GA, son William 1/12 VA, sister Elizabeth 35 VA, sister Dorine? 31 VA, MIL Lucy Delaney 58 GA VA GA and BIL Thomas J. Hines 35 GA GA GA.

Clotilde DeLaunay	Aug. 4, 1846	Nov. 24, 1926	w/o Thomas J. Hines

- Obit: died Milledgebille, GA, widow of Thomas J. Hines, d/o Gustavus DeLaunay & Mrs. Lucy Jones DeLaunay, born Stewart Co., GA, sister, Miss Corine DeLaunay, Mrs. Thomas L. Worsley, both deceased, brother Harrison, died in Civil War, leaves nieces & nephews.

Corine Worsley	Dec. 2, 1877	Mar. 5, 1907	w/o Alfred Anderson Wellborn
Moselle Worsley	Nov. 1, 1881	July 2, 1963	d/o Moselle DeLaunary & Thomas Lee Worsley

Sexton Records indicate buried in this lot:

William D. Worsley   *bur. 5/14/1954*

- William DeLaunay Worsley was born c1879. He married Henrietta Hill Blanchard, the d/o William Randolph Blanchard and Henrietta Hill Seabrook.[27]
- 1910 Muscogee Census:William DeL Worsley 29 VA VA GA (mar. 0/12), wife Henri B. 26 GA GA SC.

Lot 131, D.E. Williams on wall

William T. (Billie) Williams	Dec. 31, 1867	Aug. 24, 1941	
Sarah Emma Chaffin	Nov. 5, 1846	Dec. 19, 1905	w/o Daniel Edw. Williams

- Obit: born Columbus, GA, leaves husband, 1 son, William T. Williams, 1 dght., Mrs. Edward W. Swift, 3 brothers, Capt. Thomas Chaffin of Columbus, GA., James D. Chaffin of Pensacola, FL & George D. Chaffin of Atlanta, GA, 1 sister Mrs. J.L. Peabody.

- 1850 Muscogee Census: Thomas Chaffin 52 GA, Mrs. S. G. 46 GA, James A. 24 GA, William 22 GA, Thomas 20 GA, Miles H. 18 GA, Laura J. 16 GA, Mary F. 14 GA, George R. 10 GA and Sarah E. 8 GA.

Alma Swift	Aug. 4, 1904 Columbus, GA	May 12, 1906	d/o Edw. W. & Alma Swift
Daniel Edward Williams	Mar. 24, 1839	Feb. 20, 1914	C.S.A.

- 1880 Muscogee Census: (boarding in household of Sallie Chaffin 41 TN VA TN) Dan Williams 40 GA GA GA, wife Sarah 35 GA GA GA, Wm T. 12 GA and Alma 7 GA.

Lot 132, W.H. Williams on wall

Frances Chaffin	Oct. 8, 1895	Aug. 2, 1987	d/o Bessie W. & D.E. Williams, Jr.
Daniel Edw. Williams, Jr.	Mar. 14, 1868	May 14, 1909	

- s/o William H. and Frances Chaffin Williams; married Bessie Williams, the d/o George Morton Williams and Henrietta Lawrence Wall, 11/21/1894.

Henrietta Lawrence Williams	no dates		d/o D.E. Williams, Jr. & Bessie W. Williams SR:bur.7/28/1917, 19
Maud Williams	no dates		d/o Frances Chaffin & W.H. Williams
W.H. Williams, Jr.	no dates		s/o Frances Chaffin & W.H. Williams
George Morton Williams	Sept. 15, 1901	Dec. 10, 1950	s/o Bessie W. & D.E. Williams, Jr.
Frances Chaffin	no dates		w/o William H. Williams
William H. Williams	1841	1931	SR: bur.3/25/1931

- 1880 Muscogee Census: W. H. Williams 38 GA GA GA, dau Emma 13 GA, son D. E. Jr. 12 GA, dau Mary 11, dau Maude 9, dau Fannie 8 GA, son Tom 5 GA, son Jesse 4 GA and dau Anna 2 GA.

Sexton Records indicate buried in this lot:

Wm. Mitchell Williams   *bur. 9/18/1914*

Lot 133, Springer on wall

Little Frankie	Aug. 21, 1883	Aug. 18, 1884	nf/s/o C.P. & M.F. Springer
Mary Kate Kincaid	June 17, 1887	Jan. 20, 1971	w/o Harry C. Bize
Harry Clifton Bize	Oct. 22, 1878	Mar. 13, 1960	
Anthony William Smyth	June 13, 1909	July 10, 1967	
Louise Adelle Bize	June 15, 1897	Dec. 29, 1947	d/o R.E. & Anna S. Bize
Robert Edward Bize	Oct. 12, 1869	Mar. 31, 1937	

- 1920 Muscogee Census: Robert E. Bize 49 GA SC GA, wife Anna 52 GA France GA and dau Adele 22 GA.

- 1880 Muscogee Census: Daniel Bize 40 GA SC GA, wife Mary 32 GA SC GA, dau Lula 14 GA, son Chars. 13 GA, son Robert 10 GA, son Louis 8 GA, dau Mary 7 GA, son Frederick 3 GA and son Harry 2 GA.

Anna J. Springer	Jan. 10, 1868	Dec. 15, 1940	w/o Robert E. Bize

- 1880 Muscogee Census: F. (Frank) J. Springer 46 France France France, wife Emily GA Wartemberg Kramen, dau Adella 20 GA, son Charlie 19 GA, dau Allice 17 GA, son Philip 15 GA, dau Anna 12 GA and son Frank 7 GA.

Lot 134, Foley on steps

Ann Foley	Oct. 21, 1892	Jan. 28, 1977	w/o Richard T. Young
Joseph Gittinger Foley	Nov. 23, 1882	June 6, 1944	
Adele L. Springer	Nov. 15, 1858	May 24, 1941	w/o Theo M. Foley

- 1880 Muscogee Census: F. (Frank) J. Springer 46 France France France, wife Emily GA Wartemberg Kramen, dau Adella 20 GA, son Charlie 19 GA, dau Allice 17 GA, son Philip 15 GA, dau Anna 12 GA and son Frank 7 GA.

- 1900 Muscogee Census: Adela L. Foley Nov. 1859 GA France GA (wd, 4 children/4 living), son Joseph G. Nov. 1883 GA Iowa GA, son Theo___ M. Apr. 1886 GA, son Frank S. Aug 1888 GA, son Charlie B. June 1891 GA, mother Emlie Springer June 1837 GA Germany France(wd, 6 children/6 living) and brother Frank H. Springer Mar 1870 GA.

Frank Daniel Foley	Aug. 17, 1888	June 6, 1944	
Charles B. Foley	June 23, 1891	Feb. 5, 1939	
Theo M. Foley	Oct. 10, 1857	Jan. 28, 1898	

- Obit: Theodore (sic) M. Foley died Jan 28, 1898 after an illness of two weeks. He was born in Burlington, Iowa forty one years ago, being the s/o the late D. M. Foley. He was well known throughout the state and had a host of warm friends in every part of it. He is survived by a wife and 4 sons and one sister Miss Maggie Foley. Mr. Foley was a resident of Columbus for 19 years. He was a brilliant and able Alderman and served with distinction.

THEODORE M. FOLEY.

- Theobald (sic) Matthew Foley was the s/o Daniel Matthew Foley and Mary Fleming. He was the youngest of 13 children. He married Adele Louise Springer, the d/o Francis J. and Emilie (Guttinger) Springer on 2/16/1882 in Columbus, GA.[28]

Mary Foley	July 31, 1896	w/o D.M. Foley, age 86 yrs

- Mary Fleming Foley was the d/o John and Margaret Fleming. They were natives of County Cork Ireland and the parents of ten children, five sons and five daughters, including: Mary, wife of Daniel Foley; Ellen, wife of John O'Brien, a resident of Ireland; Michael of Burlington, Iowa; Elizabeth of New Orleans; John, who lived in St. Louis and Bridget, a widow, who also resided in New Orleans. John Fleming, the father of these children, died in 1832.

Eunice Gordy	Oct. 21, 1892	Aug. 29, 1964	w/o Frank D. Foley
Theo M. Foley, Jr.	Apr. 12, 1889	Sept. 22, 1919	

- Obit: s/o late Theo M. Foley & Mrs. Adele Foley, leaves mother, 3 brothers, Joseph of Greenville, NC, Frank D. & Charles M., both of Columbus, GA

Daniel M. Foley	Oct. 23, 1895	age 84

- Obit: At 1 o'clock this morning ??? was dicovered in the northeast front room of the Veranda Hotel at the corner of First Avenue and Tenth Street.

  The alarm was raised by a passerby, who noticed smoke leaving from the front rooms. The cry of fire woke Engineer Barry?, at No. 5 Engine House across the street, who ran down stairs and up???? the burning building. The fire seemed to be confined to the two front rooms and to to these he at once forced an entrance. The interior of the first room which he entered was completely enveloped in flames. Through this he quickly rushed to the adjoining room where he found Mrs. D. M. Foley and her daughter, Miss Mattie, whose lives were in immediate danger. He at once took them to the street below and returned in the room of Mr. Dan M. Foley, which he found it impossible to enter. In the meantime the fire department had arrived on the scene, and in a short while succeeded in extinguishing the flames, when it was found that he perished in his bed. His remains were then removed to the residence of his son, Mr. T.M. Foley on Second Avenue.

  The origin of the fire is unkown, but it is believed to have been caused by the explosion of a lamp in Mr. Foley's room.

  Mr. D.M. Foley was eighty-three years of age and was a native of Ireland, but had resided in this country for a number of years, the last sixteen of which he has spent in the city.

  He was a member of the Catholic Church, and was survived by his wife and two children, Alderman T.M. Foley and Miss Mattie Foley...

- 1880 Muscogee Census: (listed as boarder in home of James Ryan) Dan'l Foley 67 Ire

Ire Ire, Mary 67 Ire Ire Ire, Dan'l Jr. 33 Ire, Theobald 33 Ire and Margaret 21 LA

- Daniel Matthew Foley was a well-known architect and builder, having built Holy Family Church in Columbus and 16 other churchers in the United States.[29] Other churches include the 1st Presbyterian Church in Claiborn Co., MS,

Lot 135, wrought iron fence, no name

| Marian W. Davidson | June 10, 1861 | Jan. 19, 1888 | one slab |
| Mary Jo Davidson | 1855 | 1927 | |

- 1880 Muscogee Census: (boarder in household of Merritt Curlee) Marion Davidson 19 AL AL AL.

2 adult slabs, n/m

Lot 136, McDonald on wall

Willie T. McDonald	Aug. 24, 1878	Jan. 11, 1948	w/o Charles M. McDonald
Charles Leo McDonald	Apr. 30, 1911	May 16, 1974	
Charles M. McDonald	Dec. 3, 1869	July 10, 1921	
Frank L. McDonald	Jan. 26, 1917	Aug. 4, 1976	
Jesse M. McDonald	Nov. 23, 1898	Oct. 1, 1983	
A.D. McDonald	Nov. 6, 1838	June 2, 1876	

- 1870 Russell Co., AL Census: A. D. McDonald 34 GA, Charlotte 27 SC, Charley M. 1 AL.

Lot 137, open lot,

No evidence of graves

Lot 138, J.E. Ragsdale on wall

No evidence of graves

Sexton Records indicate buried in this lot:

Louis Ragsdale — *bur. 3/10/1926, 66 yrs.*

Lot 139, Huff on wall

| Lula H. Huff | Jan. 14, 1860 | May 26, 1902 | beloved sister |

John Byron Huff	Sept. 20, 1866	Apr. 4, 1903	

- 1870 Harris Co., GA Census: John A. Huff 52 SC, Nancy 39 GA, Douglas 22 GA, Daniel 12 GA, Lula 10 GA, Lizzie 8 GA, Luella 6 GA and John 4 GA.

- John A. Huff married Eliza H. Stallings 25 Sept. 1839 in Muscogee Co., GA. *(The Columbus Enquirer)*

- 1880 Muscogee Census: Nancy Huff 50 GA VA NC, son Daniel 22 GA, dau Lula 20 GA, dau Elizabeth 12 GA, dau Ella 16 GA and son John 13 GA.

Anne Reynolds		Mar. 5, 1977	w/o Gerald Lewis Huff
Martha Rebecca McCrorey	Aug. 17, 1857	Jan. 19, 1936	
Ella L. Huff	May 12, 1863	July 19, 1912	beloved sister
Sarah Virginia Ross Huff	Sept. 7, 1867	July 22, 1907	
Adela McCrorey Ramsey	June 28, 1868	Aug. 15, 1936	
Mary Lee McCrorey Ramsey	Aug. 22, 1871	Jan. 25, 1961	
Lucy Hines Payne	Aug. 7, 1852	Feb. 2, 1930	
Gerald Lewis Huff		Jan. 4, 1975	h/o Anne Reynolds

- Died in Miscogee Co, age 75.[30]

Augustus Drayton Ramsey	Mar. 29, 1869	Nov. 9, 1950	Presbyterian Elder, 41 yrs
Susan McCrorey Kingsberg	Dec. 14, 1873 Talbot Co., GA	Nov. 15, 1904 Columbus, GA	

Lot 140, one grave lot, no name

Robert H. Dixon

Martha J. Dixon

Henry Bacon Dixon   On one slab

L. Decatur Johnson

Nanne Dixon Johnson

- *SR: Henry Bacon Dixon bur. July 1861 & Nanne Dixon Johnson bur. 5/28/1879*

- 1850 Talbot Co., GA Census: Robert H. Dixon 49 GA, Martha 42 GA, Emet 20 GA, Martha 18 GA, Nancy 16 GA, Elizabeth 12 GA, Marshall 9 GA and Bacon 7 GA.

- 1860 Muscogee Census: Elizabeth D. Dixon 21 GA, Stephen M. 17 GA, Henry B. 15 GA,

- Robert Henry Dixon (8/28/1800 GA- 2/11/1856 VA) was married three times.

  o 1) Nancy H. Jones, d/o Wm. H. Jones on 12/14/1819 in Putnam Co., GA. She died 10/12/1827 in Putnam Co., GA. They had 3 children. One died as an infant and the other 2 died within 2 days of her death.

  o 2) Martha A. J. A. Marshall (2/12/1812-3/29/1851), d/o Stephen Marshall and

Elizabeth Burt on 7/13/1828 in Putnam Co., GA. They had 6 children: Robert Emmett, Martha Hine, Nancy Jones, Elizabeth Burt, Stephen Marshall and Henry Bacon Dixon.

- o 3) Eliza P. (Eason) Brown 4/19/1853 in Henry Co., GA. They had 1 daughter, Mary "Mamie" P. Dixon

- Robert Henry Dixon was the s/o Henry "Harry" Dixon (5/18/1771-4/6/1867) and Martha Hall Hines (11/6/1773-10/8/1814), both from Virginia.

- Nancy Jones Dixon (c1836-5/1879) married L. Decatur Johnson. She was buried 5/28/1879.

- 1860 Muscogee Census: L. D. Johnson 40 GA and Nancy 24 GA.

Lot 141, Pittman on wall

Mary Josephine Wright	Apr. 23, 1846	June 27, 1913	mother, wife of Thomas Jasper Pittman

- Obit: widow of late Thomas Japer Pittman of Russell Co., GA, 3 children; Mrs. Wm. D. Fraser, Mrs. Joseph J. Smith & Mrs. Randolph Struppa.

Thomas Jasper Pittman	Mar. 15, 1840	May 15, 1910	father

- Obit: died at residence of dght., Mrs.J.J. Smith of Phenix City, AL, leaves wife, 3 dghts., Mrs. J.J. Smith, Mrs. J.R. Struppa & Mrs. W.C. Fraser.

- 1880 Russell Co., AL Census: Jasper Pittman 40 GA - -, wife Elizabeth 34 AL GA SC and dau Mamie? 8 AL.

Lot 142, open lot

Jimmie (cannot read)	June 9, 1858	June 31, 1861	s/o (cannot read), headstone toppled.
1 child's brick slab			headstone toppled, cannot read

Lot 143, open lot

No evidence of graves.

Lot 144, Fraser on wall

William Donald Fraser	Sept. 7, 1880	Feb. 2, 1945	
Gertrude Pittman	Sept. 3, 1880	Feb. 10, 1952	w/o Wm. D. Fraser
Charles Wm. Woolridge, Jr.	Sept. 29, 1905	Dec. 9, 1965	

Sexton Records indicate buried in this lot:

Elizabeth Wooldridge		*bur. 10/15/1991*

Lot 145, open lot

Charles T. Noble	Mar. 5, 1848	Apr. 13, 1892
Almeida Noble		Mar. 26, 1912

- Obit: 59 years old, never married.
- 1870 Muscogee Census: Francis A. Noble (female) 42? NC, Thomas C. 23 GA, Alemina 19 GA, Kirk H. 22 GA, John F. 18 GA, Daniel S. 17 GA and Lewis E. 14 GA.

Sexton Records indicate buried in this lot:

Curt Noble	*bur. 8/15/1879, 28.*
Louis Noble	*bur. 10/15/1872, 17.*

Lot 146, open lot, no evidence of graves

Lot 147, fenced lot, no name

James D. Greenwood		Sept. 8, 1852	aged 35 yrs
Leonora Eliza Greenwood	Apr. 18, 1841	Sept. 1, 1842	d/o H.T. & Amanda Greenwood
5 adult slabs, n/m		1 child slab, n/m	

Lot 148, Sommerkamp on wall

John F. Chisolm		Nov. 12, 1852	age 36 yrs

- Obit: moved from Chambers Co., AL to Columbus, Ga in 1846.

Ferdinand Julius Summerkamps	Sept. 10, 1838	Jan. 14, 1906	

- Obit: born Eufaula, AL, childen, F.M. of Dadesville, AL, Mrs. C.L.Tolbert, Frank, both of Columbus, GA, Roland of Vidalia, GA, Ralph of Philadelphia.

Mrs. Carrie Lee Sommerkamp	Sept. 20, 1862	Dec. 28, 1937	
Roland P. Sommerkamp	1862	1914	SR: bur.7/2/1914, 54 yrs.
Lucinda J. Marcrum	Aug. 18, 1828	July 12, 1899	w/o F.J. Sommerkamp

- Obit.-died at residence of son-in-law, C.L. Torbett, leaves husband, F.J. Sommerkamp, 4 children, R.P. of Morando Co., AL, R.F. of Philadelphia, Mrs. C.L. Torbett, Frank Summerkamp of Columbus, GA, d/o James Marcrum, in Columbus, GA, sister of Mrs. S.T. Berry & Capt. B.F. Marcrum.

Lot 149, no name on wall

Van Marcus, Jr.	July 20, 1900	Feb 24, 1906	s/o Van & Mary Marcus
Joseph A. St. Louis	Feb. 19, 1894	Aug. 3, 1967	Col. U.S. Army
Van Marcus	Feb. 9, 1863	June 15, 1934	

- 1870 Muscogee Census: Van Marcus 37 GA, Harriet E. 35 GA, Bennie E. (f) 12 GA, Ella B. 7 GA and Van 6 GA.

- 1900 Muscogee Census: Van Marcus Feb 1867 GA GA GA (married 3 yrs), wife Mary May 1869 GA GA GA (1 child/1 living), dau Josephine Sept 1898 GA and mother Hattie Oct 1834 GA GA GA (widow).

- 1910 Muscogee Census: Van Marcus 44 GA GA AL (married 12 yrs), wife Mary T. 38 NY Eng NY (4 children/3 living), dau Josephine V. 11 GA, son Hassell 8 GA and dau Pauline 3 GA.

Pauline Harriet Marcus	May 1, 1906	Dec. 8, 1976	
G/M Benjamin A. Brew	Oct. 24, 1921	July 23, 1944	GA 2nd Lt. 8 Air Force, WWII
Mary Theresa Hassell	May 14, 1868	Aug. 13, 1953	w/o Van Marcus

- 1880 New York, NY Census: Samuel Hassell 61 Eng Eng Eng, wife Josephine 52 NJ Scot France, son John J. 27 NY, dau Josephine 20 NY, dau Sarah L. 18 NY, dau Grace 16 NY, son Samuel W. 15 NY, dau Mary 12 NY, dau Esther F. 10 NY, dau Pauline 6 NY, dau Caroline 5 NY and son Augustine 5 NY.

Arthur H. Brew	Nov. 9, 1891	Jan. 21, 1924

Lot 150, no name on wall

Jacob Anderson Walton	1847	1925	SR:bur. 6/2/1925

- Obit: born Toronto, Canada, married Miss Nina A. Engiedove of Lynchburg, VA, children, Charles H., Sr., Mrs. A.H. Bickerstaff, J.A. Walton, Jr., all of Columbus, GA, 6 g/ch, 1 g/g/ch.

- 1900 Muscogee Census: Jacob A. Walton Oct. 1848? Can Eng Eng (emigrated 1871 and married 28 yrs), wife Nina M. Mar 1852 VA VA VA (4 children/4 living), son Robt. O. June 1873 VA, son Chas. E. Feb. 1875 VA (married 5 yrs), DIL Mary P. Dec 1876 GA GA GA, dau Nora M. May 1879 VA, son Jacob A. Jr. Dec 1885 VA, Gson Charles E. Jr. Oct. 1896 GA and Gson Preer Jan 1900 GA.

- GA Death Index shows J. A. Walton, Jr. died 1 June 1925 in Muscogee Co., GA.

Nina May Enedove	1852	1921	w/o Jacob A. Walton SR:born 3/25/1852, VA bur.5/5//1921

Robert Oscar Walton	1873	1915	SR:bur.11/29/1915, 42
Augustus Howard Bickerstaff	1876	1965	
Nora Mary Walton	1879	1949	w/o Augustus H. Bickerstaff SR:bur.8/11/1949
Robert Gradin Eakle	1914	1974	SR:born 3/20/1914, VA, bur. 4/23/1974
Edw. Halley Eakle		1952	SR:born 4/24/1952
Marie Ann Schlauk	1884	1919	w/o Jacob A. Walton, Jr. SR?bur. 6/18/1919, 34 yrs.
Inf./o Nora Walton & Howard Bickerstaff	no dates		

Lot 151, no name on wall

1 adult slab, n/m

Lot 152, J.D. Smith on wall

Richard Lequin Smith	Jan. 19, 1882	Dec. 30, 1936	
Louisa Biehler	Dec. 4, 1856	Feb. 16, 1940	w/o J. D. Smith
James N. Smith	Mar. 13, 1866	July 21, 1958	
J. D. Smith	June 20, 1854	Apr. 12, 1917	
Maggie Belle	Aug. 21, 1883	Dec. 1, 1885	d/o J.D. & Louisa Smith
Jeanette McLendon	1910	1915	SR: bur.9/30/1915
J. D., Jr.,	Oct. 4, 1893	Mar. 1, 1907	s/o J.D. & Louisa Smith

Lot 153, no name on wall

Blanche E. Bush	July 27, 1876	Nov. 3, 1899
2 baby brick slabs, n/m	1 child brick slab, n/m	

Lot 154, no name on wall

G/M George W. Twilley	May 28, 1832	Aug. 28, 1862	Co.I, 20 Regt., GA. Inf.

- Obit: killed in battle, Thoroughfare Gap.

- 1860 Muscogee Census: James Twilley 55 GA, Catherine 25 GA and George T. 25 GA.

- James Twilley married Catherine Davis 26 Nov. 1846 in Muscogee Co. Richard P. Davis married Mary E. Twilley 23 Mar. 1848 in Muscogee Co.

G/M Robert R. Davis	Feb. 10, 1826	Sept. 3, 1863	Co.I, 20 GA Regt., GA Inf.

- Obit: born GA, bridgekeeper, disable C.S.A. soldier, lost arm at battle of Manasses.

- 1860 Census Russell Co., AL: Robert R. Davis 33 GA, Mary 32 GA, Alphonzo 9 AL, Emma 7 AL and James 5 AL.

R. A. Davis	1850	1917	SR: bur.6/27/1917, 67 yrs.

- Obit: four sons, R.A., Jr., J.W. Of Hopewell, VA, Thomas of Columbus, GA, Leo B., of Anniston, AL.

1 headstone toppled, cannot read	3 adult brick slabs, n/m	1 child slab, n/m

Sexton Records indicate buried in this lot:

Ezekial C. Davis	*bur. 3/13/1856, 33 yrs.*

- 1850 Muscogee Census: E. C. Davis 27 GA, Mary I. 28 MA.

J. E. Davis	*bur. 2/11/1892, 37 yrs.*
Mrs. M. E. Davis	*bur. 3/26/1903, 76 yrs.*

Lot 155, no name on wall

no evidence of graves

Lot 156, no name on wall

no evidence of graves

Lot 157, open lot

Anne A. Ellis	May 8, 1828	Nov. 24, 1856	w/o Roswell Ellis d/o John G. & Ann Mangham

- Roswell Ellis was born 1822 in Putnam Co., GA and died 1856 in Griffin, GA.[31] He married Frances A. Mangham 14 Sept. 1848 in Muscogee Co. They had 2 children: Annie (1850-1852) and John (1854-1876).[33]

Ann J. Mangham	Feb. 25, 1804	Dec. 24, 1853	aged 49 yr 10 mo

- Obit: wife of Capt. John C. Mangham of Griffin, GA, died in Columbus, GA.

John G. Mangham, Jr.	July 24, 1824	Nov. 18, 1851	age 27 yrs 3 mo 25 dy

1 child marker, cannot read

Lot 158, open lot

James Monroe Allen	1818	1881	father SR:bur. 3/5/1881, 65

- James M. Allen married Clementine Harper 3 April 1843 in Harris Co., GA.
- 1860 Muscogee Census: James Allen 39 GA, Mary G. 17 GA, Martin 15 GA, James 13 GA, Robert 11 GA, Eliza 7 GA, Emma 5 GA, Benjamin 3 GA, Elijah 2 and Ella 2 GA.
- 1870 Muscogee Census: Jas. M. Allen 52 GA, Clementine 47 GA, Ann Eliza 16 GA, Benj.Hill 13 GA, Elijah and Ella C. (twins) 10 GA, Clementine 8 GA, Ola Lee Allen 3 GA and Nancy Harper 68 GA.

Clementine H. Allen	1821	1907	mother SR: bur. 7/2/1907

- Obit: leaves 2 sons, 2 dghts, of Columbus, GA, pallbearers will be grandsons.

Mrs. Myrtle Allen Davis	Sept. 21, 1892	Feb. 22, 1938
Mattie Allen	Mar 16, 1861	Jan. 26, 1912

Lot 160, open lot

Mrs. Easter King	Dec. 25, 1805	Oct. 2, 1872	aged 67 yrs.

- Obit: resident of Columbus since 1833, died at the home of son, John King, a dght, Mrs. F.G. Wilkins & 7 other children.
- 1870 Muscogee Census: Easter King 65 GA, Martha 26 Ga and Frances 25 GA.

Henry King		June 14, 1849	49th yr of age

5 children markers with "Baugh" no other data.

Lot 161, Jungermann on wall

Susanna Henrietta Nagley	May 14, 1797	Aug. 18, 1850	w/o Jacob Nagley

- 1850 Muscogee Census: Jacob Nagly (sic) 50 Switzerland, Susan H. Switzerland and John (adopted) 11 GA.

Francis Jungermann	Dec. 18, 1904	July 30, 1965	w/o Everette L. Campbell MD
Robert E. Jones	Apr. 20, 1900	Aug. 10, 1967	
Katherine Jungermann	Apr. 11, 1897	Sept. 26, 1980	

Lillie A. Jungermann	1869	1964	SR:bur. 2/21/1964
Everette L. Campbell MD	Jan 30, 1899	Sept. 28, 1966	
L.M. Aenchbacher			C.S.A. 1861-1865
Ernest Jungermann	1864	1934	SR:bur.4/12/1934

- 1930 Muscogee Census: Ernest Jungermann 65 Millsunberg Germany Cassell Germany Cassell Germany (married @28 and emigrated 1881), wife Lillie 60 AL Switzerland AL (married @23) and daughter Katherine 32 GA.

Irby Miller Garner	Feb. 3, 1894	May 6, 1895	s/o A.J. & J.A. Garner
Henry Jungermann			Inf. s/o E. & L. Jungermann, age 1 week, SR:bur. 5/1/1899

Sexton Records indicate buried in this lot:

S. N. Aenchbacher			bur. 9/11/1901, 62 yrs.

- Obit: born Switzerland, about 61 yrs of age, came to America early 1840's to New Orleans, then to Columbus, GA, lived awhile in Mobile, AL, C.S.A. vet., 7th enlisted man in the confederate Marine Corps, gunner on Merrimac, 1 son, John, of Phenix City, AL, 2 dghts., Mrs. E. Jungermann & Miss Pearl Aenchbacher, 2 brothers, L.P. & G.N. both of Atlanta, GA.

Lot 162, no name on wall

Mary Nell Perry	Nov. 28, 1897	Sept. 14, 1972	w/o W. Mercer Graddy
Cora Solomon	Sept. 15, 1866	Sept. 8, 1942	w/o R.C. Perry
R.E. Perry		no dates	SR:bur. 7/12/1924, 65 yrs

1 child's brick slab, n/m

Sexton Records indicate buried in this lot:

Marion Perry			bur. 1/1/1901, 9 yrs.

Lot 163, Blankenship on wall

W. H. H. Blankenship	Sept. 2, 1840	Apr. 21, 1929	father

- Obit: born Pike co., Ga, 1st resident of Wynnton, C.S.A. Vet., Lt. in Capt. Jaceue Bat., married Miss Josephine Hollenbeck d/o Garrett Hollenbeck, who moved to Columbus 100 years ago from Albany, N.Y., leaves 3 dghts., Miss Byrd Blankenship, Mrs. Ed Wehlwender, both of Columbus, GA, Mrs. Thomas D. Meader of Atlanta, GA, 4 sons, C.D. & E.L. of Columbus, GA, H., of Hamilton, GA, Major G.H., of Los Angeles, CA.

- 1870 Muscogee Census: William H. Blankenship 29 GA, Josephine 24 GA, Millie H. 6 GA, Annie 4 GA and Grace G. 5/12 GA.

- 1880 Muscogee Census: Wm H. Blankenship 38 GA VA GA, wife Josephine 34 GA GA GA, dau Annie 14 GA, dau Birdie 6 GA, dau Willie 5 GA, son Hollenbeck 4 GA, son Earnest 2 GA and son Wm H. Jr. Feb 1880 GA.

Willie B. Wohlwender	Mar. 9, 1875	Dec. 23, 1953	
Wm. Joseph Wohlwender	Nov. 23, 1912	Dec. 31, 1913	
Josephine Hallenbeck	Apr. 21, 1846	Feb. 11, 1913	w/o W.H.H. Blankenship, mother

- Obit:born Columbus, GA, leaves husband, 3 dghts., Miss Byrd Blankenship, Mrs. Edw. Wehlwander, both of Columbus, GA, Mrs. T.D. Meadow of Atlanta, GA, 4 sons, H. of Jacksonville, FL, M.L. of Columbus, C.D. of Montgomery, AL, G.H., U.S. Navy.

- 1850 Muscogee Census: Garrett Halenbeck 52 NY, Martha A. 26 GA, Napolian 5 GA, Josephine 3 GA and Sophia 1 GA.

Ellen Parker	Dec. 10, 1811	Jan. 11, 1883	w/o James Blankenship

- Obit:born Pike Co., GA, Dec. 20, 1811, in Columbus by 1849, 2 children, W.H.H. & Mrs. Louisa Warren of Macon, GA.

Ed Wohlwender, Sr.	June 3, 1874	Dec. 9, 1962

- 1880 Harrison Co., KY Census: Joseph Wohlwender 36 Wurtenburg Wurtenburg Wurtenburg, wife Caroline 38 Hanover Hanover Hanover, dau Lillie KY, son Willie 11 KY, son Joseph 9 KY, son Eddie 6 KY, dau Mary 2 KY and boarder Fred Schumaker 18 IN Wurtenburg Wurtenburg.

Lillian Wohlwender	Nov. 21, 1914	Jan. 30, 1919	d/o Edw. & Willie V. Wohlwender

Lot 164, open lot

Mrs. Clara Meigs	Stratford, CT	Columbus, Ga	unable to read, slab patched

- Obit: widow of Professor Josiah Meigs, a daughter married Hon. John Forsyth in 1802, a son is Dr. Meigs of Philadelphia, died at the home of grandson John Forsyth.

- Josiah Meigs, s/o Return and Elizabeth Hamlin Meigs was born 21 August 1757 and died 4 Sept. 1822. He married Clara Benjamin on 21 Jan 1782. In 1778, he was a Professor at Yale College and later first President of the University of Georgia.[32] In 1812, President Madison appointed him Surveyor General of the United States. Two years later he was appointed the Commissioner of the U. S. Land Office in Washington, D.C. On his death on September 4, 1822, he was buried on the Congressional Cemetery in Washington. He was subsequently reinterred in the family plot in Section 1 of Arlington National Cemetery.

- Clara was the d/o Col. John Benjamin of Stratford, CT. She married Josiah Meigs 21 Jan 1782 and died 13 August 1849 in Columbus. [33]

Richard T. Brice	Aug. 19, 1813	Dec. 26, 1851
	Baltimore, MD	Columbus, GA

- Obit: formerly of Baltimore, 15 years in Columbus.

- 1850 Muscogee Census: Richard T. Brice 37 MD, Mrs. Julia 22 GA and Arthur D. 1/12 GA in household of Mrs. Mary A. Davis with others.

Alice Toney	Aug. 15, 1856	Oct. 15, 1890	d/o Col. A.A. & M.C.
	Lee Co., AL	Columbus, GA	Lowther

Mrs. Clara Forsyth	Sept. 25, 1784	July 17, 1853
	New Haven, CT	Columbus, GA

- Obit: widow of John Forsyth.

- Clara was the 2nd child of Josiah and Clara Benjamin Meigs. [34]

- John Forsyth was born 22 Oct. 1780 in Fredricksburg, VA. He was a Representative and Senator from Georgia. In 1808 he was elected Attorney General for the State of Georgia. Governor of Georgia 1827-1829. He was appointed Secretary of State by President Andrew Jackson and reappointed by President Martin Van Buren. John died in Washington, DC 21 Oct. 1841 and is interred in the Congressional Cemetery.

- 1850 Muscogee Census: George Hargraves 40, Virginia 30, Clara 6, Mrs. Clara Forsyth 68 CT, Miss Anna Forsyth 27 PA and Miss Rosa Forsyth 27 PA.

Col. A. A. Lowther	Nov. 29, 1826	Sept. 4, 1889	C.S.A.
	Clinton, GA	Lee Co., AL	

- 1850 Muscogee Census: A. A. Lowther 23, Mary C. 22 District of Columbia, Mary H. 1/12 GA, Mrs. Mary H. Shaaf 42 and others.

- 1870 Lee Co., AL Census: A. Lowther 44 GA, M. (f) 44 DC, Julia 16 GA, A. (f) 14 AL, J. (f) 11 AL, A. (m) 9 AL, and F. (m) 2 AL.

- 1880 Lee Co., AL Census: Alexander A. Lowther 54 GA TN SC, wife Mary C. 54 DC DC GA, dau Alice 22 AL, dau Virginia 20 AL and son Foard 12 AL.

Robert Brewer Forsyth		1855	s/o Robt. & Julia
		Columbus, GA	Forsyth, age 3 yrs.

Virginia Hargroves Lowther	Oct. 5, 1859	Feb. 4, 1928

Mary C. Shaaff	Oct. 26, 1826	May 13, 1883	w/o A.A. Lowther
	Georgetown, D.C.	Columbus, GA	

- Obit: w/o Col. A. A. Lowther, of Summerville, Al, d/o Mrs. Shaaff, g/dght of John Forsyth, 6 children, Mrs. W.B. Wise of Texas, Mrs. W.H. Bedell of Selma, AL.

- Mary Forsyth married Arthur Shaaf in Washington, DC 16 August 1825. [34] Major Arthur Shaff served 1st GA Batl. Infantry Sharp-Shooters.

1 adult slab, n/m

Lot 165, Robert P. Allen on wall

Robert P. Allen   Jan. 1, 1850   Mar. 31, 1938

- Obit: born Harris Co., GA, 4 children survive, R.L. Allen of Buena Vista, GA, Mrs. J.M. Compton, Mrs. Clyde Claborn & Mrs. Lucile D. McKinley all of Columbus, Ga, 2 sisters, Mrs. E.E. Willett of Columbus, GA, Mrs. Ola Hudson of Macon, GA.

- 1870 Census Harris Co., GA: Robert P. Allen 20 GA and Caroline 16.

- 1880 Muscogee Census: Robert P. Allen 30 GA GA GA, wife Caroline 26 GA GA GA, dau Jesse (adopted) 5 GA GA GA, son Robert 8/12 GA, father James M. 62 GA SC SC, mother Clementine 59 GA NC SC and sister Ola Lee Allen 13 GA.

Carolina May   Oct. 20, 1853   Jan. 22, 1929   w/o R.P. Allen

- 1860 Census Meriwether Co., GA: Zana (m) May 60 NC, Tampa (f) 40 NC, Lucy 30 NC, Martha 28 NC, Elizabeth 25 NC, Mary 22 NC, Zacharia 24 NC, Malissa 20 GA, Caroline 6 GA, John 6 GA, and Tampa? 1 GA. Also in household Malissa Williams 6 GA, W. E. (m) 4 GA and D. T. (f) Williams 2 GA.

Lot 166, fenced lot, no name

John T. Everett   SR: born 2/28/1838   SR: bur. 9/8/1902   C.S.A. 1861-1865

- Obit: brother of Thomas W. Everett, member of Georgia Gray's.

John Everett   Dec. 3, 1845   father

- Obit: leaves wife & 4 children.

Elizabeth Ann Louisa Everett   Jan. 11, 1846   Aug. 5, 1921   Nan

- Obit: sister of late Mrs. I.G. Strupper of Columbus, GA, 1 brother H.F. Everett.

Elizabeth Everett   Oct. 9, 1884   mother

- Obit: nee Elizabeth Sigwold, married John Everett Sept. 1, 1835 in Charleston, SC, moved to FL, then to Columbus in 1839, 6 children, 1 child died an infant, Thos. W. Everett killed in Civil War, Santa Rosa Island Battle, leaves B.F. Everett Mrs. I.G. Strupper & Lizzie Everett, all of Columbus.

- 1850 Muscogee Census: Mrs. Elizabeth Everett 35 SC, Thomas W. 14 SC, John S. 13 FL, Mary R. 10 GA, Henry F. 7 GA and Elizabeth L. 4 GA.

Henry Francis Everett   Nov. 11, 1843   June 3, 1928   Co. A, 10th GA Cav. Gen. Dearings Brig. C.S.A.

- Obit: died at residence of daughter, Mrs. Walter H. Berry, of Daytona Beach, FL, born Columbus, GA, 1 son, Edward A.

Thomas W. Everett		Oct. 9, 1861	large circle on iron pole with the following inscription: the 1st who fell from Columbus Oct. 9, 1861, Co. I, 5th GA Reg.

- Obit: member of Georgia Gray's, died in Pensacola, FL.

Lot 167, fenced lot on corner

John B. McCarty	May 15, 1844 Columbus, GA	June 2, 1862	Capt. of the Montgomery AL Grays, who fell mortally wounded at the Battle of Seven Pines, age 21 yrs, 18 days
Thomas McCarty	1798 Ballinamoic Co., Leiuim Ireland	1851 Columbus, GA	

- 1850 Muscogee Census: Thomas McCarty 50 Ireland.

Mrs. Ellen McCarty	1817 New York City	Apr. 13, 1868	age 51 yrs.

- 1860 Muscogee Census: John McCarty 50 Ireland, Ellen 45 Ireland, Thomas 22 GA, John 19 GA, Ellen 17 GA, James 12 GA, Alexander 14 GA, Mary 8 GA, Hanah 4 GA and Lydia 1 GA.

Alexander B. McCarty	Oct. 10, 1850	Sept. 25, 1878	

- Obit: s/o John McCarty, died of consumption, age 21.

James L. McCarty	May 7, 1818	Feb. 5, 1874	

- Obit: funeral notice mentions Mr. & Mrs. John McCarty.

Lydia Katie McCarty	Mar. 10, 1860	July 17, 1862	
W. J. McCarty	Jan. 8, 1846	Nov. 16, 1847	one slab
Jerome McCarty	July 20, 1854	Sept. 10, 1854	

1 adult brick slab, n/m

Lot 168, H.E. Hall on wall

Robert A. Davis	July 8, 1880	Feb. 28, 1923	
Howard E. Hall	May 19, 1861	Oct. 28, 1935	
William F. Montgomery	1884	1929	SR:bur. 1/26/1929

Mrs. Elizabeth Hall   age 87, mother, SR:
                                                                          born 1/31/1825, bur.
                                                                          3/2/1911

- Obit: Mrs. Hall was born in this city on the 31st of January 1825, and had therefore just passed her eighty sixth year. She was reared in this city and had lived here all her life. Her only child was the son in whose home she died. A number of nieces survive her.

- 1860 Muscogee Census: H. J. Hall 45 GA, Elizabeth 30 GA, Harry 3 GA and Sarah 1 GA.

- 1870 Muscogee Census: Elizabeth Hall 36 GA, Lucy Presnell? 30 AL and Howard Hall 9 GA.

Tillie G. McKnight   May 3, 1868   Dec. 19, 1959   w/o Howard E. Hall

1 upright granite marker, n/m

Lot 169, no name on wall

John A. Frazer   July 3, 1829   Oct. 2, 1920
                              Wilkes Co., GA

- 1860 Muscogee Census: John A. Frazier 31 GA, Mary 26 GA, Mary E. 5 GA and Luther C. 2 GA.

- 1880 Muscogee Census: John Frazier 51 GA GA GA, wife Mary 47 GA GA GA, son Armenius? 16 AL, son Edward 14 GA, son Luther 22 GA, dau Roena 21 GA and daughter Mabel 9/12 (born Sept).

William Thomas Tommy   Feb. 28, 1838   May 29, 1854   s/o V.R. & Eliza
                                                                    Tommy

- 1850 Muscogee Census: Vincent R. Tommy 38 GA, Eliza A. 36 GA, Mary A. 16 GA, William T. 12 GA, Elizabeth 16 GA, Henry C. 8 GA, Edwin V. 5 GA and Albert P. 1 GA. (Note 1880 Vincent Tommy found in Dekalb Co., GA)

- Vincent R. Tommy married Elizabeth Shepherd 17 Dec 1830 in Newtn Co., GA.[35]

Mary A. Tommy   1833   1915

J. A. Frazer   1853   1915

Mary I. Turrentine
                                                                    one slab
L. C. Frazer

A. H. Frazer

A. E. Frazer

- *SR indicate Mary A. Tommy bur. 4/15/1915. Headstone reads "My wife"*

- Obit: Mary A. Tommy was a member of St. Luke since 1846, born near Covington, GA, father moved to Eufaula, AL, 1845, 1 daughter, Mrs. J.F. Turrentine of Tallassee, AL, 1 son, L.C. Frazer of Birmingham, AL.

Eliza A.   d/o ? Tommy unable
                                                                    to read, child

Arad Lyman   May 10, 1810   Jan. 5, 1854

- Obit: born Mass., resident of Columbus 15 years, died in New York City.

- 1850 Muscogee Census: A. Lyman 40 MA.

- Muscogee Co., GA WB A. pp. 154-161. Arad Lyman. 10 Sep 1853/6 Mar 1854. Legatees: Mother Sarah, now w/o Samuel Smith of Granby, MA; brother Samuel J. Lyman of Warwick, Franklin Co., MA; sister-in-law Eliza, widow of Warren Lyman and her children: George Warren, William H. and Henrietta Lyman. Friends William Brooks and John G. Cater of Columbus. Also mentioned: Sarah Southworth w/o Simon G. Southworth and Maria Eliza Hatfield w/o Horace Hatfield Jr. Extrs. Vincent R. Tommey, James Ennis and John G. Carter. Wit: John R. Dickinson, Dr. Orson Thayer and Lewis Abbott all of Bingham, NY.

Sarah Eliza Ligon	1851	d/o James & Sarah A. Ligon, age 1 mo, 3 dys

- 1850 Muscogee Census: James Liggon 27 GA, Sarah 19 GA and Thomas F. Rydenhour 13 GA.

- James Ligon married Sarah A. Tommy 3 July 1850 in Muscogee Co.

Lot 170, open lot

2 adult brick slabs, n/m	3 children brick slabs, n/m

Lot 171, H.H. Barfield on wall

Marietta Barfield	1855	1921	w/o H.H. Barfield SR: born 8/4/1855, bur. 6/9/1921

- H. H. Barfield married Marietta Dodson 3 July 1876 in Chattahoochee Co., GA.[36]

- 1860 Census Chatahoochee Co., GA: Jane Dodson 32, Henrietta 11, John 9, Robt. 7, Manilla 4 and Wm. Naughton? 22 laborer. In 1870, Marietta and her brother Robert are listed as attending school in Cussetta, Chattahoochee Co., GA.

     Evidence of 1 adult grave n/m

Sexton Records indicate buried in this lot:

Holt Hines Barfield	*bur. 2/17/1937, 91 yrs.*

- 1880 Lee, Dorsey Co., Arkansas Census: H. H. (m) Barfield 27 GA SC GA, and wife M. (f) 23 GA - -.

Lot 172, Fogle-Pfohl on wall

William Lewis Pfohl	Mar. 9, 1834 Friedland, NC	Feb. 16, 1906 Columbus, GA

- Obit: born Salem, NC, leaves wife, 4 daughters, Mrs. Mary H. Law of Gainsville, GA, Mrs. Walter T. Newman, Annie & Martha Pfohl, all of Columbus, Ga, 2 brothers, & 1 sister in NC.

- Married on the 31st Jan. at the residence of Mr. U. B. Harrold, Americus, Ga., by Rev. W. B. Merritt, Miss M. A. M. Fogle of Columbus, Ga., to Mr. Wm. Lewis Pfohl, of Salem, N. C.[37]

- 1870 Surry Co., NC Census: W. L. Pfohl 33 NC and S. G. Fogle 59 NC.

- 1880 Meriwether Co., GA Census: William L. Pfohl 46 NC NC NC, wife Martha A. M. 37 GA NC GA, dau Mary H. 8 GA, dau Adalade L. 4 GA and dau Anna F. 1 GA.

Martha Douglas	Jan. 18, 1881	Oct. 21, 1921	d/o W.L. & Martha Pfohl
Sarah Gertrude Fogle	Sept. 22, 1844	Sept. 11, 1854	d/o John Jacob & Nancy Fogle
G/M J. A. Fogle			Cols. Guards C.S.A. 1861-1865
Martha Ann Mitchell Fogle	Oct. 8, 1842 Columbus, GA	Dec. 10, 1928 Atlanta, GA	w/o Wm. L. Pfohl

- Obit: died in Atlanta, GA, 3 dghts, Mrs. DeLacy Law of Gainsville, GA, Mrs. W.T. Newman of Atlanta, Ga & Miss Annie Pfohl of Columbus, GA.

John Jacob Fogle	Sept. 4, 1803 Bethabara, NC	Jan. 6, 1874 Columbus, GA	

- Obit: Doctor, funeral notice mentions Dr. W.J. Fogle & Mrs. A.S. Rutherford.

- 1850 Muscogee Census: Jacob Fogle 47 NC, Nancy L. 34 Hancock Co., Theodore 16 Baldwin Co., William J. 14 Baldwin Co., James A. 12 Musc., Mary 10 Musc., Martha 8 Musc. And Sarah Gertrude 6 Musc. Co.

- Jacob Fogle married Nancy L. Turner 10 July 1832 in Baldwin Co., GA.

Theodore Turner Fogle	Jan. 16, 1834 Milledgeville, GA	May 6, 1864	killed in Battle of Wilderness, G/M Cols. Guards 1861-1865

- Obit: Lt. Columbus Guards, 2nd GA Regt., killed in Battle of Wilderness in VA, reburied Sept. 7, 1866.

Anna Rosina Fogle	Mar. 13, 1848	July 18, 1849	one slab
Emma Fogle	June 12, 1850	June 18, 1850	inf. d/o John Jacob & Nancy Turner Fogle
Nancy Lundy Turner	June 22, 1816 Sparta, GA	Apr. 4, 1870 Columbus, GA	w/o John Jacob Fogle

- Obit: w/o Dr. Jacob Fogle, d/o J. P. Turner of Milledgeville, GA, where she was married, moved to Columbus 1834, leaves husband and a number of children.

- Mrs. Nancy L. Fogle, wife of Dr. Jacob Fogle and d/o of the late Jacob P. & Mary Turner, was born in Sparta, Ga., June 22d, 1816, married in Putnam Co. July 10th 1832. She departed this life in Columbus, Ga., April 4th 1870, leaving a husband and six children.[38]

- Jacob Turner married 1) Nancy Lundy 15 Jan 1812 in Hancock Co., GA and 2) Mary "Polly" Sanders, d/o Wm. Sanders & Mary Borden, 14 Dec 1813 in Hancock Co., GA.[39]

Lot 173, no name on wall

no evidence of graves

Lot 174, Owens on wall

Miss Regina Owens	1861	1922	SR: born 9/15/1861, bur. 11/13/1922
Victoria Hoffman	1850	1920	SR: born 4/24/1850, bur. 1920
Regina Owens	1838	1915	SR: born 12/12/1838, bur. 3/25/1915

- Obit: 2 daughters, Miss Regina Owens, Mrs. F.C. Reich, 2 sisters, Mrs. F.X. Profumo and Miss Victoria Hoffman.

- 1850 Muscogee Census: Sebastian Hoffman Germany, Anna E. 31 Bavaria, Ragenia 11 GA, Barbara H. S. 9 GA, Mary Louisa 7 GA, John J. 5 GA, Sebastian S. 2 GA and Victoria M. 1/12 GA.

- 1870 Muscogee Census: Georgia Owens 31 GA, Regina 8 GA and Anna A. 6 GA.

- 1880 Muscogee Census: Regina Owens 38 GA GA GA, dau Regina 18 GA GA GA and dau Anne 16 GA GA GA.

Anna Eva	June 18, 1818	Dec. 6, 1852	w/o Sebastian Hoffman, native of Rottenburg, Bavaria

1 adult slab, n/m

Lot 175, no name on wall

George Young Banks	Aug. 3, 1866 Stewart Co., GA	Feb. 18, 1910 Columbus, GA	
Lucile Brooks	Aug. 15, 1883	Sept. 18, 1886	d/o P.B. & S.C. Williford
Katherine Bowman Banks	Aug. 16, 1873 Lexington, KY	July 11, 1960 Columbus, GA	
Katherine Reed Banks	June 2, 1904 Columbus, GA	Feb. 11, 1972	
1 baby marker	Sept. 14, 1936	Aug. 20, 1936	Inf. d/o Sue Banks & Douglas Roden
Florence Banks	Jan. 1, 1908	June 22, 1940	w/o Henry M. Coley

Lot 176, J.H. Martin on wall

Abram W. Cozart	June 14, 1870	Feb. 6, 1936

- 1880 Loudon Co., TN Census: Abram W. Cozart 57 KY KY NJ, wife Martha G. 42 GA NC GA, son Samuel C. 23 TN, son Hugh W. 22 TN, dau Hattie A. 20 TN, son John 17 TN, son Leucian? D. 14 TN, son Abram W. Jr. 9 TN, dau Mattie R. McGhee 30 GA, grandson Joseph L. McGhee 6 TN VA GA, sister-in-law Mary Coldwell 54 GA NC GA and boarders.

Henry Martin Cozart	Feb. 24, 1898	Oct. 17, 1900
Susy Martin Cozart	Dec. 8, 1874	Nov. 16, 1960
John Henry Martin	Dec. 23, 1848	Sept. 30, 1911

- Obit: Judge of Superior Court of Chattahoochee Circuit, 2 terms, born Talbot County, GA, 4 children, Mrs. John H. McGehee of Talbotton, GA, Mrs. A.D. Brown, Mrs. A.W. Cozart, both of Columbus, GA, Mrs. Holmes Frederick of Atlanta, GA

- 1880 Talbot Co., GA Census: John H. Martin 31 GA GA GA wife Carrie 28 GA GA GA, dau Mary B. 8 GA, dau Susie E. 5 GA and dau Rosa E. 2 GA.

- Married March 28th, 1871 by Rev. Thos. T. Christian, Mr. H. J. Martin to Miss Carrie Oslin, all of Pleasant Hill, Talbot co., Ga.[40]

- 1910 Muscogee Census: John H. Martin 61 GA GA GA (M2 – 24 yrs), wife Elizabeth 55 TN TN TN (2 child/2 liv), dau Ruth 23 GA, dau Edith 21 GA, dau Lillian Brown 30 GA (widowed 1 child/1 liv), and grand son Dania? 5 GA.

Caroline Cozart	May 26, 1906	June 29, 1908
Elizabeth Toole Martin	Sept. 5, 1856	Sept. 20, 1911

Lot 177, Hooper on wall

George DeBernier Hooper	A.D. 1808 Wilmington, NC	Mar. 19, 1892 Birmingham, AL	

- Obit: Judge, d. Birmingham, AL at residence of son, John DeB. Hooper, State Mine Inspector, moved to Ala. 1833 to Chambers Co. with brother, John J. Hooper, later moved to Russell Co., AL.

- Cumberland Co., NC Marriage Bond: George D. Hooper and Caroline E. Mallett 27 Sept. 1836.

- 1860 Russell Co., AL Census: G. D.(m) Hooper 51 NC and C. E. (f) 46 NC.

Caroline Eliza Mallett	1814 A.D. Fayeteville, NC	Apr. 11, 1875	w/o George D. Hooper

- Obit: wife of Judge Geo. D. Hooper of Opelika, AL, d/o Charles Mallett of Fayetteville, NC.

Caroline A. Hooper	Apr. 11, 1857	Sept. 5, 1941	
Mary Charlotte Hooper		Apr. 4, 1864	In the 10th year of her age. d/o Geo. D. & Caroline E. Hooper

John DeBernier Hooper	Mar. 23, 1853 Russell Co., AL	Feb. 12, 1927 Birmingham, AL	s/o Geo. D. & Caroline E. Hooper.
Archibald Maclaine Hooper		Oct. 14, 1853	4 years of age. s/o Geo. D. & Caroline E. Hooper.
Archibald Maclaine Hooper		Sept. 28, 1853	Of Wilmington, NC. 77 years of age.

- Obit: born in Wilmington, NC Dec. 7, 1775, died at the home of son Geo. D. Hooper.

Charlotte Debernier		July 25, 1854	68 years of age. w/o A. M. Hooper.
Col. Charles Mallett Hooper	Apr. 27, 1842 LaFayette, Ala	Sept. 4, 1910 Jacksonville, Fla.	s/o Geo. D. & Caroline Hooper.

- Obit: died Jacksonville, Fla., 3 dghtrs, Louise, Nellie Hooper both of New York, Mrs. R. Morehead of Ocale, Fla, 2 brothers, J. Hooper & Col. Geo. W. Hooper of Ala., 1 sister, Miss Clara A. Hooper.

Lot 178, no name on wall

Virginia Gordon	Apr. 2, 1827 Eatonton, GA	Jan. 27, 1904	w/o Charles Thos. Abercrombie

- Obit: relict of Dr. Charles T. Abercrombie, 1 son, Chas. Of Montgomery, Ala., 2 daughters Mrs. Grant Wilkins of Atlanta, Ga., Mrs. Henry Chambers of Oswichee, Ala.

- d/o Charles P. Gordon and Barbara Gailbraith who were married 10 June 1817 in Carlisle, PA. Virginia married Charles Abercrombie 27 June 1849 in Russell Co., GA.

- Putnam Co., GA WB B page139. Charles P. Gordon, 4/14/1835:----. Son: Andrew G. Gordon...friend John Brown of Tennessee...my four daughters Mary Ann, Julian Barbour, Virginia and Sarah Elizabeth ...debts due my brother and myself...land in town of Eatenton...two lots in Randolph owned in common by James George (?) and myself...granted to John Garland...land in Alabama owned jointly by Eli S. Slaughter and myself...land in county of Habersham...wife and son (not named)...C. P. Gordon. Wits: Samson W. Harris, H. W. Cozant, B. W. Sanford. In addition, ..brothers James G. Gordon and George H. Gordon guardians for children...brothers (aforesd.) and John Brown of Tennessee Exrs...Wits: same as above.

- 1860 Russell Co., AL Census: Charles T. Abercrombie 36 GA, Virginia 33 GA, Barbara Gordon 63 PA, Julia T. Abercrombie 10 AL, Mary F. 9 AL, Charles T. 5 AL and Anna B. 3 AL.

Fannie Epping	Aug. 25, 1864 Columbus, GA	Jan. 15, 1891 Montgomery, AL	d/o H. H. & Isabella Epping, w/o Charles Abercrombie

- Obit: died Montgomery, Ala, nee Miss Fannie Epping d/o H. H. Epping of Montgomery, Ala., sister of H. H. Jr., E. H., Mrs. Leo Swift, all of Columbus, Ga., Mrs. Cecil Gabbitt of Savannah, Ga., 2 dghts survive (not named).

- Fannie married Charles Gordon Abercrombie 12 Jan 1887 in Muscogee Co., GA. They had 2 daughters; Fannie Virginia and Isabel.

Rebecca Epping	June 8, 1852	May 24, 1873	w/o John F. Flournoy, d/o H. H. & Isabel Epping
George Swift Hamburger	Apr. 4, 1867	Mar. 20, 1935	

- George was the s/o Louis (1831-1909) and Frances Turner Moore Hamberger.

- 1910 Muscogee Census: George S. Hamberger 39 GA Germany GA (married 14 years), wife Rebecca F. 36 GA GA GA (2 children/2 living), son Frank F. 10? GA and Francis I. 6 GA.

- 1920 Muscogee Census (very hard to read): George S. Hamburger, Rebecca F., Frank and Isabel.

Rebecca Flournoy Hamburger	May 16, 1873	Jan. 27, 1963	Wife

- d/o John Francis Flournoy and Rebecca Epping (d/o H. H. Epping)

- Mrs. Rebecca Flournoy Hamburger, DAR ID Number: 69810. Born in Columbus, Ga. Wife of George Swift Hamburger. Descendant of Chapman Gordon, of North Carolina. Daughter of John Flournoy (b. 1847) and Rebecca Epping (1852-73), his 1st wife, m. 1869. Granddaughter of John Manly Flournoy (1814-59) and Mary Ann Gordon (1823-86), his wife, m. 1843. Gr-grand-daughter of Charles Pendleton Gordon (b. 1790) and Barbary Galbraith (b. 1789), his wife, m. 1817. Gr-gr-granddaughter of Chapman Gordon and Dorothy King (1763-1859), his wife, m. 1786. Chapman Gordon (1757-1813) served at King's Mountain with his older brothers, Nathaniel and Charles. He was born in Spottsylvania County, Va.; died in Wilkes County, N. C.

Isabel Hamburger Tuggle	July 14, 1903	Jan. 4, 1956	d/o George S. & Rebecca F. Hamburger

- w/o of Thomas Tuggle.

Mary Epping	July 20, 1858 Columbus, GA	Oct. 29, 1903 Savannah, GA	w/o Cecil Gabbett, d/o H. H. & Isabel Epping
Isabelle Robertson	Dec. 24, 1825 Arbroath, Scotland	Nov. 14, 1881 Columbus, GA	w/o H. H. Epping

- Obit: born Scotland, nee Isabella Robertson, was young when arrived in America, lived in Charleston, SC, 1849 married there and moved to Columbus, leaves husband & children, Mrs. G. P. Swift, Jr., Mrs. Cecil Gabbett, Henry Epping.

H. H. Epping	Feb. 15, 1821 Oldenburg, Germany	July 31, 1904 Columbus, GA	

- Obit: Henry Herman Epping, s/o J. D. Epping, 1st married Barbara Cubbedge, d/o Stephen Cubbedge of GA, Feb. 1846, she died the same year, Jan. 1850 married Isabella Robertson of Scotland, 6 children, Leo, Rebecca, Henry Jr., Mary, Earley H. & Fannie, only 3 survive, they are H. H. Jr., Early H. & Mrs. Ed E. Swift, all of Columbus, 1 brother William Epping of Oldenburg, Germany survives.

- 1860 Russell Co., AL Census: Henry Epping 39 Oldenburg Germany, Isabella 35 GA, Leo 9 GA, Rebecca 7 GA, Henry 4 GA, Mary 2 GA and Frances H. Epping 3/12 GA.

- 1880 Muscogee Census: Henry Epping 59 Ger Ger Ger, wife Isabella 54 Sco Sco Sco, son Early 18 Al, dau 15 AL, and boarders; Henry Epping Jr. 23 AL, Dora? 23 Al, John

Flournoy 32 GA GA GA, Frank 9 GA and Beca 6 GA.

1 baby brick slab unable to read

Lot 179, Struppa on wall

William I. Struppa	Aug. 10, 1844	Sept. 18, 1906	Father

- Obit: Capt. Veteran steamboat man, died at residence of son, H. I. in Russell Co., Ala., CSA vet Gray's Co. I, 5th GA Regt., leaves wife & 7 children, H. I. Claude, Dr. J. R. of Columbus, Ga., Mrs. Earl Anderson of Atlanta, Ga., Mrs. W. Baker of Griffin, Ga., Madoline & Marguerite Struppa, 1 brother, Joe of San Antonia, Tex., 4 sisters, Mrs. Jodie Whitaker, Maggie & Georgia Struppa of Columbus, Ga., Mrs. Lizzie Colter of Montgomery, Ala.

- 1880 Muscogee Census: M. A. (f) Struppa 60 PA PA PA, dau G. E. 36 GA PA PA, dau Margaret 25 GA PA PA, son Joseph 24 GA PA PA, dau Joahana 16 GA GA GA, SIL Louis Collier(?) 24 GA GA GA and dau Lizzie 21 GA PA PA.

Lucy Estelle Struppa	Jan. 21, 1873	Oct. 2, 1880	d/o Wm. I. & Ellen C. Struppa
Alma Struppa		Oct. 9, 1898	d/o C. E. & Alma R. Struppa
J. Randolph Struppa	Feb. 7, 1879	Jan. 26, 1950	
Ida Pittman Struppa	Dec. 28, 1881	Sept. 16, 1966	
John Struppa		Sept. 12, 1881	s/o W. I. & Ellen C. Struppa, 13 hours.

Lot 180, J. B. Key on wall

Benjamin Witt Key	Apr. 3, 1890	Jan. 17, 1964	Our son.
Ozella Biggers Key	June 19, 1854	Jan. 21, 1923	w/o Howard W. Key mother

- d/o James J. W. Biggers (1823-1893) and Caroline E. Williams (1825-1909).

Howard Walton Key	Nov. 6, 1851	Mar. 13, 1911	s/o Joseph & Susie Snider Key father

- Howard was the s/o Bishop Joseph Key (1829-1920) and Susie Snider (c1832-1895). He married 22 Dec. 1824 Ozella Biggers.

- 1880 Muscogee Census: Howard Key 28 GA GA GA, wife Ozella 25 GA SC SC, Joseph 4 GA and James 2 GA.

- 1900 Muscogee Census: Howard W. Key 49 GA GA GA, wife Ozella 47 GA GA GA (7 children/7 living), son Jos. S. 25 GA, dau Ozella 19 GA, son Howard W. Jr. 16 GA, dau Emma? 14 GA, son Ben W. 10 GA and son Bascomb B. 7 GA.

Lot 181, open lot

Peter Biehler, Jr.	July 1, 1847	Mar. 5, 1882	

- Obit: died at residence of brother-in-law, John Reese, shoemaker by trade.

John Biehler	Oct. 9, 1854	July 20, 1867	
Dudley Biehler		July 11, 1860	s/o P. & M. Biehler age 8 days
Edward Biehler	Sept. 1875	Mar. 22, 1876	s/o P. & M. Biehler
Charles Henry Lequin	Jan. 11, 1842 Donainer Canton deDava, Scotland	Nov. 21, 1890	Our father

- Obit: died Macon, Ga., jewelry business, funeral notice mentions Mrs. J. D. Smith.

- 1870 Muscogee Census: Charles Lequin 20 Switzerland and George Moore 23 AL.

Margaret Biehler Lequin	May 6, 1858 Columbus, GA	Aug. 30, 1894 Columbus, GA	Our mother

- Obit: funeral notice mentions Mr. John Reese.

- Muscogee Co. MR shows Maggie Biehler married Charles H. Seguin (sic) 25 Feb 1875.

Peter Biehler	May 10, 1817 Alsace, France	May 11, 1872

- Obit: born in Germany.

- 1850 Muscogee Census: Peter Bichler 29 France, Margarett 21 Baaden, Peter 3, Emily 7/12.

- 1860 Muscogee Census: Peter Beihler 37 Germany, Margaret 31 Germany, Amey 11 GA, Louisa 4 GA, Margaret 2 GA, Peter 13 GA, Charles 7 GA. Also in HH Margaret Hubert 56 GA, Frank Kroener 35 Germany and John Danall? 40 Germany.

Margaret Biehler	Oct. 2, 1827 Bavaria	Oct. 24, 1877	46 yrs, 22 days

3 adult slabs, n/m

Lot 182, Lester on steps

Ethel Philips Lester	Feb. 19, 1875	Oct. 24, 1909
Raymond H. Lester	Aug. 11, 1868	Nov. 16, 1920

- 1920 Muscogee Census: Etheldred Philips 68 FL NC GA, dau Susie 27 GA FL AL, son Ernest 34 GA FL AL, DIL Ethel 21 GA NC AL and grandson Raymond H. Lester 10 NM GA GA.

Lot 183, open lot

No evidence of graves

Lot 184, no name on wall

Mary Johnson Hendrix	Aug. 3, 1904	Dec. 18, 1988	
Benjamin Kelly Hendrix	Feb. 15, 1905	Aug. 21, 1948	G/M Cpt. 753 CML Dep. Co. Avn. WWII
Mattie Hendrix	Nov. 8, 1876	May 19, 1936	
Robert Hendrix	Feb. 11, 1852	Jan. 22, 1915	

- 1860 Muscogee Census: Simein Hendrick 45 SC, Harrit 44 AL, Jane 20 AL, Semein 16 AL, Harriet 14 AL, Marion (m) 12 AL, Robert 9 AL, Elizabeth 4 GA and George W. 4/12 GA.

- 1910 Muscogee Census: Robert Hendrix 58 AL SC VA (marriage 2, 8 yrs), Mary ___ 32 GA GA GA (marriage 1) and son Benj? K. 5 GA.

Madelin Ware	Aug. 30, 1912	Sept. 6, 1941
Alice N. Johnson	Mar. 29, 1892	Oct. 20, 1975
Mrs. Elizabeth Land	Mar. 4, 1846	Oct. 21, 1934

- Obit: widow of Jacob Land and highly esteemed Harris county woman died at the residence of her daughter Mrs. Mattie Hendrix. She was born March 12, 1846 and lived in Harris Co. the greatest portion of her life. Surviving 2 sons William Land of Fortson, Ga. and Charles Land of Columbus, four daughters Mrs. Mattie Hendrix and Mrs. Iren Caldwell of Columbus, Mrs. Nora Woodall of Fortson and Mrs. Carrie White of Salisbury, NC; four brothers Joe Sharp of Columbus, Tom Sharp of LaGrange, GA, John Sharp of Opelika, Ala., and Allen Sharp of Talbotton, Ga; three sisters Mrs. Sarah Hardy, Mrs. Kate Morgan and Mrs. Carrie Kennon of Columbus and several nieces and nephews.

- Jacob Land was born 2 March 1848 in Harris Co., GA, the son of Jacob Land.

- 1860 Harris Co., GA Census: Jacob Land 52 SC, Ann 53 SC, Joseph 24 GA, Wm 23 GA, Jacob 18 GA, Lizzie 17 GA, John 14 GA, Jasper 13 GA and Tho. 11 GA.

- 1850 Muscogee Co. Census: Rufus Sharp 30, Malissa 23, Charlotte 4, William R. 3, Sarah F. 1 and Lemuel Conner? 24.

- 1870 Muscogee Census: Rufus Sharp 49 GA, Malissa 43 GA, Elizabeth 23 GA, William 22 GA, Sarah 20 GA, John 19 GA, Susan 17 GA, Georgia 16 GA, Nancy 14 GA, Allen 12 GA, Joseph 10 GA, Frank 8 GA, Thomas 6 GA, Carrie 5 GA and Emily 2/12 GA.

- Rufus Sharp married Malissa Canon 12 June 1845 in Muscogee Co., GA.

Jacob R. Johnson	Mar. 20, 1872	Dec. 1, 1949	
Sallie Cora Hendrix	June 29, 1852	Feb. 9, 1907	w/o Rob. Hendrix

1 baby slab, n/m

Lot 185, Robert S. Grier on wall

Robert Stuart Grier, Sr.   Dec. 29, 1850   Apr. 14, 1932

- Obit: born in Burlington, VT, s/o Thomas J. Grier, native of Dublin, Ireland & Maria Clarke Grier. Leaves wife, Mrs. Annie Fee Grier, 1 son Robert S. Jr., 3 dghtrs. Mrs. Robert Ryan of Montgomery, Ala., Mrs. Flournoy Hamburger & Mrs. Henry Bray, both of Columbus, Ga., 2 sisters Mrs. John Connors of Montgomery, Ala., Mrs. H. E. Hall of Columbus, Ga., 3 g/sons, 5 g/dghtrs.

- 1910 Muscogee Census: Robert S. Grier 59 NC Ire Ire (married 14 yrs), wife Annie 46 GA Ire Ire (5 children/3 living), dau Katie 11 GA, dau Elizabeth 8 GA and dau Ella L. 6 GA. Living next door is: Maria B. Fee 75 Ire Ire Ire (emigrated 1850, 4 children/3 living), SIL James Bivens 50 GA GA TN (married 17 yrs), wife Rachel E. Bivens 51 NY Ire Ire, son Harold F. 15 GA and son George N. Fee 48 GA.

Annie Maria Fee	Mar. 13, 1864	July 19, 1936	w/o Robt. S. Grier, Sr.
Maria Vincent Grier	May 29, 1900	Dec. 18, 1908	
Annie Angelia Grier	Dec. 21, 1906		d/o Annie Fee & Robt. S. Grier
Nieves Maria Pellan	Aug. 5, 1908	Sept. 1, 1940	w/o Robt. S. Grier Jr.
Margaret Burns	May 21, 1914	Apr. 29, 1954	w/o Robt. S. Grier Jr.

Lot 186, no name on wall

James Thos. Fee	Apr. 21, 1852	Dec. 21, 1854	s/o Patrick & Margaret Berry
Johanna Berry	June 24, 1847	Dec. 15, 1851	d/o Patrick & Margaret Berry

2 adult slabs, n/m

Lot 187, Stribling on wall

Mattie Ella Stribling	Dec. 2, 1870	Oct. 15, 1928
Joseph C. Stribling	Feb. 26, 1855	Dec. 5, 1935

- 1880 Harris Co., GA Census: Joseph Stribling 28 GA GA GA, wife Mattie 28 GA GA GA, dau Eugenia 2 GA, dau Addie 1/12 GA and Si-I-L Hattie Riley 20 GA GA G.

- 1900 Muscogee Census: Joseph C. Stribling 47 GA GA GA, wife Mattie 47 GA GA GA (married at 23, 5 children/4 living), dau Addie I. 20 GA, dau T_____ K. 18 GA and son Luther S. 13 GA.

Lot 188, no name on wall

John A. Morton	July 15, 1854	Age 39 yrs 9 mo 21 dys

- Obit: Capt. Died at the home of Capt. John E. Davis, lived in Summerville, Ala.
- 1850 Muscogee Census: John H. Morton 34 (Steam boat Capt.), George S. 30, Alexander C. 25, Jane 27, Eliza 23.
- The 1860 Muscogee Census Records show that George was born in New York.

Elizabeth M. Saunders	Nov. 11, 1863	The Pastor's Wife

- Obit: born in New York.
- 1860 Muscogee Census: in boarding house: J. C. Sanders 35 TN and Mrs. Sanders 30 NY.

1 adult brick slab, n/m

Lot 189, fenced lot, no name

Osborn Douglas	July 9, 1851	May 8, 1861	
? ?	Dec. 31, 1840	Aug. 3, 18??	d/o W. E. Douglas
Harriett Douglas	Oct. 11, 1817	Oct. 18, 1869	

- Funeral Notice mentions relict of William A. Douglas, died at residence in Dover, Lee Co., Ala.

1 adult brick slab, n/m

Sexton Records indicate buried in this lot:

William E. Douglas   12/31/1810   8/3/1858

- 1850 Muscogee Census: William A. Douglass 33 GA, Mrs. H. A. 22 GA, William E. 9 GA and Warren S. 12? GA.

Lot 190, no name on wall

William Sullivan Connolly	1901	1941	SR: bur 7/24/1941
Edna Thomas Connolly	1899	1983	SR born 7/29/1899, bur. 7/21/1983. father Jefferson D. Thomas, mother Ida Sears.
Joseph M. Connolly	1907	1953	SR: bur. 10/14/1953
Catherine Sullivan		June 29, 1854	Age 56. Native of Clogheen Ireland.
John Sullivan		Dec. 31, 1854	Age 35

Patrick Sullivan		Aug. 3, 1857	Age 29
Mary A. Connolly	1904	1966	SR: bur. 12/23/1944, 76.

- 1920 Muscogee Census: Mary Sullivan 78 Ire Ire Ire, son Will A. 45 GA, dau Rose 41 GA, James S. Connelly 55 GA Ire Can?, wife Mary 45 GA, son William 18 GA, dau Mary 14 GA, son Joseph 12 GA and son John 7 GA.

Mary E. Connolly	1872	1959	SR: born 1/5/1872 bur. 3/30/1959
John V. Connolly	Sept. 21, 1912	Feb. 14, 1976	
James S. Connolly	1865	1944	SR: bur. 3/15/1944, 76
Rosa Sullivan	1877	1921	SR: bur. 2/7/1921, 44
W. A. Sullivan	1873	1925	SR: bur. 12/7/1925, 52
Mike Sullivan	1869	1918	SR: born 10/25/1869, bur. 11/4/1918, 49 yrs

- 1910 Muscogee Census: Michael J. Sullivan 40 GA Ire Ire (married 3 yrs), wife Bertha A. 29 GA GA GA (1 child/1 living) and dau Mary E. 1 2/12 GA.

7 adult slabs, n/m   1 baby slab, n/m

Sexton Records indicate buried in this lot:

Catherine Sullivan	*Bur. 10/19/1886, 55 yrs*
Mary Nell Connolly	*Bur. 4/2/1898, 16 mo.*
Annie Sullivan	*Bur. 5/30/1895, 24 yrs.*
Dennis Sullivan	*Bur. 7/11/1868*
Dennis R. Sullivan	*Bur. 9/12/1875, 16 yrs.*
John B. Sullivan	*Bur. 5/21/1894, 8 hrs.*
Mary Sullivan	*Bur. 2/21/1920, 78 yrs.*

- Obit: born in County Meath Ireland, Sept. 4, 1841, married the late Michael J. Sullivan 1 son, W. A. Sullivan, 2 dghts. Rosa Sullivan & Mrs. J. S. Connolly, 3 g/ch.

William Sullivan	*Bur. 12/8/1891, 68 yrs.*
Mike Sullivan	*Bur. 5/4/1892, 70 yrs.*

- 1870 Muscogee Census: Michael Sullivan 48 Ire, Mary 29 Ire, Dennis 11 GA, John 3 GA and Michael 8/12 GA.

Lot 191, Crichton on wall

Name	Birth	Death	Notes
George Gronbeck Crichton	Apr. 8, 1868	Apr. 8, 1961	
Jessie Inglie Crichton	Nov. 30, 1864	June 10, 1945	
I. Schnell	1832		
Hettie Crichton		Jan. 9, 1939	w/o R. M. Harding. SR: 62 years
Frances Charlott Schnell	b. Switzerland	Jan. 24, 1909	age 75 yrs.

- Obit: born of Swiss-German parents, only surviving d/o John Schnell, at 8 she was an orphan, she and one younger brother reared by Mr. & Mrs. G. W. Parker, married B. T. Gronbeck of Copenhagen, Denmark, 3 children Thomas Andrew, George Washington & Frances Petrea, all deceased, 2nd married Charles Crichton of Amonck, Ayershire, Scotland, their children David Charles of Perrine, Fla., Miss Jessie Inglie of Columbus, Ga., Mrs. Lyman E. Wells of Jacksonville, Fla., Miss Georgia Gronbeck Crichton, Miss Hattie Elizabeth, Wm. J. McAllister Crichton, all of Columbus, Ga., Mrs. B. B. Mabson Newnam, Ga., R. H. of Jacksonville, Fla.

Name	Birth	Death	Notes
Charles Crichton	Apr. 14, 1820 Gumnock, Ayshire Scotland	Oct. 1, 1884 Columbus, GA	

- Obit: One of Columbus' oldest citizens, here in 1834, native of Cumnoc, Ayershire, Scotland, a baker, married 1856 to Mrs. Fannie Gronbeck, had 10 children, 8 living, 5 gorls, 3 boys, eldest 26, youngest is 6, Mr. John Schnell is his brother in law.

- 1860 Muscogee Census: Charles Creighton 36 Scotland, Francis 25 GA, David C. 2 GA, Thomas Groanbeck 9 GA, George Groanbeck 8 GA and Henry Stevenson 22 Scotland.

- 1880 Muscogee Census: Chars Crichton 55 Sco Sco Sco, wife Fannie 44 Ger Ger Ger, son Thomas 29 GA, son Chars 21 GA, son Jesse 16 GA, dau Lula 14 GA, (sic) dau Georgia 12 GA, dau Hettie? 10 GA, son Willis 8 GA.

Name	Birth	Death	Notes
George Washington Gronbeck	Feb. 19, 1852	Nov. 5, 1867	
Peter Anderson			CSA 1861-1865. SR: bur. 8/5/1872, 45.

- 1860 Muscogee Census: Peter Anderson 33 Denmark.

Name	Birth	Death	Notes
Frances Petrea Gronbeck	Apr. 8, 1854	Mar. 7, 1855	s/o B. T. & Frances Gronbeck
B. T. Gronbeck	Feb. 10, 1811 Copenhagen, Denmark	Apr. 10, 1857 Columbus, GA	Father

- 1850 Muscogee Census: Thomas Gronbeck 38 Denmark and Mrs. F. Gronbeck 18 NY.

Name	Birth	Death	Notes
Thomas A. Gronbeck	Sept. 17, 1850	Nov. 12, 1884	Son

- Obit: baker, step-father Charles Crichton.

Name	Birth	Death	Notes
Mary Augusta	June 15, 1861	July 11, 1863	d/o C. & ??

Lula Stanford Crichton	Mar. 6, 1866	May 9, 1938	w/o Lyman Emmett Wells
David Charles Crichton	Oct. 24, 1859 Columbus, GA	Oct. 14, 1915 Savannah, GA	

Sexton Records indicate also buried in this lot:

child of John Schnell			*bur. 9/20/1871, 9 mos.*

Lot 192, Floyd on wall

Henry Summer Floyd	Feb. 15, 1854	Jan. 16, 1914	
Lillian Clark	1869	1939	SR: bur. 12/8/1939, 70.
Martha Elizabeth Floyd	Feb. 8, 1859	Dec. 2, 1938	

Lot 193, no name on wall

Mrs. Anne M. Briggs	no dates	SR: bur. 5/25/1884, 64.	
Nancy Dolvin Johnson	1783	1872	d/o John & Rebecca Dolvin w/o Robert Johnson. SR: bur. 7/1/1872, 89 yr.

- Obit: widow for 50 years, sons John Johnson, Treasurer & Ordinary of Muscogee Co., GA, F. C. Johnson, Merchant, James G., former City Treasurer, 2 others in Muscogee Co., GA, 1 in Harris Co.

- Nancy Dolvin married Robert Johnson 4 Mar. 1800 in Greene Co., GA.

John Johnson	1801	1874	s/o Robert & Nancy Dolvin Johnson. SR: bur. 4/7/1874, 73 yrs.

- 1850 Muscogee Census: John Johnson 48 GA, Hannah 48 RI, Mary B. 8 GA, Amanda M. 20 GA, Mary A. Langford 14 GA, Mary Prathie 13 GA and Lucinda McLendon 16 GA.

Hannah Briggs Johnson	no dates	w/o John Johnson. SR: bur. 3/8/1874.	
Miss Fannie Stoddard	no dates		

- Obit: d/o David L. Barker of Milford, Mass. died May 18, 1853.

Mary Briggs Johnson	Mar. 13, 1842	June 28, 1924	d/o John & Hannah Briggs Johnson.
W. A. Douglas	Fe. 28, 1813	Oct. 8, 1868	

- 1850 Muscogee Census: William A. Douglass 33 GA, Mrs. H. A. 27? GA, William E. 9 GA and Warren S. 17 GA.

Sexton Records indicate buried in this lot:

William E. Douglas	*born 12/31/1810*		*bur. 8/3/1858*

Lot 194, Geo J. Burrus on wall

Frances Catherine Burrus	Jan. 11, 1846	June 13, 1850	d/o J. G. & C. Burrus

- 1850 Muscogee Census: Jacob G. Burrows 42 France, Catherine 40 Bavaria, Jacob G. 14 NY, Lawrence 10 NY, Mary 8 GA, William 6 GA, George 2 GA, Frances 5 GA and Peter Hemmes 71 Bavaria.

George J. Burrus Jr.	Nov. 11, 1880	Nov. 7, 1970	
Effie May Pearce	June 14, 1882	Apr. 11, 1957	w/o George J. Burrus Jr.
John L. Burrus	Dec. 10, 1874	Sept. 8, 1897	
George Joseph Burrus	July 28, 1848	Jan. 11, 1932	

- Obit: born in Columbus, Ga. 28 June 1848, s/o late Jacob George Burrus (a native of France) and the late Mrs. Catherine Hammer Burrus, brothers & sisters all deceased Jacob G., Lawrence M., Wm., Mrs. Mary L. Hartman, married Jan. 21, 1871 Miss Sarah Elizabeth Daniel of Columbus, Ga., their children Geo. J. Jr., Mrs. Emma Frances Bush, both of Columbus, Miss Bessie Burrus and John Burrus are deceased.

Sarah Elizabeth Burrus	Oct. 17, 1851	Sept. 9, 1902	w/o Geo. J. Burrus

- Obit: w/o Geogre J. Burrus, leaves husband, 1 son George Jr., 1 daughter Miss Emmie Burrus, her father J. J. Daniel of Pike Co., AL, _____ of Macon Co., AL. Mrs. H. W. Garett & Mrs. Fannie Meyer both of Columbus, Ga., 1 brother James Motley of Texarcana, Ark., who was adopted by the Motley family when a little child, born in Pike Co., Ala., married George J. Burrus Jan. 25, 1871.

Philip Henry Hartmann	July 10, 1835 ? Bavaria	May 13, 1873	38 yrs.

- Obit: died from lockjaw, stuck a nail in his foot, native of Germany, lived here 15 years, brother-in-law Jake Burrus.

- 1870 Muscogee Census: Philip Hartman 54 Bavaria, Mary 28 GA, George 19 GA, William 7 GA, Philip Jr. 5 GA, Laverna 3 GA and Mary 1 GA.

C. P. Bush	May 31, 1866	Mar. 11, 1955	

- 1860 Muscogee Census: Josie Bush 38 GA GA GA, dau Fannie 18 GA GA GA, son Homer 8 GA, son Clarence 13 GA, son Henry 4 GA and son George 1 GA.

Emmie Burrus Bush	Sept. 28, 1878	Mar. 19, 1958	w/o Clarence P. Bush

Lot 195, no name on wall

Hattie L. Wright	1862	1937	w/o Geo. E. Wilhelm, Jr. SR: bur. 9/14/1937, 35
Geo E. Wilhelm, Sr.	1854	1928	SR: bur. 1/28/1928, 74.

121

William Allen Murat	Aug. 21, 1909	Feb. 10, 1987	s/o Minnie Wilhelm Murat
Clara E. Rosecrans	no dates		adult
Sarah F. Wilhelm	no dates		SR: bur. 10/5/1881, 19
Minnie Wilhelm Murat	Nov. 28, 1882	Oct. 27, 1976	

- 1930 Fulton Co., GA Census: Hattie Wilhelm 67 GA GA GA (widowed, married @19) son Emory S. 35 GA GA GA, dau Minnie Murat 47 GA GA GA (widowed, married @23), ddau Miriam 18 FL, gdau Martha 14 FL and gson Ralph F. 22 FL.

Edwin H. Rosecrans	unable to read		2nd Lt. Co. B. 95th Regt.
Fred G. Wilhelm	1839	1928	SR: bur. 7/22/1928, 89.
George E. Wilhelm, Jr.	Nov. 22, 1888	Dec. 24, 1974	
G/M Robert Wilhelm	Mar. 30, 1891	Oct. 20, 1971	GA Pvt. US Army WWI
Jesse Wilhelm	Oct. 22, 1886	July 21, 1953	
G/M Emory Spear Wilhelm		Oct. 31, 1940	GA Yeoman, 3 c1 USNRF, SR: 45 yrs.
Unable to read	May 12, 1852	?	child
3 adult brick slabs, n/m	1 child brich slab, n/m		

Sexton Records indicate also buried in this lot:

F. Wilhelm			*bur. 10/12/1893, 86 yrs.*

1860 Muscogee Census: Frederick O. Wilhelm 52 PA, Ester 43 PA, Frederick 21 GA, Mary C. 15 GA, Clara 14 GA, Sarah 12 GA and George 6 GA.

Miss F. G. Wilhelm			*bur. 4/27/1903, 18 yrs.*

Lot 196, Chase on wall

Gertrude Belle Chase	Mar. 27, 1884	Oct. 23, 1959
Effie May Chase	Oct. 13, 1872	Aug. 24, 1948
Louis T. Chase	Feb. 7, 1869	Jan. 5, 1942

- 1920 Muscogee Census: Louis T. Chase 52 GA NY MA, sister Effie M. 47 GA NY MA, sister Gertrude 34 GA NY MA and boarders.

Geo. W. Chase	Oct. 11, 1834	Oct. 3, 1910

- Obit: Professor, established Chase's Conservatory Music, son of Louis F. Chase, born Brooklyn, NY, moved to Lagrange, Ga. when a child; sons Geo. E. of Atlanta, Ga., Frank E. of Jacksonville, Fla., Louis T. & Carl T. both of Columbus, Ga.a dght in New Rochelle, N.Y., Effie & Gertrude of Columbus, Ga., 1 sister Mrs. May E. Godwin of Dallas, TX, 2 brothers William & Lowell, both of Texas.

- 1870 Muscogee Census: George Chase 35 NY, Abbey P. 27 Mass., George E. 8 GA, Frank E. 3 GA and Louis T. 1 GA.

- 1880 Muscogee Census: George Chase 45 NY NY MA, wife Abbie 36 MA MA MA, son George 18 GA, son Frank 13 GA, son Louis 11 GA, dau Effie 7 GA and dau Myria 2.

Abbie Hoyt Chase	July 17, 1842	July 6, 1897

- Haverhill, Essex Co., MA Vital Records show Abby P. Hoyt being born 17 July 1842, the d/o Daniel and Betsy Hoyt. She married George W. Chase 30 Aug. 1860 in Haverhill, Essex Co., MA.

Sexton Records also indicate buried in this lot:

Henry Chase	*bur. 3/28/1875 s/b*
Bessie Holt Chase	*bur. 4/2/1877, 1 day*
Edgar Chase	*bur. 4/15/1871, s/b*
John Chase	*bur. 3/24/1876 s/b*
Mary Ella Chase	*bur. 10/16/1863, 3 mos.*

Lot 197, A. A. Carson on wall

Willis Gordon Carson	Oct. 2, 1877	Apr. 29, 1914	s/o Albert A. & S. A. Carson
Sarah Augustus Carson	Aug. 30 1849	Feb. 18, 1913	w/o Albert A. Carson

- Obit: died in Eufaula, Ala., at residence of dght Mrs. F. A. Pomeroy, widow of late A. A. Carson who died last Aug., 2 children, Willis of Columbus, Ga., Mrs. F. A. Pomeroy of Eufaula, Ala., brother-in-law H. A. Carson of Columbus, GA.

Albert A. Carson	Mar. 28, 1849	Aug. 18, 1912

- Obit: born in Oglethorpe, GA., s/o Major J. T. Carson who was killed in the War Between the States, leaves wife, dau. Mrs. J. F. Pomeroy of Eufaula, Ala., son Willis G. Carson of Columbus, Ga., brothers R. A., J. T. both of Columbus, Ga. Sisters Mrs. W. H. Hinton of Miami, Fla., Mrs. L. C. Waters of Columbus, Ga.

- Albert's father, John Thomas Carson married Susan Saphronia Howe 2 Feb. 1847. Maj. John Carson died 30 Sept. 1864 at Lynchburg, VA.

- 1860 Macon Co., GA Census: John T. Carson 35 GA, Susan S. 35 GA, Albert A. 11 GA, Robert A. 8 GA, Marcia E. 5 GA, Martha S. 3 GA, Lulu C. 1 GA and Charles McDaniel 15 GA.

- 1900 Muscogee Census: Albert A. Carson Mar 1849 GA GA GA (married 25 yrs), wife Sally A. August 1849 GA GA GA(4 children/3 living), dau Mabel C. Mar. 1876 GA, son Willis G. Oct. 1877, dau Carrie R. Mar. 1880 GA, MIL Rebecca S. Welch Dec 1821 GA GA GA (3 children/1 living) and boarder James Tignor Jan. 1879 AL AL AL.

Mabel Carson	Mar. 28, 1876	Sept. 26, 1908	w/o W. J. Burrus
Rebecca Serepta Welch	May 2, 1823	Feb. 21, 1906	w/o Nichols Narrell Welch. Grandmother.

- Obit: born in Greensboro, Ga. leaves daughter & 2 sisters, the last of 13 children, Mrs. H. K. Herndon of Decatur, Ga., Miss Mary Walker of Macon, GA.

- Rebecca N. Walker married Nicholas N. Welch 11 Dec. 1839 in Bartow Co., GA.

Sexton Records also indicare buried in this lot:

c/o W. Burrus	bur. 10/5/1871, 2 days.
Sarah E. Burrus	bur. 9/10/1902, 50 years.

- 1900 Muscogee Co., GA Census: George J. Burrars July 1847 GA Germany Germany (mar. 28 yrs), Sarah Oct. 1850 GA GA GA (4 children/2 living), dau ? Sept 1877 GA and son George Jr. Nov. 1880 GA.

- George Joseph Burrus was the s/o Jacob George Burrus of Alsace, France and Catherine Hammer of Germany. He was born 28 June 1848 in Columbus, GA. He married on 27 January 1871 Sarah Elizabeth Daniel, the d/o Joseph J. and Harriet Daniel.

- George J. Burrus Jr. married Effie May Pearce, the d/o George Augusta Pearce and Ida Embry.

Geo J. Burrus	bur. 10/7/1873. 2 wks.
c/o Wm. Burrus	bur. 6/21/1872

Lot 198, no name on wall

3 adult slabs, n/m	3 children slabs, n/m	1 adult tomb, unable to read

Lot 199, no name on wall

1 small granite marker, blank

Lot 200, Robinson on wall

William A. Robinson	Dec. 12, 1884	Aug. 2, 1945
Estelle Robinson Hammond	May 13, 1896	Feb. 18, 1950

Sexton Records also indicare buried in this lot:

C. Degeorge

- Obit: C. Degeorge Dies Here Sunday Night. *Prominent Artist and Photographer Passes at City Hospital Following Long Illness.*

Constantine deGeorge 47, for many years a citizen of Columbus died at the City Hospital last night at eight o'clock following a long illness. Mr. Degeorge who was an artist and photographer was widely known in Columbus where he had made many friends who will learn of his death with sincere regret. He had lived here twenty-five years.

Mr. Degeorge was a native of southern France, coming to the United States thirty years ago. He lived in New York for five years, moving to Columbus from that city. He was an accomplished painter and photographer and engaged in that business for many years here…. He left no close relatives here or in France.

- Georgia Death Records show that Mr. Degeorge died in Muscogee Co., GA 10 Aug 1924.

- 1900 Muscogee Census: Constantine DeGeorge Sept 1855 (single) Scotland Scotland Scotland, emigrated 1877, 22 years in the U.S. and boarder Thurston Hatcher Nov 1881 GA GA GA.

Lot 201, Wood on wall

Mary E. Wood	Dec. 7, 1901	June 17, 1987
Rev. Wm. S. Wood, Sr.	Dec. 22, 1902	Sept. 30, 1968
William Jefferson Wood	Feb. 29, 1885	Nov. 25, 1947
Mary O. Wood	Aug. 22, 1886	Dec. 23, 1965

Lot 202, Brown on wall

Jefferson Davis Brown	Apr. 14, 1888	Jan. 2, 1952

- 1920 Muscogee Census: Jefferson D. Brown 31 VA VA VA, wife Etta 27 GA GA GA, dau Helen 1 6/12 GA

Lot 203, Chase on wall

Mary Belle Vernoy	Dec. 27, 1862	Nov. 29, 1942	w/o Geo. E. Chase
Geo. E. Chase	1861	1937	SR: bur. 2/21/1937, 75 yrs.

- 1870 Muscogee Census: George Chase 35 NY, Abbey P. 27 Mass, Geo E. 8 GA, Frank E. 3 GA and Sonnie T. (male) 1 GA.

- The father, George Williams Chase, s/o Daniel Chase, was born 11 October 1834 in Manhattan, NY. He married Abbie Hoyt, d/o Daniel Hoyt of Haverhill, Mass. on 30 August 1860. George Williams and Abbie Hoyt Chase were the parents of George E., Louis T., Effie M., Gertrude B., Carl T., Boysen H., Frank E. and Mrs. A. M. Chase.[41]

Sexton Records indicate also buried in this lot:

Louis Chase   *bur. 12/1/1911, 21*

Geo Chase	*d. Atlanta, GA 1898, 14 yrs.*

Lot 204, open lot

Thomas Augustus Pacetty	SR: bur. 10/19/1922

- Obit: 1 son L. A. Pacetty of Columbus, Ga.

- 1860 Chatham Co., GA Census: Andrew C. Pacetty 59 St. Augustine, FL, Catherine 44 St. Augustine, FL, Mary Ann 17 St. Augustine, FL. Alexander 15 Savannah, Emeline 12 Savannah, Catherine A. 6 Savannah and Thomas A. 1 Savannah.

- 1880 Muscogee Census: Catherine Pacetty 64 FL and son Augustus 21 FL.

- WWI Draft Registrations: Louis Augustus Pacetty born April 1, 1882, wife Mary.

Sarah W. Pacetty	1856	1922	SR: born 12/4/1858, bur. 10/25/1922

- Obit: husband died about 1 week ago, 1 son L. A. of Columbus, Ga.

Sexton Records indicate also buried in this lot:

Lula Pacetty Willett	SR: bur. 3/22/1887, 22 yrs.

- 1880 Muscogee Census: Martha Willett 50 GA KY GA, son John B. GA GA GA, son Enoch 25 GA, dau Sarah M. 22 GA, son Henry 20 GA, dau Lula 15 GA, dau Hattie 11 GA and dau Emma Lavender 22 GA.

Lot 205, Chadwick on wall

Alonza Ewell Chadwick	Apr. 18, 1873	Dec. 3, 1907 Baltimore, MD	
Mary Frances Herring	July 13, 1847	June 21, 1931	w/o Wyatt Holmes Chadwick

- Obit: widow of Wyatt Holmes Chadwick who died 4 years ago, 3 dghts Mrs. W. S. Buckner of Rome, GA., Mrs. S. A. Williamson of Americus, Ga., Mrs. Leona C. Wilson of Columbus, Ga., 1 son J. W. of Columbus, Ga., 3 brothers C. H. Herring, J. L. Herring & J. T. Herring, all of Russell Co., Ala., 7 g/ch.

- Mary Frances Herring married Wyatt Chadwick 15 Nov. 1866 in Russell Co., AL. She was the d/o William Tarpley and Sarah Jane Ford Herring. William died ca 1885 in Russell Co., AL. Wyatt is buried in Blount Co., AL.

- 1860 Russell Co, AL Census: Easter Chadwick 47 SC, Elias 23 AL, Wyett 15 AL, Stephen 13 AL, William 9 AL and Emoline 7 AL.

- 1880 Blount Co., AL Census: Wyatt Chadwick 35 AL SC SC, wife Mary F. 32 GA GA GA, son William A. 12 AL, dau Princy E. 11 AL, son Alonzo E. 7 AL, son Julian W. 5 AL, dau Ader E. 4 Al and dau Eddie L. 10/12 AL.

- Atlanta Constitution 4 Jan 1903: Mrs. Wyatt Holmes Chadwick announces the intended wedding of her daughter, Leone, to Mr. John William Wilson on January 14th at her residence.

- 1910 Muscogee Census: Mary F. Chadwick 62 GA VA GA (wd 7 children/4 living), son Julian W. 32 AL, gson Wyatt M .Chapman 16 GA GA GA, SIL John W. Wilson 34 GA GA GA(m1 7yrs), dau Leonie C. 29 AL (1 child/1 living), gdau Julian 1 AL and Addie L Huff 40 AL AL AL.

Lot 206, Duncan on wall

Frank Ennis	Apr 14, 1866	Feb 16, 1931	
Walter S. Duncan		No dates	SR: bur. 12/21/1925, 57 yrs.

- AL Death Records show Walter S. Duncan as dying in Lee Co., AL Dec 1925.

- 1920 Lee Co., AL Census: Walter J? Duncan 51 AL AL AL, wife Estelle 46 GA AL AL, son Cecil 25 GA, DIL Martha 23 GA, dau Elenor 19 GA, son Forest 12 Al and boarder Frank Ennis 53 (wd) AL AL AL.

Estelle Ennis Duncan	Jan 16, 1874	Dec 30, 1932	
Willis Earl Duncan	Mar 20, 1920	Aug 5, 1933	
Walter Cecil Duncan	Mar 24, 1891	Feb 5, 1941	G/M Pvt. Co. A 115 Inf. WWI
Thomas Marion Duncan	Aug 29, 1821	Sept 18, 1895	Co. B Bonard's Bn. Arty C.S.A.

- Obit: died at residence in Lee Co., AL, leaves wife & 7 children, uncle of Mrs. C. H. Herring of Columbus.

- 1880 Russell Co., AL Census: Thomas Duncan 58 GA GA GA, wife Malissie 37 AL GA GA, son Alonzo 13 AL, son Walter 12 AL, dau Nettie 9 AL, dau Maggie 6 AL and son Blanton 5 AL.

- 1870 Lee Co., AL Census: T. M. Duncan 49 GA, M. C. (f) 25 AL, A. (m) 4 AL and W. (m) 2 AL.

- Russell Co., AL MR shows Thomas M. Duncan married Millisia Digby 7 Nov 1865.

David Ennis	G/M C.S.A. 1861-1865
	SR: bur. 7/8/1893, 42 yrs.

- 1880 Muscogee Census: David Ennis 50 GA GA GA, wife Elisa Mattie 28 GA GA GA, son Frank 14 GA, dau Bertie 12 GA, dau Lilly 10 and dau Estella 8 GA.

- 1870 Muscogee Census: David Ennis 40 GA, Elizabeth 32 GA, Marcus 7 AL, Frank 4 AL and Albert 1 AL.

- 1860 Russell Co., AL Census: David Ennis 60 GA enumerated in HH of Joshua Johns.

- 1850 Chambers Co., AL Census: David Ennis 50 NC and Elizabeth 35 unknown.

- Chambers Co., AL MR shows David Ennis married Elizabeth Williams 30 Oct 1850.

Lot 207, open lot

Bertha E.		Oct 12, 1878	d/o A. G. & Elenora Laurence, consort of James H. Conway. Age 37 yrs.

- Muscogee Co., GA MR show Bertha Elanora Laurence married James Henry Conway 16 Nov 1865. Harris Co., GA MR shows James H. Conway married Georia A. Dixon 12 Dec 1879. *See 1880 Muscogee Census for Conway line continuation.*

- 1870 Muscogee Census: James Conway 32 VA, Bertha 29 GA, Elnora 2 GA and Elizabeth McCall 37 SC.

- 1860 Muscogee Census: Augustus G. Lawrance 44 GA, Elenora 43 SC, Bertha 19 GA, John 17 GA, Eugene (f) 14 GA, Janey 12 GA, Addison 7 GA, Georgia 6 GA, William 4 GA and Mrs. E. McCall 33 SC

- 1850 Muscogee Census: A. G. Raurence (sic)32 GA, Eleanor 31 SC, Bertha L. 11 GA, Hugh G. 9 GA, Eugene A. (m) 5 GA, Francis (m) 2 GA and Miss Elizabeth McAll 22 SC.

Henry Eugene McCroan	1873	1944	SR: bur. 1/28/1944, 70 yrs.
Nina H. McCroan	1874	1940	SR: born 11/14/1874, bur. 6/4/1940, 65 yrs.

- 1900 Muscogee Census: Nina H. McCrone Nov 1874 GA GA GA, dau Henrietta Aug 1896 GA GA GA, dau Lois Sept 1899 GA and aunt Georgia Lawrence May 1855 GA.

Eugene McPherson Thomas	1936	1937	
H. M. McCroan			G/M Co. F. Cobb's Leg. GA Hampton Brig. C.S.A. 1861-1865
			SR: bur. 5/10/1884, 40 yrs.
Nannie McCroan	May 6, 1850	June 2, 1923	
7 adult slabs, n/m	3 baby brick slabs, n/m		1 child brick slab, n/m

Sexton Records indicate also buried in this lot:

Charles N. McCroan		SR: bur. 6/13/1888, 35 yrs.
Henrietta McCroan		Age 16.

Lot 208, open lot

J. C. Jordan		G/M 3rd GA Cal. 1861-1865
		SR: bur. 10/19/1890, 45 yrs.

- 1880 Muscogee Census: Julius Jordan 37 GA GA GA, wife Julia 36 GA PA SC and dau Lily 9 GA.

- 1860 Harris Co., GA Census: Martha Jourdain 36 GA Susan 21 GA, Sophronia 19 GA, Salina 17 GA, John 16 GA, Julius 15 GA, Arkansas 14 GA, Martha 10 GA, Arch 8 GA, Marcus 6 GA and Joseph 4 GA.

- 1850 Harris Co., GA Census: John M. Jordan 41 GA, Martha E. 35 GA, Columbus M. 18 GA, James H. 16 H., Sarah A. 14 GA, Mary L. 12 GA, Caroline S. 10 GA, Salina 8 GA, John F. 7 GA, Julius C. 5 GA, Arkansas 4 Ga and Emily 2 GA.

Lillian Jordan	no dates	adult
Julia Rowe Jordan	no dates	adult. SR: born 1843, bur. 3/14/1918, 75 yrs.

- Obit: Leaves 1 daughter, Lillian Jordan, 2 sisters Lizzie Rowe & Mrs. E. G. Walker, both of Columbus, GA, 1 brother Dan Walker (sic) of Atlanta, GA.

- 1910 Muscogee Census: Julie Jordan 65 (wd, 1/1 child) GA PA SC, dau Lillian 25 GA GA GA and sister Lizzie Rowe 38 GA PA SC.

Annie L. Sherwood	no dates	adult
Mary E. Rowe	no dates	adult, SR: bur. 8/10/1925, 80 yrs.

- Obit: Miss Mary E. Rowe died from injuries of an automobile accident that occurred October before, nephew Flournoy C. Walker, 1 sister Mrs. E. G. Walker of Columbus, GA, 1 brother D. M. Rowe of Atlanta, GA, born and reared in Columbus, GA.

Daniel M. Rowe	no dates	adult, SR: bur. 12/22/1930, 81 years.

- 1880 Fulton Co., GA Census: Daniel M. Rowe 27 GA PA GA, wife Louisa J. 27 AL GA GA, dau Lcula B. 3 GA and BIL E. Hurt 37 AL GA GA.

- Daniel Rowe married Louisa Jane Hurt (1853-1890), the d/o Joel Hurt (1813-1861) and Lucy Apperson Long (1822-1915). Louisa is buried in Oakland Cemetery in Atlanta, GA.

Sexton Records indicate also buried in this lot:

Mary A. Rowe	SR: bur. 4/14/1897, 75 yrs.

- 1880 Muscogee Census: Mary Rowe 57 SC Scotland NC and dau Lizzie 25 GA PA SC.

- 1870 Muscogee Census: Mary A. Rowe 49 SC, Elizabeth 23 GA, Daniel 17 GA, Julius C. Jordon 27 GA, Julia C. 26 GA, Milton J. Walker 29 GA, Ella G. 26 GA, Milly R. 6 GA and Clara C. 1 GA.

- 1860 Muscogee Census: Daniel Rowe 48 PA, Mary 38 SC, Julia 18 GA, Ella 17 GA, Elizabeth 15 GA, Laura 12 GA, Edwan 10 GA and Daniel 7 GA.

- 1850 Muscogee Census: Daniel Rowe 39 PA, M. H. Rowe (f) 27 SC, Julia 11 GA, Ella 9 GA, Elizabeth 7 GA, Laura 5 GA, Edwin 1 GA and Mrs. Nancy McAll 53 SC.

- Muscogee Co., GA MR show Daniel Rowe married Mary McCall 13 Nov 1838.

Eddie Rowe	bur. 10/10/1869, 20 yrs.

Lot 209, no name on wall

Charlie D. Wynn   Jan 2, 1851   Sept 18, 1884

Lot 210, open lot

no evidence of graves

Lot 211, J. H. Jones on wall

Lula Cobb	Jan 5, 1860	Jan 5, 1921	w/o J. H. Jones
Lula Cobb Connally	Jan 30, 1940	July 17, 1940	
James Henry Jones	Oct 13, 1853	Mar 4, 1939	

- 1910 Muscogee Census: James H. Jones 56 GA GA GA, wife Lula 50 GA GA GA (m1 31 yrs, 12/7 children), son Ronald 19 AL, son Gary 18 GA, dau Ida L. 8 GA and MIL Savannah Cobb 71 GA GA GA (wd, 3/2 children).

- 1900 Muscogee Census: J. H. Jones Oct 1854 GA GA GA, wife Lula Jan 1859 GA GA GA (m24 0, 7/7 children), dau Lena Oct 1886 GA, son Perry Feb 1888 GA, sdau Idie Oct 1891 AL, son Ronald Feb 1896 AL, son Gary July 1897 GA, dau Mary Nov 1899 and MIL Savannah Cobb Sept 1828 GA GA GA.

- 1880 Chattahoochee Co., GA Census: James H. Jones 28 GA, Lula 20 GA, son James Jr. 6/12 GA, mother Vannie Cobb 40 GA and Crawford Pollard 22 GA.

- 1870 Chattahoochee Co., GA Census: Walker P. Jones 60 GA, Tabitha 19 GA, James 17 GA, Edgar 14 GA, Nancy 12 GA, Rufus 9 GA, William 7 GA and Frances 4 GA.

- Muscogee MR shows Walker P. Jones married Frances McNaughton 27 Aug 1850.

Mrs. Savannah Cobb   Sept 27. 1838   April 18, 1919

- Obit: died at the residence of daughter Mrs. J. H. Jones, born Walker Co., GA, 1 other daughter, Mrs. E. W. Blan (sic) of Columbus.

- 1870 Chattahoochee Co., GA Census: Savannah Cobb 30 GA, Emma 12 GA, Loula 10 GA and Isaac 8 GA.

- 1860 Chattahoochee Co., GA Census: Isaac Cobb 30 GA, Savanah 20 GA, Emma 2 GA and Talula 8/12 GA.

- Marriage Record in Chattahoochee Co., GA shows Isaac H. Cobb married Savannah House 3 June 1855. Isaac H. Cobb was the s/o Seth Cobb (c1798-1852) and Martha "Patsy" Hill (c1800-1879). Seth Cobb's will is recorded in both Chattahoochee Co., GA and Muscogee Co., GA. His wife's Patsy's is in Will Book A in Chattahoochee Co., GA.

Ronald E. Jones	Feb 21, 1896	Nov 11, 1922
Adolphus Gary Jones	July 8, 1898	Dec 6, 1962
infant of Mr & Mrs. W. O. Whitaker, Jr.	Mar 11, 1927 only date	

Sexton Records indicate also buried in this lot:

Noland Jones   *SR: bur. 7/31/1898,*
                                                                18 yrs.

Lot 212, no name on wall

Mattie Evans Henry	Nov 1847	June 1903	

- 1900 Muscogee Co. Census: Martha I. Henry Jan 1845 GA GA GA, son Georgie May 1878 AL, son Bev H. June 1880 AL, dau Eula April 1883 AL, dau Jesse Aug 1885 GA and several boarders.

Beverly Marshall Henry	Mar 1845	Oct 1893	G/M C.S.A. Chapter 548 UDC

- 1880 Russell Co., AL Census: B. M. Marshall 40 GA GA GA, wife Martha 33 GA GA SC, dau Buter? 11 AL, son John 9 AL, dau Lula 6 AL and son George 2 AL.

Jesse Henry Witte	Aug 16, 1885 Columbus, GA	May 29, 1913 Georgetown, SC	
George Y. Henry	Mar 1, 1878	Dec 2, 1949	
Rosa Cobb Henry	Jan 15, 1871	Dec 2, 1945	
John Evans Henry	Dec 25, 1870	Sept 27, 1913	

Lot 213, no name on wall

Mary Effie Williams	Mar 24, 1878	Jan 24, 1965	
Ina Williams	Oct 20, 1883	Sept 26, 1948	SR: d/o Dr. C. L. & Mary L. Eavans Williams
Charles L. Williams, M.D.	Mar 26, 1844 Harris Co., GA	July 16, 1914 Columbus, GA	

- Obit: s/o Thomas A. & Mrs. Lucinda Williams, C.S.A. Co. K., 20th GA Reg., married 1st Miss Mary Evans of Russell Co., AL, 4 children, Mrs. R. L. Edmond, Misses Sallie Belle, Elle, Ina Williams, all of Columbus, GA, 2nd marriage May 1897 to a Mrs. Sarah Elizabeth Griffith of Norfolk, VA & Hamilton, GA, 2 brothers, Judge J. F. C. Williams of Harris Co., GA and Britain Williams of Columbus, GA, 2 sisters, Mrs. Lula Dozier of Morgan Co., GA and Mrs. Henry C. Cameron of Columbus, GA.

Mary Louise Evans	Feb 1, 1844 Harris Co., GA	Jan 26, 1889	w/o Charles L. Williams

- Obit: Mrs. Dr. C. L. Williams, nee Mary L. Evans, d/o late Judge John J. Evans of Russell Co., AL, sister of H. Evans of Columbus, A. Evans of Clayton, AL, Miss Eula Evans, I. C. Evans, J. L. Lewis, Mrs. E. H. Glenn, Mrs. B. M. Henry, all of Seale, AL. (Obit states that remains are to be interred in Villula, AL.)

Charles W.	Oct 14, 1872	Feb 4, 1876	s/o C. L. & M. Williams

Lot 214, H. I. Struppa on wall

Edna Crawford Struppa	Sept 23, 1898	Aug 11, 1928
James Watt Struppa	Dec 15, 1895	Dec 18, 1924

- 1900 Russell Co., AL Census: H. Struppa Jan 1870 AL AL AL, wife Alice May 1870 AL AL AL (mar. 10 yes; 4/4 children), son Dannard Jan 1891 AL, son Jack May 1895, dau Ellen May 1898 and son Randolph June 1899.

Lot 215, wrought iron fence, no name

Abner Holloway	Dec 28, 1849	Dec 11, 1851	s/o James T. and Henrietta H. Flewellen

- s/o James Thweatt Flewellen (1828-1889) and Henrietta Hargraves Fontaine (1826-1857).

Robert Hardaway	Nov 4, 1852	June 9, 1854	s/o Abner H. & Sarah E. Flewellen

- s/o Capt. Abner Holloway Flewellen (1830-1900) and Sarah Elizabeth Hardaway (1830-1899). Grandson of Maj. Robert Stanfield Hardaway (1797-1875) and Martha Bibb Jarratt (1805-1859).

- Abner and Robert Flewellen were grandsons of General William Flewellen (1787-1835) and Mary "Polly" Thweatt (1797-1834).

Henrietta Hargraves	Dec 12, 1857	30th year of age w/o James T. Flewellen, d/o John Fontaine

- d/o John Maury Fontaine (1792-1866) and Mary Stewart (c1808-1852)

Lot 216, no name on wall

Alice Goulding Crawford	Dec 26, 1896	May 8, 1921	w/o D. Stanley Parkman

- d/o Tol Y. Crawford.

George Hungerford	Jan 31, 1823 Hawington, Conn.	June 16, 1890

- Obit: born Southington, Conn., watchmaker & jeweler, married Cornelia F. Pond, d/o Dr. Asa Pond, sister of George Y. Pond, leaves wife & 4 daughters, Mrs. Tol Y. Crawford, Mrs. John H. Henderson, Mrs. John H. Johnston, all of Columbus GA, Mrs. James Coggins of Mobile, AL.

- 1850 Muscogee Census: Asa Pond 53 CT, Lucy A. 40 CT, Charles 18 GA, Henry 15 GA, Anna 13 GA, George 11 GA, Margaret 9 GA, William 3 GA, George Hungerford 27 CT, Cornelia 31 GA, Mrs. Ann Goulding 64 CT and Henrietta Goulding 20 GA.

- George Hungerford married Cornelia F. Pond 8 Nov. 1849 in Muscogee Co., GA.

George is the s/o Dana Hungerford of CT and Upson Co., GA and his wife Rachel Catlin. He was also the brother-in-law to Maj. Robert S. Hardaway's 2nd wife Mary E. Hungerford.

Cornelia Francis	Sept 26, 1829 Lexington, GA	Dec 15, 1900	w/o George Hungerford

Lot 217, no name on wall

Chapple Teasdale			C.S.A. 1861-1865
Our Mother		no name or dates	
Our Sister & precious Auntie Faithful Mary & Sarah – no dates			
H. Teasdale	Jan 1850	May 20, 1851	s/o Henry R. & Estinslade Teasdale

- 1850 Muscogee Census: Mrs. Mary M. Teasdale 55 Fl, Mary M. 30 SC, Henry R. Teasdale 28 GA, Sarah 26 GA, C. B. (m) 23 GA and boarders.
- St. John's Co., FL MR shows Henry R. Teasdale married Estanislada F. Benet 18 Dec 1848.

Lot 218, open lot

Dr. H. W. Edwards	Apr 25, 1821 Tuscsloosa, AL	Feb 10, 1882 Columbus, GA	

- 1850 Troup Co., GA Census: Hezekiah W. Edwards 29 GA and wife Ann H. 23 SC.

Ann	June 12, 1821	April 1, 1856	w/o H. W. Edwards
Edwin S.		Mar. 8, 1848 ony date	s/o H. W. & Ann H. Edwards
? ?		Dec 1847	w/o L. B. Jones
Inf			s/o H. W. & A. Edwards SR: born 3/28/1850 bur. 6/12/1850
Anna Louisa	Mar 28, 1856	Aug 20, 1856	d/o H. W. & Ann H. Edwards
Susan Wynne Dismukes	Nov 22, 1865	Oct 18, 1943	

- 1870 Muscogee Census: Thomas K. Wynn 48 NC, Mary L. 32 KY, Susan 4 GA, Ezekiah 2 GA, George Waddell 15 AL and Sallie Waddell 13 AL.
- 1880 Muscogee Census: Thomas K. Wynne 58 NC NC NC, dau Susan 14 GA, son Hezekiah E. 12 GA, son Thomas K. 10 GA, son Albert E. 6 GA, boarder Hezekiah Edwards 59 KY KY KY and niece Sallie Waddell 22 AL NC NC.

Anna Dismukes Winn	July 25, 1901	June 14, 1931	w/o Dr. John H. Winn baby buried with her.

- 1930 Muscogee Census: John H. Winn Jr. 41 Canada Canada Canada (m. @ 33), wife Ann D. 28 GA GA GA (m. @ 20), father John H. Winn 73 wd Canada Canada Canada.

William Haynes Dismukes	Nov 25, 1865	Apr 18, 1936	

- Married 1) Minnie Lu Williams (1865-1898) 23 Jul7 1887 in Troup Co., GA the d/o John M. Williams and Elizabeth Ann Moss and 2)Susan Wynne 23 Aug 1899.

Lot 219, no name on wall

Charlie Hansford	Jan 30, 1859	July 11, 1860	s/o Wm & Julia W. Andrews
Jennie Smith	May 4, 1871	May 26, 1872	d/o W. G. & Julia W. Andrews
Louise Dixon	1866 (sic)	1923	SR: bur. 12/11/1923, 35 yrs.
Sarah E. Dixon	1857	1922	SR: born 1/11/1857 bur. 12/1/1922
James T. Dixon	1882	1913	SR: bur. 5/21/1913, 30 yrs.
Julia W. Andrews		Dec 28, 1890	Our Mother, age 57 yrs.

- Obit: Died in Atlanta, widow of W. G. Andrews, 57 years old, leaves 4 daughters, Mrs. D. W. Dixon, Misses Julia, Katie & Irene, all of Columbus, GA

- Muscogee Co., GA MR William Green Andrews married Julia W. Shotwell 15 Feb 1854.

- 1850 Muscogee Census: Alexander Shotwell 46 NJ, Mrs. 46 NJ, Miss Julia 17 NJ, Jane 15, Elizabeth 22 NJ, John Wade 80 CT, Mrs. 75 CT, Elizabeth 10, Ella 3, John 1, Oliver Danforth 30 and Mrs. 24 SC. (Boarding House)

- 1860 Montgomery Co., AL Census: W. G. Andrews 34 GA, Julia W. 24 NJ, William A. 6 GA, Sarah E. 5 AL and Charles H. 1 AL.

- William Green Andrews was the s/o Samuel R. Andrews and his first wife Sally Ransom who were married 12 Jan 1821 in Hancock Co., GA.

Ellen L.	Dec 18, 1847	Oct. 14, 1877	w/o Davis A. Andrews

- Obit: d/o Jeremiah Massey

- 1850 Muscogee Census: Jeremiah Massey 37 SC, Frances 24 Hancock Co., Eleanor M. 4 Musc. Co. and William T. 2 Musc. Co. (lived next door to Eli Massey 55 SC and his family.)

Harry W. Dixon	1888	1916	SR: bur. 2/29/1916
Julia Shotwell Andrews	Aug 21, 1861	May 17, 1954	
Claude E. West	Feb 18, 1894	Feb 20, 1920	w/o Ben West
Ella Louise	June 2, 1889	Nov 5, 1894	d/o Wm H. & Mary E. West
Mary Ella West	Nov. 14, 1865	July 26, 1904	d/o Davis A. & Ellen Lenora Andrews.

Elizabeth	June 30, 1809	July 25, 1872	w/o S. R.
	Tenn.	Columbus, GA	Mother

- Obit: former Elizabeth Day, came to Columbus 22 Feb 1827, married in 1828 to Samuel R. Andrews.

- Elizabeth Day was born in Rhea Co., TN, d/o Jesse Day (1771-1835) and Hannah Howard (1774-1824). Several of Elizabeth's siblings came to Muscogee and Russell Cos. as well.

Davis A. Andrews	Jan 19, 1844	Dec 4, 1921

- Obit: born Columbus, GA, Muscogee Tax Collector 28 yrs, 1 brother, J. C. Andrews of Acadia, LA, 1 son Tom Andrews, 2 g/ch, 2 g/g/ch.

George E. Andrews	July 10, 1846	April 12, 1882

- Obit: leaves wife & child, 2 sisters, 2 beothers, Mrs. Cal Ragland, Mrs. S. E. Massey, Davis & J. C. Andrews.

S. R. Andrews, Jr.		no dates	Father

- Obit: Judge, one of Columbus' early settlers, Treasurer for Columbus, Alderman, Justice of Inferior Ct.

- Columbus Enquirer 4 Apr 1862. Death of Judge Andrews. It is with sorrow that we perform the duty of announcing the death, at his plantation near this city, of Judge Samuel R. Andrews, in the 68th year of his age. Judge Andrews was one of the early settlers of Columbus, and always enjoyed the confidence and esteem of the people of this city, and county, by whom important public trusts were at various times committed to his hands. As a public officer and as a private citizen, he ever "acted well his part," leaving behind him an honourable name and a memory long to be cherished and respected. A good man has gone to his rest, leaving a bright and unsullied record behind him.

- 1850 Muscogee Census: Samuel R. Andrews, 54, NC, Elizabeth 40 TN, James 21 GA, Amanda 17 GA, Mary 14 GA, Samuel R. Jr., 13 GA, Julius C. 11 GA, Susan 10 GA, Joseph 7 GA, Davis A. 6 GA, George 4 GA and Clarance 1 GA.

Lot 220, J. T. Johnson on wall

J. T. Johnson	Dec 30, 1862	Sept 21, 1915	Gen. Superintendent
	Caroline Co., VA	Savannah, GA	Central of GA Ry. Co.

- 1910 Chatham Co., GA Census: John T. Johnson 47 VA VA VA, wife Vetelin? 47 VA VA VA (married 24 yrs; 4/2 children), son Thomas M. 8 GA, son Henry 6 GA and nurse Mary E. Simpson 27 SC SC SC.

Elizabeth Mountcastle	Jan 27, 1863	Dec 17, 1927	w/o J. T. Johnson
Johnson	New Kent Co., VA	Orchard Hill, GA	

- 1920 Muscogee Census:.Elizabeth M. Johnson 56 (wd) VA VA VA, son Thomas M. 18 GA and son Henry B. 15 GA.

2 headstones Mary & Edgar, no other data.

Lot 221, open lot

William E.	June 16, 1877	Sept 12, 1878	s/o Mr. & Mrs. W. S. Williams
1 brick adult slab, n/m	1 adult slab, n/m		

Lot 222, no name on wall

Bessie Mary Smith	July 26, 1903	Aug 9, 1948	w/o Col. James Palmer Blakeney U.S. Army.
Gurney B. Smith	Mar 26, 1877	June 2, 1940	

- 1920 Russell Co., AL Census: Gurney Smith 42 AL AL AL, wife Mamie 36 GA GA GA, dau Elsie 19 AL, dau Bessie Mary 6 AL and son Leonard 21 AL.

- 1880 Russell Co., AL Census: Reuben Smith 52 GA NC VA, wife Penelope E. 30 AL GA GA, son Nicola A. 21 AL , dau Corell 9 AL, dau Estelle 7 AL, dau Peal E. 5 AL and son Gurney B. 3 AL.

Elizabeth Leonard	Aug 2, 1861	Oct 7, 1924	w/o Theodore E. Golden

- d/o James M. Leonard and Susie Carter. Elizabeth Antionette was born in Talbot Co., GA.

Theodore E. Golden	Nov 1, 1859	Oct 8, 1937	

- 1920 Muscogee Census: Theodore E. Golden 59 AL NC NC wife Lizzie 55 GA GA GA, dau Susie 30 AL, dau Melissa 28 AL, son Theodore Jr. 26 AL and son William P. 23 AL.

- 1880 Russell Co., AL Census: Geo J. Golden 47 SC MD SC, son Porter 23 AL, son Theodore 21 GA, son George R. 16 AL, dau Winney L. 14 AL, son Cecil S. 3 Al and other Jane Short 55 GA NC SC.

- 1870 Russell Co., AL Census: Geo Golden 37 SC, Sarah 36 GA, Parthena 12 GA, Theodore 10 AL, Robert 7 AL and Winnie 5 AL.

- Theodore was the s/o George Jasper Golden (1833-1880) and his wife Sarah Caroline Poitevent (c1834-1876) who were married 9 Dec 1852 in Russell Co., AL.

William Swift Golden	Apr 17, 1896	Sept 26, 1971	s/o Theo E. & Elizabeth Golden

Lot 223, Elledge on wall

Andrew M. Elledge	July 2, 1850 Laurens Co., SC	June 7, 1903 Columbus, GA

- Obit: Capt. Andrew Madison Elledge, b. Laurens Co., SC, s/o Joshua & Elizabeth, brothers & sisters Robert J. Elledge of SC, F. M. Elledge of SC, Mrs. Burgess of Piedmont, SC, 1 dght. Mrs. J. T. Norman.
- 1900 Muscogee Census: A. M. Elledge July 1850 SC SC SC, wife Mollie Apr 1845 GA GA GA (married 27 yrs; 1/1child), SIL John T. Norman Oct 1864 GA GA GA and stepdau Honor July 1865 AL GA GA

Mary A. Elledge   April 21, 1845   Oct 15, 1911

- Obit: died at residence of daughter, Mrs. John T. Norman, widow of A. M. Elledge who died 8 years ago, 2 sisters Mrs. A. B. Reid and Mrs. C. P. Vaugh, both of FL, member D.A.R and U.D.C.

Lot 224, open lot

no evidence of graves

Lot 225, no name on wall

John Landon Jordan   June 30, 1846   Jan 26, 1887

- 1880 Muscogee Census: John L. Jordon 35 FL FL VA.

1 adult brick slab, n/m

Lot 226, no name on wall

Madie P.	Sept 16, 1899	May 10, 1915	d/o W. L. & Minnie Gilbert
Walter Lee Gilbert	Mar 28, 1878	Sept 26, 1925	

Lot 227, J. A. Matthews on wall

Ben Frank Billings, Sr.	July 23, 1863	June 24, 1931	Father

- 1930 Muscogee Census: Ben F. Billings 66 AL GA SC (m@27), wife Minnie L. 59 GA GA GA (m@20)
- 1910 Muscogee Census: Benjamin F. Billings 46 AL GA GA, wife Minnie L. 26 GA GA GA (married 19 yrs, 3/3 children), dau Louise 17 GA, son Benjamin F. 13 GA, dau Mary F. 11 GA and father John D. 78 (wd) GA MA GA.

Minnie Matthews Billings	Oct 22, 1872	Oct 23, 1936	Mother
T. L. Matthews	June 6, 1834	Apr 23, 1891	

- Obit: died of malarial fever, born in Talbot Co., GA, leaves 2 brothers & 1 sister.

Matilda Jones	1805 Jasper Co., GA	Jan 29, 1882 Columbus, GA	First married Thomas Matthews of Pike Co., GA, 1824, 2nd to Clemons Wynn of Talbot Co., GA 1843

- 1850 Talbot Co., GA Census: Clements Wynn 58 GA, Matilda 44 GA, Clements 17 GA, Emelia 10 GA, Mary 7 GA, Frances 6 GA, Rebecca 5 GA, Stephen 3 GA and Seaborn 1 GA. Next door is Josiah Matthews 19 GA and Thomas Matthews 17 GA.

Mother		no other data	
Eldorah C. Matthews	Sept 3, 1878	Oct. 16, 1880	
J. A. Matthews	Mar 19, 1827 Upson Co., GA	May 15, 1883 Columbus, GA	

- Obit: born in Upson Co., GA, in Columbus 1 year from Stewart Co., GA, brother Judge J. M. Matthews, Talbotten, GA, J. L. Matthews of Pineville, wife & 4 children.

- 1880 Muscogee Census: James Matthews 51 GA GA GA, wife Amanda 30 GA GA GA, son Willie 10 GA, dau Minnie 8 GA, dau Mattie 4 GA, dau Dora 2 GA, mother Matilda Wynn 70 GA GA GA and niece Rebecca 24 GA GA GA

- 1850 Talbot Co., GA Census: Josiah Mathews 63 NC, Jane 34 SC, Thomas 27 GA, James 24 GA, Oliver 19 GA and Manve? 16 GA.

Lot 228, fence on 3 sides, no name

John C. Leitner	Aug 8, 1812	Apr 17, 1851

- Obit: Agent for Brunswick Bank of Augusta, GA.

- 1850 Muscogee Census: John C. Leitner 35 GA and Mrs. L. E. 24 GA.

Lot 229, Johnson on wall

Robert Lee Johnson	Dec 12, 1899	Mar 21, 1987	G/M LCDR U.S. Navy WWII
Campbell Johnson	Aug 18, 1921	Nov 28, 1984	G/M Cpl. U.S. Marine Cor. WWII
Robert Lee	July 21, 1931	July 22, 1931	s/o Sarah & Campbell Johnson
Sarah Redd	Sept 30, 1895	June 12, 1961	w/o Campbell Jackson Johnson

Lot 230, Baird on wall

John Baird	Mar. 6, 1835 Cumberland, Scotland	Mar. 9, 1889 Brownsville, AL

- Obit: leaves wife & 7 children, 54 years old.

- 1880 Brownville, Lee Co., AL Census: John Baird 45 Scotland Scotland Scotland, wife Isabella M. 35 AL AL Scotland, dau Jennie 16 AL, son Hugh 11 AL, dau Isabella 6 AL and son John 2 AL.

Mary Ann Thompson	1825	1897	w/o Wm. J. Ingersoll
			SR: bur. 3/7/1897

- 1860 Russell Co., AL Census: Stephen M. Ingersoll 66 NY, Mary A. 36 Scotland, Isabella 16 AL, Stephen M. 14 AL, William J. 12 AL, Josephine 9 AL and Isaac J. Cowl? 40 NY.

Forest Kinnett Baird	Mar. 8, 1914	Nov. 17, 1936	
Isabella Maria Baird	Feb. 10, 1845	June 6, 1904	w/o John Baird
	Russell Co., AL	Phenix City, AL	

- d/o Dr. William J. Ingersoll and Mary Ann Thompson.

Julienne L. Baird	Apr. 19, (no year)	May 20, 1961
Isabella Baird	Aug. 31, 1873	Nov. 30, 1958
S.M. Ingersoll, M.D.	Mar. 15, 1792	June 5, 1872
	Duchess Co., NY	Brownsville, AL

- Obit: resident for 40 plus years, it is said that Morse obtained his first idea of the magnetic telegraph from him while traveling in a stagecoach in Lee Co., AL helped to establish a ferry across the river in 1831

- 1850 Russell Co., AL Census: Stephen M. Ingersoll 50 VA.

- 1860 Russell Co., AL Census: Stephen M. Ingersoll 66 NY, Mary A. 36 Scotland, Isabella 16 AL, Stephen M. 14 AL, William J. 12 AL, Josephine 9 AL and Isaac J. Cowl? 40 NY.

- Atlanta Constitution Dec. 12, 1900: *Did Dr. Ingersoll Invent the Telegraph? Columbus Traditions Says He Did.* This is a wonderful article on Dr. Samuel Ingersoll which lays great credence to the fact that he may have originally given Morse the idea for the telegraph. It also speaks of Dr. Ingersoll's being the first man to erect a mill at this point of the Chattahooshee and of his great friendship with Chief McIntosh, the Great Indian Chief. They must have been very good friends as Dr. Ingersoll purchased over 6,000 acres, comprising most of what was Phenix City and Girard, for $1.50. In 1836, Dr. Ingersoll was asked by the government and did travel with the Indians on the Trail of Tears as far as New Orleans. In those days, Dr. Ingersoll was a very wealthy man and was carrying a large sum of money with him. A pickpocket in New Orleans stole $50,000 from him. Dr. Ingersoll was from a very distinguished family. He had a cousin that was a Congressman and was also a cousin to Robert G. Ingersoll, the famous thinker and philosopher. History may give the credit of the telegraph to Morse, but local tradition gives it to Dr. Stephen Miles Ingersoll. This article also gives his death as the 5th of March 1872, 10 days from his eightieth birthday.

- Now for the rest of the story...... Across the river from Dr. Stephen Miles Ingersoll was the home of his friend, Daniel Griffin. Together they flew kites and investigated the weather. Dr. Ingersoll was fascinated with electricity and had numerous inventions at his home. Griffin had acquired his fortune as President and owner of a large line of stages that ran from Milledgeville, then capital of Georgia, to Montgomery, the new capital of Alabama. His home was a great place of beauty to please his wife. As a man of importance, he entertained numerous influential and distinguished guest, of whom one was Dr. Samuel Morse, a professor at New York University. Older Columbus citizens remember that after the telegraph had been developed and generally credited to Morse, a newspaper article appeared in a northern paper where Morse admitted that the germ of his idea came from a doctor down in Georgia. When told of the article, it is said that Dr. Ingersoll became quite angry.

William J. Ingersoll, M.D.		Aug. 30, 1851	age 30 years
John Stephen Baird	Dec. 23, 1877	Mar. 31, 1935	
Frank Power Baird	Feb. 7, 1905	Mar. 9, 1907	

Lot 231, open lot

1 adult brick slab, n/m

Lot 232, open lot

Leroy Jenkins	Nov. 2, 186?	Mar. 21, 186?	s/o ? & Mary Jenkins

small baby marker, flat & partially covered

Lot 233, no name on wall

Charlie Edom Cole	Aug. 27, 1857	Jan. 31, 1919	one slab
Martha McCall Cook	Sept. 19, 1871 Greenville, AL	July 5, 1964	Martha McCall Cook w/o Charlie Edom Cole
Burrel Cook	Nov. 11, 1894	Dec. 23, 1963	
Berta Thomas Cole	Aug. 29, 1892	Feb. 29, 1980	
Mary Phillips Riley	Jan. 19, 1901	Apr. 18, 1929	w/o Geo H. Cole
Charles Edom Cole, Jr.	Nov. 11, 1896	Aug. 20, 1980	G/M YI, U.S. Navy 1896-1980

Lot 234, no name on wall

Lillian D. Hindsman	Feb. 19, 1871	Dec. 13, 1966	
W.P. Hindsman	Feb. 17, 1869	May 23, 1914	
Maria Louise Mariner	Dec. 19, 1849	Apr. 10, 1850	d/o Abner S. & Avarilla Mariner

- 1850 Muscogee Census: Abner S. Marriner 43 Maine, Mrs. A. J. 32 GA, William Owens 13 GA, M. M. Owens (female) 10 GA and Mary E. Owens 3 GA.
- Avarilla Cox was born 29 May 1819 in Jones Co., Georgia. Avarilla married 1) Robert Owens 22 Nov 1835 in Muscogee Co., GA. After his death, Avarilla married Abner S. Marinerr 25 Feb. 1849.
- In 1860 the Mariner family can be found in Cherokee Co., TX with 2 children.

Lot 235, open lot

Hariet Clara Matilda Hamill	Nov. 30, 1833	July 22, 1851	only c/o A. & Maria Hamill
Wm. ? Hamill (unable to read)			

Lot 236, no name on wall

Clara Torrance	unable to read

- 1850 Muscogee Census: Mrs. Clara Torrance 42 SC and Matilda Torrance 40 SC.
- Clara and Matilda were the daughters of Andrew N. Torrance of Scotland and Hester Howard, the d/o Nehemiah Howard and Edith Smith.
- Elbert Co., GA WB B page 34. Nehemiah Howard, 3/17/1796: Codicil 1/4/1798 proven 4/1/1798. Sons: Archer, James, Joseph, Neniah, Merle, Benjamin (land in Pendleton Co., S. C.) Friend: Elijah Owens. Daus: Sarah Putnam, Hester Torrence, Nancy Owens, Mary Woodward. Son-in-law: Elisha Owens. Exrs: Benjamin Howard, son, and son-in-law, Elisha Owens. Tests: Ralph Owens, Moses Haynes.

1 child brick slab, n/m

Lot 237, W.M. Becker on wall

William M. Becker	Oct. 29, 1869	Jan. 15, 1927	

- 1920 Muscogee Census: William M. Becker 47 AL Ger Ger, and wife Alice 36 AL AL AL.

Capt. John W. Hingle	1881	1957	SR: bur. 12/16/1957, 76 yrs
Alice Becker Myrick	Jan. 5, 1883	Nov. 17, 1946	
Emma Kate Fuller	1884	1947	w/o Capt. John W. Hingle SR: born 11/11/1884 bur. 10/30/1947, 62 yrs.

Lot 238, no name on wall

Dessie Mae	Aug. 1, 1893	Dec. 11, 1918	w/o D.V. Tippins

Lot 239, Johnson on wall & J.W. Dortch on other wall

Johnathan Niles	Apr. 11, 1776	Oct. 15, 1846

- Obit: born in Providence, RI.

- 1840 Russell Co., AL Census: Jonathan Niles 2 males 15-20, 1 male 40-50, 1 male 60-70 and 1 female 40-50.

- Jonathan Niles born 11 April 1776, the s/o Jonathan Niles and Avis Niles.[42] Marriage record in Warwick, Kent Co., RI shows Jonathan Niles marrying Avis Rice 23 Feb 1764,

John W. Dortch   Nov. 25, 1855   Jan. 5, 1940

- 1920 Muscogee Census: J. W. Dortch 65 GA GA GA and Sara 68 GA GA GA.

- 1900 Muscogee Census: Jack Dorch Nov. 1853 GA GA GA and wife Sarah Jan 1850 GA GA GA married 13 years no children.

- 1860 Washington Co., GA Census: Walter Dortch 44 GA, Elizabeth A. 33 GA, Andrew 15 GA, Walter W. 13 GA, David W. 6 GA, John W. 4 GA and Mary Jane Hanies 18 GA.

Sarah W. Johnson   Jan. 23, 1845   Oct. 28, 1929   w/o John W. Dortch

- Obit: 1 brother, J.E. Johnson of Columbus, nieces & nephews, w/o J.W. Dortch, Coroner.

- 1860 Muscogee Census: Wm Johnson 45 GA, Louisa M. 45 GA, Theo? P. 21 GA, Jacob 19 GA, Sarah 17 GA, Rebecca 14 GA, Wm R.? 11 GA and John 4 GA.

- 1850 Muscogee Census: William G. Johnson 35 Greene Co., GA, Louisa 34 Greene Co., GA, Thomas P. 10 Muscogee, Jacob 9 Muscogee, Sarah J. 7 Muscogee, Amelia R. 5 Muscogee and Robert 2 Muscogee.

Inf. s/o Nathaniel B. &   Oct. 24, 1848   Aug. 12, 1849
Mary B. Love

- 1850 Muscogee Census: N. B. (male) Love 43 RI, Mary B. 39 RI, Joseph H. 7/12 GA, Mrs. Susan Niles 69 RI and Job T. Niles 49 RI.

John E. Johnson   Dec. 18, 1856   Mar. 28, 1936

Annie Leah Jones   Feb. 28, 1875   Apr. 15, 1900

Lot 240, no name on wall

William Ligon   May 3, 1792   Feb. 1, 1860

- 1850 Muscogee Census: William Liggon 57 VA, Elizabeth H. 56 SC, Timothy Markham 21 CT, and Nancy Markham 21 GA,

Timothy Markham   Nov. 25, 1826   June 16, 1886   father

- Obit: native of CT, Treasurer for Muscogee Co., GA for 14 years till death, sons Charlie & Woodsie Markham.

- 1870 Muscogee Census: Timothy Markham 43 CT, Nancy 42 GA, Charlie 18 GA and Woodson 16 GA.

- 1880 Muscogee Census: Timothy Markham 58 CT CT Ct and wife Nancy 50 GA GA GA.

Elizabeth H. Ligon   June 14, 1793   July 29, 1863   w/o William Ligon

Nancy A. Markham   Jan. 31, 1827   May 3, 1886   w/o Timothy Markham mother

- Obit: born Henry Co., GA, married Tim Markham 36 years ago, leaves husband, 2 sons, C.H. & Woodsie Markham.

- Nancy Ligon and Timothy Markham married 1 May 1850 in Muscogee Co., GA.

3 adult brick slabs, n/m   1 baby brick slab, n/m

Lot 241, Benning on wall

| Seaborn Jones | Feb. 1, 1788 | Mar. 18, 1864 | d/o Abraham & Sarah Jones |

- Obit: Colonel, b. GA, moved from Milledgville, GA, elected to Congress 1833 & 1844.

- Seaborn is the son of Lt. Abraham Jones, Jr. (c1752 Prince George Co., VA – May 1811 Montgomery Co., GA) and his first wife Sarah Bugg (born ca 1763Lunenburg Co., VA the d/o Sherwood Bugg and Elizabeth Hobson).[43]

- Southern Recorder XI page 215 Mar 22,1864. Died Col. Seaborn Jones, formerly of Milledgeville and well known throughout the country, died in Columbus on Friday last, aged 78. He has filled many prominent positions, besides at one time a member of congress.

| Henry L. Benning | Apr. 2, 1814 | July 10, 1875 | s/o Pleasant M. & Malinda L. Benning. Maj. Gen. C.S.A. "Old Rock" |

- Obit: born Columbia Co., GA 12 Sept. 1839, married Mary H. Jones, d/o Col. Seaborn Jones of Columbus, GA, his son Capt. S.J. Benning was buried a few months ago, he leaves 3 single dghts & Mrs. Reece Crawford, Mrs. S. Spencer, 1 brother in Harris Co., GA, 1 brother-in-law H.L. Patterson of Russell Co., AL.

- Henry Lewis Benning was the s/o Pleasant Moon Benning (1783-1845) and Malinda Lewis White.[44]

- 1850 Muscogee Census: Henry L. Benning 36 Columbia Co., Mary H. 53 Baldwin Co., Seaborn J. 10 Muscogee Co., Mary H. 8 Muscogee Co., Caroline M. 4 Muscogee Co., Anna M. 3 Muscogee Co., Augusta J. and Louisa V. (twins) 2 Muscogee Co.

| Hazel Hull Hubbell | Nov. 13, 1889 | May 2, 1975 | d/o Herbert Ladson Hull & Sallie Benning |

- Obit: born Eufaula, AL, d/o Herbert & Sally Benning Hull, Sr., g/dght of late Maj. Gen. Henry L. Benning.

| Anna Caroline Benning | June 22, 1853 | Feb. 8, 1935 | d/o Henry Lewis Benning C.S.A. & Mary Howard Jones "Mother of Patriotic Organizations" |

| Mary Howard Jones | Jan. 13, 1788 | Feb. 4. 1869 | d/o John & Jane Howard w/o Seaborn Jones |

- Southern Christian Advocate 16 April 1869. Memorial of Mrs. Mary Jones. She was born in Sandersville, Ga., Jan. 13, 1788, and died in Columbus, Ga., Feb. 5, 1869, aged 81 years. Her maiden name was Howard. She came to this city with her husband Col. Seaborn Jones, in 1828. A. M. Wynn, Pastor.

- Mary Howard married Seaborn Jones 19 May 1813 in Baldwin Co., GA.Mary was the d/o John Howard (1761-1822) and Jane Vivian (1770-1837).

Seaborn Jones	July 8, 1840	Dec. 12, 1874	s/o Henry L. & Mary H. Benning, Capt. C.S.A.
Lucius Chappell Hull	Dec. 23, 1887	May 30, 1889	s/o Herbert L. Hull & Sallie Benning
Mary Howard Benning	Mar. 18, 1817	June 28, 1868	d/o Seaborn & Mary Jones w/o Henry L. Benning
Sallie Benning	Jan. 17, 1855	May 16, 1949	w/o Herbert Ladson Hull d/o Henry Lewis Benning & Mary Howard Jones
Mary Howard Benning	Nov. 23, 1841	Feb. 5, 1927	d/o Brg. Gen Henry Lewis Benning &C.S.A. & Mary Howard Jones "Ladies Memorial Association" 1866 U.D.C., 1896

- Obit: oldest d/o Gen. Henry L. Benning, born Columbus at St. Elmo, 3 sisters, Miss Anna Caroline Benning, Mrs. Reese Crawford, both of Columbus, GA, Mrs. H.L. Hull of Ft. Worth, TX member U.D.C., D.A.R., The Colonial Dames.

Lot 242, no name on wall

Sarah Mitchell		Oct. 1, 1914
Rochelle Martinier	Jan. 18, 1881	Dec. 25, 1962
Wm. Ashe Martinier	Apr. 23, 1842	Feb. 1, 1895

- 1850 Macon Co., AL Census: T. V. Rutherford 34 GA, Louisa E. 27 VA, Robert 8 GA, Hubbard 7 GA, Vivian 1/12 AL, William Martinere 7 AL and James W. Black 22.

- 1860 Macon Co., AL Census: T. V. Rutherford 43 GA, Mrs. Louisa 38 VA, Robert M. 19 GA, Ben H. 17 GA, Wm A Martinear 18 AL, Vivian A. Rutherford 9 AL and Eugenia H. 7 AL.

- 1880 Muscogee Census: Parissa J. Mitchell 80 VA? VA VA Mother, dau Sarah 50 GA NC VA, Adline 46 GA; boarders: Wm. Martinier 38 AL AL AL, Rochell 34 AL AL AL, Eugene 6 GA, Adele 4 GA and Wm 1 GA.

- GA Death Index shows Mrs. Rochelle Martiniere dies in Muscogee Co. 10 April 1922.

- 1920 Muscogee Census: Rochelle Martiniere 74 wd AL AL AL, dau Rochelle 38 GA AL AL and son Nicholas 34 GA AL AL.

- 1900 Muscogee Census: Rochelle Martinere Feb 1858 wd AL AL AL, son Eugene Sept? 1878 AL AL AL and son Nicholas Feb 1880 AL AL AL.

| Frances Eliza Rutherford | Aug. 16, 1846 | | consort of T. Rutherford d/o Isaac & Parizde Mitchell 26 yrs 5 mo 22 dys inf./d buried w/her |

- Obit: w/o T.V. Rutherford of Macon Co., AL, d/o Isaac & Parizade Mitchell, married Mar. 6, 1839 in Muscogee Co., GA.

| Janie Martinier | | | 4 years old SR: bur. 4/6/1875 |

| Adelaide Mitchell | June 17, 1916 | | |

- Obit: last survivor of a large & prominent family, born in Columbus, GA, school teacher, d/o late Isaac & Elizade (sic) Mitchell, sister, Mrs. Sallie Mitchell.

- 1850 Muscogee Census: Isaac Mitchell 56 NC, Parizade 48 GA, Sarah A. 22, Adeline 17 GA, John J. 15 GA, Caroline 7 GA.

- 1880 Muscogee Census: Parissa J. Mitchell 80 VA? VA VA Mother, dau Sarah 50 GA NC VA, Adline 46 GA; boarders: Wm. Martinier 38 AL AL AL, Rochell 34 AL AL AL, Eugene 6 GA, Adele 4 GA and Wm 1 GA.

| Nicholas G. Martinier | Mar. 12, 1885 | Jan. 18, 1964 | |

Lot 243, open area

| Virginia E. Green | 1854 | 1944 | SR:bur. 9/10/1944 |
| Eugene Rogers | Feb. 1824 Apalochie, FL | Jan. 5, 1867 Columbus, GA | |

2 adult brick slabs together

Lot 244, open lot

| Victoria R. Haynes | Aug. 16, 1839 Columbus, GA | Nov. 16, 1878? | d/o R.E. & Elizabeth Brounax w/o L.W. Haynes |

Lot 245, no name on wall

| Frances Love | | Mar. 1852 | age 76. SR:bur.5/29/1853 |

- Obit: widow of John Love, formerly of Greene Co., GA, died at residence of Isaac Mitchell. NOTE: Sexton record is in error, newspaper obit shows she died in 1852.

- Parizade Love married Isaac Mitchell 19 Jan 1819 in Greene Co., GA.

| John Love | | | C.S.A. 1861-1865 |

Lot 246, partial fence, no name

Rosaline F. Klinkerfuss   June 21, 1828   June 5, 1884

- Obit: leaves husband.

Louis Gutowsky   Feb. 17, 1825   Nov. 14, 1873

- Obit: native of Poland who arrived in Columbus 1852, jeweler by trade.

- 1870 Muscogee Census: Louis Gutowsky 45 ~~Switzerland~~ Poland, Rosaline 42 Switzerland.

Lot 247, wrought iron fence, no name

Name	Birth	Death	Notes
Robert (no last name)		Apr. 9, 1874?	age 11 yrs 5 days
Emma Terry Pollard	Jan. 28, 1855 Georgetown, GA	Nov. 24, 1917 Atlanta, GA	one slab also her daughter Gertrude
Gertrude Pollard	1882	1977	SR: Gertrude bur. 7/22/1977

- 1870 Muscogee Census: Carlisle Terry 44 CT, Elizabeth 42 GA, Carlisle 19 GA, Emma G. 15 GA and Charlie 12 GA.

- Carlisle Terry married Eliza G. Goulding 3 Dec 1846 in Muscogee Co., GA.

Name	Birth	Death	Notes
Henrietta H. Goulding	Oct. 14, 1829	May 26, 1852	d/o Rev. Thomas & Anne Goulding
Annie H. Goulding	Aug. 16, 1786	1878	w/o Thos Goulding, D.D. Our Mother

- Obit: died Maysville, Sumpter Co., SC, w/o Rev. Thos. Goulding, nee Ann H. Holbrook of CT, moved to Columbus 1838, children, Mrs. Reid, Maysville, SC, Rev. F.R. Goulding, Roswell, GA, Mrs. Terry & Mrs. Pond, both of Columbus, 91 yrs old.

- Muscogee Co., GA WB A P. 96-97. Thomas Goulding. 22 Jan 1847/2 July 1848. Legatees: wife Ann Holbrook Goulding; sons Francis R., Thomas B. Edwin R. and John C.; daus. Henrietta, Margaret Reid (w/o Wm. M. Reid), Elizabeth Terry (w/o T. C. Terry), Lucy Pond (w/o A. Pond) and Charlotte McMurray (w/o Francis McMurray). Extrs. ASll sons, A. Pond, Francis McMurray, William Reid & T. C. Terry. Wit: John Johnson, Calvin Stratton & John Bedsoe.

Name	Birth	Death	Notes
William E. Pond	Dec. 29, 1846	Aug. 9, 1885	one slab also our Sister
Anna Elizabeth Pond		no dates	SR: Anna bur. 2/13/1914

- Obit: g/dght of late Dr. Thomas Goulding, died at res. of niece Mrs. Tol G.Crawford sister of late Geo Y. Pond.

Ann Bellinger Goulding   Oct. 8, 1808   Aug. 3, 1891

- Obit: died in Rome, GA, relict of Thomas B. Goulding, aunt of Geo Y. Pond, Miss Pond & Mrs. John H. Henderson.

Dr. Asa Pond   Feb. 13, 1797   Dec. 13, 1882   our father

- Obit: had a large family, dght, Mrs. Geo Hungerford, Geo & W.E. Pond, Rev. Thos Pond, of Albany, GA, 2 unmarried daughters.

- 1830 listed in Oglethorpe Co., GA Census.   1840 in Muscogee Co., GA Census.

- 1850 Muscogee Co. Census: Asa Pond 53 CT, Lucy A. 40 CT, Charles 18 GA, Henry 15 GA, Ann 13 GA, George 11 GA, Margaret 9 GA and William Pond 3 GA. Also in household: George Hungerford 27 CT, Cornelia Hungerford 31 GA, Mrs. Ann Goulding 64 CT and Henrietta Goulding 20 GA,

- 1870 Muscogee Census: William P. Bevis 30 AL, Mary E. 24 AL, Asa Pond 72 Conn, Lucy 62 Conn, Ann E. 27 GA, George 29, GA and William A. 23 GA.

Charles Edw. Terry   Oct. 12, 1857   Oct. 23, 1873

Carlisle Terry   June 3, 1851   Mar. 10, 1887

Edw. Wadsworth Terry   Aug. 22, 1847   Aug. 22, 1868

- Obit: died at residence of Judge John H. Henderson.

George Y. Pond   June 22, 1840   Feb. 1, 1897

Thomas Baxter Goulding   Sept. 27, 1818   Jan. 20, 1884

- Obit: d. in Atlanta, GA, only member of the family now living is Mrs. Dr. Carlisle Terry of Columbus, GA, Mrs. Margaret Redd of Sumter Dist., SC, brother of Frances R. Goulding, the late Mrs. Asa Pond was his sister.

- Marriage License Mobile Co., AL: Thomas B. Goulding & Eloise Cuthbert 11/23/1848. Return of license not properly recorded.

Eloise Cuthbert Goulding   Mar. 22, 1821   June 11, 1849

- Obit: w/o Thomas B. Goulding, d/o John A. & Louise Cuthbert of Mobile, AL

- Muscogee County, GA deaths: Mrs. Eloise w/o Thomas P. Goulding 7/11/1849 (sic).

Ira Lewis Pollard   Sept. 21, 1845   June 2, 1918
                        King William Co.,
                            VA

Lucy Ann Goulding   Sept. 14, 1807   Mar. 1, 1882 | Our Mother

Charlotte M. Pond   no dates | one slab

                                                     | Our Sister

- Obit: Lucy Ann Goulding is w/o Dr. Asa Pond, 75th year, d/o Rev. Thomas R. Goulding, mother of Rev. Thomas Pond of Albany, GA, Geo Y. Pond, Wm. Pond, Mrs. Geo Hungerford, Misses Callie & Annie Pond.

- Oglethorpe Co., GA Lucy Ann Goulding married Asa Pond 4/13/1826.[45]

- 1860 Muscogee Census: Mrs. Ann Goulding 73 CT.

- Obit: Charlotte Pond died at residence of Judge John H. Henderson. SR: Charlotte bur. 4/27/1905, 73 yrs.

Quentin Carlisle Terry   Jan. 16, 1825   May 6, 1893   one slab

Elizabeth Goulding   Feb. 16, 1827   Aug. 8, 1908   and his wife
                          Lexington, GA

- Obit: Q.C. Terry -doctor, b. Hartford, CT, in Columbus, GA 1844, lived awhile in Georgetown, GA & Eufaula, AL, daughter is wife of I.L. Pollard.

- Obit: Elizabeth Goulding – w/o late Dr. Carlisle Terry, born Lexington, GA, d/o Dr. Thomas Goulding, 1 daughter, Mrs. I.L. Pollard of Atlanta, GA, 1 g/dgh, Miss Gertrude Pollard.

- 1870 Muscogee Census: Carlisle Terry 44 physician Conn, Elizabeth G. 42 GA, Carlisle 19 GA, Emma G. 15 GA and Charlie 12 GA.

- Muscogee Co., GA Marriage Licenses: Eliza Ann Goulding & Carlisle Terry 12/3/1846.

1 baby granite marker "A.T."	no dates	

Lot 248, no name

Florence Maria Johnston	Nov. 1, 1882	Apr. 14, 1979	
Capt. W.E. Cropp			Co. A C.S.A. 1861-1865

- William E. Cropp born ca 1830 and died 15 June 1864. He was a Capt. In Co. B 1 Florida Infantry.

Henry Matthews	SR: b.1802 Reading, Berkshire, England	Aug. 6, 1847	for the last 13 yrs lived Columbus age 45 yr 20 dy
John Reid Brown	Feb. 11, 1847 Wynnton, GA	Nov. 25, 1884 Columbus, GA	

- Obit: born Columbus, GA, leaves wife, no children, brother of Charles F. Brown, Mrs. Giles T. Williams, Mary & Ella Brown, all of Columbus, GA, William A. Brown of Louisville, R. L. Brown of AL.

- 1860 Muscogee Census: Wm B. Brown 60 NY, Mary J. 23 GA, Mariah A. 21 GA, William A. 19 GA, Anna A. 17 GA, Charles F. 15 GA, John R. 13 GA and Ella V. 11 GA.

- 1850 Muscogee Census: William Brown 51 NY, Mariah 28 SC, Mary J. 13 Cols GA, Antoinett 11 Cols GA, William 10 Cols GA, Anna A 8 Cols GA, Charles 6 Cols GA, John 4 Cols GA and Ella 2 Cols GA.

- William A. Brown married Martha E. Low 16 Oct 1838 in Muscogee Co., GA.

James Deveaux Johnston	Dec. 8, 1851	Jan. 12, 1883
Lemuel P. Warner	July 24, 1814	Aug. 23, 1899

- Obit: died at summer cottage at Clapp's Factory, born Uticia, N.Y., in Columbus 1835, married Charlotte F. Matthews in 1853, who survivies him, 3 children, H.H., F.H., Mrs. Nellie D. Johnson.

- 1860 Muscogee Census: L. P. Warner 40 NY, Charlott F. 22 GA, Frederick 6 GA and Ella D. 2 GA.

F.B.W.		no dates	child
Mary Branell		May 11, 1856	w/o Fraser Warner
Ann Cropp	June 23, 1797	May 19, 1885	w/o Henry Matthews

- 1850 Muscogee Census: Mrs. Ann Mathews 52 England, Elizabeth A. 25 England, Harriett A. 22 England, Allen I. 20 NY, Savannah G. 18 GA, Charlott F. 16 FL, William D. 12 GA and Frederick R. 10 GA.

Nannie Morgan Getzer	July 21, 1875	Sept. 8, 1908	w/o Frank H. Warner
Frederic B. Warner	Oct. 18, 1893	Apr. 23, 1983	
Sallie C. Warner	May 25, 1888	July 21, 1976	
Charlotte F. Warner	Jan 27, 1834	Nov. 14, 1917	w/o Lemuel P. Warner

- Obit:widow of late Lemuel P. Warner. born Florida, 1 dght, Mrs. Nellie D. Johnston, 2 sons, H.H. of Columbus, GA, F.H. Warner of Columbia, SC.

Lucy Lillian Warner	Oct. 14, 1857	Jan. 31, 1858	inf. d/o A.P. & C. F. Warner
Henry Geo Matthews	June 11, 1821	Mar. 3, 1849	s/o Henry & Ann Matthews
Harriet A. Matthews		Oct. 7, 1892	w/o Capt. W.E. Cropp, age 65 yrs

- 1860 Muscogee Census: Harriet A. Cropp 23 GA, Frederick Matthews 22 GA and William D. Matthews 24 GA.

Frank H. Warner, Sr.	Aug. 23, 1872	Oct. 9, 1957	
Ella Douglas Warner	May 30, 1859	July 14, 1945	w/o James Deveaux Johnston
2 adult slabs, n/m	1 adult brick slab, n/m		1 adult slab, badly crumbled

Lot 249, no name on wall

Col. William Barden		C.S.A. 1861-1865

- Obit: funeral notice mentions C.E. Booker & family, J.W. Barden & family.
- Funeral Notice: The friends and acquaintances of J.W. Barden and family, also of C.E. Booher and family, are respectfully invited to attend the funeral of their father, Wm. Y. Barden, at the residence of C.E. Booher, on Broad Street, this morning, September 26th, at 10 o'clock, Sept. 26, 18??
- SR show burial 8 June 1880, age 37 yrs.

James Camak	May 28, 1857	July 4, 1857	s/o Thos. & Laura Camak
Thomas B. Camak	June 26, 1858	Sept. 23, 1860	
Willie Ragland	Sept. 3, 1844	May 5, 1868	
Geo W. Hardwick	Sept. 16, 1819 Columbia Co, GA	Nov. 30, 1849	s/o Geo & Elizabeth Hardwick age 30 years

- Obit: one of the proprietors of the Enquirer, in the 31st year of his age.

Charles Augusta	May 15, 1848	Aug. 30, 1847	s/o G.W. & E.A. Hardwick
Maj. Thomas Clark	Sept. 13, 1829	July 2, 1863	

- Obit: killed in battle at Gettysburg, while in command of Cobb's Legion, reburied in Linwood 24 April, 1866.

Capt. O.S. Ragland	1841	1914	SR:bur. 8/4/1914, 73

- Obit: Captain O.S. Ragland, a former citizen of Columbus, died in Rogers, AR on last Saturday at the advanced age of 73 years. He was known among his intimate friends as "Fin" Ragland and was a gallant Confederate soldier, having worn the title of captain. He is survived by his wife and adopted daughter, Mrs. We?? of Greenfield, MO, one sister, Mrs. D. Tinsley of Macon, one nephew, Nisbet Tinsley and three nieces, Mrs. Tracey Baxter and Misses Theo and Sara Tinsley of Macon. He also had relatives residing in Talbotton.

Gilmer Ragland	July 6, 1837	May 3, 1874	G/M Capt. Nelson's Rangers, C.S.A. 1861-1865

- Obit: born Milledgeville, GA, s/o late Thomas Ragland, leaves wife & 2 young children, private in Columbus Guards, 1st Lt. Nelson's Rangers, made Capt.& Colonel.

Thomas Ragland	Oct. 4, 1798	Dec. 18, 1872	

- Obit: wife Sarah Ann, born Raleigh, NC, married in Jones Co., GA, 30th Oct. 1823 to Sarah Ann Day, Sr., proprietor of "The Columbus Enquirer".
- 1850 Muscogee Census: Thomas Ragland 51 NC, Sarah A. 40? VA, John B. 22 Baldwin Co., Sarah C. 19 Baldwin Co., Laura A. 17 Baldwin Co., Turner 15 Baldwin Co., George G. 13 Baldwin Co., Albert E. 11 Baldwin Co., Orin H. 9 Baldwin Co., William R. 7 Muscogee Co. and Ema S. 5 Muscogee Co. Also in HH Eliza A. Hardwick 24 Baldwin Co., Elizabeth M. 7 Augusta, Thomas 5 Augusta and Georgia 1 Muscogee Co.

Anna Hardwick	Apr. 17, 1846	Aug. 30, 1847	inf. d/o G.W. & E.A. Hardwick
Laura Camak	May 15, 1833	Aug. 5, 1873	

- Obit: relict of the lat Col. T.U. Camak, d/o late Judge Thomas Ragland, died in Griffin, GA.

Capt. James Ragland			C.S.A. 1861-1865
Carrie Ragland	Mar. 25, 1827	Apr. 2, 1869	

- Obit: full name Sarah Carrie Ragland.

Sarah A. Ragland	May 3, 1806	June 27, 1860	Mother

- Obit: w/o Thomas Ragland.

Eliza Agnes	Apr. 5, 1825	Jan. 21, 1853	w/o W. Hardwick, 27 years

- Obit: widow of Geo W. Hardwick, died at the home of her father, Thomas Ragland.

John Boleing	Jan. 29, 1829 Milledgeville, GA	Mar. 23 1854 Savannah, GA	s/o Thomas & Sarah A. Ragland his remains deposited in this cemetery Mar. 30, 1854.

- Obit: Junior proprietor of "The Columbus Enquirer", son of Thomas & Sarah Ragland of Columbus, GA, died in Savannah, GA.

Lot 250, Mitchell on wall

Willie Lou Ragland	May 4, 1885	Sept. 19, 1974	
Kate Crowell	Apr. 1, 1849	Jan. 17, 1929	w/o Albert E. Ragland

- Obit: widow of late Dr. Albert E. Ragland, d/o Dr. Thomas Crowell, 1 daughter, Miss Willie Ragland of Columbus, GA.

Albert E. Ragland	Sept. 14, 1839	Jan 11, 1891	G/M C.S.A. 1861-65

- 1850 Muscogee Census: Thomas Ragland 57? NC, Sarah A. 46 VA, John B. 22 Baldwin Co., Sarah C. 19 Baldwin Co., Laura A. 17 Baldwin Co., Thomas 15 Baldwin Co., George C. 13 Baldwin Co., Albert E. 11 Baldwin Co., Orin H. 9 Baldwin Co., William R. 7 Muscogee Co. and Ema S. 5 Muscogee Co..

Lot 251, no name on wall

Lizzie Cooper Mitchell	June 8, 1868	Oct. 12, 1899	w/o John Calvin West

- Obit: Mrs. John C., sister of John A. Mitchell, niece of Dr. Thomas S.
- Lizzie Cooper Mitchell married John Calvin West 8 Feb 1899 in Etowa, AL.
- Lizzie was the d/o William Mandon Alexander Mitchell (1822-1876) and the granddaughter of Joshua Snead Mitchell (1793-1838) and Mary Ann Hazelwood Alexander (c1793-1856) of Virginia and Chambers Co., AL.

Eliza Frances Cooper	Feb. 4, 1829	Apr. 24, 1904	"Auntie"
Dr. Thomas S. Mitchell	Sept. 4, 1836	June 19, 1911	Co. A, 54 Reg. GA Vol. Mercer Brig. Beaugards Div. (has Cross of Honor on slab)

- Obit: died in Pensacola, FL, born LaFayette, AL, nephew John A. Mitchell of Columbus, GA.
- Thomas S. Mitchell married Willie Susan Cooper 4 Mar 1856 in Tuskegee, AL.
- 1870 Harris Co., GA Census: Thomas S. Mitchell (Physician) 37 AL, William S. (female) 37 GA, Thomas R. 13 GA, Fannie S. 13 GA, James J. 9 GA, William C. 7 GA, Stella L. 3 GA, and Effie L. 1 GA.
- 1860 Harris Co., GA Census: Thos. S. Mitchell (MD) 26 AL, Willie S. 26 GA, Thos R. 3 AL and F. L. L. (female) 6/12 GA.
- Thomas Snead Mitchell was the s/o Joshua Snead Mitchell (1793-1838) and Mary Ann Hazelwood Alexander (c1793-1856) of Virginia and Chambers Co., AL.

Dr. Thos Rutledge Mitchell	Jan. 31, 1857	Feb. 14, 1894	
Willie Susan Mitchell	Apr. 4, 1831	July 3, 1903	w/o Dr. Thos S. Mitchell

- Obit: died Pensacola, FL, w/o Thomas S. Mitchell, nee Cooper of Harris Co., GA 2 sons, Edgar & Clifford, 3 sisters.
- 1850 Muscogee Census: Mary Cooper 50 Warren Co. GA, James 48 Warren Co. GA, Eliza 21 Putnam Co. GA, Susan 19 Muscogee Co. GA and Thomas Hanson 9 Muscogee Co. GA.

William Cooper Mitchell	Oct. 27, 1862 Hamilton, GA	Sept. 21, 1894 Columbus, GA

1 adult brick slab, n/m

Lot 252, Davis on wall

John T. Davis	Oct. 9, 1863	July 17, 1929

- John Timothy Davis was born in Marianna, FL the s/o John T. Davis (1829-1911) and Clarkie Wilson (1833-1909).
- 1900 Muscogee Census: John T. Davis Jr. Oct 1865 FL FL AL, wife Nettie A. July 1862 GA GA GA (married 15 yrs, 2/2 children), dau Ophelia A. Aug 1892 GA and son John T. Jr. Oct 1898 GA.

George William Cox	Apr. 12, 1884	May 14, 1974

- 1930 Muscogee Census: George W. Cox 45 OH OH OH (married @ 37), wife Ophelia D. 35 GA FL GA (married @ 27) and aunt Mary Adams (single) OH VA NY.

Nettie Ashford	July 2, 1865	Apr. 16, 1941	w/o John T. Davis

- 1870 Harris Co., GA Census: Thomas Ashford (Physician) 34 SC, Ophelia 32 GA, Nettie N. 4 GA and James M. 2/12 GA.
- Nettie marrie John Timothy Davis 30 Dec 1884 in Harris Co., GA.
- 1930 Muscogee Census: Nettie A. Davis 62 (widowed) GA GA GA, dau Clarkie E. 23 GA FL GA and son Thomas A. 20 GA FL GA.

Ophelia Davis	Aug. 23, 1893	Feb. 2, 1957	w/o Geo W. Cox
John T. Davis, Jr.	Oct. 17, 1896	Feb. 1, 1975	h/o Louise Bevis

Lot 253, Massey on wall

William Dowd Massey	Aug. 1, 1912	Sept. 23, 1988
Martha Edwards Massey	Nov. 14, 1917	July 10, 1990

Sexton Records indicate buried in this lot:

Mrs. J.W. Norris	*bur. 5/13/1908, 71*
J.W. Norris	*ch/o bur. 8/10/1873, 3 is buried in this lot*

- Obit: Mrs. J.W. Norris, aged 71, died at the home of her daughter Mrs. W.H. Adams on Eighth Avenue in Phenix City yesterday afternoon at 4:14 o'clock. Mrs. Norris leaves two daughters, Mrs. Adams and Mrs. Ida? Cobb, both of Phenix City: two sisters, Mrs. C. H. Johnson and Miss A. Brown both of Camp Hill, AL: one brother, Mr. B.T. Brown of Camp Hill, several grand children and other relatives to mourn her death. Mrs. Norris is preceded to the grave by a brother who departed this life about four weeks since.

Lot 254, Klinkerfuss on wall

Theresa Klinkerfuss	Oct. 24, 1866 Lucky, Hungary	Apr. 16, 1945 Columbus, GA
Frederick Klinkerfuss	Sept. 3, 1853 Baden, Nauhein, Germany	June 8, 1927 Columbus, GA

- 1900 Muscogee Census: Frederick Klinkerfuss sept 1853 Ger Ger Ger and wife Teresa Oct 1866 Hun Hun Hun (married 13 years)

- Fredserick arrived in New York in the ship Donau on 5 Oct 1872 from Bremen, Germany.

Lot 255, open lot

1 adult slab, n/m

Lot 256, open lot

Harvey King, M.D.	June 21, 1817 Greensboro, GA	Feb. 5, 1856 Barbour Co., AL	s/o Wm. & Mary King

- Obit: Doctor, Midway, AL

- 1850 Census Macon Co., AL: Harvey King (Physician) 33 GA, Sarah A. 21 GA, William 2 AL, Ann 6/12 AL and Mary 17 GA.

Mary Virginia Butt	Sept. 20, 1854	unable to read	w/o Daniel Bird
Moses Butt	Sept. 20, 1781 Halifax Co., NC	Mar. 8, 1848 Wynnton, GA	

- Obit: Captain. Died October 25, 1835 Mrs. Eliza A. Dozier, wife of John Dozier, d/o Mose Butt, age 22 years.

- 1830 Muscogee Census shows: Moses Butt 2 males 5-10, 1 male 15-20, 1 male 40-50; 1 female 0-5, 3 females 10-15 and 1 female 20-30.

- Moses Butt married Elizabeth Brown 30 Dec 1806 in Upson Co., GA. He married secondly Priscilla Banks 28 July 1822 in Columbia Co., GA.

- Muscogee Co., GA WB A P. 93-94. Moses Butt; 14 Jan 1848/1 May 1848. Legatees: wife Priscilla; sons Frederick, William B., John H. and Richard; daus Sarah A. King and Mary Virginia. Harvey King is to sell land in Alabama. John H. Butt is trustee for Georgia P., Moses E., Willis B. and James E. Butt minors (relationship not stated). Extrs: John Banks & John H. Butt. Wit: D. F. Wilcox, Arad Lyman and M. S. Patterson.

James Butt			C.S.A. 1861-1865
Priscilla Banks	Sept. 3, 1802 Elbert Co., GA	Feb. 2, 1853 Wynnton, GA	

- 1850 Muscogee Census: Priscilla Butt 45 Elbert Co. GA, John H. 26 Columbia Co. GA, Caroline Virginia M. 16 Muscogee Co. GA, Elizabeth Georgia T. 15 Muscogee Co. GA, Moses E. 12 Muscogee Co. GA, Willis B. 10 Muscogee Co. GA and James E. 8 Muscogee Co. GA.

- Ralph Banks (1) married Rachel Alston Jones , of North Carolina. (Her mother was of the celebrated Alston family, famous in North and South Carolina, of who it was said "the men all died in their boots." Theodosia Alston, wife of Aaron Burr , was her cousin). They removed to the Broad river settlement, Elbert county, Ga., and had ten sons and three daughters, including Priscilla.
  1. John Henry Butt (3), m. Johngeline Winter . No issue.
  2. Richard Lemuel Butt (3), m. (I) Eliz. Leonard , and m. (II) Patty Gamewell , and m. (III) Mary Henderson . Issue, six children.
  3. Sarah Alabama Butt (3), m. Dr. Harvey King ; three children.
  4. Mary Virginia Butt (3), m. Daniel Butler Bird , of Florida; two children.
  5. Georgia Priscilla Butt (3), m. Thomas Erskine Young , son of Colonel George and Susan (Watkins) Young , of "Waverly," Columbus, Miss. , a bright and lovely woman, who has given many of the above notes of her family. Issue, six daughters.
  6. Rev. Moses Edward Butt (3), of Alabama M. E. Church South, m. (I) Henrietta Allen , of Alabama, and had two children. He m. (II) Jerusha Reedy , and had four children.
  7. Willis Banks Butt (3), m. Julia Treutlen . No issue.
  8. James Eldridge Butt (3), C. S. A.; killed in battle.[46]

- Muscogee Co., GA WB A P. 140. Priscilla Butt. 10 Oct 1852/7 Feb 1853 Legatees: sons John H. and Richard L. Butt; daus.: Sarah A. King and Mary V. Bird; stepsons: Fredrick A. and William B. Mentions 10 children and grandchildren. Extr. John H. Butt. Wit: John Banks, Sarah Banks & John T. Banks.

Burlington B. West	Aug. 17, 1892	July 10, 1973	d/o Judge Wm. B. Butt

Sexton Records indicate buried in this lot:

A.T. Butt	*bur. 5/23/1921, 68*
Geo G. Butt	*bur. 2/22/1956, 62 yrs*
W.B. Butt	*born 11/14/1840 bur. 5/1/1905, 65*

- Obit: born Marion Co., GA, Mar. 14, 1840, s/o William Burlington Butt formerly of Warren Co., GA & Elizabeth ? formerly of Louisville, GA, leaves wife & 3 children, Jamie, Burlington & Grimes, 1 adopted daughter, Elizabeth Grace Butt. Senator from 24th Senatorial district, represented Muscogee Co. in legislature, married Miss Annie Tillman of Columbus, Sept. 1885, Judge of the Superior Ct. of the Chattahoochee Circuit.

Inf. d/o Lt. & Mrs. H.L. Coates

Lot 257, Sapp on wall

W.P. Sapp	1847	1915	SR: bur. 1/27/1915

- Obit: died at residence of W.F. Matheney, 2 daughters, Mrs. Cantrell, Mrs. Lewis, of Dallas, GA, 3 sons, Theo, Bradley & Hines, all of Columbus & wife.

- 1880 Census Chattahoochee Co., GA: Phillip Sapp 34 GA GA GA, wife Stellie 29 GA GA GA, dau Annie 13 GA, dau Fannie 11 GA, son Theophilus 8 GA, son Hines 5 GA and dau Estelle 3 GA.

- William Phillip Sapp was born 2 Oct 1846 and died Jan 1915. He was the s/o Theophillus Sapp (1808-1807) and his first wife Narcissa Frances Clark (1813-1862). William's wife Stella is mentioned in Theophilus' will of 1877 in Chattahoochee Co., GA.

Erin Sapp	no dates		child, SR: bur. 10/21/1871
Elizabeth Sapp	no dates		baby
William Andrew Weems	Nov. 23, 1857	Dec. 12, 1921	

- Teressa Ann Elizabeth Sapp, d/o Theophilus and Narcissa Sapp, married Edward Mortimer Weems 27 Jan 1853 in Muscogee Co., GA.

Narcissa Sapp	Mar. 30, 1812	May 23, 1862	w/o Theopliu Sapp

- Obit: wife of Theophilus Sapp, leaves 3 children.

- 1860 Chattahoochee Co., GA Census: The. Sapp 50, Narcissa 44, Henry 19, Philip 14 and William Clark 66.

- Narcissa Francis Clark was the d/o William Clark (1792-c1881) and Rebecca Peddy (1792-1857) who were married 26 Mar 1812 in Jasper Co., GA. Narcissa married Theophilus Sapp 26 July 1832 in Muscogee Co., GA. Narcissa's sister, Theresa Ann M. Clark was the wife of Forbes Bradley. William and Rebecca Clark are buried in the Peddy Cemetery in Chattahoochee Co., GA.

Sexton Records indicate buried in this lot:

Martha Sapp		*bur. 8/3/1911*

- Obit: died in Chattahoochee Co., GA

Stilla Sapp		*bur. 4/27/1890, 41 yrs.*
H. Sapp		*bur. 11/19/1877, 70*

Lot 258, Pomeroy on wall

Little Eddie Charles			Edward s/o Capt. C.E. & ? Mims age 8 mo 6 days
Margaret Elizabeth Pomeroy	June 16, 1839	Oct. 3, 1897	w/o F.A. Pomeroy, sister

- 1850 Census Richmond Co., GA: Robert F. Boyer 37 GA, Mary A. 26 GA, Margaret E. 11 GA, Laura G. 8 GA, John M. 4 GA and Robert E. 2 GA.

Sarah Rochelle	May 24, 1912	Feb. 20, 1917	d/o J.T. & R.C. Pomeroy
Frederick Alphonso Pomeroy	Aug. 28, 1831	Jan. 12, 1902	father

- born East Hampton, MA, lived in Augusta before coming to Columbus, where he married Miss Bouyer, she died about 4 years ago, pattern maker by trade, 4 chldren, J.F., Mrs. G.R. Golden, Mrs. Charles J. Eifler, all of Columbus, H. Frank of Madison, FL.

- 1870 Muscogee Census: Frederick A. Pomeroy 38 Mass, Margaret E. 30 GA, Ella 7 GA, Annie 4 GA and Frederick 2 GA.

- 1880 Muscogee Census: F. A. Pomeroy 45 PA PA PA, wife M. E. 40 GA GA GA, dau Ella 17 GA, dau Annie 14 GA, dau Maggie 9 GA and son Frank 4 GA.

- Listed as s/o Julius Pomeroy (1802-1886) and Maria Clark (1805-1842).[47]

Lot 259, open lot

2 adult brick slabs, n/m

Lot 260, Owen McArdle on wall

Owen McArdle	Sept. 4, 1868	June 10, 1928

- 1920 Muscogee Census: Owen McArdle 47 GA Scot Scot, wife Daisy J. 27 GA GA GA, dau Josephine 1 3/12 GA and son Owen Jr. 3 6/12 GA.

- 1900 Muscogee Census: F. Jo Mcardall (female, widow, 9/7 children) Nov 1837 Ire Ire Ire, dau Alice Dec 1865 GA, son Owen Sept 1871 GA, son Henry Apr 1873 GA, dau Katie Dec 1876 GA and dau Annie July 1878.

- 1870 Muscogee Census: Frank McArdle 32 Ire, Catherine 33 Ire, Margaret 8 AL, Alice 6 GA, Mollie 3 GA and Owen 1 GA.

Inf./o Henry & Jessie Stevenson	Feb. 6, 1870	May 29, 1871

- 1870 Muscogee Census: Henry Stephens 34 Scot, Jenett 30 Scot and Henry Jr. 4/12 GA. (Note: Census taken 15 June)

Lot 261, W.L. Nunn on wall

Walter Luna Nunn		Apr. 13, 1923	
Sarah Mullins	Feb. 5, 1877	Jan. 4, 1948	w/o W.L. Nunn

Lot 262, Wellborn on wall

Samuel M. Wellborn	Aug. 24, 1835	Jan 21, 1875	one slab w/ Florida

- Obit: died at the former residence of Gen. Abercrombie in Russell Co., AL. He owned considerable property in Meriwether Co., G., married Miss Florida, d/o Gen, Abercrombie, leaves 3 children.

- Samuel Marshall Wellborn was the s/o Alfred Wellborn (ca 1797-1857) and Elizabeth Martin Terry (c1801-1848). He married Florida Abercrombie 1 Mar 1864.

Florida Abercrombie Smith	Feb. 1, 1840	Dec. 15, 1925	one slab with Sammuel Wellborn

- Obit: widow of former Gov. of GA James Milton Smith, died in Aiken, SC, d/o Gen. & Mrs. Anderson Abercrombie, born Russell Co., AL, married Samuel Marshall Wellborn, Mar. 1, 1864, who died in 1874, married James Milton Smith in 1881, 1 dght, Mrs. Thomas H. Morgan of SC, 1 son, S. Marshall Wellborn of Columbus, GA, 4 g/ch.

- 1880 Muscogee Census: (enumerated as boarders in the HH of Robert Ware) Florida Welborn 39 AL GA GA, Florida 13 AL GA GA and Marshall 11 AL GA GA.

1 baby slab, n/m

Lot 263, Dr. Gardner on wall

Martha A. Gardner	May 13, 1828	Apr. 25, 1907	w/o Dr. Joseph M. Gardner

- Obit: widow of late Dr. J.M. Gardner, nee Weeks, of Talbotton, GA, dghts, Misses Bird, Willie, Mrs. W.G. Jones of Elberton, GA.

- 1850 Talbot Co., GA Census: William Mullins 40 VA, Nancy 17 GA, William 8 GA, Virginia 3 GA, William Weeks 28 GA, Martha Weeks 19 GA and Julia 2 GA.

Wilhelmina E. Gardner		Nov. 17, 1921	d/o Joseph & Martha Gardner

- Obit: 2 sisters, Miss Bird Gardner of Columbus, GA, Mrs. A.C. Jones of Elberton, GA.

Dr. Joseph M. Gardner	Apr. 12, 1816	Oct. 20, 1900	

- Obit: born Savannah, GA, surgeon in C.S.A. service, leaves wife, 3 dghts, Mrs. W.O. Jones, Miss Bird & Woolley Gardner.

Thomas Flounoy Foster	Nov. 23, 1796 Greensboro, GA	Sept. 24, 1848	In memory of our dear father.

- Obit: begin career as a lawyer in Greensboro, GA.

- Thomas Flournoy Foster was the s/o George Wells Foster (1764-1847) and Julia Elizabeth Flournoy (1767-1836). He married Elizabeth Gardner 9 Jan 1839 in Richmond Co., GA.

- Reseaqrchers of this family may want to read Southern Historical Collection, #2783-z, Julia McKinne Foster Weed papers. She was the d/o Thomas F. Flournoy and was president-general of the United Daughters of the Confederacy from 1899 to 1901.

- Thomas' sister, Ann Martin Foster, was the wife of Rev. Lovick Pierce.

William Joseph Foster		Nov. 12, 1847	In the grave w/his father Thomas Flounoy Foster. age 5 months
Miss Anna Bird Gardner	July 22, 1859	Nov. 16, 1924	
Thomas M. Gardner	Feb. 3, 1853	Jan. 17, 1901	

Lot 264, no name on wall

Lillie Spencer		Mar. 27, 1932	w/o L.A. Camp

- Obit: daughter of late Perry Spencer, b. Columbus, GA., 2 sisters, Mrs. Richard Massey of Birmingham, AL, Mrs. Arthur P. Gordy of Columbus, GA, 6 nieces, 3 nephews.

Edna Spencer Gordy		Feb. 7, 1964	
Adela DuBose	Mar. 16, 1846	Sept. 1, 1875	d/o W.E. & E.T. DuBose
Perry Spencer	Nov. 7, 1893	Oct. 12, 1895	s/o Richard W. & Bessie Massey
Mamie DuBose	Enon, AL	Mar. 10, 1923 Columbus, GA	w/o Perry Spencer
Dr. Arthur Perry Gordy	Apr. 30, 1875	Nov. 3, 1929	
William E. DuBose	Nov. 8, 1809	Sept. 1, 1875	

- Obit: married Elizabeth T. Alston, Colonel, lived in Columbus but a few years.

- 1860 Muscogee Co. Census: Wm E Dubose 50 SC, Elizabeth 34 GA, James C. 19 GA, Edwin P. 16 AL, Adella E. 14 AL, Mary E. 13 AL and Walter E. 2 AL.

- William DuBose married 1) Amanda Elizabeth Walton 27 June 1831 Lincoln Co., GA and had 5 children; 2) Mary Elizabeth Cantelou 25 Sep 1839 Lincoln Co., GA and had 1 child; and 3) Elizabeth T. Alston 26 July 1842.

Perry Spencer	Mar. 3, 1823 Talbot Co., MD	May 26, 1891 Columbus, GA

- Obit: born Talbot Co., Maryland, came to Columbus in 1836, married twice, 1st to Janie S. Carter, Sept. 1851, 2nd wife, Mamie E. DuBose, Apr. 2, 1871, she survives him, 1 son, his namesake by 1st marriage, 4 children by 2nd marriage (not named).

- Perry Spencer was the s/o Lambert Wickes Spencer (1776-1836) and Anna Spencer (ca 1786-1858).

- Old Kent: The Eastern Shore of Maryland; George A Hanson, Call Number: R929.1H25. Lambert Wickes Spencer, son of Richard Spencer and Martha Wickes, settled in Talbot County, and m. Anna Spencer, dau. of Col. Perry Spencer, of Perry Hall, Talbot, and had child., viz., Dr. Samuel Wickes,--Perry,--Lambert,--George,--Martha, and Anne Spencer.

- Muscogee Co., GA – Will of Anna Spencer 9/22/1857:11/1/1858, p. 241-244 Sons: Samuel W., Richard P., Lambert, Perry, George H. Daus: Martha W. Philips, wife of James; Lydia Murdock, wife of Robert B.; Anna Spencer, Jr. Grson: George C. Sherwood, son of Martha (now Martha Philips) and James Sherwood. Trustee for George C. Sherwood. Wit: Lambert Spencer. Exrs: Samuel W. Spencer, Richard P. Spencer. Wits: James Robinson, R. W. James, J. Rhodes Brown.

Elizabeth T. DuBose	Oct. 15, 1824 Elbert Co., GA	Apr. 12, 1886 Columbus, GA

- Obit: married William E. DuBose, July 26, 1842, nee Alston, died at residence of son-in-law, Perry Spencer, Sr., d/o Capt. F.H. Alston, who was one of the Commissioners appointed by the Governor in 1827 to lay out the City of Columbus, born Columbus, 3 children, Mrs. Perry Spencer, W.E. DuBose, both of columbus, GA, E. P. DuBose of

Tuskegee, AL.

- 1880 Muscogee Census: Elizabeth DuBose 55 GA SC GA, son Walter 20 AL, SIL Perry Spencer 57 MD MD MD, dau Mary 32 AL GA GA, gdau Bessie 6 GA, gdau Lillie 5 GA and gdau Edna 2 GA.

- Elizabeth was the d/o William Hinton Alston (born ca 1793 NC, the s/o Lt. Col. Wm Alston and Charity Alston) and Elizabeth Rucker (born ca 1795, the d/o John Rucker and Betsy Tinsley). They were married ca 1774 in Halifax Co., NC.

| Marie DuBose | May 8, 1872 | Aug. 12, 1878 | d/o Perry & Marie Spencer |

Lot 265, wrought iron fence, no name

| William Nelson Carter | Jan 23, 1848 Wynnton, GA | June 22, 1869 Key West, FL | 21 years old |
| Maj. Thomas M. Nelson | Sept. 25, 1782 Williamsburg, Va | Nov. 10, 1853 Wynnton, GA | 1812 Representative in Congress until he resigned 1819 |

- Obit: born Virginia, veteran of War of 1812, received a sword from Va. Legislature for his gallantry at Battle of Lacolis Mile & Chatuaugay.

- Thomas Maduit Nelson, a Representative from Virginia; born in Oak Hill, Mecklenburg County, Va., September 27, 1782; attended the common schools; commissioned a captain in the Tenth Infantry Regiment and subsequently a major in the Thirtieth and Eighteenth Infantry Regiments in the War of 1812; after the war was reduced to the grade of captain, and resigned his commission May 15, 1815; elected as a Republican to the Fourteenth Congress to fill the vacancy caused by the death of Thomas Gholson, Jr.; reelected to the Fifteenth Congress and served from December 4, 1816, to March 3, 1819; was not a candidate for renomination in 1818; died near Columbus, Muscogee County, Ga., November 10, 1853; interment in Linwood Cemetery.[48]

- Thomas Nelson married 1) Sarah Page Walker (1790-1834) 6 Oct 1816 in Frederick Co., VA and 2) Anna M. ? (1805-1872).

| Mrs. Anna Nelson | A.D. 1805 Richmond, VA | A.D. 1872 Wynnton, GA | widow of Maj. Thos. M. Nelson |
| Evelyn Page Carter | Apr. 9, 1819 | Jan. 8, 1896 | |

- Obit: w/o late Robert Carter, 78 years old, d/o Maj. Thomas M. Nelson of VA, moved with family to Columbus in 1838, married Robert Carter in Augusta, 2 sons, Robert Carter of Columbus, T.M. Carter of Albany, GA, 2 sisters, Mrs. F.O. Ticknor, & Mrs. W.G. Woolfolk.

| Robert E. Carter | Dec. 1842 | Dec. 20, 1919 Carter Place | Nelson's Rangers C.S.A. |

- Obit: druggist by trade, C.S.A., Nelson's Rangers, leaves wife, Mrs. Belle Power Carter, 1 son, Robert, Jr., 1 daughter, Mrs. Mercer Blanchard, both of Columbus, 1 brother, T.M. Carter of Albany, GA.

Thomas M. Nelson	July 14, 1864		fell leading the 6th Miss. Cav. at Harrisburg near Tupelo, MS. 1861-1865

- Nelson, Thomas M.-Private Apr.28, 1861. Appointed Surgeon May 10, 1861. Resigned Nov.4, 1861. Elected Captain of Nelson's Company Ga. Cavalry Apr.18, 1862. Appointed Major of Corps of Scouts and Guards, C.S.A., June 27, 1864 Elected Lieutenant Colonel of the 6th Regt. Mississippi Cavalry July 1864. Killed at Tupelo,Miss. July 14, 1864.[49]

- Marker at Linwood Cemetery. Buried Oak View Cemetery, Albany, Dougherty Co., GA.

- Married Frances Tift 30 Dec 1863 in Dougherty Co., GA.

Robert Carter	Oct. 3, 1818 Augusta, GA	Apr. 13, 1894 Columbus, GA	

- 1850 Muscogee Census: Robert Carter 38 Augusta GA, Evelyn 31 Clarke Co GA, Anna M. 70 VA, Thomas N. 9 Augusta GA, Robert E. 7 Muscogee Co. and William N. 2 Muscogee Co.

- Robert Carter married Evelyn Byrd Page Nelson 30 Dec. 1839 in Augusta, Richmond Co., GA.

Belle Carter Blanchard	Jan. 4, 1893 Carter Place	May 28, 1936 Carter's Place	d/o Robert e. & Belle Powers Carter. Mar. Dr. Mercer Blanchard May 9, 1916
Mrs. Anna Matilda Carter	Oct. 21, 1779 Williamsburg, VA	Jan. 18, 1855 Wynnton, GA	

- Nee Anna Matilda Wray, the widow of John Carter (1761- c1820).

- Muscogee Co., GA WB A P. 182-183. Anna Matilda Carter. 26 Sep 1847/10 Mar 1855. Legatees: sons Robert, Charles & Nelson Carter; dau.: Anna M. Nelson; grandchildren: Thomas Mitchell Carter, James Henry Carter, Matilda Carter, Jane McKenzie Carter, Nancy Carter and Martha H. Carter. Also mentioned: Cary Carter, Mrs. Anna M. Robinson, Eliza Carter, Flournoy Carter, Robert Elliott Carter, John Barrett Carter & Evelyn Carter. Extr: R. Carter. Wit: William Nelson, Maria B. Woolfolk, Anna M. Nelson and W. G. Woolfolk.

5 baby slabs, n/m

Lot 266, Geo H. Whiteside on wall

2 adult brick slabs, n/m

Lot 267, no name on wall

Sarah R. Fry	1853	1915	*SR: bur. 10/9/1916, 63*

3 children's brick slabs, n/m	1 adult brick slab, n/m

Lot 268, Leonard-Garrard on wall

Guy Garrard	June 20, 1883	Sept. 15, 1960	s/o Louise F. & Annie L. Garrard, h/o Edith Powell
Adeline P. Reynolds		May 13, 1847	w/o Benj. H. Reynolds, d/o Thos & Eliz Ford, 42 years of age

- Obit: w/o Benjamin H. Reynolds, of Russell Co., AL, d/o Thomas & Elizabeth Ford.

Mary Evans	Jan. 14, 1863	July 17, 1864	d/o A.P. & B.E. Rood
Mary Louisa Jones	June 17, 1853	Nov. 3, 1903	w/o Wm. Wallace Bruce
Helen Garrard Rucker	Apr. 2, 1886	Oct. 19, 1958	d/o Louis F. & Annie L. Garrard. Mar. Col. Kyle Rucker U.S. Army Oct, 1910 interred in Sunset Mausoleum, Berkeley, Cal.
Edith Powell Garrard	Jan. 13, 1887	Nov. 12, 1869	d/o Thos W. & Rebecca E. Powell, w/o Guy Howard
Mary Judith Groves		Dec. 11, 1847	d/o L.J. & M.L. Groves, age 19 years
Harman Wayne Patterson	May 1, 1889	Mar. 31, 1987	
May Louisa Leonard	Mar. 8, 1825	Apr. 15, 1875	w/o John A. Jones

- Obit: married John A. Jones, Oct. 5, 1843, nee Leonard, died at the residence of Gen. Henry L. Benning, d/o Van Leonard, widow of Col. Jack Jones, who died at Gettysburg, the only son of Seaborn Jones, leaves 3 sons, 2 dghts.

Harman Wayne Patterson II	Jan. 12, 1922	Jan. 13, 1922	s/o Harman W. & Isabel Garrard
Van DeVan, inf. d/o Louis F. & Annie L. Garrard	Oct. 30, 1887	Nov. 5, 1889	
Col. Van Leonard	May 27, 1790 Petersburg, VA	Aug. 2, 1861	

- Obit: Colonel

- 1850 Muscogee Census: Van Leonard 60 VA, Fanny 47 Baldwin Co. GA, Hernietta 21 Morgan Co. GA, Van 17 Morgan Co. GA and Anna 1 Muscogee Co. GA.

- Muscogee Co., GA WB A:299-304. Van Leonard, 8/7/1856:8/20/1861. Wife: Frances R. Sons: James, Van A. Daus: Mary S. Jones, wife of John A.; Henrietta S. Whitaker, wife of Samuel E.; Elizabeth C. Butt, wife of Dr. Richard L.; Ann Foster Leonard. Grson: Seaborn Leonard Jones. Codicil dtd 7/5/1860 says that Richard L. Butt has left the

State. Exrs: Wife, sons, and sons-in-law. Wits: B. F. Coleman, Wiley Williams, T. G. Holt. Wits to Codicil: Thomas Ragland, James Venoy, Wiley Williams.

- VandeVan Leonard married 1)Elizabeth Ballard Gilbert (1794-1816) 25 Apr 1811 in Greene Co., GA, 2) Jeanette Harvie (1802-1835) 27 Mar 1817 in Oglethorpe Co., GA and 3) Frances Ramsey Darnell 13 May 1836 in Baldwin Co., GA.

E. C. Leonard, M.D.	July 27, 1845	22 years of age

- Obit: doctor, died at the residence of his father in Eugenia, NC

Henry Gardner	Feb. 5, 1847	s/o Van & Frances Leonard, 9 months
Thomas Powell Garrard	July 28, 1916	Dec. 25, 1948	s/o Edith Powell & Guy Garrard
Mary P. Reynolds	? ?, 1815	?? unable to read	w/o ? ?, d/o Benj. & Adeline Reynolds
Capt. Van Asbury Leonard	Dec. 8, 1831	July 17, 1862	Co. I, 20th GA Regt. GA Vol. C.S.A. 1861-1865

- Obit: died of wounds in battle near Richmond, VA, Co. I, 20th GA Regt. "Southern Guards".

- s/o Van Leonard and Jeanette Harvie. He married Georgianna Flournoy, the d/o Josiah Flournoy and Martha Rosser, 30 Jan 1835 in Putnam Co., GA.

Frances Isabel Garrard	Dec. 23, 1894	Jan. 6, 1955	w/o Harman Wayne Patterson, "MIZPAH"
William Leonard Garrard	Aug. 17, 1870	Aug. 20, 1883	s/o Louis F. & Annie L. Garrard
Louis Ford Garrard	Nov. 25, 1847	Aug. 1, 1908	

- Obit: s/o William W. & Frances Isabel Garrard, moved to Savannah, GA, at age 3, returned to Columbus several years later, married Anna Foster Leonard, May 20, 1863, d/o Van deVan Leonard & Frances Ramsey Darnell Leonard, children, Louis Ford, Jr., Frank Urqhart, Annie Leonard (Mrs. Frank G. Lumpkin), Guy, Helen Gertrude, & Frances Isabel Garrard, 2 children deceased, William Leonard & Van deVan Leonard Garrard, 2 sisters, Mrs. Helen G. Glenn of New York, Mrs. Gertrude G. Harris, of Jackson, MS, 1 brother, Col. William Garrard of Savannah, GA.

- Louis Garrad was the s/o William Waters Garrard (1818-1866) and Frances Isabella Garteray Urquhart (1818-1890)

Frances R. Leonard	Jan. 4, 1804 Milledgeville, GA	May 27, 1877 near Columbus, GA

- Obit: w/o Van Leonard, deceased, 1 child, Mrs. L.F. Garrard of Columbus, GA.

- Southern Christian Advocate 3 July 1877. Obituary. Mrs. Francis R. Leonard nee Darnell, relict of the late Van Leonard, was born in Milledgeville, Ga., January 4, 1804; died near Columbus, Ga., May 29, 1877. J. S. Key

- Frances Ramsey Darnell married 1) to Henry Malone (c1799-1835) on 29 Nov 1820 Baldwin Co., GA and 2) VandeVan Leonard 13 May 1836 in Baldwin Co., GA.

- 1850 Muscogee Census: Van Leonard 60 VA, Fanny 47 Baldwin Co. GA, Hernietta 21 Morgan Co. GA, Van 17 Morgan Co. GA and Anna 1 Muscogee Co. GA.

- Muscogee Co., GA WB A:299-304. Van Leonard 7 Aug 1856/20 Aug 1861.

Legatees: wife: Frances R. Sons: James, Van A. Daus: Mary S. Jones, wife of John A.; Henrietta S. Whitaker, w/o of Samuel E.; Elizabeth C. Butt, w/o Dr. Richard L.; Ann Foster Leonard. Grson: Seaborn Leonard Jones. Codicil dtd 7/5/1860 says that Richard L. Butt has left the State. Exrs: Wife, sons, and sons-in-law. Wits: B. F. Coleman, Wiley Williams, T. G. Holt. Wits to Codicil: Thomas Ragland, James Venoy, Wiley Williams.

2 adult brick slabs, n/m   4 baby slabs, n/m

Lot 269, no name on wall

Mary L. Wynne		May 27, 1877
Thomas Knibb Wynne	Aug. 21, 1870	Apr. 11, 1895
Hezekial Edwards Wynne	Dec. 31, 1867	Apr. 22, 1904
Albert Edwards Wynn	Dec. 4, 1873	July 31, 1962
Martha Lamar Wynne	Aug. 2, 1884	June 19, 1956

one slab

- 1880 Muscogee Census: Thomas K. Wynne (editor paper) 58 NC NC NC, dau Susan 14 GA, son Hezekiah E. 12, son Thomas K. 10 GA, son Albert E. 6 GA, boarder Hezekiah Edwards 59 KY KY KY and niece Salli Waddell 22 AL NC NC.

- 1870 Muscogee Census: Thomas K. Wynn 48 NC, Mary L. 32 KY, Susan 4 GA, Ezakiah 2 GA, George Waddell 15 AL and Sallie Waddell 13 AL.

Lot 270, no name on wall

Charles Dexter Jordan III	Dec. 9, 1959	May 17, 1979?
Geo Dexter Jordan	May 20, 1886	Nov. 4, 1911
Oscar Sylvester Jordan	Dec. 24, 1849	Dec. 23, 1941

- 1910 Muscogee Census: Oscar S. Jordan 60 (wd) GA MA GA, dau Clara G. 34 GA GA GA, dau Maud D. 30 GA GA GA, son George D. 23 GA GA GA, dau Bessie D. 23 GA GA GA and son Edward B. 19 GA GA GA.

- 1900 Muscogee Census: Oscar S. Jordon (sic) Dec 1850 GA MA GA, wife Bettie? Dec 1858 GA MA GA, dau Clara Sept 1877 GA, - Maud Apr 1880 GA, son George May 1886 GA, dau Bessie May 1888 and son Edward Aug 1891 GA.

- 1880 Muscogee Census: Oscar S. Jordon (sic) 30 GA MA GA, wife Elizabeth B. 26 GA MA GA, son Charles F. 6 GA, dau Clara G. 4 GA and dau Maud D. 1 GA.

- 1850 Hancock Co., GA Census: Sylvester F. Jordan 49 MA, Rachel 41 GA, Robert P. 13 GA, William F. 11 GA, Delia D. 7 GA, George G. 4 GA, Oscar S. 7/12 GA, James N. Stanford 23 GA and Elizabeth A. Stanford 22 GA.

- Sylvester F. Jordan married Rachel Gunby 1 Mar 1836 in Columbia Co., GA.

Elizabeth Blake Dexter	Dec. 3, 1853	Feb. 27, 1908
Bessie Dexter Jordan	May 20, 1886	Nov. 21, 1932
Clara Gunby Jordan	Sept. 20, 1875	Nov. 28, 1946

Clara Matilda Hodges   Mar. 1, 1831   Oct. 22, 1909

- 1850 Muscogee Census: Elizabeth Hodges 53 Charleston SC, Wesley I. 20 Wilkes Co. GA, John W. 23 Putnam Co. GA, Henrietta 22 Baldwin Co. GA, Clara 18 Muscogee Co. GA and Mary 16 Muscogee Co., GA.

Eliz. Dexter Jordan   Sept. 8, 1941   d/o Dexter & Rebecca Jordan

Edw. Blake Jordan   Aug. 29, 1897   Feb. 17, 1927

Maude Dexter Jordan   Apr. 14, 1879   June 24, 1945

Charles Edw. Dexter   Apr. 30, 1823   June 6, 1881
                             Boston, Mass.   Columbus, GA

- 1880 Muscogee Census: Charles E. Dexter 57 MA MA MA and wife Clara M. 48 GA NC SC.

- 1870 Muscogee Census: Charles E. Dexter 47 MA, Clara M. 39 GA, Elizabeth 16 GA and Richard P. 14 GA.

- 1860 Muscogee Census: Chas E. Dexter 37 Boston, Clara 29 GA, Elizabeth 6 GA and Richard 4 GA.

- Charles Dexter married Clara M. Hodges 17 Feb 1853 in Muscogee Co., GA.

1 baby slab & marker   unable to read

SECTION B

Paved Rd
Paved Rd
Care Taker
Linwood Blvd

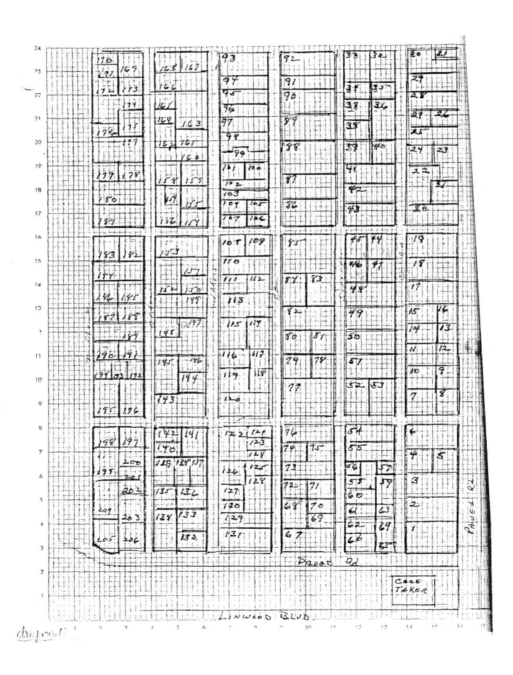

Lot 1, no name on wall

Rebecca T. Taliaferro   Feb. 24, 1836   Sept. 15, 1898   w/o Wm. H. Broyles

- 1880 Russell Co., AL Census: William H. Broyles 48 SC - -, wife Rebecca 44 GA SC GA, dau Minnie 22 TN, dau Gussie 19 TN, dau Rebecca 17 AL, son Charles 13 AL, son Bruce 11 AL, son Oze 9 AL and son John 6 GA.

- William Henry Broyles (1832-1875) was the son of Ozey Broyles and Elizabeth Ann Taliaferro. He and Rebecca were cousins.

Charles B. Taliaferro   June 3, 1809   June 28, 1882

- Obit: Charles B. Taliaferro – born SC, to Oglethorpe Co., GA., married Mildred B. Meriwether, moved to Coweta Co., GA., wife survives, 5 children, Mrs. M. C. Wooten of Columbus, GA., Mrs. Dr. Weatherly of Montgomery, AL., Mrs. Wm. H. Broyles of Russell Co., AL.

- Col. Charles Boutwell Taliaferro was the son of Warren Wilmer Taliaferro (1760-1815) and his wife Mary Meriwether Gilmer (1786-1856) of Pendleton District, SC.

   o Original papers Oglethorpe Co, Inferior Court. Warren Taliaferro. Division of property, July 10, 1819. Distributes: To Peachy R. Gilmer [brother of Mary Meriwether Gilmer Taliaferro VV p 12] in trust for minor children of said Warren, dec.: Lucy G. Taliaferro, Zachariah, Sally, Sophia Taliaferro; Nicholas Powers in right of his wife, Mary M. Powers, widow and relict of said Warren Taliaferro, dec'd; Thomas Rainey in right of his wife, Mary E., formerly Taliaferro. Record recites the division was made according to the last will of Warren Taliaferro.

- *Letter written by Sophia Taliaferro born c1816, wife of James Meriwether, and sister to Charles B. Taliagerro:*
"My Ma [Mary Meriwether Gilmer] was married when quite young to Mr. Warren Taliaferro. She lived in Wilkes, Co, but her health became so bad they moved to Pendleton Dis. S. Carolina where they remained until his death. Ma had six children by her first marriage. Mary Elizabeth [died 1863] was born March 1804. She married T. [Thomas] Rainey. Lucy Gilmer born 1816 she married Ishmael Dunn now living, no children. Zachariah Thomas was a Dr. He died 1824?. The fourth Charles B. [Boutwell] was born 1811 and married Miss Mildred Meriwether lives in Coweta Co. The fifth Pollie Harvey, born 1814 married Mr. Floyd T. Landrum. She is left a widow with ten children, five sons and five daughters. And the sixth Sophia Ann born 1816 married James Meriwether (a cousin of Brother Charles' wife.) They live in the State of Alabama." *Note: Mary Meriwether Gilmer married secondly Rev. Nicholas Powers (1783 Ireland – 1843 Oglethorpe Co., GA)*

- 1850 Coweta Co., GA Census: Chas. B. Taliferro (sic) 41 SC, Mildred B. 37 GA, Valentine H. 19 GA, Elizabeth G. G. 17 GA, Rebecca T. 15 GA, Charles F. 12 GA, Mary B. 10 GA, Lucy M. 8 GA, Walker B. 5 GA, teacher Albert Rowland 21 GA, Margaret Rowland 17 SC

- 1870 Muscogee Census: Charles Taliafero Jr. 61 SC and Mildred B. 58 GA.

- 1880 Muscogee Census: Charles Talliafend (sic) 71 SC VA VA, wife Mildred 68 GA VA VA and other Joe Durham 30 GA VA VA.

Mildred B. Taliaferro   Nov. 3, 1812   July 2, 1882

- Obit: Mildred Taliaferro – w/o late Col. C. B. Taliaferro, about 70, nee Mildred Meriwether, married about 50 years ago in Oglethorpe Co., GA, 5 children.

- Mildred Barrett Meriwether was the daughter of Valentine Ham Meriwether and Barbara Minor Cosby.

Bouttie Wooten	Mar. 27, 1868	Oct. 4, 1871	d/o M. C. & L. M. Wooten
Warren Boutwell Taliaferro	Dec. 18, 1844	Sep. 5, 1862	s/o Charles B. & Mildred B. Taliaferro
Charles Taliaferro Wooten	Fe. 18, 1870	July 2, 1882	
Pearl T. Lee	1878	1915	SR: bur. 1/20/1915, 37
Efie Malone Taliaferro	July 12, 1867	Dec. 17, 1929	
Charles F. Taliaferro	Nov. 1, 1864	Dec. 12, 1912	
C. F. Taliaferro	May 16, 1838	July 22, 1881	

- 1870 Muscogee Census: Charles F. Taliaferro 30 GA, Lucy H. 22 AL, Charles F. 5 GA, and Sterling B. 1 GA.

- 1880 Muscogee Census: Rich. (sic) Taliaferro 44 GA, wife Lucy 32 AL, son Chas. 15 GA, son Sterling 11 GA, dau Mary 9 GA, and dau Pearl 3 GA.

Lucy H. Bass	1847	1925	w/o Charles F. Taliaferro. SR: bur. 10/10/1925

- Lucy Bass, d/o Dr. Sterling Bass, Jr. and Mary Ann Freeman of Russell Co., Alabama. She married Charles F. Taliaferro April 14, 1846 in Barbour Co., AL.

- 1860 Macon Co., AL Census: Sterling Bass 42 GA (Physician), Mary A. 25 GA, Lucy H. 13 AL, Elizabeth 10 AL, Sterling 7 AL, Mary A. Jr. 5 AL, Allen 3 GA and Samuel 1 AL.

- 1850 Census Russell Co., AL: Sterling Bass 31 GA, Mary 20 GA, Lucy 3 AL and Elizabeth 1 AL.

Mary Katherine Daniel	Nov. 28, 1893	June 6, 1978	
Mary Wooten	Sept. 3, 1873	May 4, 1904	w/o W. F. Moss
Ben Jennings Daniel	1865	1908	
Mary Taliaferro	1871	1944	w/o Ben J. Daniel
Floyd Idus Chambliss, Jr.	1912	1944	1st Lt. Inf., bur. St. James Cem. Reaves, France

1 child slab, n/m	3 adult slabs, n/m	2 baby brick slabs, n/m

Sexton Records Indicate buried in this lot:

Mrs. L. M. Wooten	*bur. 9/20/1884*
M. C. Wooten	*bur. 11/8/1888, 51*
M. B. Wooten	*c/o M. C. Wooten, bur. 10/5/1871, 3*

- 1870 Muscogee Census: Matthew C. Wooten 36 AL, Lucy M. 26 GA, Mildred B. 2 GA and Charles T. 3/12 GA. (next door to Charles and Mildred Taliaferro)
- 1880 Muscogee Census: Mart (sic) Wooten 45 AL NC NC, wife Lucy 37 GA SC GA, son Charles 10 GA, dau Mary 6 GA, dau Lucy 2 GA and dau Crowell 3/12 GA. (next door to Charles and Mildred Taliaferro.)

Lot 2, no name on wall

Lula L. Bethune	Sept. 9, 1877	Aug. 15, 1950
Angus J. Bethune	May 26, 1833	Aug. 4, 1926

- Obit: Angus Bethune – born Sumter Co., SC, s/o Robert & Nancy Bethune, C.S.A. vet, 45th Ala. Vol., in 1860 married Miss Margaret A. Warnock, d/o Rev. John W. Warnock of Aberfold, Ala., she died two years ago, dghtrs, Miss Lula Bethune, Mrs. J. O. Pennell, Mrs. J. L. Thomas, all of Columbus, GA., sons, C. L., S. A., A. J. Jr., all of Columbus, GA, 6 gr/ch.
- 1870 Bulloch Co., AL Census: Angus Bethune 32 SC, Anna 30 GA, Beulah 7 AL, Samuel 5 AL, John 3 Al, infant male 2/12 AL and William McLeod 10 AL.
- 1900 Muscogee Census: J. Angus Bethune June 1833 SC Scotland NC, wife Margaret A. 40 GA Ireland Ireland (married 40 years; 9/6 children), son Samuel A. April 1864 GA, son Charles Larry? April 1875 GA, dau Lula L. April 1877 GA, dau Florrie March 1875 GA, son Angus J. April 1872 GA, DIL Alva May 1876 GA GA GA(married 3 years; 1/1 child), gson James R. Oct 1899 GA, dau Bula C. Thomas April 1862 GA (married 2 years; 1/1 child), SIL John L. Thomas Feb 1859 AL AL GA and gson John B. Thomas Feb 1899 GA.
- 1920 Muscogee Census: Angus Bethune 86 NC Scot Scot, wife Margaret 83 GA Ire Ire, son Samuel 52 AL, son Charles 43 GA, dau Loela 40 GA, dau Florrie Pennell 34 GA, husband Joseph Pennell 38 NC, dau Beulah Thomas 40 AL and granddaughter Margaret 16 GA.

Margaret A. Warnock	Apr. 9, 1837	June 22, 1924	w/o A. J. Bethune

- Obit: Margaret Bethune – born Rome, GA, d/o Rev. John Warnock, on Dec. 13, 1860 married A. J. Bethune, leaves husband & sons A. J., C. L., dghts, Mrs. J. O. Pennell, Mrs. J. L. Thomas & Miss Lula Bethune.

John B. Thomas	Feb. 26, 1899	Apr. 14, 1901	
James R.		Nov. 3, 1894	"their son"
Our baby		Apr. 12, 1879	
A. J. Bethune, Jr.	Apr. 6, 1872	Apr. 11, 1928	
Samuel A. Bethune	Nov. 5, 1864	Aug. 12, 1948	
Charles L. Bethune	Oct. 17, 1875	Feb. 28, 1950	
Margaret T. Barnes	Jan. 1, 1903	Nov. 11, 1984	
Frank S. Barnes	Feb. 14, 1904	May 31, 1978	
Margaret Mary Barnes		Jan. 4, 1935	d/o Margaret & Frank Barnes
John L. Thomas	Feb. 23, 1859	Feb. 15, 1942	

- Atlanta Constitution 23 Jan 1898. Columbus, GA, January 22nd. The marriage of Mr.

John L. Thomas and Miss Beaulah C. Bethune occurred Thursday evening at the home of the Bride's parents on lower Broad Street.

Beulah Bethune Thomas   Sept. 3, 1862   June 10, 1927

Lot 3, partial brick wall, no name

Lt. A. M. Kimbrough   City Light Guards, CSA.
                                                             1861-1865

- Obit: A. M. Kimbrough – on roll of dead "City Light Guards", 24 Apr. 1870 paper.
- City Light Guards: Alexander M. Kimbrough, private May 2, 1861. Elected Jr. 2nd Lt. Mar. 1862. Died at Columbus, GA Jan. 9, 1865.

Capt. O. S. Kimbrough   10th GA Regt. CSA 1861-
                                                             1865

- Owen S. Kimbrough Co. A, 10th Regt. GA Volunteer Infantry, Army of Southern Virginia. Enlisted as a private May 10, 1861. Elected 2nd Lt. July 19, 1861. Capt. Nov. 27. 1861. Absent without leave in Columbus, GA Jan. 20-Mar. 31, 1865. No later record.
- Buried 10/19/1866.
- Alexander and Owen S. Kimbrough are sons of William H. Kimbrough (1795-1877) and Nancy Garrett (1799-1850), both of whom are also buried in Linwood.[50]
- 1850 Muscogee census: Julia Byington 23 GA, William H. Kimbrough 55 GA, Mrs. Nancy 52 GA, O. S. 23 GA, Nancy G. 21 GA, Mary I. 16 GA, Alexander M. 13 GA, and Lenore 6 GA.

2 children brick slabs, n/m   2 baby brick slabs, n/m

Lot 4, open ended lot, no name

E. B. McCrary   Dec. 10, 1835   May 9, 1904

1 baby marker, n/m   1 child marker, n/m

Sexton records indicate buried in this lot

George W. McCrary   *bur. 12/12/1906, 67 yrs*

- Obit: George McCrary – died in Montgomery, AL, died Dec. 7, 1906.

Lot 5, G. M. Craig on wall

Anna Elmore Craig   Oct. 31, 1903   Aug. 9, 1928

Moody Hagins Craig   June 11, 1908   June 12, 1909   s/o G. M. & L. M. Craig

- Obit: s/o Mr. & Mrs. Geo. M. Craig. Besides his parents he leaves three brothers G. M. Jr., Alonza and Gurley and one sister Clara.

Charles Thomas Craig   Sept. 6, 1910   Dec. 25, 1913   s/o Geo M. & Lucy Craig

Lucy May Hagins   May 26, 1877   Feb. 6, 1964   w/o Geo Milton Craig
                         Harris Co., GA

- 1880 Harris Co., GA Census: J. S. Hagins 31 GA NC GA, wife H. A. 30 GA SC GA, son J. R. 8 GA, dau M. F. 6 GA, dau A. E. 4 GA, son (sic) L. M. 2 GA, dau W. J. 1 GA. Mother Ann C. 68 GA SC GA and boarder T. C. Grant (male) 32 SC SC GA.

- 1910 Muscogee Census: George M. Craig 38 GA GA GA (m. 10), wife Lucy 32 GA GA GA (m. 10, 6ch/4liv), dau Clara 8 GA, son George 7 GA, son Alton 6 GA and son Gurly 3 GA.

- 1920 Muscogee Census: Lucy Craig 44 GA GA GA wd, dau Clara 18 GA, son George 16 GA, son Alton 14 GA, son Gurly? 12 GA, son M____ 7 GA, son Mary R. 4 GA and son John Robert 3 GA.

- George Milton Craig was born in Fulton Co., GA 7 Dec 1871, the s/o George W. Craig and Sarah Layfield. He married Miss Lucy Hagins, d/o James S. Hagins and Hulda Grant, on 6 July 1899. He died 23 May 1916. [51]

Lot 6, no name on wall

Howard Key MacMillan   Oct. 5, 1860   July 22, 1862   s/o G. W. & Mary Macillan

Paul A. C. Adams   Nov. 22, 1896   Nov. 6, 1981

Mamie Lou Huff   Sept. 1, 1888   Aug. 13, 1977
Henderson

Eliza Gammell   Apr. 14, 1832   Feb. 18, 1901

- Atlanta Constitution 2/16/1901 Columbus, GA Feb 15 (Special). Mrs. Eliza Gammel, wife of Mr. A. Gammel died at their home east of the city yesterday. She is survived by her husband and three daughters, - Mrs. A. C. Bowles, Mrs. Daniel Hughes (sic) and Mrs. J. T. Fletcher. The funeral services occurred today.

I. L. Henderson   July 9, 1886   Feb. 20, 1919

Abelena Gammel   Jan. 4, 1862   Jan. 25, 1863   d/o Abraham & Eliza
                                                           Gammel

Gammel Huff   July 7, 1883   July 22, 1887   s/o Daniel & Tallulah Huff

Abraham Gammell   Sept. 15, 1819   June 18, 1902   Father

- Obit: Abraham Gammel – born in Upson Co., GA, wife died last year, 3 dghts, Mrs. J. T. Fletcher, Mrs. Daniel Huff, Mrs. A. C. Bowles.

- Atlanta Constitution June 21, 1902
  Columbus, GA, June 20 (Special)
  Abraham Gammel, aged 80 years, one of the best known residents of Muscogee county, and for many years a prominent livery stable man of Columbus, died at his home east of the city Wednesday night. He was buried yesterday afternoon.

- Abraham Gammel married 1) Mary Ann Ray Mar 10, 1840 in Upson Co., GA.

- 1850 Muscogee census: Abraham Gammell (sic) 27 GA, Mary A. 32 GA, Berry Ray 19 MA, Jeremiah Bunnell? 19 GA and Charles Hooker 25 GA.

- 1870 Muscogee census: Abraham Gammell (sic) 50 GA, Eliza 39 GA, Flora 14 GA, Talulah 11 GA and Mary 9 GA. Also in the household: Simeon Walker 84 OH, Thomas Gammell 47 GA, Mary Gammell 46 GA, George Bugg 19 GA, and (servant) Ann Carter

37 GA.

- Thomas A. Gammell married Mrs. Mary Odom 1/20/1849 in Muscogee.

- 1880 Muscogee census: Abraham Gammell (sic) 59 GA GA GA, wife Eliza 45 GA GA GA, dau Lula 19 GA, dau Bettie 17 GA and son Oska 9 GA.

- 1880 Muscogee census: Augustus Bowles 27 GA GA GA, wife Ella 24 GA GA GA and dau Bettie 2/12 GA.

- The Southern Christian Advocate, January 8, 1878
  Married by By Rev. F. A. Branch on December 19, 1877, at the residence of Mr. A. Gamewell (sic), near Columbus, Ga., Mr. Augustus C. Bowles to Miss Ella Gammell.

Tallulah Huff	July 3, 1859	May 26, 1925	w/o Daniel Huff
Daniel Huff	Nov. 9, 1857	June 26, 1939	

- 1900 Muscogee census Nov. 1857 GA AL AL, wife Talulah July 1859 GA GA FL (married 17 years; 4/3 children), son Joseph W. July 1884 GA, dau Mary L. Aug. 1888, and son Stanford Oct. 1891.

- 1880 Muscogee census: Nancy Huff 50 VA NC, son Daniel 22 GA SC GA, dau Lula 20 GA, dau Elizabeth 18 GA, dau Ella 16 GA and son John 13 GA.

- 1870 Harris Co., GA Census: John A. Huff 53 SC, Nancy 39 GA, Douglas 22 GA, Daniel 12 GA, Lula 10 GA, Lizzie 8 GA, Louella 6 GA, John 4 GA and boarder Lucy Parham 17 GA.

- 1850 Muscogee Census: John Huff 32 SC, Elizabeth 30 VA, Cincinatus 10 Musc. Co., Nathaniel 8 Musc. Co., Leonard 6 Musc. Co., and Douglas 2 Musc. Co.

Jack Weston Huff	Jan. 18, 1918	Dec. 12, 1918
Joseph Weston Huff	Aug. 27, 1884	Nov. 4, 1929

Lot 7, Summersgill on wall

Jesse M. Payne, Jr.	July 31, 1878	Nov. 12, 1951	Papa
John Summersgill	July 15, 1852	July 7, 1923	Father

- 1880 Lee Co., AL census: John Summergill 28 GA GA England, wife Amarilla 24 AL SC SC, son William H. 3 AL, dau Almerta 6/12 AL.

- 1900 Lee Co., AL Census: John Summersgill July 1857 GA England GA, wife Dora Feb 1858 AL AL AL (married 25 years; 4/4 children), dau Ina M. Nov 1880 AL, son Clinton Nov 1883 AL, dau Katy B. Feb 1887 AL and dau Eulala Sept 1890 AL.

Dora Belle Summersgill	Sept. 15, 1856	Oct. 31, 1921	Mother
Ina Mae Payne	Nov. 19, 1879	Jan. 26, 1960	
Henry T. Summersgill	Nov. 21, 1876	Mar. 21, 1950	
Lala S. Parker	Sept. 29, 1890	June 10, 1982	
Dee F. Parker	Apr. 8, 1880	Nov. 1, 1955	
Our baby girl		Aug. 30, 1941	born to Myra & Richard Payne

1 baby slab, n/m

Lot 8, open lot

Baby Thad	Aug. 14, 1903	Sept. 2, 1904	s/o Richard J. & Lucy P. Belser
Little Susie	May 31, 1896	July 14, 1908	d/o Richard J. & Lucy P. Belser

1 adult brick slab, n/m

Lot 9, open lot

Therol Rhunett DePaschal	Feb. 28, 1907	Mar. 24, 1964	
Katherine Russell	July 31, 1892	Dec. 14, 1943	w/o Lansing Shewfelt

- 1910 New York Co., NY census shows Lansing Shewfelt (single) 28 MI KY KY soldier.
- 1920 Chattahoochee Co., GA census shows Lansing Shewfelt 42 (single) MI MI MI soldier at Campe Benning.

1 child slab "Jeanett"   no dates

Lot 10, open lot

W. B. Smith		Nov. 8, 1880	age 32

- Funeral notice mentioned that he worked at Eagle & Phenix Mills.
- 1880 Muscogee census: William Smith 30 SC SC SC (working in cotton mill), wife Hattie 28 SC SC SC, Mother Martha Randal 63 SC SC SC.

W. E. Randall	July 27, 1853 Harrisburg, SC	Nov. 8, 1880

Martha Randall	unable to read	Mother, w/o Thomas R. Randall. SR: bur. 5/6/1882, 65 yrs.

- 1850 Edgefield Co., SC census: Thos. Randal (sic) 34 SC, Martha 30 SC, Joseph 13 SC, Frances 11 SC, Elizabeth 9 SC, Mary 7 SC and Adaline 5 SC.
- 1860 Edgefield Co., SC census: M Randall (f) 40 SC, H. B. (f) 13 SC, W. (m) 7 SC and E. (f) 3 SC.
- 1870 Edgefield Co., SC Census: living in the HH of James D. Benson: Martha Randal 50 SC, Hattie B. 21 SC and William 16 SC.

1 adult grave, unable to read

Lot 11, Ben Wardlow on wall

Benjamin F. Wardlow   July 9, 1887   July 12, 1958

- 1900 Muscogee Census: W. E. Wardlow Dec 1844 GA GA GA, wife Clara Nov 1850 GA GA GA (married 27 years; 8/4 children), son Albert F. Oct. 1876 GA, son Charles H. Nov 1878, dau ___ Belle Oct 1883 GA, son Benjamin July 1887 GA, MIL Sarah A. Frederick Feb 1824 GA VA SC and boarder Charles R. Russell Mar 1873 GA GA AL.

- 1880 Chattahoochee Co., GA Census: William Wardlow 34 AL GA GA, wife Clara 27 GA GA GA, dau Aylma 6 GA, son Albert 3 GA, son Charlie 1 GA, MIL Sallie Frederick 56 GA GA GA, boarders: Hellen Girdner 21 GA GA GA, Ruth Girdner 20 GA GA GA, Natt Frederick 25 GA GA GA and his wife Millie 19 GA GA GA.

- 1850 Muscogee Census: Sarah Fredrich 34 GA, Clara 10 GA, Frances 8 GA and Nathaniel 5 GA.

Annie Munn Wardlow   May 3, 1888   Mar. 1, 1980

Benjamin F. Wardlow, Jr.   Feb. 9, 1916   Jan. 22, 1944   GA Capt. Air Corps, WW II A. M.

Lot 12, open lot

George VanDoren Girdner   Sept. 11, 1858   Sept. 15, 1861   s/o James A. & Helen A. Girdner

- 1850 Muscogee Census: James A. Girdner 20 GA.

- 1860 Muscogee Census: Jas A. Girdner 29 GA, Hellen 21 GA, Hellen 2 GA, George 1 GA and Chas. Frederick 13 GA.

David E. Pease   June 12, 1843 Talbotton, GA   July 20, 1862 Richmond, VA   Member of City Light Guards, Co. I, 2nd GA Regt.

- "Eddie", nephew of J. W. Pease, of Columbus, GA.

- David E. Pease was the son of David E. Pease of Somers, CT and Caroline W. Herst of Georgia, VT, who were married 4/16/1838. David E. Pease, Sr. was a merchant in Georgia and died 3/27/1846, age 31 years. Children of David and Caroline: Amelia H. 1/3/1839, Spencer 4/4/1840, Mariette A. 6/14/1842, David E. 6/12/1843 and Olivia born 1845 d. 1846. David and John W. Pease were sons of Jonathan S. Pease. [52]

- Marriage record in Talbot Co., GA David E. Pease and Caroline Hunt (sic) dated 9/28/1837.

- Co. A. 2nd Bat. "City Light Guards: David E. Pease; Private enlisted Apr. 20, 1861.

2 children slabs, n/m

Lot 13, Blakely on wall

no evidence of graves

Lot 14, Calhoun on wall

Lula Belle Harris	July 23, 1880	Aug. 8, 1882	d/o J. F. & M. C. Harris
John F. Harris	1853	1912	SR: bur. 12/22/1912, 59
Mary G. Harris	1861	1929	SR: bur. 4/12/1929
Alice Jane Calhoun	Nov. 18, 1834	Dec. 12, 1880	w/o J. G. Calhoun

- 1880 Harris Co., GA Census: James G. Calhoun 45 GA NC NC, wife Alice J. 40 GA NC NC and dau Sarah E. 12 GA.
- James Gamble Calhoun was born 1836 in Talbot Co., GA, the son of Duncan Calhoun and Sarah McNeal originally from New Hanover Co., NC, then Talbot Co., GA. James married first Alice Jane Miller 8 May 1856.

Lot 15, open lot

5 adult brick slabs, n/m

Lot 16, Whiteside on wall

Edwina Whiteside	Dec. 16, 1902	Jan. 3, 1903	d/o L. W. & G. S. Whiteside
Edwina Whiteside		Oct. 4, 1926 only date	inf. d/o Wilson Jr. & Elsie Whiteside
E. Wilson Whiteside	Oct. 18, 1874	Jan. 20, 1937	

- 1900 Muscogee census: Wilson Whiteside May 1870 GA GA GA and wife Mary Oct 1877 GA GA GA (m. 2 yrs).
- 1920 Muscogee census: Wilson E. Whiteside 45 GA NY AL, wife Cary S. 40 AL AL GA, son Thomas B. 15 GA, son Wilson E. Jr. 11 GA, son Joseph B. 8 GA, son Flournoy? 5 GA and boarder Louis Rowe 18 GA.
- Cary Stratford (1879-1941), d/o William Eli Stratford (1850-1915) and Martha Amanda Godwin (d/o William Godwin and his wife Henrietta Sarah Traylor) married Wilson W. Whiteside.[53]

Thomas B. Whiteside	Feb. 14, 1871	Mar. 27, 1902	

- 1900 Muscogee census: Thos. B. Whiteside Feb 1871 AL NY AL, wife Carrie R. Dec 1874 (m. 6 yrs)

Hannah Hiatt	1798, NC	Sept. 25, 1865	

- 1850 Muscogee census: Harriett Hiat 56 NC, Mary 25 NC and Georgia C. 4 GA.

Mrs. Rosa Whiteside	1849	1934	SR: bur. 1/20/1934, 84 yrs.
Thomas J. Whiteside	June 16, 1848 New York, NY	Sept. 30, 1923 Columbus, GA	

- Obit: Thomas Whiteside – steamboat Capt., married 1869 to Mrs. ? Berry, d/o late Wilson W. Berry & Dorothy T. Berry of Russell Co., AL, leaves wife, children, E. Wilson

& Mrs. E. N. Quinn, both of Columbus, GA, 1 brother, Samuel J. Whiteside, deceased.

- AL Death Index shows that Thomas J. died in Mobile Co., AL.

- 1880 Muscogee census: Thomas J. Whiteside 32 NY NY NY, wife Rosa 31 AL AL AL, son Thomas B. 9 GA, Edward W. 6 GA and dau. Dodie M. 3 GA.

- 1900 Muscogee census: Thomas J. Whiteside June 1848 NY Eng PA, wife Rosa April 1849 AL VA AL (married 31 years 3child/3 liv.), dau May Quick Sep 1876 GA and SIL Edgar Quick Jan 1872 NJ.

Lot 17, open lot

3 adult brick slabs, n/m   4 baby brick slabs, n/m   2 children brick slabs, n/m

Lot 18, open lot

1 adult brick slab, n/m

Lot 19, R. S. Hardaway on fence

Benjamin Kemp Hurt   Dec. 31, 1860   s/o William & Elizabeth Bass
                                            Columbus, GA   Hurt

- Funeral notice mentions Mr. & Mrs. J. E. Hurt.

- In 1850 Muscogee Census Benjamin K. Hurt 11 AL and William Hurt 8 AL in the household of Thomas Shivers. These boys were orphaned by 1848 in Russell Co., AL.

Robert Archelaus   Feb. 2, 1829   Apr. 27, 1899   71 yrs.
Hardaway   Columbus, GA

- Was Adjt. in the Mex. War & Col. of the 2nd VA Reg. of Art. in the CSA was professor of civil engineering for more than 20 yrs in the State College & in the University of AL, s/o R. S. & M. B. Hardaway.

- Obit: Robert Hardaway – died at residence of his sister, Mrs. C. E. Johnston, Colonel, came here last Oct. w/son, B. H. Hardaway (built North Hardaway dam), old resident of Columbus before 1835, married Miss Rebecca Hurt, 2 sons, Early H. & B.H., 3 sisters, Mrs. A. H. Flewellen of Eufaula, AL, Mrs. C. E. Johnston of Columbus, Mrs. John W. Wright of Marian, Ark.

- *"Memoirs of Robert Archelaus Hardaway". It contains the notation, "Memoirs copied by Marjorie B. Molloy for the Lizzie Rutherford Chapter, UDC, ca 1968." The dates in the memoirs range from 10 July 1879 to 22 Oct 1887.*

  - I was born in Morgan County, Georgia, on the 2nd, February 1829. I was the eldest child of my mother, who was the second wife of my father. (m. Miss Martha Bibb Jarratt 5/8/1828 Elbert Co., GA, d/o Archelaus Jarratt and Sarah Booker Bibb.) My father removed from the County of Brunswick in Virginia to Morgan Co., Ga. about 1826; thence to Harris Co., Ga., in 1831, probably, and to Columbus, Ga. in the fall of 1833. My father was from Brunswick Co., Virginia. On the 17th June 1857 I was happily married to Miss Rebecca Elizabeth Hurt of Wynnton, near Columbus, Ga. Benjamin K. Hurt died Jan. 1st, 1861.

My first child, Robert Early Hardaway was born in Columbus, Georgia, April 26th 1858. George Stanfield, second child, was born at the Jones place on Talbotton road, near Columbus, Georgia, November 7th 1859. ... died at the plantation in Macon Co., Alabama, August 26th, 1860 about 4 P.M. Aged 9 months and nineteen days. My mother died at my father's plantation and residence near Jamestown in Chattahoochee Co., Georgia at sunset Sept. 25th, 1859. Aged 53 years, 10 mos. 22 days. Benjamin K. Hurt, my wife's brother was graduated at the University of Nashville in June 1859.

The children of William Hurt, Senior, my wife's father, were: Rebecca Elizabeth, guardian Joel Early Hurt; Benjamin Kemp guardian being John W. Hurt; William Barlow, guardian George Troup Hurt; Mary Louisa guardian Clement Walker. Three of the guardians were sons of Joel Hurt, who was a half-brother of William Hurt, Senior, and was guardian of my wife, Rebecca E. Hurt.

On the morning of the 1st of January 1861 about 2 A.M. Benjamin K. Hurt, brother of my wife died of diptheria at the residence of Joel Early Hurt in Wynnton near Columbus, Georgia. He was twenty-one years old in the preceding November. He was unmarried, and had returned from Europe in the fall of 1860.

Mr. William Hurt, Senior had married the daughter, Elizabeth, of Edmund Bass, formerly of Brunswick Co., Virginia, but then of Hancock Co., Georgia about the latter part of 1836 (Dec. 4th, probably). She died on a visit to Hancock in 1847 and Mr. William Hurt, Senior died at his plantation, one mile west of Uchee P. O. Russell Co., Ala. about Aug. 28th, 1848. My wife Rebecca Elizabeth Hurt was born on Sholderbone [sic] Creek in Hancock Co., Ga. Nov. 12th, 1837.

Rebecca Hurt Hardaway	Nov. 12, 1837 Hancock Co., GA	Sept. 17, 1887 Gainesville, GA	

- Obit: Rebecca Hardaway - Adopted daughter of Mr. & Mrs. Early Hurt of Wynnton, about 45 yrs., 2 sons, Early Hardaway, Decatur, AL, Benjamin Hardaway.

- Benjamin K. Hurt, William Barlow Hurt and Rebecca Eizabeth Hurt, wife of Robert A. Hardaway were c/o William Hardaway Hurt (1795 VA-1848 Russell Co., AL) who married Elizabeth Bass (c1808-1846 Hancock Co., GA) 11/24/1836 in Hancock Co., GA. William H. Hurt was the son of William Hurt (1756-1812) and Mary Bass (c1770 - after 1813).

George Hardaway		Aug. 26, 1860	s/o Robert A. & Rebecca Hurt Hardaway. 9 mos, 19 dys

Dr. William Lowther DesPortes	July 16, 1869 Ridgeway, SC	Mar. 26, 1930 Columbus, GA	s/o Richard S. & Susan Lowther DesPortes

- 1880 Fairfield Co., SC census: R. S. Desportes 37 SC France SC, wife Susan L. 32 AL GA AL, son Wm. Louther 10 SC and Richard S. 5 SC.

- William Lowther Desportes was the son of Richard Smallwood Desportes (1841-1898) and Harriett Susan Lowther (1845-1921) who were married 11/6/1867 in Lee Co., AL. Harriett Susan was the daughter of William Lowther (1816-1889) and Elizabeth Sarah Gibson (c1820-1890), who are also buried in Linwood, Section G., Lot #88.

- William Desportes married Virginia Johnston on 12/8/1897.

- 1920 Muscogee census: William L. Desportes 55 SC SC SC, wife Jennie J. 44 GA GA

AL, son Richard 21 AL, Calvin 19 GA and mother Virginia H. Johnston 80 AL VA GA.

Virginia M. Johnston	Aug. 25, 1875	June 3, 1952	w/o Wm. L. DesPortes, d/o Calvin E. & Virginia Hardaway Johnston
William Barlow Hurt	Sept. 15, 1841 Russell Co., AL	Feb. 15, 1917 Columbus, GA	s/o Wm. & Eliza Bass Hurt Capt. Art. C.S.A.

- Obit: William B. Hurt – CSA vet, Capt., nephew B. H. Hardaway, 1 sister Mrs. S. S. Scott of College Park, GA.

Woodford H. Johnston	Jan. 2, 1870	Aug. 21, 1910	
Virginia M. Hardaway	Apr. 14, 1839	Feb. 29, 1924	w/o Calvin Evans Johnston, d/o Robert Hardaway & Martha Bibb Jarratt.

- Obit: Virginia Johnston – Sister of late Col. Robert A. Hardaway, aunt of B. H. Hardaway, in 1871 married Calvin E. Johnston who died 1901, children; Woodford H., H., Virginia M. (Mrs. W. L. DesPortes).

Calvin Evans Johnston	May 28, 1827 Morgan Co., GA	July 19, 1901 Columbus, GA	

- Calvin Johnston was the s/o Lancelot Johnston and Margaret Jones. He married 1st in 7/19/1854 Mary Lewis Redd, the d/o James Kelsoe Redd and Mary Elizabeth Lewis. He married 2nd Virginia M. Hardaway on 4/12/1871 in Muscogee.

- Morgan Co., GA Will of Lancelot Johnston: 20 May 1858/7 May 1866. Legatees: My children; William J., Elizabeth J. Poullian, Calvin, Julian, and Lancelot Johnston, granddaughter, Woodford Anna Johnston, dau. of dec'd son, Woodford A. Executors, son, William J. Johnston & SIL, Antoine Poullian.

- 1850 Macon Co., AL Census: (next door to bro. Lancelot Johnston) William Johnston 27 GA & Calvin Johnston 26 GA

- 1860 Muscogee Census: Calvin Johnson (sic) 33 GA, Mary 23 AL, James 5 AL, Calvin 3 AL and Launcelot 1 AL.

- 1880 Muscogee census: Calvin E. Johnston 53 GA NC GA, wife Virginia M. 41 AL VA GA, son Willie R. 18 GA, son Julian 17 GA, son Antoine? P. 14 GA, son Woodson 8 GA, son Stanfield 7 GA and dau Virginia M. 4 GA.

Henry Buckner Wright	Oct. 15, 1882 Russell Co., AL	Sept. 25, 1883 Columbus, GA	s/o John Wright
James Bennett Wright	Feb. 19, 1875 Russell Co., AL	Nov. 12, 1892 Searcy, Ark.	s/o John Hesley & Mary Hardaway Wright
John W. Wright	June 8, 1838 Caroline Co., VA	Oct. 3, 1914	

- Obit: John Wright – died at residence of daughter Mrs. J. T. Robertson, Marianna, Ark.

Mary Hardaway Wright	1842	1910	w/o John Wright

George Archelus Wright	May 28, 1878 Russell Co., AL	May 11, 1905 Union Spgs, AL	s/o John Wesley & Mary Hardaway Wright
Maj. Robert Stanfield Hardaway	Mar. 27, 1797 Brunswick Co., VA	Apr. 20, 1875 Columbus, GA	officer Creek War 1836, State Senator from Barbour Co. & Russell Co., AL in 1842, Pres. of Mobile & Girard RR 1849-1854.

- Obit: Maj. R. S. Hardaway – Maj. R. S. Hardaway died at the residence of Mr. Calvin Johnston in Columbus. He was about 70 years old. He was one of the oldest inhabitants of this city and section. Before the war he was a rich planter. He had been married twice and by his first wife was the father of a highly respected family of children, among them was Capt. R. A. Hardaway. Brother of the late Samuel Hardaway of Montgomery.

- Robert Stanfield Hardaway married 1) Martha Bibb Jarratt/Jarrett as above and 2) 12/5/1865 Mary E. Hungerford, the (c1819 CT – 1873 Chambers Co., AL).

- Obit: Mary E. Hardaway - Mrs. Mary E. Hardaway, wife of Robt. S. Hardaway of Columbus, Ga., died in Lafayette, Chambers Co., Ala., September 9, 1873, aged fifty-four years. She was the daughter of Dana and Rachel Hungerford, and was born in Harwinton, Connecticut. Soon after her birth, her parents removed to Greensboro, Ga., at which place and in Columbus and Thomaston, her father was engaged in the mercantile business. She was married to Daniel Grant, Feb. 29, 1861 (sic). Mr. Grant died in Columbus, Ga., Nov. 4, 1864. Mrs. Grant was married to Major Robert S. Hardaway, Dec. 5, 1865. She had no children. She united with the Baptist Church in Columbus, Ga.

Martha Bibb Hardaway	Nov. 3, 1805 Elbert Co., GA	Sept. 25, 1859 Chattahoochee Co., GA	w/o Robert S. Hardaway, d/o Archelus & Sally Booker Bibb Jarrett. 53 yrs 10 mo 22 days
Dr. James Jarrett Hardaway	June 30, 1848 Columbus, GA	Dec. 20, 1877 Bibb Co., GA	s/o Martha Bibb Jarrett & Robert Stanfield Hardaway

- Obit: Dr. James Hardaway – died at residence of his sister Mrs. Redding in Macon, GA, s/o Col. R. S. Hardaway, graduate U. of VA, brother-in-law Calvin Johnston.

Dr. George S. Hardaway	Feb. 11, 1834 Columbus, GA	Oct. 16, 1859 Chattahoochee Co., GA	s/o R. S. & M. B. Hardaway

Lot 20, John I. Ridgeway, 1850, on wall

Aurelia R. Bain	Mar. 5, 1833	Feb. 9, 1878	
Myra Semmes Clark	no dates		baby
Laura Belle Clark	July 18, 1876	Jan. 24, 1892	d/o Wm. L. & Pauline Clark
John Ridgeway Clark	Nov. 15, 1858	Feb. 2, 1879	
Robin Key Clark	July 18, 1876	Jan. 24, 1892	s/o Wm. L. & Pauline Ridgeway Clark
Pauline Ridgeway Clark	Feb. 10, 1840	June 10, 1901	w/o Wm. Lawrence Clark

- Obit: - Pauline Clark – nee Pauline Ridgeway, d/o Col. J. I. & Martha Ridgeway, leaves husband, 1 sister Miss Lucy Ridgeway, 6 sons; F. A. of Mexico, Paul of Washington, DC, Ira. Harry & Robin all of Columbus, GA, W. L. Jr. of New Orleans, LA.

Wm. Lawrence Clark   Oct. 15, 1827   Dec. 18, 1908

- Obit: Wm. Clark – born Savannah, GA, s/o John Lawrence Clark & Harriet Frances Clark, married Pauline Ridgeway d/o John Ira & Martha Angelica Ridgeway Feb. 10, 1856, wife died June 16, 1901, sons, Frederick Adams Clark, William Lawrence, Paul of Washington, D.C., Ira P., Harry Marshall, John Gilbert, sisters Mrs. Laura Fickling of Allendale, SC, Miss Lucy Ridgeway.

- John Lawrence Clark (c1803 NY – 1860 Savannah) married Harriet Frances Poullen 11/22/1826 in Chatham Co., GA. He is buried in Laurel Grove Cem. in Savannah, along with Laura B. Clarke who married David Fickling 3/12/1852.

- 1880 Muscogee census: William Clark 53 GA GA GA, wife Pauline 40 GA GA GA, son Freddie 16 GA, son Willie 12 GA, son Paul 10 GA, son Ira 7 GA, dau Laura 4 GA, son Harry 2 GA, boarder Martha Ridgeway 60 GA GA GA, and boarder Lucy Ridgeway 26 GA GA GA.

John Ira Ridgeway   Sept. 28. 1811   Apr. 24, 1856

- Obit: John Ridgeway – born Clarke Co., GA, merchant, married Martha Angelica Kimbrough May 30, 1839.

- 1850 Muscogee census: J. I. Ridgeway 39 GA, Martha 30 GA and Pauline 10 GA.

- Muscogee Co., GA. John Ridgeway Nuncupative will April 24,1856/May 10, 5/10/1865 Legatees: Wife Martha A. and daus. Anna Pauline and Lucy (both minors); father-in-law William Kimbrough, brother-in-law Owen S. Kimbrough and sisters-in-law Ann G. Kimbrough & Lenora Kimbrough, both unmarried. Wit: John J. Boswell MD, Francis G. Wilkins and Alfred O. Blackman.

Martha A. Ridgeway   Aug. 11, 1819   Jan. 7, 1886

- 1860 Muscogee census: Martha Ridgeway 41 GA, William L. Clark 31 GA, Pauline 21 GA, Miriam 7 GA, Lucy Ridgeway 7 GA, and John R. Clark 2 GA.

- Martha Angelica was the d/o William H. Kimbrough and Nancy Garrett.

Mrs. Nancy Kimbrough   June 6, 1850   w/o Wm. H. Kimbrough

- see Section B, Lot 3.

- 1850 Muscogee census: Julia Byington 23 GA, William H. Kimbrough 55 GA, Mrs. Nancy 52 GA, O. S. 23 GA, Nancy G. 21 GA, Mary I. 16 GA, Alexander M. 13 GA, and Lenore 6 GA.

Lot 21, Davis on wall

Mrs. J. B. Smith   Nov. 10, 1830   Aug. 1, 1877   mother

- Funeral Notice – Mrs. Isabelle B. Smith

- 1870 Muscogee Census: John S. Smith 40 GA, Margaret 20 GA, Belle 39 GA, Anna M. Davis 63 GA and Richard Smith 13 GA.

- 1860 Muscogee Census: John Smith 40 NY, Isabella 30 GA, Mary Ann 11 GA, John 6 GA and Richard 3 GA.

W. S. Davis   Co. G, 2nd GA. Inf. CSA. SR: bur. 4/20/1875, 37.

- Private W. S. Davis - enlisted April 16, 1871. Killed at Cold Harbor, VA May 27, 1864.

Thomas F. Ridenhour, Jr.   June 25, 1861   Sept. 17, 1883

- 1870 Muscogee Census: Thomas F. Ridenhour 33 GA, Charlotte 25 GA, William S. 7 GA, Harriet M. 4 GA and Thomas F. 2 GA.
- s/o Thomas F. Ridenhour and Charlotte Taylor Davis.

Richard Henry Davis   Nov. 5, 1842   Nov. 6, 1865

Aunt Ann Kirkley   no dates

- 1850 Muscogee Census: Enumerated in the household of William Dougherty, Miss Ann Kirkley 67 GA.

Nathaniel Gleason Davis   Jan. 17, 1838   June 11, 1871

- Obit: Nathaniel Davis – resident of Texas since the war, former member of "Nelson's Rangers", CSA, s/o Mrs. A. B. Davis died in Columbus, GA.

Arthur B. Davis   Nov. 5, 1802   Jan. 23, 1846

- Obit: Arthur Davis – leaves wife & 9 children, one of the earliest settlers of Columbus, GA.

A. B. Davis, Jr.   Co. G, 2nd GA, Inf. CSA

- Obit: A. B. Davis, Jr. – member of "Columbus Guards", he had shot & killed the Capt. of a S.C. company, while under arrest he was shot by a member of the Capt.'s Co. His brother-in-law T. F. Ridenhour was also a member of the same outfit, died 8 Aug 1861.
- 1850 Muscogee census: Mrs. M. A. Davis 42, John H. 24, Martha H. 23, George S. 22, Mrs. M. V. 20, Arthur B. 18, William 15, Nathaniel 12, Charlott 5 and Henry R. 8. Also in the boarding house: William K. Schley 38, Mary Schley 31, Anna Schley 10, William Schley 8, Charlott Schley 6, Sarah Schley 4, H. Van Virghton (male) 36 NY, Mrs. N. Van Virghton 27 CT, L. T. Woodruff (male) 38 NJ, and Aurora Woodruff 24 VA.

Martha Ann   May 5, 1820   Nov 8, 1851   d/o James S. & Caroline Calhoun, w/o John H. Davis.

Anna M. Davis   Nov. 13, 1807   Apr. 21, 1879   w/o Arthur B. Davis

- Obit: Anna Davis – died at the residence of son-in-law T. F. Ridenhour, d/o ex-Gov. Wm. Schley, came to Columbus 1828, w/o Arthur B. Davis, 1st cashier of the Bank of Columbus, a daughter survives her.
- Anna Maud Schley married Arthur B. Davis 1/13/1825 in Jefferson Co., GA.
- The Hon. William Schley (1786 MD – 1858 Augusta, GA) was Governor of Georgia from 1835-1837. He and his brother John Jacob Schley, Jr.; sons of John Jacob Schley, were pioneers in the history of the railroads and the cotton mills of GA.

Lot 22, Mustian on wall

George Mustian Wilkins   Oct. 2, 1851   June 20, 1959?   s/o Charles B. & Julia Davis Wilkins

John H. Davis   Oct. 24, 1826   July 23, 1859

- *see Section B Lot 21*

Charles Lamar Davis	May 11, 1856	Aug. 26, 1923	s/o John H. & Georgia Mustian Davis
Julia Mustian Wilkins	Feb. 5, 1858	Feb. 10, 1884	w/o Charles B. Wilkens, d/o John H. & Julia F. Mustian
Georgia C. Mustian	Feb. 22, 1834	Mar. 2, 1859	w/o John H. Davis, d/o John L. & Julia F. Mustian
Julia Frances Mustian	Nov. 28, 1814 Milledgeville, GA	June 6, 1911 Columbus, GA	w/o John L. Mustian

- Obit: Julia F. Mustian – One daughter Mrs. John H. Davis who was the mother of Mrs. Charles L. Davis, who has been the proprietor of Warm Springs for years. She is survived by her granddaughter Miss Georgia Wilkins of Columbus.

- Julia Jeter married John L. Mustain (sic) 1/24/1833 in Bibb Co., GA. Julia was the d/o Francis Jeter of Baldwin and Meriwether counties and his first wife, Judith Staunton. Francis Jeter married 2nd in 1848, Dorothy Rutherford Wiggins, the widow of Joshua Bingham and a sister to John Rutherford.

John Lloyd Mustian	Feb. 3, 1805 Warren Co., NC	May 23, 1881 Warm Spgs, GA

- Obit: John L. Mustian – Colonel, help build Muscogee R. R., born NC, moved to Columbus 1840, legislator married Miss Jeter, 1 child who married John Davis and had 2 children Charley Davis of Warm Springs, GA, Mrs. Julia Wilken (sic) of Montgomery, AL, brother-in-law R. L. Mott.

- John Mustian's land is part of what is now Warm Springs Foundation. The last heir of John Mustian, Georgia Wilkins, sold the Warms Springs property to George Peabody.

- 1850 Meriwether Co., GA census: John L. Mustian 45 NC, Julia F. 33 GA, Georgia C. 16 GA and Martha F. Drumnight 16 GA.

Lot 23, open lot

Louisa V. Mulford	Jan. ?, 1829	Sept. 12, 1871	w/o Davis Mulford, d/o R. ?

- 1860 Muscogee Census: David (sic) Mulford 40 NY, Louisa V. 30 GA, Randolph 12 GA, Hattie 9 GA, and John Cargill 21 GA & John Mulford 30 GA.

- 1870 Muscogee census: Davis Mulford 54 NY, Louisa V. 35 GA, Randolph 22 GA and Mary Mustian 37 (mul.) SC.

5 adult slabs, n/m

Lot 24, open lot

Elizabeth A. Porter nee Rossiter	Feb. 20, 1874	relict of John B. Peabody, w/o David S. Porter

- Obit: Mrs. D. S. Porter – Feb. 21, 1874, This estimable lady, the wife of Mr. D. S. Porter, the well known foreman of the *Sun* Job office, died, suddenly, yesterday afternoon, of heart disease. She had been visiting not an hour before, and shortly after returning home received the fatal attack. She was born in Bridgeport, Conn., and had reached the age of fifty-nine. Her maiden name was Miss E. L. Rossiter. She was one of the earliest settlers of Columbus, and one of the few who sought refuge in the Oglethorpe House when it was rumored the Indians were attacking on the village. She had seen Columbus grow from a few shanties to the proportions of a city, and her own life has been one of usefulness. Being an ardent Episcopalian and desirous of doing good, she was mainly instrumental in establishing the parish school for poor children, which is the pride of the Columbus church. The highest praise that can be given any woman belongs to her, and that is, "She made home happy." Twice married, she has many children and grandchildren to lament her loss and honor her memory.

- 1850 Muscogee Census: Mrs. Elizabeth Peabody 35 NY, Edward R. 16 CT, Ruth 7 GA, Mary L. 5 GA, John 3 AL, Callie 1 GA and George Peabody 43 CT.

- Elizabeth Rossiter was born 4/8/1815 and married John Boadicea Peabody 4/8/1833 in Bridgeport, CT. Their children: Edward Rossiter 1834, William Henry 1837, Leila Prentiss 1838, Sarah Jane Hill 1840, Ruth Isabella Buckley 1842, Mary Louise Clinton 1845, John Ward 1847 and Callie Boadicea Peabody 1849. Elizabeth married David Porter 4/8/1855.

- The George Foster enumerated with this household is George Henry Peabody who subsequently married Elvira Canfield of CT. George and Elvira were the parents of noted philanthropist, George Foster Peabody.

  o George Foster Peabody (July 27, 1852-Mar. 4, 1938), banker, philanthropist, was born in Columbus, Ga., the first of four children of George Henry and Elvira (Canfield) Peabody. Both parents were native New Englanders of colonial ancestry. The elder Peabody, who came from a line of merchants, bankers, and professional men, had moved from Connecticut to Columbus, Ga., where he ran a prosperous general store. After attending private school in Columbus, young Peabody spent a few months at Deer Hill Institute, Danbury, Conn. The devastation of the Civil War, however, had impoverished his family; in 1866 they moved to Brooklyn, N. Y., and young Peabody went to work in a Brooklyn wholesale dry goods firm.[54]

Augustus Peabody	July 3, 1764 Woodbury, CT	Oct. 10, 1848
Katie & David Porter	no dates	baby headstones

- 1870 Muscogee Census: David S. Porter 65 CT, Elizabeth 55 NY, Leila Cory 33 GA and Edward D. Porter 25 CT.

- 1860 Muscogee Census: David S. Porter 54 CT, Elizabeth 44 NY, Sarah J. Peabody 20 AL, John Peabody 13 Al and Caroline Peabody 11 GA.

- 1850 Hartford Co., CT Census: David S. Porter 45 CT, Charlotte A. 44 CT, Charlotte H. 13 CT, Edward B. 4 CT and Sarah Harvey 20 Ireland.

Lot 25, Boswell on wall

1 adult brick slab, n/m   1 baby brick slab, n/m

Lot 26, Wilkens on wall

Mrs. Permelia P. Wilkens   Feb. 7, 1821   May 30, 1851   w/o Col. Francis G. Wilkens

- 1850 Muscogee census: F. G. Wilkens 34, Permelia P. 27, Miss M. Wilkens 40, and Alexander Robinson 3.

- Francis Wilkins (sic) married Permelia P. McClary 8/28/1835 in Putnam Co., GA.

4 adult brick slabs, n/m   2 baby brick slabs, n/m   1 child brick slab, n/m

Lot 27, no name on wall

Marshall Sturgis   no dates   baby

Carrie Sturgis   no dates   baby

Orpha W. & W. Hogan   no dates   double slab

- Thomas M. Hogan (1809 SC-1886 Lee Co. AL) and Orpha Judson Whitten (1817 SC – 1878 Lee Co., AL). Thomas Hogan married Orpha 12/2/1838 in Harris Co., GA.

- 1850 Muscogee Census: Thomsa M. Hogan 39 SC, Orpha 33 SC, James 7 GA, John 3 GA, Eliza 6/12 GA, Miss Eliza Whitton 21 GA and Lafayette Dicken 16 GA.

- 1880 Muscogee census: Thomas M. Hogan 60 SC, Orphus 52 SC, John L. 23 GA, Eliza S. 20 GA, Susan E. 16 GA, Rebecca E. 14 GA and Mary E. 10 GA.

Rebecca C. Hogan   no dates   SR: bur. 10/15/1872, 15 yrs

Emily T. Bell   Nov. 14, 1839   Sept. 7, 1916

Rev. James Whitten   Jan. 15, 1784   Nov. 17, 1859

- Funeral Notice mentions T. M. Hogan.

- James Whitten was born Jan 26, 1785 (sic) in Spartanburg District, SC, the son of John Whitten (1762 VA – 1837 TN) and Mary Reagan (1766 VA – 1836 TN). He married Elizabeth Ann Thompson 10/5/1809. He and his family moved ca 1833 to Hall Co., GA where he was the minister of Yellow Creek Baptist Church. After Elizabeth's death in 1835, he moved to Whitesville, Harris Co., GA. Elizabeth was the mother of 10 children. After Elizabeth's death, Rev. Whitten moved to Harris Co. GA and married a second time to Sarah.[55]

Eliza A. Whitten   no dates   adult

Mary Orphya Whitten   no dates   baby

Peyton E. Moore   no dates   SR: bur. 11/11/1883, 33

- 1880 Muscogee census: Eliza Hogan 26 GA SC SC, boarders: Peyton Moore 27 GA GA GA, Susie Moore 24 GA SC SC, Mary Hogan 18 GA GA GA, John Hogan 32 GA GA GA, Mimes? Hogan (m) 23 GA Scotland GA, Becka Hogan 3 GA GA GA. (large boarding house, not all residents reflected here.)

- Peyton E. Moore married Susie Hogan, the d/o Thomas & Orpha Hogan.

Mary Mica Yorston   no dates   baby

Orpha H. Moore   no dates   baby

Lot 28, partial fence lot, no name

Thos. Barnard   Cols. Guards CSA

- T. M. Barnard, private, enlisted Apr. 16, 1861. Absent without leave Oct. 31, 1861.

Jenny Barnard   June 10, 1841   Nov. 9, 1850   c/o Edw. & Lucy Barnard

Jacob Barnard   Nov. 1, 1842   Sept. 17, 1844   c/o Edw. & Lucy Barnard

- 1850 Muscogee census: Edward Barnard 38, Lucy J. 29, Thomas M. 11, Mary E. 9, Jeannette 6, Lucy 4, Edward 2 and Catterena 8mos.

- Edward Barnard married Lucy J. Barrow 11/19/1838 in Muscogee Co.

Sexton records indicate buried in this lot

Sallie T. Barnard   *SR: bur. 12/3/1907, 42 yrs.*

Lot 29, no name on wall

Charles Philips   Feb. 16, 1841   Jan. 17, 1927

- Obit: Charles Philips – married 1st to Miss Carrie E. Lewis of Columbus, GA, she died Aug. 1, 1919, 2nd married Mrs. A. J. Skinner, she survives, children: C. K. of Fla., Charles, Jr. of Griffin, GA, Edwin R. of new York, Louis of Thomasville, GA, 2 dghts, Mrs. T. J. Brooks of Griffin, GA and Miss Mary G. Philips of Paris. CSA.

- 1880 Muscogee census: Charles Philips 39 FL NC GA, wife Carrie 35 AL GA GA, son Timothy 7 AL, dau Ruth 5 GA, son John 3 GA and Charlie 1 GA.

Carrie E. Lewis   Jan. 4, 1843   July 10, 1918   w/o Charles Philips

- 1860 Muscogee Census: B. A. Sorsby 54 NC, Emma D. (sic) 44 GA, Caroline Lewis 17 AL and Sarah E. Thomas 16 GA.

- 1870 Muscogee Census: Elvira Sorsby 48 GA (widow) and Carrie Bellamy 27 AL (widow).

- Caroline Elvira is the d/o Pierce Lovick Lewis (1815-1852) and Caroline Elizabeth Cook (1820-1850) Carrie Lewis' mother was a sister to Elvira Cook, the wife of Battle Augustus Sorsby (Sowersby).

Paul Philips   Mar. 10, 1885   Oct. 4, 1919   s/o Charles & Carrie Philips

John Philips   age 4 mos. s/o Charles & Carrie Philips.

Lot 30, no name on wall

Wm. Edwards Carter   Lt. Barnwell Bat. CSA

Zoononia Darwin Hoxey   1819   1866   w/o John Davis Carter

- Muscogee Marriage records state Zoonomia D. Hoxey married John D. Carter 4 Feb. 1841.

Irby Randolph Banks	Feb. 6, 1880 Banks, AL	Feb. 22, 1937 Atlanta, GA
James Darwin Carter		Pemberton Cav. CSA. U.C.V. Camp 159. SR: b. 2/16/1849, bur. 7/10/1922
Randolph Carter Banks	Dec. 19, 1902	Feb. 11, 1950
Thomas Hoxey, M.D.		Aug. 1, 1856 62 yrs.

- Obit: Thomas Hoxey – in 1842 fought in Texas against the Mexicans, battle of Lapaticin.

- Dr. Thomas Hoxey was the son of Asa Hoxie and Sarah Ann Toxey.[56] He served from 1813 to 1814 in the Creek War as Lieut under Captain John Broadnax. He served as Major of Georgia Militia in the Creek War in 1836.

- Wilkes Co., GA probated 3/5/1825. Asa Hoxie. To Lewis S. Brown in trust for sole and separate use of my dau. Caroline Willey, four slaves, household goods, etc. Residue to be divided into four lots, to dau. Sarah Browning, Lot No. 1; to son Asa Hoxie, Lot No. 2; to son Thomas Hoxie Lot No. 3; Lot No. 4 in trust as above for dau. Caroline Willey. As wife Sarah is old and infirm all property to be kept together for her use for her natural life. Signed Sept. 8, 1824. Probated Mar. 5, 1825. Lewis S. Brown and James Willey, Exrs. Wm. Jones, Thos. Eudaley, Margaret Eudaley, Test.

Mary R. Hoxey	Jan. 27, 1795	Oct. 25, 1860

- Mary Hoxey was the d/o Brice Gaither (c1765 MD – 1823 Putnam Co., GA) and Elizabeth Reid, d/o Alexander Reid.

- Putnam Co., GA WB B pages 11-15. Brice Gaither of Putnam Co., GA. WW 10/21/1823 – WP 11/3/1823.
  Legatees: son: Greenbury, dau: Mary Hoxey, wife of Doctor Thomas Hozey (sic), daus.: Mary, Sarah D., and Nancy until they attain age of 21; son Henry (underage), dau. Sarah D. Park, w/o Dr. Andrew Park, dau. Nancy w/o John Hudson, dau. Elizabeth, dau. Margaret, son Eli, son Brice B. H. Exrs. wife Elizabeth, sons Greenbury & Henry, when the latter becomes of age, Simon Holt and Stephen W. Harris. Wits: John H. Williamson, Irby Hudson, Stephen W. Harris.

Thomas Hoxey, Jr.	Sept. 12, 1827	June 5, 1848
Dr. J. J. Bulow Hoxey	Sept. 26, 1816	Dec. 1, 1852

- Obit: Dr. J. J. B. Hoxey – surgeon during the Mex. War, sity Physician 1852, married Sarah S. Terry Oct. 10, 1838[57], 2nd wife Caroline C. Cotton, Jan. 15, 1843.

- Sarah Terry was the d/o Joseph M. Terry formerly of Edgefield District, SC.

- Caroline E. Cotton married John J. B. Hoxey 15 Jan 1843 in Muscogee Co., GA.

- John J. B. Hoxey, surg 1 Ga Inf.[58]

Brice Asa Hoxey	Oct. 22, 1825	June 21, 1855

1 child slab, n/m

Lot 31, no name on wall

W. Thomas Andrews	Dec. 9, 1870	Aug. 12, 1930
Jack Jones Pease	June 8, 1891	Jan. 13, 1964

- Jack J. Pease was married to Margaret Lenora Andrews c. 1920.

| Belle Shaw | Sept. 29, 1868 | Mar. 23, 1940 | w/o Thomas Andrews |

- 1920 Muscogee census: Tom Cr. Andrews 49 GA GA GA, wife Belle 50 GA GA GA and dau Margaret 18 GA.

Lot 32, Grimes on wall

| Willie Sterling Pope | Oct. 8, 1872 | Oct. 27, 1875 | s/o R. C. & A. G. Pope |
| Robert C. Pope | June 17, 1839 | July 23, 1891 | |

- Funeral notice mentions Cliff B. Grimes.

- 1880 Muscogee census: There is "a" Robert Pope 42 GA GA GA in the household of Grace Bennett 42. Annie and her children are enumerated in the household of Clifford Grimes.

Annie Grimes Pope	1846	1925	SR: bur. 5/24/1925. 80 yrs.
Epsey Grimes Key	Aug. 2, 1846	June 19, 1930	
William M. Key	Oct. 28, 1836 Madison, GA	Sept. 12, 1904 Atlanta, GA	

- Obit: Wm. Key – died Atlanta, GA, brother of Bishop Joseph S. Key, leaves wife & 1 son, Cliff G. Key, both of Atlanta, GA.

- William McKendrie Key was the son of Caleb Witt Key (1806-1881) and his wife Elizabeth J. Hames (1813-1837). Elizabeth Hames' father was Rev. Joshua Hames (1779-1854).

Miss Lila Pope	Aug. 26, 1870	Nov. 6, 1958	
Berta B. Grimes	1849	1923	SR: bur. 7/14/1923, 74
Sterling F. Grimes		Dec. 17, 1856	

- s/o Sterling Grimes was the s/o Dr. Sterling Grimes (1782 Hanover Co., VA – 1826 Greene Co., GA) and Mariah Fountain (1789 Louisa Co., VA – 1822).

- 1850 Muscogee census: Sterling F. Grimes 37 GA, Sarah J. 28 GA, Clifford B. 9 GA, Ann A. 7 GA, Epsey B. 5 GA, Alberta 3 GA and Fountaine 1 GA.

- Sterling married Sarah Bowdre in Greene Co., GA on 5/5/1841. Her father, Thomas Bowdre's will proved in Columbia Co., GA, 9/16/1846. Thomas Bowdre – Legatees: wife Ephata. Dau: Sarah Grimes, wife of Sterling. Sons: Albert I. R., Benjamin, Thomas. Grandchildren: Thomas and Martha Emily Hamilton, children of James F. Hamilton. Exr: Son, Benjamin Bowdre. Wits: Thomas Wynne, Jr., John Smith, Gabriel Jones. Thomas Bowdre married Ephatha Rees 6/19/1805 in Columbia Co., GA.

| Lucy Barnett Grimes | Mar. 12, 1860 | Mar., 24, 1945 | w/o Clifford Bowdre Grimes |

- Lucy is the d/o John Barnett (1818-1889) and his wife Lucy Pitts (1828-1875).

Charles Grimes	Apr. 16, 1851	Apr. 25, 1851	s/o S. F. & S. J. Grimes
Sarah J. Grimes	May 10, 1817	Dec. 4, 1878	w/o Sterling F. Grimes
David Adams	Jan. 6, 1810 Washington Co., NY	July 13, 1882 Rome, GA	

- Obit: David Adams – died in Rome, GA, was born in Washington Co., NY, came to Columbus in 1835/1836, moved to Atlanta 1869, then to Rome in 1870, leaves 1 nephew Mayor Cliff B. Grimes. (Another obituary may be found in the Atlanta Constitution 14 July 1882.)

- 1850 Muscogee census: (in household of Nat McRobinson) David Adams 40 NY, Ann A. 26 GA and Frederick G. 2 GA.

Ann America Adams	Nov. 2, 1818 Greensboro, GA	July 10, 1865 Columbus, GA	w/o David Adams. 46 ye, 8 mo 8 dy

- Ann America was a sister to Sterling Fountain Grimes (1813-1856) and d/o Sterling Grimes.

Frederick Gale Adams	Jan. 17, 1848 Columbus, GA	Apr. 10, 1864 Tuscaloosa, AL	s/o David & Ann A. Adams
Lucy Grimes	Apr. 28, 1884	Aug. 5, 1885	d/o Cliff B. & Lucy B. Grimes
Clifford Bowdre Grimes	Aug. 10, 1842	Aug. 27, 1915	

- Obit: Clifford B. Grimes – s/o Sterling F. & Sarah Bowdre Grimes, CSA, 46th GA Regt., Co. K., Mayor of Columbus 1881, later City Recorder, and City Marshal, married Miss Lucy Barnett, Feb. 24, 1882, 2 children, Miss Annie Lou Grimes, Cecil Grimes, both of Columbus.

- 1880 Muscogee Census: Clifford B. Grimes 37 GA GA GA, sister Alberta B. Grimes 28 GA, sister Annie Pope 25 GA, nephew Clifford G. Pope 13 GA, nephew Robert C. Pope 11 GA and niece Lila Pope 9 GA.

Clifford Grimes	May 8, 1886	May 6, 1888	s/o Cliff & Lucy B. Grimes

1 adult slab, n/m

Lot 33, no name on wall

4 baby slabs, n/m

?? Hall		Sept. 18, 18??	age 22 yrs
Mary Pomroy Hall		Oct. 12, 1857	21 yrs. w/o Geo. W. Dillingham
Rosa Nelson Dillingham	Feb. 19, 1872	Mar. 24, 1963	
George Walker Dillingham	Jan. 16, 1868	Feb. 16, 1915	
Charles H. Dillingham	Aug. 18, 1866	Aug. 14, 1911	
Mary Eugenia Montague		May 2, 1864	w/o Geo Hall

- Funeral Notice mentions Mr. George I. Hall & Mrs. Cairnes.

Mary Pomroy Hall	June 28, 1862	19 mos.	
George I. Hall	Nov. 12, 1837 Columbus, GA	Oct. 7, 1917 Parhyba, Brazil	
Anna Louise Hall	Dec. 4, 1842	May 12, 1904	w/o Geo. W. Dillingham

- Obit: Ann Hall – relict of Geo. W. Dillingham, d/o Mr. & Mrs. Harvey Hall of Columbus, GA. on June 1, 1861 married in Gainesville, GA, leaves 7 children, Charles, Walker,

Miss Rosa Dillingham, all of Columbus, Robert of Chattanooga, TN, Mrs. T. M. Ticknor, of Albany, GA, Mrs. Eugene Daniel, Mrs. Joe Schumaker, all of Columbus.

Geo. W. Dillingham	July 28, 1833	Dec. 28, 1896

- Obit: Member of Columbus Guards, 2nd GA Regt., married Anna Hall, d/o Henry & Jane Hall of Columbus, GA, 8 children, Charles, George Walker, Mrs. L. Carnes, Rosa Nelson, Kate Dexter, Charlotte Elvira, Robert Clifton, one deceased.

- Muscogee Co. Superior Ct. Oct. 1842. George W. Dillingham (1804-1834). Left wife Lucy E. (d/o Harriet C. Tichnor) and son George Jr. John Dillingham appointed administrator. The records mention a William Dillingham of Westchester, PA, a brother of John. Lucy (1814-1864), George Sr.'s widow married 2nd. William D. Carnes.

- George Sr. married Lucy E. Ticknor 7/13/1832 in Jones Co., GA.

- 1850 Muscogee census: George Dillingham 17 GA.

- 1880 Muscogee census: G. W. Dillingham 46 GA GA GA, wife Anna L. 36 GA GA GA, son Chas. H. 13 GA, son Geo. M. 12 GA, dau Lucy E. 9 GA, dau Rosa M. 8 GA, dau Katie 5 GA, Charlotte B. 3 and son Robt. 9/12.

Eugene Henry Daniel	May 16, 1908	Apr. 10, 1912	s/o Katie D. & Eugene H. Daniel
Charles Walker Schuessler	Mar. 19, 1906	Nov. 1, 1915	

Lot 34, E. M. Smith on wall

no evidence of graves

Lot 35, Pierce on wall

Charles Henry Pierce	Mar. 23, 1862	June 9, 1919	
Josephine Pierce		July 2, 1914	baby

Lot 36, Clayton on wall

Lily Clayton Beall	no dates		SR: bur. 3/14/1927, 83
Henry G. Beall	no dates		SR: bur. 3/13/1939, 82

- Obit: Henry Gaither Beall, b. 5/31/1856 in Hamilton, d. 1939 in Columbus, buried at Linwood. He was s/o Gen. Elias H. Beall (and his 2nd wife,) Sarah Gaither Park. Grandson of Gen. Elias Beall who, as one of 5 commissioners appointed by Governor John Forsyth helped to lay off the city of Columbus in 1828. Henry married Lily Clayton who died 3/12/1927.[59]

- 1880 Muscogee census: Henry G. Beall 24 GA GA GA (single).

- 1920 Muscogee census: Henry G. Beall 64 GA GA GA, wife Elebeth 64 GA GA GA, dau Mary Beall 33 GA.

Mary Beall	Sept. 3, 1886	May 18, 1972	w/o Dozier Fuller, Sr.

Dozier Fuller, Sr.   Oct. 31, 1877   Aug. 23, 1959

- 1880 Talbot Co., GA Census: John Fuller 46 GA GA GA, wife Susan 35 GA GA GA, son Willie 17 GA, son Dozier 2 GA.

Mary C. Lary   1839   1919   SR: bur. 7/21/1919, 80 yrs

- 1900 Muscogee Census: Mary C. Lary Aug 1842 GA GA GA (widow; 1/1 child), sister Elizabeth Beall Sept. 1856 GA GA GA (Married 8 years; 2/2 children), nephew Stanford Beall Feb 1883 GA, niece Mary G. Beall Sept 1886 GA and boarders.

3 adult graves, n/m   2 child brick slabs, n/m

Lot 37, no name

S. Hatcher Flournoy   Apr. 4, 1906   Aug. 27, 1922

Josiah Flournoy   Mar. 12, 1886   Jan. 13, 1954

Mary Flournoy   Nov. 22, 1908   Sept. 27, 1989
Passailague

- d/o M. Reynolds & Mattie Flournoy. Married Jack M. Passailague, Sr.

M. Reynolds Flournoy   Oct. 15, 1882   Apr. 26, 1920

- Josiah Flournoy and Mallory Reynolds Flournoy were sons of John Francis Flournoy (1847-1936) and his 2nd wife Mary Reynolds (1852-1926). John Francis Flournoy married 1st 1869, Rebecca Epping (1852-1873) and had 2 children by that marriage.

Mattie Hatcher   Oct. 29, 1882   May 6, 1956   w/o M. Reynolds Flournoy

- Mattie was the d/o Samuel Bass Hatcher (1850 Chesterfield Co., VA-1937) and Mary Lou Taylor (1855-1887).

Jeanette S. Martin   Apr. 18, 1885   June 13, 1931   w/o Josiah Flournoy

Lot 38, no name on wall

4 adult brick clabs, n/m   1 baby brick slab, n/m

Lot 39, open lot

no evidence of graves

Lot 40, Hogan on wall

Mrs. Isabella Hogan   no dates   SR: bur. 10/24/1923, 78

- 1920 Muscogee Census: Irene Wilson 68 GA PA Ire (single), sister Belle W. Hogan 70 GA PA Ire (widowed), niece Belle Murphy 40 GA GA GA (single) and niece Mary Murphy 35 GA GA GA.

- 1880 Muscogee Census: Lottie Wilson 22 GA GA GA, sister Irene Wilson 28 GA GA GA, sister Belle Hogan 30 GA GA GA, mother Mary Beckwith 51 GA GA GA, nephew

Jos. Hogan 10 GA and orphan May Murphy 9 GA.

- 1870 Muscogee Census: Charlotta Wilson 40 Ireland, Irene 23 GA, Lottie 14 GA and Nellie Murphy 6 GA.

James Hogan   Columbus Guards 1861-1865

- James C. Hogan – Co. I. 64th Regt. GA Vol. Inf. – Private enlisted Mar. 24, 1863. Appt. Sergeant. Roll for Oct. 31, 1864, last roll on file shows him sick in Columbus, GA hospital since Oct. 1, 1864. In Marshall Hospital in Columbus Nov. 30, 1864.
- 1870 Muscogee Census: James C. Hogan 28 GA, Isabella C. 25 GA and James 1 GA.
- 1850 Muscogee census: Thomas M. Hogan 39 SC, Orpha 33 SC, James 7, John 3, and Eliza 6 mos. Also in household Miss Eliza Whitten 21 GA and Lafayette Dicken 16 GA. James was born 7/14/1844 and married Belle Wilson 4/11/1868.

J. W. Hogan   1918   SR: bur. 1/4/1918

- Obit: died Jan. 3, 1918, popular showman, owned Dream Theatre, 49 yrs. old, leaves wife, mother Mrs. Belle Hogan, 2 aunts, Lottie & Irene Wilson.

Lot 41, Fuller on wall

Mrs. Emma L. Dudley   1840   1924   SR: bur. /13/1924

- 1910 Muscogee Census: Davis A. Andrews 66 GA GA GA (m2@31), wife Alice A. 60 GA IO GA (m1@31; 0/0 children), SIL Emma L. Dudly 70 GA IO GA (widowed), niece Julia H. Fuller 30 GA GA AL and gdau Claudia West 16 GA GA GA.
- 1860 Chattahoochee Co., GA Census: H. Fuller 62 NY, Geo 22 GA, Emma 20, Joseph 19, Carry 17, Allis 10 and Edwin 8.
- 1850 Muscogee Census: Hyram Fuller 51 Musc. Co. GA, Caroline 35 Edgefield SC, Elizabeth 14 Musc Co, George 12 Musc Co, Emma 11 Musc Co., Joseph 10 Musc. Co., Caroline 7 Musc Co. and Alice 2 Musc Co.
- Harris Co., GA MR Hiram Fuller married Mary Ann Simons 10 Jan 1832. He was probably married before this and married Caroline after this. In 1880, Hiram is in Jasper Co., Iowa listed as a stepfather in the HH of John Kesler.

Alice A. Andrews   Dec. 24, 1848   Nov. 24, 1910   w/o Davis A. Andrews

- Obit: husband, D. A. Andrews survives her, 1 step-son, W. T., 2 sisters, Mrs. J. M. Brannon of Seale, AL, Mrs. Emma L. Dudley of Columbus, GA, 2 brothers, J. P. Fuller of Columbus, GA, E. H. Fuller of Juniper, GA.
- 1850 Muscogee census: Samuel R. Andrews 54 NC, Elizabeth 40 TN, James 21 GA, Amanda 17 GA, Mary J. 14 GA, Saml. R. 13 GA, Julius C. 11 GA, __ Susan 10 GA, D. A. 6 GA, George E. 4 GA, Clarance 1 GA and Joseph 7 GA.
- 1860 Muscogee Co., GA: Judge S. A. Andrews 64 NC, Elizabeth 57 TN, Joseph C. 19 GA, Davis E. 17 GA, George E. 15 GA and Clarance H. 11 GA.
- 1870 Muscogee census: Davis Andrews 26 GA, Ellen 23 GA and Ella 5 GA.
- 1880 Muscogee census: Davis A. Andrews 36 GA TN NC, wife Allice A. 28 GA GA GA, dau Ella 13 GA, son Wm. Thomas 9 GA and boarder Emma H. Hill 38 GA (widowed).

5 adult brick slabs, n/m   2 baby brick slabs, n/m

Lot 42, open lot

John L. Barringer	Apr. 2, 1804 Cabarrus Co., NC	Atlanta, GA	

- 1850 Muscogee Census: John L. Barenger46 NC, Mathias 41 NC.

Sarah Ann Chapman	Aug. 26, 1842	Mar. 31, 1851	d/o C. W. & S. A. Chapman
Charles Chapman	May 29, 1805 Southampton, Mass.	Apr. 26, 1871 Columbus, GA	

- Obit: Asst. Assessor of Internal Rev. for Columbus District, in city by 1849.

- 1870 Muscogee census: Charles W. Chapman 65 Mass, Susan E. 63 Mass and several school teachers.

- 1860 Muscogee Census: C. T. Chapman 54 NY, Susan A. 52 MA and Harriet S. Pomroy 28 GA.

- 1850 Richmond Co., GA Census: Charles W. Chapman 45 MA, Susan A. 43 MA, Sarah 8 GA and Martha Humphrey 37 PA.

Moses Taylor	Mar. 1, 1878	SR: 80 years

- 1860 Muscogee Census: Moses Taylor 61 NC, Miles W. 21 GA and Herzula G. 19 GA.

- 1850 Muscogee census: Moses Taylor 50 NC, Sally 40 GA, Miles W. 11 Musc Co.. and Angeline G. 10 Musc Co.

1 adult brick slab, n/m   1 triple adult brick slab, n/m

Sexton Records indicate buried in this lot:

Mrs. S. A. Chapman   *bur. 9/5/1878, 65 yrs.*

Mat Barringer   *bur. 5/15/1872, 62 yrs.*

- 1870 Muscogee Census: Matthius Barringer 53 GA.

- 1860 Muscogee Census: Matt Barringer 42 NC.

- Matthias Barringer married Sarah Pryer 13 Dec 1850 in Muscogee Co., GA.

Lot 43, fenced lot, no name

Leila Rose Slade	Apr. 13, 1872	Sept. 9, 1874	d/o James J. & Leila B. Slade
John Henry Slade	Sept. 3, 1865	Apr. 26, 1867	s/o James J. & Leila B. Slade
James Jeremiah Slade	Apr. 28, 1831 Clinton, Jones Co., GA	Apr. 30, 1917	s/o Rev. Thomas B. Slade & Anne Jaqueline Blount. Maj. CSA

- Obit – Capt. Slade's Life
Capt. Slade, there was no better known man in this little section of Georgia, though a native of Jones County, had lived in this city since 1847, residing for a short time in

Macon during his boyhood days where his father, the late T. B. Slade with the late Bishop Pierce founded the Wesleyan Female college. Captain Slade's higher education was received at North Carolina University from which institution he graduated with honors. He also served as an alderman of this city.

At the outbreak of the Civil War he was a cotton planter in Carroll Parish, Louisiana. He raised a company of volunteers and offered it to the state being commissioned at that time. He served in Virginia and was with Lee in Maryland. Later as Capt. and adjutant with General Paul J. Semmes.

Capt. Slade was married to Miss Leila Bonner, d/o the late Seymour Bonner and she with ten children survive him; Messrs Wm. B. Slade of Columbus, Thomas B. Slade of Florida, Jas. J. Slade Jr. of Mexico, Chas. B. Slade of New York, Mrs. Nettie Leither, Mrs. Marion Townsend, Mrs. Effie May Dozier and Miss Florence Slade of this city, Mrs. Nora Screvens of Birmingham and Mrs. Louise West of Florida. Twenty seven grandchildren also survive him.

After the war, Capt. Slade returned to Columbus where he taught school. Capt. Slade also served as Mayor of Columbus in 1892-1895.

- James Slade first married Annie Graham the d/o John Graham of north GA. Their only child died in infancy.[60] Conflicting information is reported in Helen M. Prescott, Genealogical Memoir of the Roulhac Family in America, (Atlanta, Ga.: American Pub. & Engraving Co., 1894) which stated that James married Annie Gertrude Graham (1835-1856) 19 July 1855, the d/o William P. Graham and Margaret Graves.

Seymour B. Slade		July 16, 1887	16 yrs. s/o James J. & Leila B. Slade
Leila Birchett Bonner	Dec. 12, 1841	Dec. 8, 1921	consort of James J. Slade

- Obit: nee Bonner, married James J. Slade Jan. 12 1859, widow, children; William B. of Atlanta, GA, Thos. B. of Jacksonville, FL, James J. of Mexico City, Charles B. of New York, Mrs. R. H. Screvens of Marianna, FL, Mrs. Minnie Lightner, Mrs. K. R. Townsend, Mrs. J. Laurence Dozier, Jr. & Miss Florence Slade, all of Columbus, GA.

- d/o Col. Seymour R. Bonner (1809-1856) and his first wife

Florence Slade Daffin	Aug. 9, 1881	June 15, 1963	
G. Y. Tigner	Oct. 2, 1856	May 1, 1938	

- 1920 Muscogee Census: G. Young Tigner 62 GA GA GA, Johnny L. 54 AL GA GA.

- 1910 Muscogee Census: Germancius Tigner 52 GA GA GA, wife Johnny L. 45 AL GA GA (married 21 yrs; 2/2 children) da Helen 17 GA, son John L. 15 GA and MIL Helen R. Lindsay 64 GA NC NC (widowed; 1/1 child).

Johnny L. Tigner	Aug 25, 1864	Oct. 2, 1942	d/o J. B. Lindsay & Helen Der. Slade. w/o G. Y. Tigner
Helen Lindsay Tigner	Dec. 23, 1891	Mar. 10, 1920	
Helen Der. Slade	Feb. 15, 1841	Nov. 7, 1917	d/o Thomas B. & Ann J. Slade. w/o John B. Lindsay.

- Obit: d/o late Rev. Thos. B. Slade of Columbus, GA, widow of John B. Lindsay a CSA vet., 1 daughter Miss Helen Tigner, 2 sisters Mrs. G. E. Thomas of Columbus, GA and Mrs. Emma Prescott of Atlanta, GA, 1 brother Thomas B. Slade of Carrollton.

Anna Persons Dozier	Dec. 8, 1905	Apr. 16, 1976

John B. Lindsay   Mar. 9, 1840   Feb. 18, 1865   CSA

- John Bright Lindsay was the son of Sherwood C. Lindsay and Elizabeth Bright Cooper. He enlisted in the CSA as a private in the Columbus Guards. He saw many battles, Yorktown, VA, TN and GA. For his gallantry at Chickamauga, he was given a furlough signed by the immortal Lee. During this furlough he was shot and killed by a Home Guard in Columbus. The indignation was so great that the Commander of the Post narrowly escaped being mobbed by citizens.

Mrs. Anne G. Slade	Aug. 2, 1835	May 9, 1856	consort of James J. Slade.
Anne Graham Slade	Apr. 11, 1856	June 30, 1856	d/o James J. and Ann C. Slade.
Ann Jaqueline Blount	Feb. 16, 1805 Washington Co., NC	Feb. 12, 1891 Columbus, GA	w/o Rev. Thomas B. Slade

- Obit –died at the residence of her daughter, Mrs. H. C. McKee, 85 years old, married Thomas B. Slade, mother of Capt. J. J. Slade, Thomas B. Slade, Mrs. H. C. McKee, Mrs. J. E. Giguilliat, Mrs. Grigsby E. Thomas, Mrs. Helen D. Lindsay, Mrs. Emma Prescott.

- Ann Blount married Rev. Thomas Bog Slade 4/1/1824 in Jones Co., GA.

- "A History of Savannah and South Georgia". Harden, William,. Chicago. Lewis Pub. Co.. 1913, Vol 2:917-918 shows a biography of James J. Slade which relates that Ann Jacqueline Blount was the d/o James Blount who migrated from NC to GA and settled permanently in Blountsville, Clinton, GA.

Florence Slade Dozier	Dec. 15, 1907	Dec. 9, 1990	
Rev. Thomas B. Slade	Martin Co., NC	May 5, 1882	s/o Jeremiah & Janet Slade. Moved to GA Jan. 1824.

- Obit – born Martin Co., NC 26 June 1800, pioneer of female education in GA, leaves wife and several children.

- GA Baptists: Slade, Thomas B., born, Martin Co., NC, June 26, 1800. His father was a Brig. Gen., in War of 1812. The subject graduated from U. of N. C., in 1820 with first honors, then studied and practiced law with his father. In 1824 he moved to Jones Co., Ga., where he and Anne Jacquelin Blount were m. Apr 1, 1824. In 1828 he became principal of Clinton Male Academy, and with the exception of the last two years of the war, he spent 50 years engaged in educational activities, including a professorship at Weslyan in Macon. He was ordained in 1835, and devoted much time preaching to destitute churches. Three sons and four sons-in-law served in CSA. The youngest son, John, being killed at the battle of Sharpsburg. Several children.

- Thomas Bog Slade was the son of General Jeremiah Slade and Janet Bog. Maj. Gen. Slade served in the War of 1812 from Mecklenburg Co., NC.

- The school in Columbus of Rev. Thomas Slade was called Sladeville Hall was begun in the 1840's and was alternately a boy's and girl's school. It was rated as a High Scool in 1844. In 1845, the Slade school was listed as Slade Female Institute. In 1868-1869, Sladeville Hall was a school for boys and it was here that Thomas' son James J. Slade was an instructor.

- 1860 Muscogee Census: Thomas B. Slade 60 NC, Ann G. 55 NC, Tammett E. 30 GA, Mary L. 28 GA, Stella B. 20 GA, Hellen 18 GA and John H. ___ GA.

- 1850 Muscogee Census: Thomas B. Slade 50 NC, Mrs. Ann J. Slade 45 NC, Janett E. 25 GA, Mary L. 23 GA, Ann J. 21 GA, James J. 19 GA, Emma J. 17 GA, Thomas B. 16

GA, Stella B. 11 GA, Martha B. 13 GA, Helen B. 9 GA, John H. 7 GA, Miss Catherine A. Shields 17 GA and long list of students.

Stella Blount Slade	July 19, 1839 Macon, GA	Sept. 13, 1911	d/o Thos. B. & Ann J. Slade. Wife of H. C. McKee.

- Obit – widow of Hockley C. McKee, d/o Rev. T. B. Slade, born Macon, GA, married July 16, 1861, he died about 3 years ago, 2 brothers, Capt. James J. Sledge of Columbus, GA Thomas Slade of Carrollton, GA, 4 sisters, Mrs. G. E. Thomas, Mrs. Helen Lindsay, both of Columbus, Mrs. Gegvilliat (sic) of Macon, GA & Mrs. Prescott of Atlanta.

Hockley Cloyd McKee	Dec. 6, 1839 Columbus, GA	June 3, 1908	CSA

- Obit – Capt. in Terrell's Art., "Uncle Hock" born in Columbus s/o H. C. & Elizabeth B. McKee, father from Philadelphia and was in Columbus about 2 years after the City was laid out. Married Miss Stella B. Slade July 16, 1861, wife survives, 2 brothers James & Joseph A., both of Philadelphia, sisters Miss Elizabeth McKee of Philadelphia, Mrs. Priscilla Hamill of Georgetown, Colo.

- Hockley Cloyd McKee, Jr. was the son of Hockley Cloyd McKee (1810-1863) and Elizabeth Ballinger Atkinson (c1814-1886). Hockley Sr. and his 2 sons Hockley Jr. and John Grubb McKee were carriage makers.

Constance Thill	June 22, 1877	Apr. 18, 1962	w/o C. B. Slade
Charles Blount Slade	May 15, 1874	Aug. 23, 1942	

one large slab

Annie Slade Thomas, age 4	Jennett Eliza Thomas, age 1
John Grigsby Thomas, age 6	Grigsby Eskridge Thomas, 5 weeks.

- Children of Grigsby Eskridge Thomas and Martha Bog Slade who were married 8/2/1859 in Muscogee Co., GA.

- 1880 Muscogee Census: Grigsby E. Thomas 46 GA GA GA, Martha B. 42 GA NC NC, Emma 13 GA, Hockley 11 GA, Thomas 9 GA, Helen 6 GA, Stella 4 GA.

John Henry Slade	Jan., 11, 1843 Columbus, GA	Apr. 5, 1862	Member Cols. Guards, end regt. Ga Bat. at the Battle of Sharpsburg. s/o Thos. B. & Ann J. Slade.

- Member of Columbus Guards, killed in battle, reinterrment from Sharpsburg, MD 3/23/1869.

- Enlisted private April 16, 1861. Wounded and captured at Sharpsburg Sept. 17, 1862. Died of wounds at David Smith's farm near Sharpsburg 1862.

Mary Lavinia Slade	Dec. 11, 1826 Clinton, GA	Feb. 6, 1863 Columbus, GA	d/o Thos. R. & Ann J. Slade. SR: bur. 2/14/1863.
Amelia Slade	Nov. 1, 1830	Apr. 5, 1845	d/o Dr. James B. Slade of New Orleans, LA
Anne L. Ellis	Aug. 21, 1829	Feb. 16, 1858	w/o Roswell Ellis. d/o Rev. Thos. B. & Ann J. Slade.

- Roswell Ellis was born 4/8/1822 in Putnam Co., GA, the son of Dr. Iddo Ellis (b. NH d. 1877 Cols., GA) and Lucy Phelps (1786 New Haven, CT – 1824 Putnam Co., GA). Dr. Iddo Ellis was a physician and lived in New York until 1817 when he removed to

Edenton, Putnam Co., GA.

- Roswell married 1) Frances Ann Mangham 9/14/1848 in Muscogee. She died 1856. He married 3) 11/23/1868 Elizabeth "Lizzie" Rutherford (1833-1873).

- Roswell Ellis was a First Captain in the Columbus Guards. He also served as a 2nd Lt. in the Mexican War.

2 adult slabs, n/m   1 baby markers, n/m

For more information on this family, I suggest reading; Prescott, Helen M., "Genealogical memoir of the Roulhac family in America", Atlanta, Ga.: (American Pub. & Engraving Co., 1894).

Lot 44, open lot

Wiley Adams   July 18, 1859   50th year of age

- Wiley Adams married Eminade Dunn 1/17/1841 in Muscogee Co.[61] He married 2nd Sarah A. E. Tooke 11/27/1850 in Muscogee Co..

- 1850 Muscogee Census: Wiley Adams 37 SC, Emanuel 9, Georgia Ann 6.

Esende Adams   May 10, 1820   Feb. 25, 1848   w/o Wiley Adams, d/o Wm. ? (unable to read) married Jan. 19, 1841.

S. A. E. Adams   Nov. 30, 1903   widow of Wiley Adams, 68 yrs.

- Obit – died Montgomery, AL at the residence of daughter, Mrs. George W. Burkes, other daughters Mrs. G. H. Burkes, Mrs. I. E. Bunn of Montgomery, AL, 1 son Nathan B. Adams of Chattanooga, TN.

- 1850 Muscogee Census: James A. McDonald 46, Agnes M. 39, Thomas J. 22, Rosabella 11, John T. 13, Eugenia H. 9, Pauline H. A. McDonald 5 and Sarah A. Tooke 15.

1 baby brick slab, n/m

Lot 45, Boland on wall

Ellen Cleland   Oct. 18, 1895   85 years

- Obit: born County Carlow, Ireland, in Columbus 45 years, leaves Mrs. Annie Elter of Anderson, Ind., Jack of Chicago, Ill., Mrs. Eliz Fitzgibbon & Mrs. Grace Boland of Columbus.

- 1880 Muscogee Census: Ellen Cleland 70 VA VA VA, daughter Eliza Fitzgibbon 36 Ire Ire Ire, daughter Grace Boland 33 LA Ire Ire, GS Lee? 10 LA Ire Ire, GS Walker 8 GA LA LA, Geo 6 GA LA LA and GS Garcia? 3 GA LA LA.

Grace R. Boland   1847   1924   SR: bur. 6/9/1924

- New Orleans, LA Birth Index: father Alexander Cleland, mother Helen Ramsey

   o   Grace born 2/13/1847

   o   Anna born 1/6/1841

   o   Jeanette born 2/13/1847

- 1850 Census New Orleans, LA: Alexander Cleland 25 Scotland, Ellen 35 Canada, Anna 9 LA, Eliza 7 LA, Grace 3 LA and John 6/12 LA.

A. J. Boland	July 4, 1882	Color Sgt., 2nd GA Batt., Sharpshooter CSA, 36 yrs.

- Obit: one time proprietor of White Sulphur Springs.

- Montgomery Advertiser 4 July 1982. "On this date 100 years ago (1882)" Today's Independence Day barbecue at Pickett Springs Park will be conducted by Mr. Walker on account of the sudden death after a three-day illness of the lessee, Mr. A.J. Boland, whose remains will be carried to Columbus, Ga. for interment.

- 1870 Muscogee Census: Ellen Lealand (sic) 60 Ireland, Andrew Boland 24 GA, Grace Boland 23 LA and Lee Boland 2/12 GA.

- Andrew Jackson Boland was the son of Jacob Boland and Mary Tinsley.

Lot 46, open lot

Mary Elizabeth Griswold	Apr. 11, 1829	Mar. 10, 1848	w/o Wm. H. Griswold, d/o Dr. L. F. W. & Jane Andrews.

- Obit: wife of William H. Griswold, d/o L. W. F. Andrews, 21st Mar. paper.

- 1850 Muscogee Census: William H. Griswold 30 CT, Caroline M. 18 PA.

- William H. Griswold married Mary E. Andrews 2/21/1847 and Caroline M. Andrews 6/16/1849 in Muscogee County.

Horace Griswold	Dec. 11, 1847	Apr. 30, 1848	inf. s/o Wm. H. & Mary E. Griswold

2 adult slabs, n/m	1 baby brick slab, m/m	1 child's brick slab, n/m

- Obit Caroline M. Andrews: 26 Mar 1856: Died at Beallwood, near Columbus, on the 21st inst. in the 24th year of her age, Mrs. Caroline Matilda Griswold, w/o Wm. H. Griswold, Esq., Junior Proprietor of the Columbus Enquirer, and daughter of Dr. L. F. W. Andrews of Macon.

- June 12, 1827 Pittsburgh Reporter: "Married Wednesday last, Dr. Lewis F.W. Andrews to Jane, eldest daughter of James Gray Esquire. Both of Alleghenytown, Pa."

- The Rev. L. F. W. Andrews (1802-1875) was a Universalist minister through much of the antebellum period in the Southern States. His Two Opinions, or Salvation or Damnation (Macon, Ga., 1837) is a good glimpse into the theology of the time and place.

Lot 47, open lot

Ellen J. Verstille	Jan. 11, 1832	May 18, 1871	w/o Henry W. Verstille
Addie Verstille		no dates	d/o Walter H. & Florence Johnson

2 adult brick slabs, n/m	3 baby brick slabs, n/m

- 1870 Muscogee Census: Henry W. Verstille 41 SC, Ellen J. 38 GA, Rosa E. 15 GA, Florence 12 TN?, William Roberts 23 AL, Susan Roberts 16 GA, Jerome W. Roberts

2/12 GA and Ponder? Roberts 54 SC.

- 1880 Muscogee Census: Henry Verstille 50 SC CT SC and wife Sarah 45 GA GA GA.

- Henry W. Verstille, the son of Col. Tristam Verstille and Rebecca (step-daughter to Tarlton Brown of Barnwell Dist., SC and was a desc. of William Jennings with her mother being Frances Jennings who m. Brannon.), was born 8/10/1828. He attended college at Athens, GA and Harvard Law School, m. Ellen Lockhart of Columbus, Minn. (sic) 8/6/1851. Res. 1861 Louisiana.[62]

Lot 48. open lot

2 adult brick slabs, n/m   1 baby brick slab, n/m

Lot 49, Lewis on wall

Name	Born	Died	Notes
Hettie Hunter Ingram	Sept. 2, 1874	Mar. 25, 1933	
Thomas J. Lewis	Mar. 11, 1827	Dec. 13, 1862	Father. Fell mortally wounded in the Battle of Fredericksburg, VA.

- Obit – died Fredericksburg, VA, Lt. in CSA.

- Thomas Jefferson Lewis was the s/o Ulysses Lewis (1799-1856) and Sarah Ann Abercrombie (c1809-1876).

Name	Born	Died	Notes
Henry F. Mather, Esq.	1853 Marlboro, VT	Feb. 10, 1883 Columbus, GA	s/o Henry & Lucy Ingram Mather

- Henry F. Mather was born 10/31/1852 the s/o Henry Taylor Mather (s/o Capt. Rufus) who married Lucy Ingram in Marlboro VT. 10/12/1841. Lucy I. Mather, widow of Henry, married Capt. Dan. Mather (s/o Timothy) 12/7/1858. [63]

Name	Born	Died	Notes
Alabama Thomasine Lewis	June 21, 1862	May 23, 1926	d/o Thos. J. & Nannie M. Lewis. Sister
Leila E. Lewis	Feb. 9, 1857 Russell Co., AL	Jan. 11, 1909	d/o T. J. & N. M. Lewis
Nannie M. Eiland	June 20, 1831	Dec. 22, 1915	w/o Thomas J. Lewis. Mother.

- Nannie M. Lewis applied for a Widow's Pension for Thomas Jefferson Lewis, a soldier in the CSA, Co. D. 5th Battl. of AL. He enlisted in Nov. 1862 and was in the Virginia Army up to Dec. 13, 1862 when he was killed. Nannie had his remains brought to Columbus and he was buried Dec. 25, 1862.

- Nancy Murray Eiland was the d/o Stephen Eiland (1788-1853) and Mary Allen (1789-1865).

- 1880 Muscogee Census: Nannie Lewis 48 GA GA SC, dau Arma 28 Al, dau Mary 26 AL, dau Lela 23 AL, son John 21 AL, dau Alabama 17 AL

Name	Born	Died	Notes
Annabell Lee	Apr. 14, 1851	Oct. 9, 1918	d/o Thos. J. & Nannie M. Lewis

Susan Eliz Rainey	Apr. 1, 1942	May 28, 1977
Hiram Wason Rainey, Jr.	Oct. 1, 1917	Dec. 27, 1979
Bessie Ingram Heuer	July 18, 1870	Jan. 9, 1955
Lucy Palmer	1852	1862
Aline Ingram Chambers	Dec. 6, 1898	Nov. 18, 1966
Elizabeth Lewis Ingram	June 23, 1829	Jan. 26, 1908

- Obit: w/o Porter Ingram, Judge, born Columbus, 79 years old, nee Miss Elizabeth Martin Lewis d/o Judge Ulysses Lewis, 1 son, Thomas L. of Atlanta, GA, 1 daughter Bessie Ingram of Columbus, GA, 1 step-daughter Mrs. W. W. Benning of Opelika, AL.

John Allen Lewis	Dec. 19, 1858	July 18, 1921	
Wm. Thompson Lewis	Nov. 25, 1892	Nov. 21, 1941	s/o John A. & Willie T. Lewis
Porter Ingram	Apr. 2, 1810	Dec. 3, 1893	

- Obit: born Marlboro, VA, twice married, 2nd wife survives him, children; Tom L., Miss Bessie both of Columbus, Mrs. W. W. Barnes of Opelika, AL.

- 1880 Muscogee Census: Porter Ingram 70 VT MA MA, wife Elizabeth 50 GA GA GA, son Thomas 16 GA, dau Bessie 10 GA and dau Jennie 6 GA.

- 1870 Muscogee Census: Porter Ingram 55 VT, Elizabeth 40 AL, Mary 18 GA, Tommie (f) 5 GA, Jane Cowdery 29 AL, Claude 14 AL, and Sallie 9 AL.

- Porter Ingram s/o Jonathan & Polly (Underwood) Ingram, b. 4/2/1810 Marlborough Vermont, d. 12/3/1893. Graduated from Yale 1831 and taught school in NY until 1836. Came to Harris Co and began practicing law. He m. 1) Sarah Ann Jarrett in 1849, d/o Dr. J.D. & Sarah (Heard) Jarrett. She was b. 10/17/1830, d. 8/5/1855 and buried Bethel Methodist Church Cemetery Pine Mountain Valley Harris Co. He moved to Columbus and was Judge of the Columbus City Court. He m. 2) Elizabeth Lewis. Barfield says they married in 1843. She was the d/o Ulysses Lewis. Porter was a member of the "Home Guard" at the time of Wilson's Raid. Elizabeth d. 1/26/1908, both are buried Linwood.[64]
    - NOTE:
    Dr James D. Jarrett's Bible record reads that he married Sarah A. Heard 5 Jan 1825. Heard Family Bible Records[65] show that Sarah Hammond Heard, w/o James D. Jarrett died 16 August 1825. Dr. Jarrett married secondly 7 July 1829 Jane Jack in Elbert Co., GA.
    - Dr. James D. Jarrett (Jarratt) was the s/o Archelous and Sarah Booker Bibb Jarrett.

Willie Thompson Lewis	May 12, 1861	July 10, 1924	w/o John Allen Lewis
Jane Hall Murdock	Sept. 12, 1840	Aug. 26, 1873	d/o Ulysses & Sarah A. Lewis

- Obit: d/o U. & Sarah Lewis, died at Mt. Meigs, Montgomery Co., AL, sister of Mrs. Porter Ingram, before her marriage to Mr. Murdock some years since, she was the widow of L. P. Cowley (sic).

Sarah Ella Cowdery	Mar. 28, 1861	June 3, 1909	w/o L. C. Freeny
Sarah E. Cowdery	July 10, 1835	Mar. 28, 1861	w/o L. P. Cowdery. d/o U. & S. A. Lewis

- 1860 Russell Co., AL Census: Lymon P. Cowdry 30 OH, Sarah 25 AL and Claud 4 AL.

Ulysses Lewis	Feb. 5, 1799 Jefferson Co., GA	Aug. 8, 1856 Russell Co., AL	He was a direct descendant of Fielding Lewis & his wife Betty Washington Lewis, a sister of George Washington who lived at Fredricksburg, VA, in the historic home Kenmore which they built. He was the first Mayor of Columbus, GA year 1829.

- Baldwin Co. WB A (1806-1829) P. 120. Col. John Lewis ww 1/1/1817 wp 9/15/1817. Wife: Elizabeth. Exrs: Wife, Elizabeth. Ch: William, Fielding, Charley, Augustin, also others. Grdau: Elizabeth Lewis Sturges. Wits: Hiram Starrs, John L. Harris, Stephen Sanders.

- Baldwin Co. WB A (1806-1829) P. 219. Elizabeth Lewis ww 1/10/1825 wp 1/24/1825. Sons: William, Fielding, Richard, Fauntleroy, Ulysses. Son-in-law: William Kennon, D. Stone, --- Dawson? Dau-in-law: Lucy Lewis. Exrs: Sons, Willian, Fielding, Ulysses. Wits: William H. Torrance.

NOTE:
Georgia Journal - Sep 16,1817 Departed this life on the 29th ult, at the close of his 64th year, after two days painful illness, Col John Lewis, a native of Halifax Co, Virginia, but for many years a citizen of Georgia.

The Alderman Library at the University of Virginia has Col. Fielding Lewis' Bible Records. It states: Fielding Lewis was married to Miss Catharine Washington 1746. 22 June 1747 - Our First Son John Lewis was born 22d Day June 1747 His Uncle John Lewis and Mr Charles Dick God Fathers. Mrs Mary Washington & Mrs Lee God Mothers. There is no other son John listed as a child of Miss Betty Washington.

Col. John Lewis, father of Ulysses Lewis was born 31 Feb. 1753. Fielding and Catherine Washington's son, John, was married multiple times and died 23 Nov 1825 in Logan Co., KY.

While Ulysses was definitely related many times to Col. Fielding Lewis, the husband of Catherine Washington, available records do not seem to support him to be a direct descendant, especially as written to be the son of Fielding and Betsy Washington.

Carrie Roper Ingram	Oct. 29, 1871	Sept. 1, 1921	
Sara Abercrombie Lewis	1807 Hancock Co., GA	Aug. 6, 1876 Columbus, GA	w/o Ulysses Lewis

- Sarah Abercrombie was the d/o John Booth Abercrombie (1785-1817).

Thomas Lewis Ingram	Mar. 13, 1864	Nov. 23, 1939	
Annie Abercrombie	May 12, 1862	Apr. 29, 1864	
Bessie Bell	Oct. 8, 1866	May 11, 1868	children of Porter & Elizabeth M. Ingram
Mattie Freeny	June 1, 1865	Oct. 28, 1868	
Jennie Ella Ingram	Jan. 30, 1874	Apr. 21, 1892	d/o Porter & Eliz Lewis Ingram

Lot 50, no name on wall

Mary L. Johnston	Sept. 3, 1837 LaGrange, GA	Apr. 1, 1867 Columbus, GA	w/o Calvin E. Johnston, d/o James A. & Mary E. Redd

- 1860 Muscogee Census: Calvin Johnson 33 GA, Mary 23 AL, James 5 AL, Calvin 3 AL, and Lancelot 1 AL.

- 1880 Muscogee census: Calvin E. Johnston 53 GA NC GA, wife Virginia M. 41 AL VA GA, son Willie R. 18 GA, son Julian 17 GA, son Antoine? P. 14 GA, son Woodson 8 GA, son Stanfield 7 GA and dau Virginia M. 4 GA.

- Mary Lewis Redd married Calvin Evans Johnston 7/19/1854 in Muscogee. Calvin married 2nd, Virginia M. Hardaway 12 April 1871.

N. L. Redd	Nov. 23, 1843	Mar. 8, 1884	s/o J. K. & M. E. Redd
Rebecca Ferguson Redd	Mar. 17, 1844	May 7, 1905	w/o N. L. Redd

- Obit: nee Ferguson, Authoress, born Athens, AL, d/o Rev. Frederick Guthrie Ferguson. Children: Louis, Cliff G. both of Columbus, GA, Charles F. of Memphis, TN, 2 brothers, Judge Charles W. Ferguson & Capt. Fred Ferguson of Birmingham, AL, sister-in-law of Capt. William Redd, Jr. & Soule Redd.

James K. Redd	Mar. 8, 1803	Sept. 18, 1874

- Obit: born Greene Co., GA, near 72nd year.

- James Kelsoe Redd, s/o William Anderson Redd (1775-1839) and Elizabeth Ann Daniel (1780-1850). Greene Co., GA MR shows that James married Mary Elizabeth Lewis 28 May 1830.

- 1850 Muscogee Census: James K. Redd 47 Green Co., GA, Mary E. 37 Green Co., GA, Augusta F. 15 Troup, Mary 13 Troup, William 11 Troup, Nicholas 8 Troup, James 6 Troup and Charles 3 Muscogee.

- 1860 Muscogee Census: James Redd 58 GA, Mary E. 46, William 21 GA, Nicholas 17 GA, Charles 13 and Tulay (f) 9 GA.

Charles Redd	June 5, 1847 Columbus, GA	July 9, 1865	s/o Jas. K. & Mary E. Redd
James K. Redd, Jr.	Apr. 19, 1845 LaGrange, GA	May 2, 1860 Columbus, GA	s/o James K. & Mary Redd

- Obit: s/o James K. Redd & Mary Redd, age 15 years, member "Columbus Guards".

Mary E. Lewis	May 10, 1814	Dec. 16, 1878	w/o James K. Redd

- Obit: nee Lewis, w/o late J. K. Redd, 60 years old, mother of N. L. & Soule Redd, both of Columbus, GA.

- Mary Elizabeth Lewis was born in Greene Co., GA, the d/o Nicholas Meriwether Lewis (c1780-1832) and his second wife Harriet Grimes.

- Mrs. Willie Redd Crowell
  DAR ID Number 37603
  Born in Columbus, Georgia
  wife of Henry B. Crowell
  Descendant of Robert Lewis
  Daughter of William Redd, Jr., and Sarah Hines Holt, his wife

Granddaughter of James Kelso Redd and Mary Elizabeth Lewis, his wife
Gr-granddaughter of Nicholas Meriwether Lewis and Harriet W. Grimes, his 2nd wife
Gr.gr-granddaughter of Robert Lewis and Mary Frances Lewis, his wife (cousins)
Robert Lewis (1730-80), was a member of the Constitutional Convention of North Carolina 1776. He was born in Albemarle County, Va. His will was probated in Greenville county, N.C.

3 adult brick slabs, n/m   1 child brick slab, n/m

Sexton records indicate buried in this lot

Louis Redd   *SR: bur. 4/17/1908, 38 yrs.*

Lot 51, no name on wall

Thomas Randolph Rusk	Mar. 11, 1851 Jackson Co., FL	Mar. 17, 1910 Augusta, GA	our life-long friend

- 1880 Barbour Co., AL Census: Thomas R. Rusk 28 FL Eng FL, teacher.

Ethelred Philips	Mar. 6, 1851 Marianna, FL	May 3, 1923 Columbus, GA	
Frank Appler Philips	Jan. 5, 1882	Oct. 12, 1944	
Susan Gauther Philips		June 7, 1880	w/o Dr. Ethelred Philips. Our Mother.

- Ethelred Philips married Mrs. Susan Philips 12/1/1846 in Pulaski Co., GA.

- 1880 Muscogee Census: Ethelred Phillips (sic) 29 FL NC GA, wife Mary 24 AL VA AL, Mary E. 5 MS and son George 2 GA.

Mary Collier Benagh	Sept. 15, 1856 Tuscaloosa, AL	Mar. 4, 1919 Columbus, GA	w/o Ethelred Philips

- Mary is the d/o Prof. George Wm. Benugh (sic) of the Univ. of Al and his wife Mary Williams Collier.[66]

- Tuscaloosa Co., AL marriage records show George Benagh married Mary W. Collier 14 October 1852.

Lot 52, no name on wall

Sally Letitia Wright	Aug. 2, 1834	July 22, 1861	w/o Rev. Arminius Wright
Rev. Arminius Wright	Mar. 4, 1829	June 18, 1879	"of the South GA Conference"

- 1860 Spalding Co., GA Census: Arminius Wright 35 GA, Sallie 26 GA, Homer 10 GA, Alice 8 GA, Ella 7 GA, Arminius Jr. 3 GA and Fannie 1 GA.

- 1870 Spalding Co., GA Census: Armenius (sic) Wright 41 GA, Amelia 35 GA, Alice 18 GA, Sallie 16 GA, Armenius (sic) 13 GA, Fannie 11 GA, Ralph 3 GA and Amelia 11/12 GA.

- *Southern Christian Advocate July 9, 1873* – James Arminius Wright was drowned on the

7th of June last, in the seventeenth year of his age. He was a son of the esteemed Rev. Arminius Wright of Columbus, Ga., and was a sophomore in Emory College. He was born February 6th 1857.

- *Southern Christian Advocate November 6, 1872-* At St. Paul's Church, Columbus, Ga., Oct. 22d, by Rev. Joseph S. Key, Mr. John W. Collier, of Atlanta, Ga., to Miss Sallie E. Wright, daughter of Rev. Arminius Wright, pastor of St. Paul's Church.

- *Southern Christian Advocate April 7, 1875-* In Macon, Ga., March 20th, 1875, by Rev. W. C. Bass, D. C., Rev. W. B. Bonnell and Miss Alice J. Wright, eldest daughter of Rev. Arminius Wright.

- *Nashville Christian Advocate May 1, 1908-* Mrs. Joel T. Daves, whose husband was presiding elder of the Atlanta District, died April 16, 1908; daughter of Rev. Arminius Wright and a native of Columbus, Ga.

Sarah Amelia Wright   July 10, 1836   Sept. 29, 1884   w/o Rev. Arminius Wright

- Obit – relict of Rev. Arminius Wright, 48 years old, leaves 4 orphan children, 5 step-children, one of whom is Mrs. Barnwell, sister of Dr. E. (Edward) L.(Livingston) Bardwell of Talbotton, GA.

- Sarah Amelia (Bardwell) Taft married Arminius Wright 12/4/1862 in Columbus, GA. Amelia was born in Augusta, GA. Amelia was first married to Horatio Taft.[67]

Ralph E. Wright   Apr. 29, 1867   Oct. 19, 1907

James Arminius Wright   Feb. 6, 1857   June 7, 1873

1 baby brick slab, n/m

Lot 53, T. W. Smith on wall

Geo. H. Parks   June 19, 1857   Aug. 7, 1861   inf. s/o Rev. H. H. & S. Parks

Thomas William Smith   July 15, 1860   Sept. 17, 1926

- 1920 Muscogee Census: Thomas W. Smith 59 MS GA AL, wife Minnie 58 AL Ger Ger, son Earnest 27 GA, son Thomas W. Jr. 20 GA and son Frank W. GA,.

Minnie F. Smith   Oct. 3, 1860   July 18, 1935   w/o Thomas W. Smith

Philip Smith   Apr. 13, 1887   Jan. 30, 1889   s/o T. W. & M. L. Smith

1 adult slab, n/m

Lot 54, J. F. Flournoy on wall

John Manly Flournoy   Dec. 29, 1890   July 6, 1943

- s/o John Francis Flournoy (1847-1936) and his 2nd wife Mary Welch Reynolds (1852-1956).

Rose G. Boynton   Aug. 1, 1889   Sept. 1, 1966   w/o John M. Flournoy

Walker Reynolds Flournoy   Dec. 31, 1892   Mar. 17, 1940

Gordon Flournoy   Dec. 27, 1887   Feb. 4, 1930

J. A. Strother	no dates	adult

- Obit – Col. J. A. Strother remains arrived, Tuesday Apr. 22, 1879 paper.

- Enlisted as a Captain on 23 May 1861, Commission in Company B, 20th Infantry Regiment Georgia on 23 May 1861. Resigned Company B, 20th Infantry Regiment Georgia on 16 January 1862.

- 1870 Russell Co., AL Census: John Strother 50 GA.

Mary Wheat Flournoy	Jan. 11, 1894	Apr. 30, 1986	

- Married Walker Reynolds Flournoy 8/19/1917.

Susette Joerg Flournoy	May 9, 1891	Jan. 5, 1972	
Infant		Feb. 16, 1926	s/o John M. & Rose B. Flournoy
John Francis Flournoy	Jan. 24, 1924	Jan. 28, 1924	Inf. s/o Susette Joerg & Gordon Flournoy
Infant		Dec. 1, 1923	s/o John M. & Rose B. Flournoy
Mary Ann Flournoy Strother	no dates	adult	

- Mary Ann Flournoy married John A. Strother 6/25/1847 in Dallas Co., AL

1 adult slab, n/m

Lot 55, no name on wall

Dr. James S. Ware			Sample Arty CSA 1861-1865. SR: bur. 7/16/1883, 52 years.

1 baby brick slab, n/m

Sexton records indicate buried in this lot

Mrs. James Ware			*SR: bur. 10/14/1883*

Lot 56, open lot

2 adult graves, marked with small granite stones at head & feet.

Lot 57, no name on wall

Allen Cameron Matthews	Sept. 26, 1940	Oct. 5, 1940	
Henry G. Cameron	1847	1931	SR: bur. 1/30/1931

- Obit – Judge, former city attorney, died in Atlanta, GA, 83 years old, b. Whitesville, GA, leaves 2 dghts, Mrs. J. G. Carter of Oklahoma, OK, Mrs. T. B. Matthews of Columbus, GA, 1 son, H. C. Jr. of Albany, GA, 9 g/ch., 4 g/g/ch.

- Enlisted CSA Co. B. Bat., GA Cadets August 1864 in Milledgeville, GA. His 1910 pension stated that he had lived in Georgia for 40 years and that he spent 1871 in Texas.

Joel William Cameron	1851	1918

1 adult brick slab, n/m

Sexton records indicate buried in this lot

Mrs. N. C. Cameron	*SR: bur. 6/20/1890, 39 yrs.*
Mrs. Henry Cameron	*SR: bur. 12/13/1918, 63 yrs.*

Lot 58, Philips on wall

Mabel M. Philips	Sept. 23, 1900	Feb. 9, 1987	w/o Lovick W. Philips
Lovick Wynn Philips	Oct. 10, 1895	Oct. 19, 1945	
Julia L. Gaither	Dec. 28, 1846	Jan. 24, 1894	w/o L. W. Philips

- Obit: b. Wetumpka, Ala., married Dr. L. W. Philips, 1880, leaves husband & several brothers & sisters.
- Julia S. Gaither married Dr. Lovick Wynn Philips 6/9/1880 Wetumpka, Russell Co., AL.

Lovick W. Philips MD	Jan. 7, 1838	Jan. 22, 1920

- Obit – died Russell Co., AL, CSA surgeon Co. K, 32nd GA Regt., raised a company of Cav. in Lee & Russell Co., leaves wife, 1 dghtr Miss Georgia Bert Phillips (sic), 2 sons, L. W. J. & Abram, all of Russell Co.
- Dr. Philips is the s/o James Philips (1795-1863) and Margaret Mariah Lewis (1805-1853) who were married 4/20/1823 in Jones Co., GA. He is the maternal grandson of Pearce A. Lewis (1774-1852) and his wife Phoebe Langdon (1776-1858). His paternal grandparents are Col. Abram Philips (1754-1831) and his wife Cynthia Lanier (1761-1837). Dr. Philips attended Tulane University School of Medicine, New Orleans: Univ. of LA Med. Dept., 1861, and Univ. of NY, Ophth. Sch. of Med., NY, 1860.
- CSA Service record: Lovick W. Phillips (sic): Promoted to Full Lieutenant 2nd Class, Enlisted as a Private on 19 December 1861, Promoted to Full Quartermaster Sergeant on 19 December 1861, Enlisted in Company B, 31st Infantry Regiment Georgia on 19 December 1861. Promoted to Full Assistant Surgeon on 11 April 1862, Discharged Company B, 31st Infantry Regiment Georgia on 12 May 1862 in Beaulieu, Savannah, GA, Promoted to Full Captain on 10 September 1862, Surrendered Company K, 10th Cavalry Regiment Georgia on 26 April 1865 in Greensboro, NC.

Georgia Bert Philips	June 19, 1899	Oct. 3, 1912	
Georgia S. Davis	Feb. 16, 1878	Jan. 11, 1931	Mother. w/o L. W. Philips

- Georgia Searcy Davis married Dr. Lovick Wynn Philips 10/17/1894 in Dale Co., AL.

Lot 59, F. B. Brooks on wall

Geo. W. Lips	Jan. 16, 1836 Philadelphia	Nov. 7, 1880

- 1880 Muscogee Census: C. A. Klink (m) 50 PA PA PA, nephew George Lipp 32 PA PA PA, wife Emma 26 PA PA PA and son Geo Jr. 3 GA.

Ethel Willis	Mar. 5, 1889	Feb. 13, 1957	w/o H. G. Brooks
Charles A. Klink	Aug. 2, 1827 Germany	May 22, 1889 Columbus, GA	"Our Uncle"

- Obit – father, John Klink, immigrated to this country 1829 with family, settled in Philadelphia. His mother died 1840, he left home then, went to St. Louis, then to Louisville, KY, and in 1843 to Columbus on steamer Charleston, 1851 made Capt. of Retrieva, helped raise a company, "Columbus Guards". 17th Regt. under Col. Benning.

- 1850 Philadelphia, PA Census: John H. Klink 53 Ger, Christina 47 Ger. and Fredericka 20 Ger.

- 1860 Muscogee Census: Charles Klink 34? GA is enumerated as a bar keeper in the home of Capt. Stapler, Capt. of SS Bias?.

- 1880 Muscogee Census: C. A. Klink 50 PA PA PA steamboat Capt.; nephew George Lipp (sic) 32 PA PA PA, wife Emma 26 PA PA PA, son George Jr. 3; Jack Brooks 25 GA GA GA, wife Pauline 24 PA PA PA, son Charles 2 GA and BIL Henry Kennedy 21 GA GA GA.

H. G. Brooks, Sr.	Sept. 2, 1891	Apr. 28, 1940
F. B. Brooks	Aug. 14, 1855	Dec. 14, 1917

- 1910 Muscogee Census: Florence Brooks (male) 54 wd GA PA GA, son Harry G. 18 GA GA GA, sister-in-law Emma P. Lips 58 PA Ger Ger .

- 1900 Muscogee Census: Florance B. Brooks Aug 1855 GA PA GA, wife Pauline C. July 1857 PA Germany Germany (married 21 yrs; 3/2/children), son Clarina J. Dec 1886 GA, son Harry C. Sept 1891 GA and SIL Emma E. Lipps Oct 1852 PA Germany Germany (widow; 8/7 children).

- 1870 Muscogee Census: Stephen Brooks 44 PA, Ann 43 GA, Leonard R. 19 GA, Laura E. 18 GA, Florence B. (m) 15 GA and George E. 12 GA.

- Marriage Record in Muscogee Co., GA shows Stephen S. Brooks and Nancy A. Henley 7 June 1848.

Emma E. Lips	Oct. 13, 1852	Feb. 15, 1920	
Pauline C. Brooks	July 27, 1855 Philadelphia	Jan. 25, 1910 Columbus, GA	
Charlie Brooks	Sept. 29, 1877	Mar. 31, 1880	s/o F. B. & P. C. Brooks

Lot 60, no name on wall

2 adult brick slabs, n/m

Lot 61, no name on wall

Francis Marion Bagley	Nov. 18, 1845	May 6, 1903

- Obit: born Chattahoochee Co., GA, CSA vet. Co. H., leaves wife, eight children, Wm. W. of Atlanta, GA, Albert S., Worth Bagley, both of Columbus, Mrs. M. M. Massey, Misses Lula, Etta, Mabel & Marion Bagley all of Columbus, GA.
- 1850 Muscogee Census: William Bagley 39 Jasper Co., Johannah 35 Warren Co., John 14 Musc., Samuel M. 13 Musc. William W. 12 Musc., Priscilla C. 11 Musc., James M. 10 Musc., Lucy A. 9 Musc., Francis M. 8 Musc (marked over), Thomas J. 7 Musc., Benjamin F. 3 Musc. and Amy Sheffield 22 Musc.

Sophronia Reeves	Oct. 17, 1854	Jan. 17, 1929	w/o F. M. Bagley
Rollin Jefferson Bagley	Jan. 10, 1884	Jan. 28, 1885	s/o F. M. & S. Bagley
Julius Walker Bagley	Oct. 23, 1881	Oct. 13, 1882	s/o F. M. & S. Bagley

Lot 62, no name on wall

| Abbie Yarbrough | July 21, 1870 | Oct. 15, 1883 | s/o T. C. & M. A. Yarbrough |

1 baby clab, n/m

Sexton Records indicate buried in this lot:

John S. Yarbrough		*bur. 5/9/1899, 18 yrs.*
Mrs. T. G. Yarbrough		*bur. 9/9/1895, 38 yrs.*
T. G. Yarbrough		*bur. 10/13/1932, 77 yrs.*

- 1880 Russell Co., AL Census: Tho. Yarbrough 24 GA SC GA, wife Mattie 22 GA – SC, son Thomas E. 2 AL, son Albert G. 10/12 AL.
  - Prior Household: Carrie Yarbrough 45 GA GA SC, son John F. 22 AL, sister Eva Butler 37 GA GA GA, nephew William W. 14 GA, niece Ida 13 GA, niece Ellen D. 11 GA, 3 boarders, and father William Roggers (sic) 84 GA SC SC.
  - 1850 Muscogee Census: William Rogers 54 Jefferson Co., Mary 50 SC, Jesse 20 Musc., Caroline 16 Musc., Eliza Ann 14 Musc., Martha Ann 12 Musc., Evalina 10 Musc., Harriett 8 Musc., Augustine 6 Musc., and Robert Pry 20 SC.
- 1900 Muscogee Census: Thomas G. Yarbrough Sept. 1855 GA GA GA, son Roy C. Mar. 1885 GA, son George M. June 1894 GA, son-in-law Charles C. Phelps July 1876 VA, dau. Jesse L. July 1883 GA and mother Carrie Yarbrough Sept. 1835 (3 children/2 living).
- 1920 Muscogee Census: Thomas Yarbrough 63 GA SC GA, and mother Carrie 83 GA GA GA.

Lot 63, no name on wall

| Ben Edmunds | Aug. 7, 1876 | Sept. 7, 1944 | |
| Georgia P. Edmunds | | Mar. 29, 1911 | |

- 1880 Russell Co., AL Census: Benjamin W. Edmunds 43 AL VA VA, wife Josephine 28 AL GA Scotland, son Turner 9 AL, son John 6 AL and son Benjamin 3 AL.
- 1900 Lee Co., AL Census: Benj. Edmunds Aug. 1877 AL AL AL, wife Georgia Feb. 1878 TX GA AL.

Lot 64, no name on wall

Mary O. Chalmers		Oct. 14, 1898	

- Obit: Died at residence of son George E. Chalmers.

Wm. Ponce Chalmers	May 26, 1886	July 16, 1887	s/o W. E. & Nettie P. Chalmers
William E. Chalmers		Jan. 16, 1916	Lt. Co. C, 63rd AL Regt. CSA
Nettie P. Chalmers		Dec. 21, 1934	

- 1880 Russell Co., AL Census: Mary Chalmers 56 VA VA VA, son Wm. E. 33 AL Scotland VA, son Louis M. 31 AL, d-i-l Jennie 22 GA, sister Sarah Harris 50 VA VA VA, nephew Robt. J. 26 AL, nephew Chas. E. 21 AL and gdau Bernice 1 GA.
  - 1880 Russell Co., AL Census: (Prior Household) Geo. Chalmers 30 GA Scot VA and wife Mollie 23 GA GA GA.
- 1900 Muscogee Census: Wm. E. Nov 1849 AL Scot VA (m. 14 yrs), wife Antonette Aug. 1867 GA Spain Eng, dau Katherine Jan 1888 GA, son Wm. D. Jan. 1891 GA and son Albert D. Apl. 1898 GA.
- 1910 CSA Pension filed in Muscogee Co.: W. E. Chalmers served Co. C. 63rd AL Regt. He served about 11 months and was taken prisoner Apr. 1865 at Blakely, AL. He was held prisoner on Ship Island until the close of the war.

Lot 65, no name on wall

Celeste Dismuke Key	Aug. 26, 1888	Dec. 31, 1954	w/o Howard W. Key

- Celeste Dismuke married Howard Walton Key, Jr. 8/28/1906 in Muscogee Co.
- d/o William Haynes Dismukes (1865-1936) and Minnie Lou Williams (1865-1898).
- 1920 Muscogee Census: H. W. Key 35 GA GA GA, wife Dismuke 30 GA GA GA, child Walter 12 AL, child William 9 GA and child Joe Stanford 4 GA.

Minnie Dismuke	July 16, 1865	Aug. 6, 1898	w/o W. H. Dismuke

- Minnie Lou Williams, d/o John M. Williams and Elizabeth A. Moss, married William Haynes Dismuke (1865-1936) on 7/23/1887 in Troup Co., GA. William married 2nd Susan Wynn (1865-1943) on 8/28/1889. John M. Williams (b. c1823 GA) and Eliza Moss who were married 11/30/1847 in Meriwether Co., GA.

Joe Key	Feb. 14, 1916	Dec. 23, 1922	s/o Howard W. & Celeste D. Key

Lot 66, no name on wall

Mrs. Sophronia Hudson	Apr. 6, 18??	Feb. 29, 1890?	sister
J. W. Davis	July 26, 1882	Dec. 29, 1918	
James & Bessie Davis		no dates	same slab

1 adult brick slab, n/m   1 child's brick slab, n/m

Lot 67, no name on wall

Joseph Leo Dillard	Feb. 11, 1900	Sept. 6, 1982	
James A. Curry, Sr.	1869	1945	
Katherine C. Curry	1879	1929	
Mary A. Curry	1843	1916	
William H. Blalock	1902	1927	SR: bur. 2/14/1927

- GA Death Records show William H. Blalock died 2/13/1927 in Muscogee Co.
- 1920 Census Meriwether Co., GA: John H. Blalock 50 GA GA GA, wife Lula 43 GA AL AL and son William

James T. Curry	Feb. 28, 1836	July 31, 1882
	London, Eng.	

- 1850 Muscogee Census: Thomas Curry 50 Ire, Ellen 40 Ire and James 14 Eng.
- 1870 Muscogee Census: James Curry 34 Eng, Mary A. 27 GA, George T. 9 GA, Willia E. 7 GA, Alice I. 3 GA and James 1 GA.
- 1880 Muscogee Census: James Curry 35 Eng. Ire Ire, wife Mary 37 GA Ger Ger, son George 19 GA, son William 17 GA, dau Allice 14 GA, son James 11 GA, dau Mary 7 GA and son Leo 4 GA.

Leo H. Curry	1875	1926	
Mary Curry Brannan	1872	1960	w/o James R. Brannan. SR: bur. 5/4/1960

4 baby brick slabs, n/m   2 aadult brick slabs, n/m

Sexton Records indicate buried in this lot:

Wm. David Dillard   *SR: bur. 12/23/50, 1 day.*

Lot 68, no name on wall

2 adult slabs, n/m   4 children slabs, n/m

Lot 69, McKnight on wall

W. S. McKnight	Jan. 4, 1895	31 years

- Winfield McKnight married Tillie Grier.
  - 1870 Muscogee Census: Thomas Grier 49 Ire, Maria 39 Ire, Mary 18 VT, Lizzie 16 VT, Katie 4 GA and Tillie 2 GA.

Children of W. S. & Tillie McKnight

Arthur	age 4 months

Marie   age 19 months

- 1900 Muscogee Census: Howard Hall May 1861 GA GA GA, Tillie May 1863 GA GA GA (married 7 mos.), mother Elizabeth Jan 1829 GA GA GA, step-dau Hazel McKnight Jan 1887 GA, step-son Robt. July 1890 GA, step-dau Ermine Dec. 1892 GA and step-dau (sic) Wynn Sept. 1895 (male) GA.
- 1880 Muscogee Census: Lizzie Hall 51 GA GA GA, son Howard S. Hall 19 GA GA GA.

Lot 70, no name on wall

J. W. Barber   13th AL Regt. CSA 1861-1865. SR: bur. 12/9/1888

- Obit: Justice, one time Clerk of Superior Ct., Justice of Peace, leaves wife & several children.
- James W. Barber served in Co. A, 13th AL Inf. as a private.
- 1870 Muscogee Census: James Barber 27 GA, Mary 25 GA and Chipley 2 GA.
- 1880 Muscogee Census: Jas. Barber 37 GA GA GA, wife Mary 34 G MS MS, son Chipley 12 GA, son Hunley? 10 GA, dau Ida 7 GA, son Gordon 3 GA, son 1/12 GA and son 1/12 GA

1 adult slab, n/m   1 child's brick slab, n/m

Lot 71, open lot

Samuel Pirrie   July 23, 1882   age 48 years

- Obit: died at the residence of William Dawson in Russell Co., AL, native of Scotland, grocer, had no relatives in this country, in Columbus 15 years.

4 adult brick slabs, n/m

Lot 72, Bedell on wall

Wm. Richard Bedell	Jan. 8, 1835	Nov. 15, 1903	s/o G. G. & C. K. Bedell. Adjuant 46 Regt. GA Vol. CSA
Maggie Ware Bedell	Apr. 27, 1843	June 18, 1898	d/o Dr. R. A. & M. C. Ware w/o W. R. Bedell.

- Last night's fire had a sad sequel – one that will occasion geniuine and sincere sorrow throughout the entire city. Mrs. W. R. Bedell is dead. This true, noble and generous Christian woman has passed away. Very few people, even among those who witnessed the fire, knew of the tragic death of this devoted wife and mother. The news of the death comes like a clap of thunder from a clear sky. Her death occurred shortly before 11 o'clock. She had rushed out to the scene of the fire, and it seems that she was taken suddenly ill. She immediately returned to her home and expired in a few minutes. Medical aid was summonded, but it was beyond human aid to revive her. It was the opinion of the doctors that Mrs. Bedell died from an attack of apopplexy.

Mrs. W. R. Bedell was born in this city on the 27th of April 1843. She was the daughter of the late Dr. and Mrs. R. A. Ware of this city, and an aunt of Mrs. J. S. Harrison also of this city. The deceased was a consistent member of St. Luke church of which she had been faithful member for a good many years. Mrs. Bedell was married to Mr. W. R. Bedell of this city on the 19th day of June 1866, and today would have been the thirty-second anniversary of her marriage. Mrs. Bedell leaves a heart broken husband and four children, three sons and one daughter. Her children are Messrs. James Bedell and W. A. Bedell of San Antonio, TX, Mr. Robert Bedell of Montgomery and Miss Ellie May Bedell. They have the heartfelt sympathy of the entire community in the hour of theirsad affliction. She is also survived by two sisters and one brother, Mrs. Jane Martin of this city, Mrs. M. V. Willis of Macon and Mr. Robert Ware also of Macon. The sad news of the death of this good woman will cast a gloom over the entire city.

Sarah A. Bedell   Apr. 24, 1821   Apr. 2, 1894   w/o W. A. Bedell

- Obit: died at the residence of Mrs. Nesbitt, w/o Col. W. A. Bedell, born Eatonton, Apr. 1821, d/o Judge William Switzer, married 4 Dec. 1838 in Columbus, GA.
- William Bedell married Sarah Switzer 14 Dec. 1838 in Harris Co., GA.[68]

Robert Clinton Bedell   May 16, 1871   Oct. 29, 1949

Sexton Records indicate also buried in this lot

ch/o W. R. Bedell   *bur. 7/14/1874*

William A. Bedell   *bur. 9/23/1903, 85 yrs.*

- Obit: died at the residence of Mrs. C. A. Etheridge, no near relatives, 2 nephews, W. R. Bedell of Columbus, GA, G., W. H. Bedell of Dallas, TX, 2 nieces, Mrs. A. E. Wright & Mrs. M. E. Thompson of AL, born Jones Co., GA Jan 11, 1818, moved to Harris Co., GA when 15, moved to Columbus 1844, 1 brother A. G. Bedell.

Lot 73, no name on wall

Edward C. Sauls   Nov. 27, 1858   Nov. 1, 1940

- Obit: born Quincy, FL, s/o William M. & Sarah Jane Brown Sauls.
- 1920 Muscogee Census: Edward Sauls 61 FL SC SC, wife Emmie 41 AL AL GA. son James Sauls 10 GA and boarder Nina Pitts 22 AL AL AL.

Emma Fuller Sauls   Feb. 25, 1876   Nov. 12, 1953

- Obit: d/o Joseph P. & Eliza Turner Fuller.
- 1880 Russell Co., AL Census: Joe Fuller 38 GA NY SC, wife Annie 24 AL VA GA, dau Mary 12 GA, dau Alice 9 GA, dau Anna 7 AL, dau Emma 4 AL and dau Luellen 1 AL.

Mattie Wagner   1833   1918   SR: bur. 10/21/1918, 85 yrs.

1 baby brick slab, n/m

Sexton Records indicate also buried in this lot

Tobe Wagner   *bur. 4/29/1902*

Lot 74, Mullins on wall

Sarah America Mullins Duke	Apr. 10, 1832	May 30, 1905

- Obit: w/o G. S. Duke, 2 sisters Mrs. Cornelia Nelson, Mrs. Laura Binns, both of Harris Co., GA.

3 adult brick slabs, n/m

Sexton Records also indicate buried in this lot:

J. Warren Mullins   *bur. 1/28/1898, 67 yrs.*

- Obit: CSA vet, member of Camp Benning, a Mason.

Elizabeth Mullins   *bur. 8/10/1879, 74 yrs.*

Lot 75, no name on wall

Francis M. Sharp	Dec. 17, 1857	Sept. 29, 1906	
Mary Julia Bridges	Mar. 17, 1858	Dec. 16, 1929	w/o Francis Marion Sharp

- Francis M. Sharp married M. Julia Bridges 12/15/1881 in Houston Co., GA.

- 1880 Houston Co., GA Census: Benj. F. Bridges 55 GA GA GA, wife Sallie P. 42 GA GA GA, dau Julia M. 21 GA, dau Celia 20 GA, dau Sallie 8 GA and boarder Bryant Hansell 60 SC SC SC.

Lot 76, John M. Flournoy on wall

Barbara C. Gordon	Jan. 11, 1793 near Carhill, TN	July 22, 1876 AL	w/o Charles P. Gordon of Eatonton, GA.

- Obit: w/o Hon. Charles G. Gordon, lived at Eatonton, GA, mother of Mrs. John M. Flournoy, Virginia Abercrombie & Mrs. Sarah Wilkins.

- Barbara Gailbraith, the d/o Andrew Gailbraith and Barbara Work married Charles P. Gordon on 6/10/1817 in Carlisle, PA.

  o Putnam Co., GA WB B page 139, Charles P. Gordon, 4/14/1835-_____: Legatees - Son: Andrew G. Gordon; friend John Brown of TN; my four daughters Mary Ann, Julian Barbour, Virginia and Sarah Elizabeth; wife and son (not named)...C. P. Gordon. Wits: Samson W. Harris, H. W. Cozant, B. W. Sanford. Brothers James G. Gordon and George H. Gordon guardians for children...brothers (aforesd.) and John Brown of Tennessee Exrs...Wits: same as above.

Sarah Gordon Wilkins	Apr. 1831	Sept. 1871	w/o Joseph C. Wilkins of Liberty Co., GA.

- Sarah Elizabeth Gordon, d/o Charles P. and Barbara Gordon married Joseph C. Wilken 12/10/1851 in Russell Co., AL.

- Joseph Campbell Wilkins was the s/o Paul Hamilton Wilkins and Margaret Campbell. He was first married to Mary Grant 6/27/1837 in Clarke Co., GA.

Name	Birth	Death	Notes
Charles Gordon Flournoy	Dec. 24, 1844	Apr. 5, 1902	Soldier of the South Nelson's Rangers.

- Obit: leaves wife, 2 children, Susan May & Lee, 2 brothers, J. F. of Columbus & Josiah.

Name	Birth	Death	Notes
Maud Flournoy Dixon	Apr. 12, 1884	June 23, 1976	w/o S. Marshall Dixon
Addie Gillespie Flournoy	Aug. 10, 1859	Jan. 9, 1920	w/o Charles Gordon Flournoy

- Addie P. Gillespie married Charles G. Flournoy 5/11/1885 in Meriwether Co., GA.

- 1880 Meriwether Co., GA: John L. Gillespie 50 SC SC SC, wife Sue D. 49 GA GA GA, dau Addie P. 19 GA, dau Susie H. 17 GA, son Charlie R. 16 GA, dau Sallie I. 11 GA and dau Willie Fannie 9 GA.

Name	Birth	Death	Notes
Mary Hannah Flournoy	Mar. 22, 1889	Feb. 19, 1983	d/o Mary Welch Reynolds & John F. Flournoy.
Stephen Marshall Dixon	Nov. 23, 1878	Jan. 8, 1954	

- Son of Stephen Marshall Dixon Sr. and Fannie E. McDougald. Husband of Maud Flournoy.

Name	Birth	Death	Notes
Josiah Flournoy	Jan. 25, 1850	Sept. 9, 1922	Soldier of the South Nelson's Rangers.

- Obit: 72 years old, civil & mining engineer, surveyor, born in Columbus, 1 brother John F. Flournoy, nieces & nephews.

Name	Birth	Death	Notes
Frances Maury Fontaine	Sept. 4, 1871	Apr. 24, 1891	
Mary Flournoy Fontaine	May 7, 1852	Feb. 20, 1875	w/o Francis Fontaine d/o John M. & Mary A. Flournoy.
John Francis Flournoy	Mar. 13, 1847	July 15, 1936	Soldier of the South Nelson's Rangers

- Obit: second son of John Manly and Mary Gordon Flournoy, CSA, Nelson's Rangers, 1st (Nov. 1869) married Rebecca Epping of Columbus, GA, after her death, mar. Miss Mary Welch Reynolds of Alpine, AL (Sept. 1881), 4 sons, J. F. of New Orleans, LA, Josiah, John Manly & Walker R., all of Columbus, GA, dghts, Mrs. Rebecca F. Hamburger, Mrs. S. M. Dixon, Miss Mary Hannah Flournoy, all of Columbus, GA.

- 1880 Muscogee Census: Henry Epping 59 Ger Ger Ger, wife Isabella 54 Sco Sco Sco, son Early 18 Al, dau 15 AL, and boarders; Henry Epping Jr. 23 AL, Dora? 23 Al, John Flournoy 32 GA GA GA, Frank 9 GA and Beca 6 GA.

Name	Birth	Death	Notes
Mary Welch Reynolds	May 1, 1852	Mar. 11, 1926	w/o John F. Flournoy
Virginia G. Flournoy	Oct. 7, 1855	Aug. 20, 1857	d/o John M. & Mary A. Flournoy
John Manly Flournoy	Jan. 14, 1814 Putnam Co., GA	Sept. 14, 1859 Wynnton, GA	

- Muscogee Co., GA WB A:266-268. John M. Flournoy. 7/19/1858:1/9/1860. Wife: Mary A., extrx. Son: Charles Gordon Flournoy. Other ch. Bro: Robert. Bro-in-law: Joel E. Hurt. Mentions Dr. Charles T. Abercrombie. Wits: C. W. Chapman, Beverly A. Thornton, Wiley Williams.

- 1850 Russell Co., AL Census: John M. Flournoy 36 GA, Mary 35 GA, Charles 5, John 3, Josiah 1, Mary Gordon 60 PA, Sarah Gordon 20 PA and Alfred Thompson (overseer) 35 GA.

Martha D. Flournoy	Oct. 1, 1789 Virginia	Apr. 27, 1877	w/o Josiah Flournoy

- Obit: mother of Mrs. Fannie Hurt & Robert Flournoy.

- Southern Christian Advocate, 24 Mar 1875: Martha Dixon Flournoy, relict of Josiah Flournoy, deceased, was born in Dinwiddie County, Va., and died at the residence of Col. L. A. Jordan in Lee County, Ga., in the eighty-fifth year of her age. After the decease of her husband in 1852 [sic]. W. R. Branham.

- Martha Manley married Josiah Flournoy 8/17/1808 in Putnam Co., GA.

- Putnam Co., GA Bk B:166 Josiah Flournoy, 1/25/1842:9/17/1842. Wife: Martha. Exrs: sons Thomas and John M. and sons- in- law, Nathan Bass, Walter R. Branham and Early Hurt, granddaughter Evelina Tombs, two children of my deceased son Josiah. Wits: S. A. Wales, D. R. Adams. Stephen B. Marshall.

- Putnam Co., GA OCR Bk 2:28 & 98. Will & Inventory of Josiah Flournoy, Sr. of Putnam Co., GA. Wife Martha. Sons: Thomas and John M. Sons-in-law Nathan Bass, Walter R. Branham and Early Hurt. Granddaughter Evalina Powels, Georgianne Flournoy. Grandson Samuel Josiah Flournoy.

Mary Ann Gordon Flournoy	Mar. 10, 1823 Eatonton, GA	July 28, 1886 Wynnton, GA	w/o John Manly Flournoy

- Obit: born Putnam Co., GA, mother of John F. of Columbus, GA, Charles G. of Chipley, GA, Josiah Flournoy of CA, sister of Mrs. Charles Abercrombie.

- Mary Ann Gordon, d/o Charles P. Gordon and Barbara Gailbraith. Married John Manley Flournoy 10/26/1843.

Lot 77, J. Kyle on wall

Henry Barry	Sept. 21, 1891	June 2, 1893	s/o Henry B. & ? Woolfolk
Catherine Lydia Kyle	Nov. 7, 1842	Mar. 3, 1920	

- Obit: died at residence of dght. Mrs. H. H. Woolfolk, d/o Capt. Isaac P. Moragne of Gadiston, AL, b. St. Clair Co., AL, married Aug 20, 1861 to John Hunter Kyle, s/o Joseph Kyle, husband died Oct. 1874, 2 dghts Mrs. Geo L. Candler of Savannah, Mrs. Henry B. Woolfolk of Columbus, GA, 6 g/ch, 4 g/g/ch.

- 1850 St. Clair Co., AL Census: Isaac P. Moragne 33 SC, Louisa 25 AL, Lydia K. 8 AL, Washington? A. 6 AL, Mary L. 4 AL, Eliza J. 2 AL, Isaac 2/12 AL and James Gaston 25 SC.

Blanchard Ball Battle, Jr.	Jan. 12, 1921	Mar. 26, 1983	
Robert Elliott Carter, Jr.	Jan. 6, 1896	Apr. 5, 1969	s/o Belle Powers & Robert Elliott Carter

Catherine Woolfolk	Jan. 10, 1898	Mar. 14, 1987	d/o Annie Wise Kyle & Henry Barry Woolfolk w/o Robert Elliott Carter, Jr.
Infant	June 14, 1950 (only date)		s/o Albert & Romeyn Woolfolk
Elizabeth Pamela Kyle			Age 14 mo 17 days
John H. Kyle	Apr. 2, 1838	Oct. 29, 1874	

- Obit: s/o Joseph Kyle, 35 years old, born Columbus, GA.

Joseph Kyle	Feb. 16, 1874	June 22, 1911	s/o John H. & Catherine Kyle
Henry Barry Woolfolk	Oct. 15, 1859	Jan. 26, 1931	

- Henry was the s/o William Gray Woolfolk and Maria Byrd Nelson who were married Jan. 16, 1846. Muscogee Co. MR showed Henry married Annie Wise Kyle Dec. 11, 1888.

- 1900 Muscogee Census: Henry B. Woolfolk Oct. 1859 GA GA VA, wife Annie Oct. 1866 GA GA GA, son Joseph Oct. 1889 GA, son Albert May 1893 GA and dau Kate Jan 1898 GA.

Elizabeth Lee		Apr. 5, 1875	w/o Joseph Kyle
Joseph Kyle	July 24, 1812	Feb. 1, 1903	

- Obit: The Atlanta Constitution 2 Feb 1903. Columbus, GA Feb 1. Joseph Kyle one of Columbus' oldest and estimable citizens passed at his home at 2 o'clock at his home on Twelfth Street. He was 90 years old having been born on July 24, 1812 in Omega, County of Tyrone in Ireland. His parentage was Scottish. At the age of 17 he came to America and settled in North Carolina. In 1838 he came to Columbus. Mr. Kyle and his brother John were the youngest of 10 children; 5 sons and 5 daughters. When they emigrated in 1851, they went to Rockingham Co., NC.

- Joseph Kyle was the s/o Robert Kyle and Sarah Hunter. [69]

- 1860 Muscogee Census: Joseph Kyle 43 Ireland, Elizabeth 41 Ireland and John H. 21 AL.

- 1850 Muscogee Census: Joseph Kyle 35 Ireland, Elizabeth 30 VA, John H. 10 AL and Elizabeth 8 GA.

Ruth Battle Woolfolk	Oct. 7, 1893	Jan. 8, 1988	
Joseph Moragne Kyle			Age 3 yrs 10 mo
A. Hunter		Oct. 31, 1866	

- 1860 Muscogee Census shows A. Hunter aged 45 born in Ireland as a merchant living in Thos. Brassell's boarding house.

- 1850 Muscogee Census: A. Hunter 38 Ireland, F. W. Goulden (m) 19 New York City.

John Kyle	Jan. 24, 1891	July 11, 1906	s/o John H. & Catherine L. Kyle
Annie Wise Kyle	Oct. 31, 1866	Mar. 6, 1953	w/o Henry B. Woolfolk
Lizzie P. Nuckolls	Aug. 2, 1839	Feb. 23, 1863	

- Muscogee MR show that Elizabeth P. Kyle married Nathaniel Nuckolls Aug 3, 1858.

Albert Sidney Woolfolk	May 3, 1893	Mar. 14, 1959	
Albert Sidney Woolfolk	Feb. 18, 1920	Apr. 11, 1953	

Lot 78, no name on wall

Lawrence Joseph Rafferty	no dates	SR: bur. 12/12/1893

- 1880 Muscogee Census: L. J. Rafferty 27 Ire Ire Ire, wife E. A. 23 GA Ire Ire, son Jos. W. 2 GA and dau. Mary B. 10/12 GA.

- Living in prior household 1880: C. E. (f) Deignan 48 Ire Ire Ire, son Thos. 25 GA, dau M. A. 25 GA, dau Katie 21 GA, dau Teresa 19 GA and dau Lizzie 19 GA.

Ellen Deignan Rafferty	no dates	SR: bur. 4/27/1927, 68 yrs.
Katherine Mary Deignan	no dates	d/o Wm. & Catherine Deignan
Elizabeth Sarah Deignan		d/o Wm. & Catherine Deignan

- SR: born 11/18/1866 and buried 2/19/1946, 79 years.

Theresa Mary Deignan		d/o Wm. & Catherine Deignan

- SR: born 12/19/1859 and bur. 3/1/1948, 88 yrs.

5 adult brick slabs, n/m	1 small marker, unable to read. d. Oct. 18, 1849.

Sexton Records indicate buried in this lot:

Catherine M. Deignan	*bur. 4/19/1950, 90 yrs.*
Thomas M. Deignan	*bur. 7/21/1898, 46 yrs.*

- 1870 Muscogee Census: Catherine Deignan 41 Ireland, Mary A. 19 GA, Thomas M. 17 GA, Ellen 14 GA, Katie 12 GA, Theresa 10 GA and Lizzie 6 GA.

- 1860 Muscogee Census: William Degnan (sic) 40 Ireland, Catherine 34 Ireland, Mary 9 GA, Thomas M. 7 GA, Ellen 4 GA, Catherine 2 GA, Teresa 1 GA, Patrick 66 Ireland, Richard 26 Ireland and Patrick 23 Ireland.

- 1850 Muscogee Census: HH 321/341 Hugh Doland 27 Ireland. HH 321/342 William Degnan (sic) 30 Ireland, Catherine 26 Ireland and Bridget Doland 16 Ireland.

Lot 79, Lynch on wall

Joseph Arthur Lynch	Oct. 28, 1895	Dec. 26, 1953	

- 1930 Muscogee Co.: J. Arthur Lynch 35 GA GA GA (married @25), wife Georgia F. 35 GA GA GA (married @25) and son J. Arthur Jr. 8 GA.

Joseph A. Lynch, Jr.	Nov. 24, 1920	Mar. 17, 1954	GA Capt. 3200 Proof Test Gp. A. F. WWII AM & OLC-PH
Roger O'Melia		May 18, 1864	age 25 yrs.
Franck Curran Lynch	Feb. 21, 1881	Dec. 17, 1939	

Georgia Flewellen Mitchell	June 20, 1897	May 9, 1934	w/o Arthur Lynch

Lot 80, Durkin on wall

Mary Margret Byrne	1928	1989	SR: bur. 2/22/1989
John Durkin, Jr.	1868	1902	SR: bur. 11/9/1901
Mary M. Bryant	1867	1959	SR: born 3/8/1867, bur. 5/20/1958
John Durkin	1821	1905	SR: born 1815 Ireland bur. 3/25/1905

- Obit: born Sligo Co., Ireland, June 21, 1815, 89 years old, to Columbus in 1844, rock mason by trade, laid a portion of the foundation of the Eagle & Phenix Mill, worked on old dam at Clapp's Factory, an Alderman for a number of years, planted oak trees around the old Catholic Church at 2nd Ave. & 7th Street, leaves wife & 2 dghtrs, Mrs. A. M. Bryant, Miss Lavira Durkin.

- 1850 Muscogee Census: John Durkin 35 Ireland, Ann 34 Ireland, John 10 Ireland, Mary Ann 5 Ireland and James 11/12 Ireland.

- 1870 Muscogee Census: John Durkin 50 IRE, Lavira 34 GA, Mary M. 3 GA, John T. 1 GA and Savanna B. 2/12 GA.

Alaric M. Bryant	1858	1939	SR: bur. 8/29/1939. GA Death Index: Died Muscogee Co. 8/29/1839, 81 years.

- 1880 Muscogee Census: T. M. Bryant 48 GA GA GA, wife Martha 42 GA GA GA, son A. M. 21 GA, son T. B. 19 GA and dau M. E. 6 GA.

- 1920 Muscogee Census: Alaric M. Bryant 63 GA GA AL, wife Mary M. 52 GA IRE GA, son Jacob A. 29 GA, dau Margaret G. 16 GA and DIL Elna 20 SC SC SC. (next door to Lavira Durkin)

Lavira T. McCrary	1835	1922	his wife SR: bur. 6/27/1922, 87.

- 1920 Muscogee Census: Lavira T. Durkin 84 GA GA GA wd, dau Lavira T. Jr. GA IRE GA, boarder William H. Wise 20 IN IN IN and boarder Clarissa M. Wise 19 MS MS MS.

Mary Eugenia Bryant	1892	1918	SR: bur. 10/21/1918
Lavira Theresa Durkin			SR: 1/8/1929, 57 yrs.

Lot 81, open lot

unable to read		8/30/1851	age 31 years
Patrick Tierney		9/7/1850	age 21. Native of Ballyduff Co., Tippewary, Ireland

- Obit: born Durrough Co., Tipperay, Ireland.

Lot 82, no name on wall

Myra Hawkins Birdsong	1838	1920	SR: bur. 12/19/1920, born 12/19/1838

- Edward Birdsong married Nancy Susan Hawkins 5/15/1834 Oglethorpe Co., GA. Edward was born 5 May 1804 in Oglethorpe Co., GA the s/o Freeman and Frances Finn Birdsong. Freeman died 6/25/1841 in Upson Co., GA. Edward died 1/26/1859 in Russell Co., AL.

- 1850 Muscogee Census: Edward Birdsong 40 GA, Mrs. Nancy 30 GA, Ann E. 13 GA, Alvira 12 GA, Cawkin (f) 11 GA, Louisa 7 GA and Mary 4 GA.

- 1860 Muscogee Census: Nancy S. Birdsong 43 GA, Anna 23 GA, Elmira 22 GA, Hawkin? (f) 21 GA, Louisa 18 GA, Mary 14 GA, Henry 10 GA and Charles 8 GA.

- 1870 Muscogee Census: Nancy S. Birdsong 53 GA, Myra H. 30 GA, Henry G. 18 GA, Edgar H. 10 GA and several other boarders.

Ruth Weeks		7/1872	age 2 mo., infant d/o Lyman & Mary E. Wells
Mary Birdsong Wells	Oct. 23, 1847	Nov. 14, 1897	w/o Lyman Printup Wells

- 1870 Bullock Co., AL in household of Henry Haynes: Lyman Wells 28 GA, Mary B. 22 GA and Everett 2 AL.

Myra Birdsong Schussler	1866	1934	
Kate Schussler	1868	1958	SR: bur. 3/5/1958, 89.
Lula Birdsong	1842	1917	w/o Lewis G. Schuessler. SR: bur. 1/22/1917, 75.

- Obit: sied Jan. 21, 1917, widow of late Louis G. Schuessler, 2 dghtrs, Misses Myra & Kate, 1 sister Miss Myra Birdsong.

Thomas Emmett Madden		Aug. 28, 1849	age 1 yr 2 mo 29 days. s/o J. H. & A. M. Madden.

- 1850 Muscogee Census: John H. Madden 33 NY, Ann 29 Ireland, Patrick H. 4, Henry 29 NY, Hubbard 39 Ireland other boarders.

Lewis G. Schuessler	1836	1908	

- 1880 Muscogee Census: L. G. Schussler 42 GA GER GER, wife Louisa 34 GA GA GA, dau Myra 14 GA, dau Ann 12 GA, dau Katie 10 GA and sister Myra Birdsong 37 GA GA GA.

Nannie Schuessler	Oct. 19, 1858	July 3, 1889	
2 children slabs, n/m	4 adult brick slabs, n/m		

Lot 83, Owens on wall

Elzadia R. Worrell	Mar. 11, 1862	Nov. 23, 1900	w/o H. T. Owens

Lot 84, no name on wall

Mrs. Mary A. Sharp   Feb. 8, 1838   Feb. 11, 1913

- 1880 Lee Co., AL Census: Mary A. Sharp 42 AL GA GA, dau Misouri 23 AL GA AL, son Frank M. 22 AL, dau Mollie 21 AL, dau Martha 20 AL, son Warren 18 AL, dau Eliza 16, dau Ella Porter 25 AL, grandson Warren Porter 8 AL and grandson Lewis Porter 5 AL.

1 adult slab, n/m

Sexton Records indicate buried in this lot:

Warren Sharp   *bur. 5/5/1886, 23 yrs.*

Lot 85, no name on wall

Mary B. (Bridges)   July 11, 1843   July 16, 1931
Murdock Wright

- Obit: widow of Julius W. Wright of Wilmington, NC, d/o Lydia Spencer & Robert Bridges Murdock, born Columbus, GA July 11, 1843, cousins survive.

- Julius Walker Wright (1838-1878) was the son of Joshua Grainger and Mary Ann Walker Wright of Wilmington, NC. He married Mary "Mollie" in 1868 and they moved to Kansas City, MO.[70]

Arthur Culpepper   Oct. 16, 1859   Oct. 16, 1925
Murdock

Lydia Murdock   June 9, 1817   Apr. 11, 1883   d/o Lambert W. & Ann
                 Talbot Co., GA   Columbus, GA   Spencer

- Obit: w/o R. B. Murdock Sr. born in Talbot Co., MD 1818, in Columbus Dec. 1837 with uncle Col. Richard Spencer, 4 children, 2 brothers, Perry Spencer of Summitt, Miss. (only 1 mentioned.)

Robert Bridges Murdock   Nov. 12, 1893   age 78 yrs

- Obit: born March 25, 1815 in Philadelphia, PA, in Columbus 1839, married Lillian Spencer in 1842, sister of late Lambert Spencer & the late Perry Spencer, Sr, his wife died in 1883, children, R. B. Murdock Jr., Mrs. Mary B. Wright, Arthur C. Murdock.

- Robert B. Murdock & Lydia Spencer married 6/8/1842 Muscogee Co., GA.

- 1850 Muscogee Census: Robert B. Murdock 34 PA, Lydia 32 MD, Mary A. 7 Muscogee, Robert 5 Muscogee and Emila 37 PA.

- 1870 Muscogee Census: Rob B. Murdock 55 PA, Lellia 50 MD, Mary B. 25 GA, Julius Wright Sr. 32 NC, Rob B. Murdock Jr. 23 GA, Samuel Murdock 16 GA and Arthur C. Murdock 10 GA.

- 1880 Muscogee Census: Robert B. Murdock 64 PA PA PA, wife Lydia 60 MD MD MD, dau Mary B. Wright 35 GA, son Robert Murdock 33 GA, son Samuel 29 GA, son Arthur 20 GA and sister Harriet Murdock 69 PA PA PA.

Robert Bridges Murdock   Aug. 14, 1895   age 50 yrs

- Obit: died Hot Springs, Ark., s/o late R. B. Murdock, 1 sister Mrs. W. R. Wright of Columbus, GA, 1 brother Arthur C. Murdock of Columbus, GA, member Nelson Rangers.

Helen Lindsley Spencer	Apr. 16, 1841 New Orleans, LA	Nov. 4, 1899 Columbus, GA	d/o Helen A. & Henry R. Backus, w/o Lambert Spencer

- Obit: died at the residence of Mrs. M. B. Wright, nee Helen L. Backus, born New Orleans LA Apr. 16, 1841, married in 1870, husband died in 1881, 2 dghts., Agnes Spencer of Columbus, GA and Mrs. Frank Ervin Calloway of Atlanta, GA, step-son Samuel Spencer of New York, sister Mrs. John B. Holst, Miss Annie J. Backus of Columbus, GA & Mrs. W. R. Mason of Richmond, VA.

- Married Lambert Spencer 11/11/1869 in Chatham Co., GA.

Henry Perry Spencer	Apr. 12, 1854 Columbus, GA	Jan. 13, 1892	s/o Perry & Jinnie Spencer
Samuel Spencer Murdock	Apr. 3, 1851	Sept. 19, 1883	s/o Robert B. & Lydia Murdock
Verona Spencer	Aug. 24, 1824	Feb. 13, 1857	d/o Isaac & Parizade Mitchell, w/o Lambert Spencer

- Obit: w/o Lambert Spencer, died at the home of her father Isaac Mitchell.

- 1850 Muscogee Census: Isaac Mitchell 56 NC, Parizade 48 GA, Sarah A. 22, Adaline 17 GA, John J. 15 GA, Caroline 7 GA and others.

Lambert Spencer	Feb. 14, 1821 Easton, MD	June 25, 1881 Columbus, GA	s/o Lambert & Anna Spencer.

- Obit: wife Verona Mitchell Spencer, funeral notice mentions he left a family. A tribute of respect from GA Home Ins. Co., born Easton, Maryland, died June 25, 1881, 68 years old, 1 brother Perry, 1 son Samuel.

- 1870 Muscogee Census: Lambert Spencer 49 MD, Helen 29 LA.

- 1880 Muscogee Census: Lambert Spencer 56 MD MD MD, wife Helen 39 LA NY MA, dau Agnes 9 and dau Helena 8.

Lambert W. Spencer	SR: bur. 2/22/1887, 45 yrs. Co. F., 2nd Regt., FL Vol. CSA 1861-1865

- 1850 Chatham Co., GA Census: Henrietta Spencer 65 MD MD MD and son Samuel 38 FL MD MD.

- s/o Dr. Samuel Wickes Spencer and Henrietta Maria Chamberlain Hayward who were married Nov. 22, 1828 in Talbot Co., MD.

Mrs. Anna Spencer	Nov. 21, 1858	73 yrs. w/o Lambert Spencer of Maryland.

- Anna Spencer was born in Talbot Co., MD, the d/o Perry Spencer and Mary Hopkins. She married Lambert Wickes Spencer 9/13/1804 in Easton, Talbot Co., MD. Lambert was the s/o Richard Spencer and Martha Wickes, born 7/11/1776 in Easton, MD and died 10/5/1836 in Easton.

Lot 86, no name on wall

Henry Lockhart   SR: bur. 1/15/1862, age 67.

- Obit: Doctor, formerly of Warren Co., GA & Apalachicola, FL, died Jan. 15, 1862.

- Henry Lockhart was born ca 1794 in Hancock Co., GA, s/o Richard Hancock and Mary Pope. He married Mary Ann Beall 12/12/1820 in Warren Co., GA.

- Muscogee Co., GA WB A pages 313-316. Henry Lockhart. 3/1/1860:1/20/1862. Legatees: wife: Mary Ann. Extr. Sons: Robert B., Dr. Richard H. Daus: Rowena M. Lockhart, Anna Thomas, wife of Joseph W. Thomas, Ellen Jane Verstille, wife of Henry W. Verstille, and Mary Cornelia Hudson, wife of John F. Hudson. Wits: William H. Hughes, Jr. Alfred Young, Robert M. Gunby.

Edwin Beall Booth   June 20, 1886   Dec. 12, 1915

Mrs. Mary A. Lockhart   Jan. 9, 1803   June 14, 1888   w/o Henry Lockhart

- Mary Ann Beall is the d/o Robert Augustus Beall (1767-1832) and Elizabeth Marshall (1774-1840).

- 1870 Muscogee Co., GA: Mary Lockhart 67 MD, Annie E. Chapman 43 GA, Thomas Chapman 33 GA, Mary J. Thomas 24 GA, William H. Thomas 20 GA, Anna E. Thomas 10 GA and numerous boarders.

- 1880 Muscogee Census: Tom Chapman 50 GA GA GA, wife Anna 54 GA GA GA, dau Mary Thomas 33 GA, dau Nannie Thomas 21 GA, son Robert Thomas 28 GA, boarders: Willie Thomas 30 GA, Georgia Thomas 25 GA, Marie Thomas 4 GA and Maud Thomas 2 GA, mother Mary Lockhart 77 GA GA GA and numerous other boarders.

Rowena L. Echols   age 45

- Funeral notice mentions Mrs. Mary A. Lockhart, died Oct. 27, 1866.

Josephus Echols   age 58

- 1850 Muscogee Census: Josephus Echols 43 VA, attorney.

- 1860 Russell Co., AL Census: Josephus D. Echols 53 VA, Mary E. 53 SC and Edward Fishburn 12 Canada.

- Josephus Echols married Rowena Lockhart 10/12/1863 Muscogee Co., GA.

Georgia A. Thomas   No Dates   SR: died 6/24/1881, 32 yrs.

- Obit: d/o late George W. Hardwick, 32nd year, leaves husband, 2 children, d. 24 June 1881.

- Georgia A. Hardwick married William Thomas 5/29/1873 in Muscogee Co., GA.

Henry L. Thomas   age 19

- Obit: s/o late Joseph W. & Ann Thomas.

Clare Marie Booth   Oct. 15, 1889   Jan. 6, 1947

Robert Rast Cole   Sept. 29, 1914   June 2, 1916   s/o R. & Hazel B. Cole

Clare Beall Thomas   No Dates   baby

Willie Booth   Jan. 3, 1884   Aug. 27, 1884   s/o John & Nannie Booth

Joseph W. Thomas   Sept. 5, 1817   Mar. 6, 1859
                          New York City   Columbus, GA

- Obit: former editor of the Enquirer.

- Muscogee Co. WB A: 247-249. Joseph W. Thomas. 2/20/1859:3/10/1859. Legatees: wife Anna Elizabeth. Sons: Henry Lockhart Thomas, William Hampton Thomas and Robert Beall Thomas. Daus: Josephine and Anna Elizabeth. Bros: William H. Thomas of NYC and Robert H. Thomas now of NYC. Father-in-law: Dr. Henry Lockhart. Exrs: wife, Anna E. Thomas, Dr. Henry Lockhart, Robert B. Lockhart. Wits: Michael Woodruff, Julius R. Clapp, Robert B. Lockhart.

- Joseph Thomas married Anna Lockhart 9/24/1842 in Warren Co., GA.

- Joseph's widow, Anna Elizabeth Lockhart married 2) Tom Chapman.

Richard Henry Lockhart   Mar 27, 1826   Sept. 24, 1859

- Obit: doctor, had been on a trip to restore health, died 24 Sept. 1859, Knoxville, Tenn.

- 1850 Muscogee Census: Richard H. Lockhart 24 GA, physician.

3 adult brick slabs, n/m   2 baby brick slabs, n/m

Sexton Records indicate buried in this plot:

Anna Eliz Booth   *bur: 2/14/1914, 55 yrs.*

- 1900 Muscogee Census: Boarding house of Mary Thomas June 1844 GA NY GA, among others: boarder John Booth May 1848 GA GA GA, Anna Apr 1844 GA GA GA, Edwin Jul 1866, Jean? June 1890 GA, Hazel June 1892, Mary June 1899 and Maud Thomas Oct. 1878.

Miss Mary J. Thomas   *bur. 3/22/1902, 58 yrs.*

- Obit: born Warrenton, GA 1844, d/o Joseph W. Thomas & Ann E. Chapman, 1 brother, R. B. Thomas of Atlanta, GA, 1 sister, Mrs. John E. Booth.

Lot 87, no name on wall

Margaret Bozeman   Dec. 22, 1787   Aug. 30, 1864
                          Prince William
                          Co., VA

- 1850 Muscogee Census: Mrs. M. Bozeman 62 VA.

- Margaret's maiden name was either Trent or Trate and I will leave it to someone else to decide that one. She first married ? Shelton and married secondly James Bozeman (1774-1834) 2/20/1820 in Greene Co., GA.

Lot 88, open lot

Pauline Dillard Coart   May 13, 1860   Jan. 19, 1943   w/o Wm. C. Coart

- 1910 Muscogee Census: William C. Court 63 NC US US (m^2 23), wife Pauline 48 GA GA GA (m^1 23 7ch/6 liv), dau Pauline 21 GA, dau Vurtice? 20 GA, son William C. J. 16 GA, son George 15 GA, dau Margaret 13 GA and day Florence 11 GA.

- William Coart married 1) ca 1870 Mary Ann Holt, d/o Dr. Leroy Holt and Mary Chandler.

Florence Coart Whitaker	May 12, 1899	Feb. 24, 1971	Mother of Mary Eliza Hille
Goode Holt	June 5, 1864	July 14, 1864	s/o T. G. & N. Holt
Wm. Chandler Holt	July 8, 1860	Feb. 7, 1861	s/o T. G. & N. Holt
Thaddie G. Holt	Aug. 7, 1870	Aug. 21, 1877	s/o T. G. & N. Holt
Mary Holt	Aug. 21, 1856	July 12, 1857	d/o T. G. & N. Holt
Wm. Chandler Holt	Feb. 26, 1821	Apr. 3, 1848	died from military wounds in Mexico.

- Obit: attorney, died from illness contracted in Mexican War as a member of Columbus Guards.

Mary Sankey	May 30, 1810	Mar. 23, 1870	Step-mother. 2nd wife of Dr. Leroy Holt

- Obit: died in Montgomery, AL

Dr. Leroy Holt	Apr. 9, 1796	Apr. 30, 1861	Father.

- Obit: lived in Union Springs, AL, formerly of Columbus, at the home of Mrs. A. J. Dawson, married Mary Ann Sankey July 15, 1840.

- Dr. Leroy Fowler Holt, s/o Thaddeus Holt (c1768-1813) and Martha Goode married 1) Mary Chandler (1807-1835) and 2) Mary Ann Sankey 7/15/1840 Muscogee Co., GA.

- 1850 Russell Co., AL Census: Leroy Holt 53 GA, Mary 39 GA, Elizabeth 22 GA, Martha 20 GA and Mary 1 AL.

Mary Chandler	Aug. 19, 1807	July 13, 1835	1st wife of Leroy Holt

3 adult slabs, n/m

Sexton Records indicate the following also buried in this lot:

Lena Coart	*SR: bur. 9/10/1896, 5 yrs*
Mrs. N. B. Holt	*SR bur. 3/29/1912, 73 yrs*

- Obit: died in Atlanta, GA, Mrs. Narcissa Boykin Holt, died July 15, 1912 at the residence of Mrs. P. E. Bruce, widow of the late T. G. Holt and last surviving child of the late Dr. Samuel Boykins of Columbus, 1 son, Samuel Holt of Hot Springs, Ark., leaves the children of deceased son, Leroy Holt, formery of Birmingham, AL, several nieces and nephews.

Martha Holt	*SR: bur. 3/29/1914, 85 yrs*

- Obit: died Mar. 27, 1914 at the residence of R. B. Turman in Atlanta, GA, d/o late Dr. Leroy Holt, related to the W. C. Coart family.

William C. Coart	*SR: bur. 2/27/1919, 71 yrs*

- Obit:secretary of the GA Home Ins. Co., born July 4, 1847 in New Berne, NC, s/o John C. Coart & Margaret Templeton Coart, CSA, father killed in Battle of New Berne 1861, brother of late John C. Jr., T. Singleton, uncle of late Rev. Wm. M. Hawks, CSA, Gen. Philips command, twice married, Mary Amonet Holt of Columbus, 2nd Pauline Dillard, d/o late George Dillard of Auburn, AL, leaves widow, sons John C. of Seattle, WA, Major Leroy, Mrs. Dr. A. A. Williams of Columbus, GA, Mrs. P. L. Hopkins of Chipley, FL, Mrs. E. S. Brinson of Columbus, Lt. W. C. Jr. US Army Lt., Geo H. of US Army, Miss Margaret & Miss Florence, both of Columbus, GA.

- 1910 Muscogee Census: William C. Coart 63 NC US US (m2 23), wife Pauline 48 GA GA GA (m1 23 7ch/6 liv), dau Pauline 21 GA, dau Vurtice? 20 GA, son William C. J. 16

GA, son George 15 GA, dau Margaret 13 GA and day Florence 11 GA.

T. G. Holt   *SR: bur. 11/12/1898, 74 yrs*

- Obit: died at residence of son, Lee Holt in Sumpterville, AL, 1 brother-in-law W. C. Coart, married in Columbus to Miss Boykins, 75 years old.

- Thaddeus Goode Holt married Narcissa Boykins (1833-1912), the d/o Dr. Samuel Boykin (1786-1848) and Narcissa Cooper (1803-1859) 12/14/1854.

    o Married in Russell Co., ALA, on the morning of the 14th inst., at the country residence of Mrs. Boykin, by the Rev. John E. Dawson, Mr. Thaddeus G. Holt to Miss Narcissa Boykin, all of Columbus, GA.[71]

- 1880 Shelby Co., AL Census: Thadius G. Holt 51 GA GA GA, wife Narcissa 45 GA SC GA, son Lee 21 GA, niece Bell Boykin 5 AL and other boarders.

Mary Ann Holt   *SR: bur. 3/26/1870, 47 yrs*

- Obit: died Montgomery, AL at the residence of T. G. Holt, funeral notice mentions Mrs. John R. Dawson..

Lot 89, open lot

Col. A. P. Mooty   Aug. 1, 1889

- A. Percival Mooty was the s/o James Mooty (1790 SC – 1879 Troup Co., GA) and Margaret Hawthorne (1800 SC – 1842 Troup Co., GA). A. P. was Co-Principal of LaGrange High School in 1868 with his brother-in-law Leonidas Jones.[72] A. P. married Elizabeth Johnson ca 1852. His sister, Mary Antoinette Mooty (1821-1902) married Joel Gibson (1821-1902).

- 1860 Meriwether Co., GA Census: A. P. Mooty 33 SC, E. M. (f) 23 SC, Wm. F. 2 GA and Martin J. 6/12 GA.

- 1870 Troup Co., GA Census: A. P. Mooty 42 SC, M. S. (f) 32 SC, Willie 12 GA, James 10 GA, R. L. (m) FL, M. H. (f) SC, Chas. 3 GA and Hugh 1 GA.

Elizabeth J. Mooty	1835	1929	SR: b. SC, bur. 1/12/1929, 93 yrs.
Mattie E. Barr	May 25, 1854	Feb. 18, 1896	w/o J. T. Gibson
J. T. Gibson	Apr. 24, 1856	Feb. 25, 1901	s/o Thomas & Emily Gibson
Mary E. Barr	Dec. 25, 1850	Aug. 22, 1901	w/o J. T. Gibson

- Obit: widow of late J. T. Gibson, died at residence of Mr. & Mrs. W. J. Barr in Summerville, about 50 years old, d/o Mr. & Mrs. W. J. Barr, 4 brothers, Geo. F., W. T. both of Columbus, GA, Charles F. of Summerville, AL, J. W. of Cedartown, 2 sisters, Mrs. Charles Lowther, Miss Lizzie Barr.

Wiley Jones Gibson	Dec. 13, 1866	Mar. 11, 1896	
Charles P. Mooty	1866	1941	SR: bur. 4/8/1941, 73
G. W. Gafford	Jan. 13, 1834	Aug. 1, 1879	
Tower Dawson			Columbus Guards 1861-65

- Obit: s/o Mrs. John R. Dawson, died march 7, 1867

Elizabeth Gafford	Dec. 25, 1837	Dec. 27, 1896

- 1870 Russell Co., AL Census: E. W. Gafford 36 GA and Elizabeth 34 GA.

- 1880 Muscogee Census: Elisabeth Gafford 40 GA GA GA widowed.

| John R. Dawson | Dec. 20, 1810 | Oct. 27, 1852 |
| | Greensboro, GA | Wynnton |

- Obit: 42 years old.

- Muscogee Co., GA WB A:137-139. John R. Dawson, 8/17/1852:12/11/1852.Legatees: wife and ch mentioned. Exr: Thomas H. Dawson, brother. Wits: Joseph B. Hill, Thadeus G. Holt, Thomas M. Watt.

- 1850 Muscogee Census: John R. Dawson 40 Greene Co, GA, Jane A. 32 Greene, Henry R. 13 Musc., David T. 11 Musc., Mary E. 9 Musc., John F. 7 Musc., Annoitt (f) 2 Musc. and Miss A. Sankey 14 AL.

- John Rogers Dawson, s/o Thomas Henry Dawson (1784-1846) and Suzannah Rogers (d. 10/1/1864) who were married 1 Dec. 1803 of Greene Co., GA.

| 2 adult slabs, n/m | 1 adult brick slab, n/m | 1 baby brick slab, n/m |

Sexton records indicate also buried in this lot:

| *Minnie Mooty* | | *SR: bur. 3/28/1941, 75 yrs.* |

Lot 90, no name on wall

| Col. P. W. Alexander | Mar. 21, 1825 | Sept. 23, 1886 | CSA, s/o P. W. & Mary Banks Alexander |

- Obit: died Marietta, GA, married Theresa Shorter.

- 1880 Cobb Co., GA Census: P. W. Alexander 55 GA VA GA, wife M. Teresa 40 AL VA GA, dau Sallie 7 AL, son George S. 5 AL, son Paul 4 GA and niece Lizzie Shorter 13 AL AL GA.

| Maria Theresa Shorter | Aug. 14, 1840 | Aug. 9, 1918 | w/o Col. P. W. Alexander, d/o James H. & Eliz. Hargraves Shorter. |

- Obit: died New York, one of the founders of United Daughters of the Confederacy, arrived with the remains from New York, Mr. & Mrs. Paul Alexander, Mr. & Mrs. Geo. Alexander, Miss Sarah Alexander, D. B. Jones, joined in Atlanta by Mr. & Mrs. Samuel T. Weyman and in Macon by Dr. & Mrs. Shorter, closely connected with the Fountain, Stewart, Hargraves & Meigs families.

| Sarah S. A. Allen | Dec. 28, 1872 | Apr. 10, 1940 | d/o Col. P. W. & Theresa S. Alexander, w/o John H. Allen |

| Virginia Hargraves | Sept. 2, 1819 | June 4, 1858 | w/o Geo. Hargraves, d/o Hon. John Forsyth |
| | Washington City | | |

- Obit: w/o Geo. Hargraves, d/o late Hon. John Forsyth.

- Virginia Forsyth was the d/o Hon. John Forsyth born in Fredericksburg 10/10/1780 and died in Washington 10/22/1841. Among other positions, he was Governor of Georgia. John married Clara Meigs, the d/o Hon. Josiah Meigs, LL D, the first President of the University of GA.[73]

| Geo. Hargraves Jr. | Apr. 28, 1810 | Dec. 1, 1884 | mar. Virginia Forsyth in |
| | Warrenton, GA | Ivy, Albermarle | Columbus 1843, s/o Geo. & |

	Co., VA	Theresa Hargraves

- Obit: wife, Virginia Forsyth.

- 1850 Muscogee Census: George Hargraves 40 GA, Virginia 30 GA, Clara 6 GA, Mrs. Clara Forsyth 68 CT, Miss Anna Forsyth 27 PA and Miss Rosa Forsyth 27 PA.

- George Hargraves married Virginia Forsyth 4/19/1843 Muscogee Co., GA.

Mary Eliz. Jones	Oct. 8, 1866	Mar. 23, 1946	d/o Charles S. Shorter & Sallie Shepherd, w/o Donald B. Jones
Geo. Hargraves	July 25, 1772 Charles Co., MD	Sept. ?, 1849 Columbus, GA	

- Muscogee Co., GA Will Book A Pages 109-110. George Hargraves, Sr., 7/3/1847:11/5/1849. Legatees: son George, Jr., dau: Elizabeth M. Shorter of Russell Co., Ala., widow of James H. Shorter. Exrs: George Hargraves, Jr., John C. Thompson, Joseph B. Hill. Wits: L. D. Johnson, J. R. Dawson, J. R. Jones.

- George Hargraves Sr. married Elizabeth Thompson 2/13/1806 in Warren Co., GA.

- Wilkes Co., GA WB HH page 33: Joseph Thompson. Dec. 9, 1809. Probated May 7, 1810. Legatees: son William Thompson, grandson Joseph Thompson. On the decease of their father   William, I give to grandson William Thompson, grandaus. Julia and Eliza Thompson, certain slaves. Wife Elizabeth, son James B. Thompson, son Henry Bradford Thompson, dau. Fenson Hargraves, grandau. Annes Semmes, not 16, mentions son-in-law George Hargraves, son Henry Bradford, grandson George Hargraves. Mentions a deed of gift from Ignatius Semmes to his daughters Annie and Henriette Semmes of slaves. Wife Elizabeth and son Henry Bradford Thompson, Excrs. Wit: John McLaughlin, John Brooks, A.Giver.

James Hargraves Shorter	Oct. 4, 1844 Summerville, AL	Feb. 2, 1922 Macon, GA	s/o Eliz Hargraves & James Hurt Shorter

- 1870 Muscogee Census: John E. Pleasant 27 VA, James H. Shorter 26 AL, Mary E. Shorter 56 AL, Maria T. Shorter 26 AL, Mary E. Shorter 3 AL, and Peter W (sic). Alexander 46 GA among others.

Elizabeth Swift Shorter	July 4, 1856 Waynmanville, GA	Feb. 1, 1929 Paris, France	d/o Geo. Parker Swift & Adelaide Jewett Swift
Elizabeth Hargraves	1805	1890	w/o James H. Shorter. SR: bur. 5/9/1890

- Elizabeth Hargraves of Maryland, wife of James H. Shorter, was the mother of Mrs. Benjamin Fontaine. Mr. James H. Shorter came to Columbus from Maryland shortly after he graduated from Yale in the 1830's, to join his uncle Eli S. Shorter, a prominent lawyer.[74]

- 17 Mar 1836 At this city, James H. Short (sic) to Miss Mary E. Hargraves, d/o George Hargraves Sr., of Columbus by Rev. Mr. O'Riley.[75]

James H. Shorter	Mar. 23, 1810	June 30, 1846	

- James Hurt Shorter was the only child of James Hurt Shorter and Dorothy Napier.[76]

one marker CHS CSA 1861-1865

Lot 91, open lot

James Meeler   Mar. 23, 1808   July 21, 1885

- James Meeler married Catherine M. Williams 9/11/1845 in Muscogee Co., GA.

- 1850 Muscogee Census: James Mealer (sic) 40 GA, Catherine 24 GA, Sarah H. 12 GA and Wesley 9 GA.

- 1860 Muscogee Census: James Mealer (sic) 50 GA, Catherine 30 GA and Lucinda Mealer 40 GA.

Catherine M. Meeler   Jan. 6, 1828   Nov. 4, 1906

- Obit: married the late James Meeler when 18, nearest living relative is a grandson, Joseph T. Carruthers, a step-son, Dr. Sam May of Brantley, AL, 1 niece Mrs. John Scott of Grapevine, TX.

- 1900 Muscogee Census: Catherine Meeler Jan. 1827 GA GA GA and grandson Joseph Caruthers (sic) Dec. 1877 GA GA GA.

Tinnie F. Meeler   Jan. 9, 1857   Dec. 18, 1877   wife of (unable to read), married Feb. 22, 1877, d/o James & Catherine Meeler

Lot 92, fenced lot, no name

unable to read   Nov. 1, 18??   Nov. 22, 18??   (adult)

Gen. Daniel McDougald   Cumberland Co., NC   Sept. 8, 1849   age 50 years

- Obit: Mayor in 1839, Senator 1840, native of NC, removed to Washington Co., GA. when only 18 years of age & then to western GA. He represented Harris Co. in the Senate of GA.

- Born 1799 in Cumberland Co., NC, the s/o Duncan McDougald and his wife Sarah.

- Major General Daniel MacDougald, who had been in temporary command of all the troops at Columbus, was one of the earliest settlers. with his brothers, Alexander and Duncan, he moved to Georgia from North Carolina. The father of these three young men was a Scottish highlander, and their mother was born on the Island of Skye. The three brothers became prominent citizens of Columbus. They came together from the Cape Fear River in NC, first to Washington County, thence to Harris County. Duncan McDougald, the oldest, remained bachelor. Daniel, born 1799 Cumberland County, NC was destined top play an important role in the boomtown on the Chattahoochee. When he came to Georgia, Daniel was only 18 years old.[77]

- On Tombstone: " his extraordinary powers of mind, his great energy of character, and his extended feeling of benovelence of action had assigned to him a large space in the public mind, and gathered around him in every struggle of his life a host of as true warm-hearted, and devoted friends as ever clung to the fortune of the living, or gathered around the grave of the dead. In his social and domestic relations his virtues were conspicuous, few were his equal, and none his superior. He lived and died with a conscience void of offense to God."

Ann Eliza Alexander   Dec. 9, 1809   Nov. 22, 1889   w/o Gen. Daniel McDougald
                           Putnam Co., GA   Brooklyn, NY

- Obit: Entered into rest of Sunday, 22nd instant, at the residence of her daughter, Mrs. Mary Dixon. Ann E. Billings. aged 77 yrs. Interment at Columbus, GA. Brooklyn Daily Eagle.
- d/o Maj. William Henry Alexander (1780-1857) and his first wife, Elizabeth Lane (1784-1833). She married 1) Gen. Daniel McDougald 12/24/1831 in Putnam Co., GA and 2) Dr. Samuel A. Billings 11/11/1885 in Brooklyn, NY. Swift Kyle House, 303 12th Street built in 1857 by Dr. Samuel F. Billings, a physician of the town, when he married the widow of Gen. Daniel MacDougald.
- 1850 Muscogee Census: Mrs. Eliza A. McDougald 37 GA, Miss Mary 15 GA, William 13 GA and Duncan 4 GA.

Mary Lizzie Dixon		De. 13, 1855	d/o Robert E. & Mary Dixon (child)
Duncan McDougald, II	Nov. 11, 1848	Sept. 1862	s/o Gen. Dan & Eliz A. McDougald

- Obit: a cadet at GA Military Institute, died in the home of R. E. Dixon.

Robert Emmet Dixon	1832 Talbot Co., GA	Apr. 24, 1863 Richmond, VA	s/o Robert E. & Martha McDougald Dixon

- Georgia Journal & Messenger 4/29/1863: Killed-Robert Emmett Dixon, Clerk of the House of Representatives, was killed in Richmond by R. E. Forde of Kentucky, on April 24. Dixon was a native of Talbot Co, Ga, and a resident of Columbus.

- s/o Robert Henry Dixon (1800-1856) and his 2nd wife Martha A. J. A. Marshall (1812-1851).

- Talbot Co., GA WB B:35. Robert H. Dixon Sept 18, 1855. Wife - Eliza P [Eliza P. Eason Brown] - Household and kitchen furniture, all the property she brought into the marriage, slaves, $1,000. Parker Eason [prob her brother] Henry Co., in trust for unborn child 1/13 of estate Joseph B. Roulac trust for my d Martha Hines Roulac, slaves and enough of estate to make 1/6. 1/6 to Robert E Dixon and James J. Marshall - trust for my d Nancy Jones Dixon – same 1/6 RED/ JJM my d Elizabeth Burt Dixon – same 1/6 RED/JJM my son Stephen Marshall Dixon, 1/6 RED/JJM my s Henry Bacon Dixon, 1/6 Robert E. Dixon. Robert E. Dixon, John L. Dixon, William B. Marshall - executors. "A Codicil to my last and testament which is in the possession of John C Mount of Talbot Co. I do hereby give and devise to my six children named in said will to wit: Robert E, Martha H, Nancy J, Elizabeth B, Stephen M, and Henry B my intero interest in the Copper Mines of Raburn Co, Ga subject to the same restrictions and limitations as the legacy in the body of said will near prospect of death, but in the full possession of my mental facilities being of sound and desp{/} mind and memory d at Rockbridge Alum Springs, Va this 1st day of Nov in the year of our lord 1856. Robert H. Dixon." Witnesses: William Fragen, Jno w. Bordan, H. G. Davidson[78]

Mary McDougald Dixon	July 1835 Putnam Co., GA	Dec. 7, 1900 Brooklyn, NY	d/o Daniel & Eliz. McDougald, w/o Robert Emmet Dixon

- Obit: leaves sons David & Emmett Dixon, 1 dght, Mrs. Fred Little, wife of R. Emmet Dixon, d/o Gen. Daniel McDougald * sister of late Col. W. A. McDougald.

- death certificate #5698 Brooklyn (NYC Archives) for Daniel McDougald Dixon: sick from Dec 24 - Chronic Nephritis, 45yrs, 4 mos, broker, b-Columbus, GA. father Robert E. Dixon, mother-Mary McD.

- Children: Mary Elizabeth (Died as Infant) (1854-1855), Daniel McDougald (1856-1902), Robert Emmet (1858-1901) and Bacon Adele 1 (1861-1929)[79]

Robert Emmet Dixon	Sept. 1858 Columbus, GA	Nov. 11, 1901 Brooklyn, NY	s/o Robert Emmet & Mary McDougald Dixon
Adele Dixon Little	1861	1929	w/o Frederick Scrymser Little. SR: bur. 2/6/1929, 66
Duncan McDougald	Nov. 13, 1795 Cumberland Co., NC	May 3, 1872 Russell Co., AL	

- Obit: born NC, moved to Washington Co., GA, then to Harris Co., GA, was older brother of late Col. Dan. McDougald & uncle of W. A. McDougald.

William A. McDougald	July 4, 1838 Russell Co., AL	Sept. 17, 1887	

- Obit: s/o Gen. McDougald, born Columbus July 4, 1838, 1868 married Emily Fitten d/o Maj. Fitten of Adairsville, 5 sons & 2 dghtrs, Mrs. Mary McDougald Dixon in NY is his sister.

- William MacDougald, s/o Daniel & Ann Eliza McDougald, whose home was on the Alabama side facing the river, married Emily Fitten of Athens, a brilliant young woman, who, after rearing her large family and after her husband's death moved to Atlanta, where she became the head of the Woman's Suffrage movement in Georgia.[80]

- 1880 Russell Co., AL Census: William A. McDougald 41 AL, wife Emily C. 31 GA, dau Annie 10 GA, son Duncan 7 GA, son William 5 Al, dau Emily C. 3/12 AL and son John 5 AL.

Emily Fitten McDougald	Nov. 11, 1848 Augusta, GA	Jan. 13, 1938	

- Obit: died Atlanta, GA. Led in the woman's suffrage, d/o late Col. & Mrs. John Fitten.

- Mrs. Emily Fitten Macdougald. DAR ID Number: 114658. Born in Augusta, Ga. Wife of William Alexander MacDougald. Descendant of Lieut. Isaac DuBose, as follows: John Holmes Fitten (1818-99) m. 1843 Anne Sophia Martin (1823-1902). Alexander Martin (1775-1815) m. Anne DuBose (1790-1866). Isaac DuBose m. Sarah DuBose (cousins). Isaac DuBose was 2nd lieutenant under Generals Marion and Sumter, South Carolina Line. He was born in South Carolina; died in Columbia County, Ga.

Mary McDougald	Feb. 17, 1885	June 9, 1885	d/o Wm. A. & E. C. McDougald
John Fitten McDougald	Dec. 14, 1876 Russell Co., AL	June 29, 1931 Atlanta, GA	s/o Emily Fitten & Wm. A. McDougald
Wm. A. McDougald, Jr.	Feb. 3, 1875 Russell Co., AL	June 11, 1901 Atlanta, GA	s/o Emily Fitten & Wm. A. McDougald

Lot 93, no name on wall

N. M. Robinson	Mar. 31, 1809	Sept. 23, 1851

- A tribute from Chattahoochee, Division #17, Sons of Temperants.

- 1850 Muscogee Census: Nat Mc. Robinson 40 GA, Ann E. 36 GA, William J. 12 GA, Ann E. 7 GA, Miss E. D. Jernigan 25 GA, Amanda C. Jernigan 18 GA, Henry M. Jernigan 24 GA, P.? A. S. Jernigan 17 GA.

- Muscogee Co., GA WB A: Nathaniel Mc. Robinson 9/17/1851:11/4/1851. Legatees: son, William J. Robinson, dau: Ann Eliza. Sisters-in-law: Eliza D. Jernigan and Amanda C. Jernigan. Nephew: Isaac T. Robinson (exr). Wits: Abram B. Ragan, Alpha K. Ayer, Jordan L. Howell.

Anne Robinson	Dec. 3, 1837	Nov. 29, 1854	died by accident in Tuscaloosa, AL
Alexander Robinson	Apr. 1, 1850	June 25, 1853	s/o W. M. Robinson
Philetus N. Jernigan	May 9, 1826	Sept. 23, 1851	

Lot 94, Whatley on wall

John T. Whatley	Apr. 11, 1858	Feb. 2, 1930

- 1900 Muscogee Census: John T. Whatley Apr. 1858 GA GA GA, wife Lillie Jan 1863 GA GA GA (5 ch/5 liv), dau Lillie Apr. 1884 GA, dau Laura Nov. 1885 GA, son John T. Jr. Sept. 1887 GA, dau Hannah Oct. 1890 GA and dau Nettie Sept. 1893 GA.

- 1920 Muscogee Census: J. T. Whatley Sr. 62 GA AL AL, wife Lillie 56 GA GA GA and dau Hannah 24 GA.

Lillie O. Whatley	Jan. 28, 1862	May 4, 1932

- 1930 Muscogee Census: Lillie O. Whatley 67 GA GA GA and dau Hannah E. 32 GA AL GA.

Hannah W. Lowe	Oct. 2, 1890	June 5, 1966
Charles F. McCoy	Mar. 10, 1884	Feb. 14, 1946

- 1920 Muscogee Census: Charles F. McCoy 36 GA AL GA, wife Laura 34 AL GA GA and dau Frances 5 GA.

Laura Whatley McCoy	Nov. 3, 1886	Mar. 12, 1974
Frances McCoy	Oct. 14, 1908	Oct. 5, 1976

Lot 95, no name on wall

Augustus Wm. Heuer	Sept. 19, 1864	Jan. 2, 1938	
Anneliza Griggs Heuer		Apr. 14, 1913	d/o Elizabeth B. Henry & Wm. M. Griggs
Cordelia (Doucie) Griggs		July 10, 1924	d/o Wm. M. & Elizabeth Henry Griggs, w/o John J. Speed
John Joseph Speed	Dec. 11, 1868 Granville, NC	Feb. 14, 1922	s/o Cynthia Tunstall & John Joseph Speed

- Brother to Ida Tunstall Speed that married Richard Perry Spencer. Both are children of John J. Speed (c1803-1870) and his second wife, Cynthia Tunstall (1822-1872). John Sr. died in Granville Co., NC.

- 1880 Census Granville Co., NC Census listed John is listed in Sassafras Town 12 yo boarder in the household of Thos. M. Watkins with his brother Henry age 14. Henry is actually William Henry Speed born 8/8/1865.

Tallulah Henry Griggs	Feb. 1, 1919	w/o John Haywood

- Obit: died in Wetumpka, AL, d/o late William M. & Elizabeth Griggs of Columbus, GA, leaves husband, 1 brother, J. S. B. Griggs of Jacksonville, FL, 5 sisters, Misses Mamie & Bessie Griggs, Mrs. John Speed, all of Columbus, GA. (only 3 named)

- William Maxwell Griggs, s/o Judge William & Louise C. Griggs, was born 8/6/1832; married Elizabeth Henry. He died 10/23/1897. She died 6/19/1893. Their children: Mary Louise, Tallulah Haseltine (sic), James Fenemore C., Ann Eliza (sic), Elizabeth Britt, Lillie Howard, Cordelia Hill and Sarah Outlaw Griggs.[81]

Lot 96, open lot

Martha L. Hogan	1840	1920	SR: born SC 1840

- 1900 Lee Co., AL Census: Martha L. Hogan Mar. 1840 wd SC SC SC (2 ch/2liv), lodger Jackson C. Rice May 1862 SC SC SC and lodger Mattie Rice May 1866 SC SC SC (0 ch/0 liv.).

Jacob L. Hogan	Mar. 23, 1829	Mar. 11, 1890

- Obit: died in Lee Co., AL, born SC.

John A. Hogan	Nov. 24, 1858	Oct. 5, 1877	s/o J. L. & M. L. Hogan
Jackson C. Rice	1863	1935	SR: bur. 10/4/1935, 73 yrs

2 adult brick slabs, n/m

Sexton records indicate also buried in this lot:

Mrs. Mattie Rice	*bur. 9/23/1941, 68 yrs*

Lot 97, Goetchus on wall

Mary Ann Bennett	Feb. 26, 1819	June 29, 1878	w/o Richard R. Goetchus

- Obit: nee Mary A. Bennett, married 11 Sept. 1839, died near Tuscaloosa, AL at the home of her father Micajah Bennett from Virginia, leaves 7 children, John & Edw. killed in late war, 4 surviving, Rev. Geo. T. Goetchus of Milledgeville, GA, Henry K. of this city.

Richard Rose Goetchus	Mar. 9, 1814	Nov. 21, 1875
	Ulster Co., NY	Columbus, GA

- Obit: Born in Ulster Co., NY March 19, 1814 hence he was 61 years of age. Settled in Columbus 1837. Before the war he established the Columbus Steam Planing Mills. In 1839 Mr. G. married Mary Bennett of Columbus. Seven children were born to this union. One of his noble sons fell at Gettysburg and another at Petersburg. One of his sons is now pastor of the Presbyterian Church in Milledgeville and another a lawyer in our city.

- 1850 Muscogee Census: R. R. Goetchus 36 NY, Mary A. 30 AL, John W. 8 GA, William

E. 6 GA, George F. 4 GA and Charles R. 2 GA.

- 1860 Muscogee Census: R. R. Goetchius (sic) 48 NY, Mary 35 AL, John M. 19 GA, Wm. E. 17 GA, Geo. F. 15 GA, Richard H. 10 GA, Mary E. 3 GA, Mrs. Polly Bennett 60 VA, Anna Bennett 28 GA and William Bennett 24 GA.

- 1870 Muscogee Census: Richard R. Goetcheus (sic) 55 NY, Mary A. 57 AL, Mary E. 13 GA, Charles B. 9 GA and Anna Bennett 40 AL.

Mary McKinley	Sept. 3, 1856 Columbus, GA	Mar. 29, 1882 Milledgeville, GA	d/o Richard & Mary Goetchus, w/o Guy McKinley

- 1870 Baldwin Co., GA Census: William McKinley 50 SC, Lucy L. A. 45 CT, Catherine 23 GA, Archibald 18 GA, Mary 15 GA, Sarah 12 GA, Julia 10 GA, William 8 GA, Andrew 6 GA, Guy 2 GA and Gracey A. ____ 16 CT.

Wm. Richard McKinley MD	Sept. 9, 1880 Milledgeville, GA	Oct. 24, 1906 Augusta, GA	s/o Guy C. & Mary McKinley
Anna Cora Bennett		Sept. 10, 1875	age 46 years
John Micajah Goetchus	Apr. 11, 1841	July 3, 1863	d. Gettysburg

- Obit: member "City Light Guards" killed in action, s/o Richard R. Goetchus, died in Gettsysburg, PA.

Wm. Edward Goetchus	Aug. 13, 1843	Dec. 22, 1868	s/o Richard & Mary Goetchus
Capt. M. Bennett	Aug. 7, 1836	Dec. 22, 1868	17 Regt., GA Vol. CSA

- Obit: died of fatal disease of which he contracted while being confined in a Northern prison.

Micajah Bennett		Feb. 15, 1858	age 70 years

- 1850 Muscogee Census: Micajah Bennett 65 VA, Mrs. Polly 60 GA, Anna 21 AL and William 12.

Mary Powell Bowles		Feb. 28, 1870	w/o Micajah Bennett, age 76 years

- Obit: born GA, husband was from Virginia, moved from Tuscaloosa, AL to Columbus, GA with family in 1829, mother-in-law of R. R. Goetchus.

2 baby graves, unable to read

Lot 98, Pease on wall

Helen Pease	No Dates, adult	SR: bur. 2/5/1926, 53
Leah A. Pease	No Dates, adult	SR: bur. 6/15/1926, 83 yrs.

- John W. Pease married 1) Jane A. Norman 1/11/1848 Muscogee Co., GA and 2) Leah A. Norman 5/2/1855 Russell Co., AL.

- 1870 Muscogee Census: John M. Pease 51 CT, Leah 27 GA, Dorah 20 GA, Willie 13 GA, Norman 11 GA, Maggie 8 GA, Eddie 3 GA, Helen 6/12 GA, Leah Norman 56 GA, Richard 22 GA, Jacunitha? 31 GA, Cornelia 18 GA and Annie Norman 14 GA.

- 1880 Muscogee Census: John Pease 58 CT CT CT, wife Lea 36 GA GA GA, son Norman 21 GA, dau Maggie 18 GA, son Eddie 12 GA, dau Helen 10 GA, son Walter 5

GA, son Willie 23 GA, dau Addie 23 GA and sister Cynthia Norman 42 GA.

6 adult slabs, n/m   4 children's slabs, n/m

Lot 100, A. R. Callahan on wall

Our Baby   Feb. 22, 1901   Mar. 25, 1904

Adolphus R. Callahan   Aug. 22, 1856   Feb. 26, 1912

- Adolphus R. Callahan married Mollie A. Sharp 12/4/1884 in Muscogee Co., GA.

- 1850 Rutherford Co., NC Census: Alfred B. Callahan 57 NC, Ethlinda 50 NC, Samuel C. 23 NC, William A. 20 NC, Thomas 17 NC, Charity E. 18 NC, Adolphus R. 13 NC, Nelson 11 NC, Edward L. 8 NC and George L. 5 NC.

Claudia C. Edwards   Sept. 29, 1879   Mar. 21, 1962   w/o A. W. Polley

- 1880 Houston Co., GA Census: William Edwards 23 GA GA GA, wife Fannie 20 GA GA GA and dau Claudia 9/12 GA.

- 1900 Muscogee Census: Adolphus R. Callahan Aug. 1857 (sic) NC NC NC, wife Claudia C. Sept. 1879 GA GA GA, dau Minnie L. Oct. 1886 GA and dau Annie M. Sept. 1897 GA.

Mollie A. Callahan   May 8, 1859   Aug. 7, 1899   w/o A. R. Callahan

- 1880 Lee Co., AL Census: Mary A. Sharp 42 AL GA GA, dau Mosouri 23 AL, son Frank M. 22 AL, dau Mollie 21 AL, dau Martha 20 AL, son Warren 18 AL, dau Eliza 16 AL, dau Ella Porter 25 AL, grandson Warren 8 AL and grandson Lewis Porter 5 AL.

Lot 101, open lot

evidence of 2 adult graves, n/m

Lot 102, A. M. Brannon on wall

Alonzo Augustus Brannon   June 4, 1842   Oct. 23, 1845   s/o Thomas A. & Julia M. Brannon

- Thomas Albert Brannon married Julia Martin Mims, d/o Drury Mims of Muscogee County on 9 April 1835 Muscogee Co., GA by Rev. T. J. Hand. They are listed in the 1860 Barbour Co., AL Census. There is "a" Thomas Brannan listed in the 1830 Harris Co., GA Census and Thomas A. Brannon in the 1840 Muscogee Census.

- 7/1/1858 - Departed this life, in the city of Eufaula, Ala., on the 18th inst., Deacon Drury Mims, aged 75 years, 5 months and 2 days. Father Mims was born in Edgefield District, S. C., 1/16/1783. In 1830 he moved to Muscogee Co., Ga., and to Russell Co., Alabama in 1837, where he lived until 1/1855. Having been bereft of his companion, he sold his property and dividing most of the proceeds thereof among his children, he selected the home of Thomas A. Brannon, who married his second daughter, as his future home. In Sept. last, Brother Brannon moved to Eufaula and was soon followed by Brother Mims....[82]

Little Mac Brannon   Feb. 9, 1860   Sept. 24, 1863   s/o A. M. & Julia M. Brannon

Minnie Lee Brannon   Aug. 22, 1866   Sept. 9, 1868   s/o A. M. & Julia M. Brannon

Robert A. Carson   Jan. 18, 1853   Oct. 4, 1914

- Robert Carson married Ida C. Brannon 6/12/1877 in Muscogee Co., GA.

- 1910 Muscogee Census: Robert A. Carson 56 GA GA GA and niece Madge Norman 22 AL AL GA.

Infant   1878   Inf. s/o R. A. & Ida C. Carson

A. M. Brannon   Sept. 27, 1831   May 8, 1905

- Obit: Alexander Means Brannon was born Sept. 27, 1831, 73 years ago in Newton Co., GA. When he was 4 years old his father moved to Ridgeway community in Harris County, and there he grew in manhood. He came to Columbus in 1851 and for 54 years was continuously in the drug business in this city. Mr. Brannon was the last of seven children. Four brothers have passed in the last ___ years; Judge W. H. Brannon of Columbus in spring of 1900, Col. John M. Brannon of Seale, AL in April 1904, and Judge S. M. Brannan of Waverly Hall on Oct. 27, 1904.

- Mr. A. M. Brannon was associated at one time with Dr. John Pemberton who originated the Coca-Cola formula. His granddaughter Miss Madge Norman married Henry E. Weathers.[83]

- 1850 Harris Co., GA Census: Calvin G. Brannon 46 NC, Catherine 52 NC, A. M. 19 GA, John M. 17 GA, William H. 14 GA, Emily P. 16 GA, Tolliver J. 12 GA and Frances C. 9 GA.

- Calvin John Brannon, s/o John Brannon and Nancy Parker, was born in SC on 11/9/1804 and lived there until 1825. In 1835 he married Katherine Croucher. Their children: Sephas Marion, Alexander Means, John Manson, William Henry, Margaret, Emily P. and Frances C. Brannon.[84]

- 1860 Muscogee Census: Means A. Brannon 28 GA, Julia A. 25 GA, Ida 4 GA and Ellen M. 5/12 GA.

- 1880 Muscogee Census: A. Means Brannon 48 GA, wife Julia 46 GA, son-in-law Robert Carson 28 GA, daughter Ida Carson 23 GA, daughter Margaret Brannon 17 GA, son William M. 11 GA and son Means 7 GA.

Frederick Norman   June 17, 1862   Apr. 2, 1899

- 1870 Bullock Co., AL Census: James Norman 42 GA, Mary 37 GA, Jacinthea 15 GA, James 14 GA, Frederick 7 AL, Mary 5 AL and Thomas 1 AL.

Julia A. Brannon   Feb. 25, 1833   Mar. 19, 1891   w/o A. M. Brannon, d/o Hiram & Mary A. Fuller

- Obit: nee Julia Fuller, d/o late Col. Hiram Fuller of Chattahoochee Co., GA, mar. A. M. Brannon, Sept. 22, 1831, 4 children, Mrs. R. A. Carson of Columbus, GA, Mrs. F. A. Norman of Clayton, AL, W. H. Jr., R. Means Brannon of Columbus, GA, 4 sisters, 3 brothers; Mrs. Davis A. Andrews, Joseph Edward of Columbus, GA, Mrs. David Dudley, Mrs. John M. Brannon, both of Russell Co., AL, Mrs. Mary Olmstead of Nens, Wisc., J. M. of Seale, AL, A. M. of Columbus, 1 sister dec'd.

- 1850 Muscogee Census: Hyram Fulter (sic) 51 Musc GA, Caroline 34 Edgefield SC, Elizabeth 14 Musc. GA, George 12 Musc. GA, Emma 11 Musc. GA, Joseph 10 Musc. GA, Caroline 7 Musc. GA and Alice 2 Musc. GA.

- Hiram Fuller married Mary Ann Simons 1/10/1832 in Harris Co., GA. Julia's sister, Elizabeth married Alexander's brother John M. Brannon.

Ida C. Brannon	July 12, 1856	Mar. 1, 1910	w/o Robert A. Carson
Maggie J. Brannon	Jan. 21, 1863	July 12, 1901	w/o F. Norman
Henry Edgar Weathers	Dec. 21, 1879	July 9, 1965	"Tip"
Madge N. Weathers	Dec. 21, 1887	Dec. 30, 1968	
William H. Brannon	Oct. 25, 1836	May 30, 1900	

- Obit: d. in Atlanta, GA, May 29, 1900, 63 years of age, Judge, born Harris Co., GA, near Ridgeway, s/o Calvin Brannon, 1877 Mayor of Columbus, 3 brothers, Judge S. M. of Ridgeway, J. M. Seale, AL and A. M. of Columbus, 1 sister dec'd.

Lot 103, J. W. Ferguson on wall

Cliff M. Ferguson	1887	1947	SR: bur. 5/22/1947
Fannie C. Lauderber	1854	1934	w/o J. W. Ferguson

- 1900 Muscogee Census: Fanny C. Ferguson Feb. 1854 GA GA SC, dau Fontana Jan 1878 GA, son Homer Apr 1881 AL and son Clifford June 1887 GA.

John W. Ferguson	1849	1897

1 baby brick slab, n/m

Lot 104, open lot

Richard Henry Hooper	May 5, 1841	June 4, 1846	s/o Richard L. Hooper
Geo. Pendleton	Mar. 3, 184?	July 20, 184?	

3 adult slabs, unable to read   1 child brick slab, n/m

- Richard Hooper married Louisa P. Shivers 4/23/1835 in Muscogee Co., GA.[85] Richard Hooper was the grandson of William Hooper, one of the three delegates from North Carolina who signed the Declaration of Independence.[86]
- 1850 Muscogee Census: Richard Hooper 41 SC, Louisa 34 GA, Louisa W. 14 GA, William F. 11 GA and Robert A. 2/12 GA.

Lot 105, no name on wall

Shelby Compton	Dec. 9, 1857	Dec. 24, 1901

- 1870 Rapides Parish, LA Census: John Lederwick Compton 24 LA, Mary 22 LA, George 6/12 LA, Peter B. 22 LA, Alexander H. Mason 33 VA, Annie E. Mason 31 KY, Shelby Compton 13 LA, Amelia Compton 6 LA, Ralf Mason 4 LA and Alexander Mason 9/12 LA.
- 1900 Muscogee Census: Shelby Compton Dec. 1857 LA GA KY, wife Juliette July 1865 GA GA GA (married 12 years), dau Amalie Sept. 1889 GA, dau Ann Feb. 1892 GA, dau Ellen Nov 1893 GA, son Shelby Aug 1896 GA, dau Juliette May 1899 GA and dau Mary May 1899.

Juliette Hudson Compton	July 16, 1865	Dec. 13, 1909
Benjamin Hall Hudson	Aug. 7, 1836	Dec. 11, 1904	Civil Engineer

- Obit: Capt., wife died 3 years ago, 4 children, Mrs. Juliete Compton, Miss Nellie Hudson, Thomas C. all of Columbus, GA and R. H. Jr. of Ft. Wayne, Ind., R. R. Colsey of Columbus is a nephew, born Augusta, GA, 70 years old, s/o late Henry Hall Hudson, attended West Point Military Academy.

- 1880 Muscogee Census: Ben Hudson 42 GA NJ GA, wife Ellen 39 GA GA GA, dau Juliet 10 GA, dau Sallie 10 GA, son Ben 7 GA, dau Ellen 5 GA, son Thomas 1 GA and mother Sarah Charlton 89 GA Eng Eng.

- 1900 Muscogee Census: Ben H. Hudson Aug 1838 GA NJ GA (married 35 yrs.), wife Ellen July 1839 GA GA GA (5 children/4 living), dau Nellie Dec. 1865 GA and son T. Charlton Nov. 1878 GA.

David Hudson		Mar. 23, 1873

- 1850 Muscogee Census: David Hudson 44 NJ, Juliette 38 GA, Benjamin H. 14 GA, Mary 12 GA, Henry D. 1 GA and William M. 2 GA.

- 1860 Muscogee Census: David Hudson 54 NY, Juliet 46 GA, Benjamin 24 GA, Mary 22 GA and William 11 GA.

- 1870 Muscogee Census: David Hudson 63 GA, Benj. H. 32 GA, Ellen 29 GA, Juliet 4 GA and Sallie 9/12 GA.

Ellen Charlton	July 31, 1835	Dec. 19, 1901	One slab w/o Benjamin H. Hudson
Sallie Waters		July 22, 1881	step-dght. of B. H. & E. C. Hudson. Age ___ yr, 10 mo.

- Obit: Ellen Charlton Hudson died from results of burns, 60 years old, nee Ellen Charlton of Savannah, GA, d/o Dr. Thomas J. Charlton & g/dau of Hon. ? & N. P. Hudson, leaves husband & 4 children, Mrs. Shelby Compton, B. H. Jr of Petosky Mich., Miss Nellie & Thomas both of Columbus.

- 1860 Chatham Co., GA Census: Sarah Charlton 56 Bryan Co., GA and Ellen 25 Savannah, GA living at the Savage House.

- Thomas Jackson Charlton died 22 SEP 1835 in Hardwicke, Bryan Co., GA and is buried at the Whitehall Plantation Cemetery in Bryan Co., GA.

Dr. E. F. Colzey	Dec. 25, 1878	One slab
Mary Hudson	May 23, 1864	his wife
Juliette	Nov. 21, 1865	their inf. dau

- Obit: Dr. Colzey: married Mary Hudson Oct. 18, 1860, came to Columbus 1861, surgeon of Col. M. J. Crawford, Cav. Reg., 46 years old, born Charleston, SC, is of Huguenot family, sister in Paris, France, leaves wife, son, daughter, the son is the only male descendant of the line now living.

Sexton records indicate also buried in this lot:

Juliette Hall Hudson	*1812*	*1864*	*Age 52*
William (Willie) M. Hudson	*1849*	*1880*	*Age 30*
Henry David Hudson	*1844*	*1852*	*Age 7*

Lot 106, no name on wall

William E. Preston Nov. 9, 1844 Dec. 30, 1933

- Obit: CSA vet, 3 daus, Mrs. Mollie Epps of Columbus, GA, Mrs. Gray Wells, Mrs. Reiner Leutje both of Atlanta, GA, 3 sons, J. E. of Ozark, AL, E. E. & R. F. both of Columbus, GA.

- 1900 CSA Pension records: states W. E. Preston or W. E. Matthews Co. B 33rd AL Lowery's Brig. Claiborne Division. Pension board questioned his application. He stated that his name was changed in 1892 from W. E. Matthews by Muscogee Superior Court to W. E. Preston. He has lives in State of GA since 1880. He enlisted in Clopton, AL 3/11/1862.

- Transfer of Pension 26 July 1932 from W. E. Preston to R. F. Preston for care and attention.[87]

- 1880 Dale Co., AL Census: William Matthews 34 GA GA GA, wife Nancy 32 GA South South, son James E. 8 AL, son Whit 7 AL, dau Mary 4 AL, dau Willie 2 AL and son Earnest 3/12 AL.

- 1870 Dale Co., AL Census: W. E. Matthews is listed as 25 GA single and in the HH of J. W. Stuckey 55 SC and family.

Nancy A. Preston Mar. 15, 1847 Feb. 1, 1910

- Obit: born March 15, 1847, moved to Muscogee Co. from Mt. Andrew, AL, survived by husband and children; Messrs. Ernest B. and Robert P. of Columbus and J. Ed Preston of Ozark, AL, Mrs. J. W. Epps, Mrs. R. Leutje and Miss Emma Preston of Columbus, GA.

Whitfield E. Preston	Mar. 28, 1874	Sept. 26, 1898	Co. H, 13 GA Vol. Inf.
John Epps Preston		Oct. 16, 1916	age 3
Robert Preston, Jr.	Dec. 31, 1917	Aug. 8, 1921	
Theo W. Luetje	Oct. 5, 1917	Nov. 8, 1917	

Lot 107, no name on wall

1 double adult slab, n/m

Lot 108, Worrill on wall

Joseph S. Key	Sept. 28, 1875	Mar. 19, 1901	s/o Howard W. & Ozella B. Key

- 1880 Muscogee Census: Howard Key 28 GA GA GA, wife Ozella 25 GA SC SC, son Joseph 4 GA and son James 2.

- Howard Walton Key, s/o Bishop Joseph Staunton Key and Susie M. Snider, married Ozella Biggers Dec. 22, 1874.

Susie Lee Biggers	Aug. 6, 1857	July 10, 1879	d/o J. J. W. & C. E. Biggers One slab
Lolah Walton Biggers	Mar. 12, 1859	Mar. 15, 1873	d/o J. J. W. & C. E. Biggers
James J. W. Biggers	July 9. 1823	Dec. 5, 1898	

- Obit: married Caroline E. Williams, Dec. 23, 1851

- 1870 Harris Co., GA Census: James J. W. Biggers 46 SC, Caroline 45 SC, Susan L. 12 GA, Lola W. 12 GA and Bascomb 9 GA.

- 1850 Muscogee Census: Elizabeth Biggers 67 SC, James J. W. 26 SC, Susan 55 NC, A. Jackson 33 SC and William McGehee 18 overseer.

- s/o Joseph Biggers (c1780-1850) and Elizabeth Countryman (c1783-1851).

- 1850 Mortality Schedule shows Joseph R. M. Biggers age 70, born SC died July in Muscogee Co.

Caroline E. Williams	Mar. 10, 1825	Dec. 8, 1909	w/o James J. W. Biggers

- Obit: nee Williams, died Fortson, GA, 86 years old, 3 children Mrs. Howard B. Key, Mrs. E. B. Worrill, B. H. Biggers, all of Columbus, GA.

Edmund Harper Worrill	Nov. 17, 1885	Feb. 19, 1935	
James Harper Worrill		June 16, 1903 Columbus, GA	age 48 years

- 1880 Harris Co., GA Census: Edmund Worrill 66 GA VA GA, wife Mary E. 58 GA GA GA, dau Sallie 31 GA and son James H. 24 GA.

Joseph Walton Worrill	Aug. 17, 1887	Sept. 25, 1890	inf. s/o James H. & Emma B. Worrill
Emma Biggers Worrill	June 19, 1854	Apr. 29, 1934	w/o James Harper Worrill

Lot 109, no name on wall

Horace H. Taft	June 10, 1826	Jan. 30, 1861	

- Tribute from Y.M.C.A., funeral notice mentions Mrs. Taft and Mr. & Mrs. Bardwell.

- Muscogee Co., MR shows Horace H. Taft married Sarah Amelia Bardwell 1 July 1858.

- 1860 Muscogee Census: Horace H. Taft 34 Mass., Amelia 28 GA and Edwd. L. Bardwell 21 GA.

Sarah S. Bardwell	Nov. 25, 1809	Dec. 4, 1879	w/o R. N. R. Bardwell mother

- Obit: Two children; Dr. E. L. Bardwell of Talbotton, GA and Mrs. Amelia Wright of Columbus. Wife of N. R. Bardwell, came to this city 1836-1837.

- According to Franklin Co., MA MR, Sarah Sophia Sherman married Reuben Newton

Ranson Bardwell 8 Oct. 1832 in Montague, MA. Their daughter Sarah Amelia married secondly Armenius Wright 4 Dec. 1862.

R. N. R. Bardwell	Oct. 27, 1808 Montagville, Mass.	Columbus, GA age 61 years

- 1860 Muscogee Census: Sarah S. Bardwell 50 Mass and Sarah E. Jones 22 GA.

- 1850 Muscogee Census: R. N. R. Bardwell 42 Mass., Mrs. S. S. 41 Mass., Sarah A. 14 GA, Edward L. 21 GA, Sarah Reynolds 20 GA and Caroline Oakney 20 France.

Lot 110 Woodruff-Willingham on wall

Eugene W. Dews	June 19, 1864	Apr. 16, 1881	Our son
Our Louisa M. Evans	no dates		Child
Anna	June 26, 1846	Oct. 8, 1862	d/o Dr. M. & Mrs. Woodruff
Sophronia Farrington Woodruff	Jan. 6, 1835 Augusta, GA	Aug. 6, 1913 Chattanooga, TN	w/o Geo M. Dews

- Obit: died inNashville, TN, widow of late Prof. Geo M. Dews died 1881, SIL Mrs. Mary Woodruff, niece Miss Ruby Willingham, Miss Banks of Chattanooga, TN.

Dr. M. Woodruff	Oct. 2, 1810 Newark, NJ	Apr. 27, 1870 Columbus, GA	Our father

- President of Muscogee Bible Society.

- 1860 Muscogee Census: M. W. Woodruff 50 NJ, Abbigil G. 50 NJ, Sophronia L. 24 GA, Mary J. 22 GA, Anna B. 13 GA, Henry W. 10 GA, Ella B. 6 GA, Wm H. Griswold 43 CT and Thos. J. Garrison 19 GA.

- 1850 Muscogee Census: M. Woodruff 40 NJ, Mrs. A. T. 40 NJ, Miss S. F. 14 GA, Mary J. 12 GA, Ann L. 4 GA and Henry W. 7/12 GA.

Geo. M. Dews	June 1, 1830 Savannah, GA	Apr. 15, 1891 Forsyth, GA	s/o John J. & Harriett Dews

- 1880 Muscogee Census: George Dews 50 GA GA GA, wife Safronia 45 GA NJ NJ and son Eugene 16 GA GA GA.

Ruby	June 27, 1879	Oct. 14, 1956	d/o W. A. & M. J. Willingham

- William A. Willingham, of Chattanooga, was born in Beaufort County, S. C., July 6, 1837, son of Thomas and Phoebe S. (Lawton) Willingham, both natives of South Carolina. Our subject was reared and educated in his native State. In 1859 he married Miss Emilie F. Dews, of Daugherty County, Ga. She died in 1868 leaving four children, three now living: John T., Edward G. and Maxie Belle (wife of J. K. Nuckells, wholesale shoe merchant, of Columbus, Ga). In 1862 our subject enlisted in the Third South Carolina Cavalry, and served one year as a non-commissioned officer. In 1865 he left South Carolina, and spent three years in agricultural pursuits in southwest Georgia. In 1869 he engaged in the lumber business at Forsyth, Ga., where he continued until 1876, after which he engaged in the same business at Columbus, Ga. In January 1885, he established a sash, door, blind and general lumber business at Chattanooga. In 1869 Mr. Willingham married his present wife, Mary J. Woodruff, of Columbus, Ga., who bore him three children: Furman D., Florence and Ruby. (Mary the eldest is deceased.) Mr. Willingham is a director in the Chattanooga Savings Bank, a Democrat, an ancient

Mason, a member of the A. O. U. W. and K. of P., and a deacon in the First Baptist Church of Chattanooga.[88]

Mrs. A. T. Woodruff	April 19, 1810 Patterson, NJ	Nov. 1, 1879 Forsyth, GA	Our mother
Margaret Ann	Nov. 22, 1839	July 16, 1842	
Stephen Thomas	Aug. 10, 1841	June 16, 1842	c/o Dr. M. & A. T. Woodruff
Wilbur Fisk	Dec. 25, 1843	July 23, 1845	
Charles D. Schoonmaker	Sept. 1826 Flat Bush, LI, NY	Mar. 18, 1853 Columbus, GA	

- Engineer of Muscogee R.R., died from train falling from a trestle.

Lot 111, no name on wall

no evidence of graves

Lot 112, no name on wall

Mrs. E. Skinner   age 80 yrs., our mother.

SR: bur. 8/23/1882

- Eleanor Humphries married Willis Skinner 6/25/1831 in Newton Co., GA.

- 1850 Muscogee Census: Willis Skinner 50 Putnam Co. GA, Eleanor 48 Jackson Co GA, Sarah A. 18 Newton Co GA, Hester 17 Musc., Joseph H. 16 Musc., Mary R. 14 Musc., Willis 12 Musc., Rebecca C. 10 Musc., Elizabeth 8, Musc., Charlotte 7 Musc. and Emily 4 Musc.

- 1880 Muscogee Census: Ellen Skinner 78 GA NC NC, dau Emma 30 GA VA NC, granddau. (sic) Homer Poe (m) 14 GA, Alice Snow 8 granddau and boarders.

- June 18, 1873 - Mrs. Lottie A. Snow, wife of Wm. M. Snow and daughter of Willis and Ellen H. Skinner, was born in Muscogee county, near Columbus, Ga., July 28th 1841, and died in Opelika, Ala., March 3d 1873, aged twenty-eight years, seven months and six days. O. L. Smith

2 adult brick slabs

Lot 113, no name on wall

James J. Henry   1878   1930   SR: bur. 7/7/1930, 57 yrs.

- 1880 Muscogee Census: Patrick Henry 48 Ire Ire Ire, wife Hannah 40 Ire Ire Ire, dau Sallie 10 GA, son James 8 GA, dau Mary 5 GA, dau Ellen 3 GA and dau Fannie 1 GA.

F. McVey Hoffman   no dates   SR: bur. 4/30/1902, 22 yrs.

S. J. Hoffman   Oct. 20, 1847   May 1, 1913   Father

- Obit: 1 dau. Miss Mamie Hoffman, 3 sisters, Mrs. Prufomo, Mrs. R. Owens, Miss Victoria Hoffman, all of Columbus.

- 1880 Muscogee Census: John Hofman 31 GA France France, wife Mary 27 GA Ire Ire, son James 10 GA, son William 9 GA, son George 6, son John 4 GA and dau Maggie 2.

- 1850 Muscogee Census: Sebastian Hoffman 34 Germany, Anna E. 31 Bavaria, Ragenia 11 GA, Barbara H. S. 9 GA, Mary Louisa 7 GA, John J. 5 GA, Sebastion J. 2 GA and Victoria M. 1/12 GA.

Bridgett C. Dolan   no dates   SR: bur. 5/24/1939, 84

Mary T. Hoffman   no dates   Mother

Margaret Dolan   no dates   adult

Annie L. Dolan   Dec. 5, 1870   Dec. 6, 1952

Bernard Dolan   SR: bur. 7/1/1870

- 1870 Muscogee Census: Bernard Dolan 40 Ire, Bridget 39 Ire, Bridget 15 GA, Mary 13 GA, Burnet 2 GA and John 2 GA.

Margaret Dolan   no dates   adult

Charlie   Apr. 22, 1881   July 19, 1881

Mary Ann Dolan   Apr. 22, 1883   w/o J. A. Gab??   one
                                                                         slab
Bernard E. Dolan   1868   1926   SR: bur. 1/7/1928, 58 yrs.

Lula W. Dolan   1875   1965   Mother
                                             SR: born 1/7/1874, bur. 8/21/1961, 87 yrs.

Hugh Dolan   May 1, 1857   age 38

- Muscogee Co. WB A P. 222-225. Hugh Dolan. 4 Apr 1857/1 Jun 1857. Legatees: wife Catherine formerly Catherine Kane; mother Bridget Dolan now in Ireland; dau Mary Anne; brothers Michael Dolan in Ireland and Bernard Dolan; sisters Catherine Degman w/o William Degman, Anne Dolan in Ireland, Mary Greenan of Ireland & Bridget Flynn of Ireland and uncle John McCarty. Extr. John McCarty. Wit: John Flynn, Michael McCarty & L. T. Downing.

- 1850 Muscogee Census: HH 321/341 Hugh Doland 27 Ireland. HH 321/342 William Degnan (sic) 30 Ireland, Catherine 26 Ireland and Bridget Doland 16 Ireland.

Catherine   July 10, 1852   age 27. w/o Hugh Dolan.

Mary Hoffman Henry   Dec. 12, 1877   Oct. 5, 1939

Lot 114, Deignan on wall

William J. Deignan   Aug. 9, 1873   Dec. 13, 1960

- 1920 Muscogee Census: Alice M. Lee 40 GA Ire Ire, sister Ella M. 45 GA Ire Ire, Will J. Deignan 42 GA Ire Ire, wife Mary Lee 35 GA GA GA, son William Jr. 13 GA, son Richard 11 GA and son Arthur 5 GA.

- 1880 Muscogee Census: Patrick Deignan 40 Ire Ire Ire, wife Mary 30 GA Ire Ire, dau Mary 12 GA, dau Annie 11 GA, dau Ida 8 GA, son Willie 6 GA, dau Christina 3 GA and son Richd 1/12 (May) GA.

Mary H. Lee	May 11, 1875	Dec. 26, 1944	w/o W. J. Deignan

- 1880 Muscogee Census: Michael H. Lee 50 Ire Ire Ire, wife Lizzie A. 38 Ire Ire Ire, son John Burnett Lee 16 GA, dau Ellen M. 13 GA, son Frederick F. 11 GA, dau Maggie M. 9 GA, dau Alice S. 7 GA and dau Mary Charlotte 4 GA.

William J. Deignan, Jr.	Nov. 25, 1906	Sept. 27, 1947
Richard A. Deignan	July 14, 1909	Jan. 24, 1967
Arthur L. Deignan	Oct. 4, 1914	Dec. 6, 1973
Charles		
Joe		Inf. s/o
Marion		W. J. & Mary L. Deignan
1 slab, no dates, baby		

Lot 115, Needham on wall

Marie C. Hefferman	Nov. 8, 1886	Apr. 13, 1962
Patrick Joseph McSorley	Sept. 1, 1858	Oct. 3, 1930

- 1930 Muscogee Census: Patrick J. McSorley 71 (m@38) Ire Ire Ire and wife Alice N. 70 (m@32) Mass Mass Ire.

- 1910 Muscogee Census: Patrick J. McSorley 51 Ire Ire Ire (m1. 15 yrs), wife Alice N. 48 Mass Ire Ire (m.1 15 yrs), nephew Richard Needham 16 Mass Ire NY.

Nellie Dempsey	Sept. 12, 1871	Dec. 8, 1944	w/o R. W. Needham
Marie Dempsey Needham	Jan. 20, 1896	Aug. 13, 1947	
Wm. Stokes Needham	Mar. 13, 1810 Tipperay, Ireland	Jan. 18, 1896 Columbus, GA	In memory of our dear uncle.

- Obit: William Stokes Needham was born in Tipperay, Ireland in March 1816 and was in his eighty-sixth year. His family are accounted among the most ancient of the Irish landed gentry. He was educated ath that famous Irish school of learning, "Ourlow College", where he graduated the degree of Masters of Arts.

  Besides a number of more distant relatives, Mr. Needham is survived by two mephews and two nieces, Mr. Richard Needham and Miss Alice Needham of this city, Mr. William Needham of California and Mr. James Diffour? Of Massachusetts. The funeral will occur from the Church of the Holy Family tomorrow morning at 10 o'clock.

- 1880 Muscogee Census: William Needam (sis) 55 Ire Ire Ire and nephew Richd Needam 28 ire Ire Ire.

- 1870 Muscogee Census: William Needham 50 Ire and Richard Needham 21 Ireland.

Alice Needham	Feb. 2, 1855	Sept. 9, 1941	w/o P. J. McSorley
Richard Welch Needham	May 15, 1849	June 6, 1930	

- Obit: Mr. Needham was born in County Tipperary , Ireland May 15, 1844 and was brought to America at an early age by his parents. He settled in Columbus after the War Between the States having come here to visit W. S. Needham, an uncle.
  After removing to Columbus, Mr. Needham studied under a private tutor for some time. Then his uncle, a former professor of classical languages in Columbia, SC noticed his aptitude for business, placed him in charge of the W. S. Needham Grocery company. Mr. Needham had acquired the business establishment in this city in 18?4 from his former partners, Messrs. Quinn and Correran.

- 1900 Muscogee Census: Richard Needham May 1852 Ire Ire Ire, wife Elleanor Sept 1872 (m. 5 yrs 1/1 child.) GA Ire GA, dau Marie D. Jan 1895 GA Ire GA and nephew Frank Hefferman Sept. 1876 Mass. Mass. Ire.

Lot 116, Tarver on wall

James Monroe Tarver	Aug 27, 1881 Enon, AL	Aug 2, 1898 Columbus, GA	s/o James B. & Sallie B. Tarver
Newton Banks Tarver	Aug 13, 1876 Enon, AL	Jan 17, 1906 El Paso, TX	s/o James B. & Sallie B. Tarver

- Atlanta Constitution 21 Jan 1906: Banks Tarver Funeral. Columbus, GA January 20 (Special).
  The funeral of Banks Tarver, a well known young man of Columbus , who died 3 or 4 days ago in Texas took place at noon today from the union depot upon the arrival of the Mobile and Girard train. His mother, Mrs. J. B. Tarver accompanied the remains from Texas to Columbus.

Annie Belle Tarver	Nov 19, 1890 Columbus, GA	Aug 4, 1907 Charlotte, NC	d/o James B. & Sallie B. Tarver
Sallie Banks Tarver	Nov. 17, 1853 Enon, AL	July 24, 1935 Atlanta, GA	

- d/o Dr. Newton Paley Banks & Fanny Jernigan.
- Sarah Banks married James B. Tarver 10 Feb 1874.[89]

James Banks Tarver	Feb 10, 1854 Enon, AL	June 17, 1917 Columbus, GA	

- Obit: born Enon, Bullock Co., AL, leaves wife, d/o Dr. N. P. Banks of Enon, AL, 1 dau, Mrs. H. M. Wade, 2 sons W. H. of California and Clifford Tarver of Columbus.

- 1900 Muscogee Census: Jas B. Tarver Feb 1854 AL GA GA, wife Sarah B. Nov 1858 (married 25 yrs; 6/5 children), son J. Banks Aug 1876 AL, dau Rosa Lee Dec 1878 AL, son William Feb 1884 GA, son Clifford May 1887 GA and dau Anna Belle Nov 1891 GA.

- s/o James Monroe Tarver and Rachel Jones Banks (1826-1893) who were married 9 Oct 1845 in Enon, AL.[90] Newton Paley Banks and Rachel Jones Banks were siblings, c/o James Jones Banks and Hannah Alston.[91]

Lot 119, no name on wall

evidence of 1 grave, brick at head

Lot 120, no name on wall

Walter Lawrence Pou	Mar 3, 1865	Aug 27, 1895	
John Beall Dozier	Mar 15, 1807 Warren Co., GA	Oct 24, 1873 Muscogee Co., GA	Husband-Father

- Obit: John Bell (sic) Dozier died on 24th October 1873. Had he lived until the 15th of March next, he would have been 67 years of age.

- 1850 Muscogee Census: John B. Dozier 43 Warren Co., Emalie E. 27 SC, Antoinette 10 Muscogee Co., Laurence 7 Muscogee Co., S. Virginia 6 Muscogee Co., Daniel P. 2 Muscogee Co. and Josiah Grimes 20 Muscogee Co.

- John Beall Dozier was the s/o Richard Talley Dozier (February 22, 1779 Virginia - January 19, 1855 Harris County, GA.) and Richard's first wife, Elizabeth "Betsy" Beall (June 14, 1804 Warren County, GA. She was the d/o John and Mary Beall born February 26, 1782 in Warren County, GA, and died October 30, 1833 in Harris County, GA.

- John Beall Dozier married Emily Eliza Huff 16 May 1839 in Muscogee Co., GA.

Emily E. Dozier	Feb 8, 1823	July 19, 1884	w/o John B. Dozier Mother
Emily			
Herschel		no dates	Infs./o John B. & Emily E. Dozier
Charlie			
Robert			
Antionette Dozier	Nov 5, 1840	Jan 23, 1912	w/o Joseph Felder Pou

- Antoinette married Joseph F. Pou 13 Dec 1858 in Talbot Co., GA. Joseph (16 June 1836 – 22 Feb 1908) was the s/o Joseph Pou and Elizabeth Margaret Felder who were married 25 Oct 1827 in Orangeburg Co., SC.

- 1880 Muscogee Census: Joseph F. Pou 44 GA SC SC, wife Nettie D. 39 GA GA SC, son Phelder 20 GA, son Dozier 17 GA, son Walter L. 15 GA, son Joseph 12 GA, son Robert E. 8 GA and son John B. 4 GA.

- 1870 Muscogee Census: Joseph Pou 34 GA, Antoinette 29 GA, Felder 10 GA, John 7 GA, Walter 5 GA and Joseph 2 GA.

Joseph Felder Pou	Sept 16, 1867	Oct 27, 1918	
Felder Pou	Dec. 7, 1859	Oct. 9, 1935	
Loulie Redd	June 23, 1874	Feb. 4, 1940	w/o Felder Pou

- Louise Hansell Redd was the d/o Charles Anderson Redd and Eugenia Almira Weems.

Robert Edw. Pou	Feb. 1, 1872	July 2, 1962

John B.	May 8, 1876	Dec. 26, 1884	s/o Joseph & Nettie D. Pou
Joseph Felder	June 12, 1910	May 1, 1912	s/o Felder & Loulie Pou
Antoinette	Apr. 3, 1900	May 26, 1901	d/o Felder & Loulie Pou
Emily Dozier	Feb. 26, 1907	Sept. 3, 1912	d/o Felder & Loulie Pou

1 adult brick slab w/large obelisk, unable to read 1 side other side.

Elizabeth	Apr. 5, 1821	May 2, 1858	w/o Ezekial Hollis, d/o Robert & Sandal McGough

- Ezekiel Hollis married Elizabeth McGough 25 Nov 1842 in Monroe Co., GA. Robert McGough (1786-1881) married Sandal Cabaniss (b. ca 1786) 10 Aug 1811.

- 1850 Monroe Co., GA Census: Ezekiel Hollis 30 M GA and Elisabeth 28 F GA

Lot 121, open lot

No evidence of graves.

Lot 122, open lot

Virginia C. Renfroe	1827	Feb. 26, 1885	w/o G.M. Renfroe
Geo. M. Renfroe	Jan. 19, 1827	Dec. 28, 1871	

- 1870 Muscogee Census: (in private boarding house) George M. Renfro 43 GA, Virginia 42 GA and Dorah 13 GA.

- 1860 Muscogee Census: George Renfroe 34 GA, Virginia 34 GA, Lilla D. 3 GA and Walter 1 GA.

Walter Clare		Sept. 29, 1859	1 yr 9 mo 1 d. s/o Geo. M. & Virginia C. Renfroe
Dora R. Trippe	Jan. 8, 1857	July 30, 1887	w/o Robert B. Trippe
			(Robert Renfroe & Clarence)
			No other data.

- Obit: Atlanta Constitution 31 July 1887: Died yesterday afternoon at 1:30 o'clock, Mrs. Dora Renfro Trippe, wife of Mr. R. B. Trippe, after an illness of several months. Remains to be taken to Columbus for burial at 6:45 this morning.

- Atlanta Constitution 5 Aug 1887: In Memorium for Mrs. Dora Renfroe Trippe, a tribute by her husband.

- 1880 Bartow Co., GA Census: Robert B. Trippe 30 GA GA GA, wife Dora R. 23 GA GA GA, MIL Virginia C. Renfroe 52 GA VA VA and son George R. Trippe 6/12/ GA.

Lot 123, Charles R. Humber on wall

Charles R. Humber	Oct. 3, 1881	Jan. 17, 1950	

- 1920 Muscogee Census: Charles R. Hunber (sic) 37 GA GA GA, wife Sadie 34 GA GA

GA and Charles R. Jr. 9 GA.

Sadie Hunt Humber	Aug. 17, 1884	July 15, 1960	

- 1900 Muscogee Census: Thomas J. Hunt June 1848 GA GA GA, wife Sarah B. Apr 1848 GA GA GA (m. 32 yrs; 7/6/ children), Renean C. (m) Sept 1849 GA, dau Sadie R. Aug 1883 GA, and dau Nellie L. May 1886 GA.

Charles R. Humber, Jr.	June 24, 1910	Feb. 16, 1945	Sgt. 5th Air Force. Nat'l Mem. Cemetery of the Pacific, Territory of Hawaii Island of Oahu, died in action.

Lot 124, Joseph C. Russell on wall

Jennie Hudson Russell	Aug. 16, 1874	May 25, 1960	Mother
Joseph C. Russell, Sr.	Nov. 25, 1866	Nov. 17, 1924	Father

- 1910 Muscogee Census: John O. Willis 33 GA G GA (M2-4), wife Jennie 22 GA GA GA (m1-4; 3/1 children), mother Jennie Russell 44 GA GA GA (wd; 8/6 children) half brother Cyril Russell 13 GA, boarder Dozier O'Niel 24 GA GA GA and boarder Mattie Boyd 32 GA.

- 1900 Muscogee Census: Joe Russell Nov 1869 AL SC SC, wife Jennie C. Aug 1869 GA SC GA (m14; 5/4 children), dau Jennie M. Aug 1890 GA, son Joe C. Nov 1892 GA, dau Ethel A. Jan 1896 GA, dau Annie L. Dec 1899 GA and mother Eliza June 1834 SC SC FL (wd; 4/4 children).

Lot 125, no name on wall

John Bethune	Sept. 8, 1770 Isle of Skye, Scotland	Oct. 11, 1861 Columbus, Ga.	

- 1860 Muscogee Census: John Bethune 89 Scotland, Cherry 70 NC, Elizabeth 14 GA, Benjamin T. 12 GA. William L. 13 GA, Anna C. 17 GA and Mary M. 14 GA.

- 1850 Milledgeville, Baldwin Co., GA Census: Benjamin Bethune 34 GA, Mary 9 GA, Ann 7 GA, Martin 5 GA, William 3 GA, Benjamin T. 2 GA, John 80 GA, Cherry 66 GA, Sarah S. Dean 32 GA and Elizabeth Bethune 4/12 GA.

Cherry Little	Feb. 6, 1783	Dec. 24, 1864	w/o John Bethune
Mrs. Henrietta Matilda Tompkins	Oct. 21, 1821	Apr. 23, 1866	d/o John & Cherry Bethune of Ga. w/o H.M. Tompkins of Ala.
Henry Mercer Tompkins	Mar. 11, 1804 Edgefield Dist., S.C.	Apr. 7, 1885 Alabama	

- 1860 Barbour Co., AL Census: Henry M. Tompkins 47 SC, H. M. (f) 36 GA, Henry B. 15 AL, Mary A. 4 AL and Hamilton M. 23 AL.

- 1850 Barbour Co., AL Census: Henry M. Tompkins 40 SC, Henrietta 24 GA, Henry B. 4

AL and John Swan 60 VA.

Lot 126, fenced lot, no name

Fannie Adell   Feb. 20, 1867   Age 38 years. d/o Dana
                                                                 Hungerford, w/o J.S. Parks

- Frances A. Hungerford married James S. Parks 20 July 1849 in Upson Co., GA. James S. Parks was the s/o James G. Parks (d. 1830) and Elizabeth Biggers Woolfolk (d. ca 1836).

Dana Hungerford   Nov. 24, 1860   Age 70 years. Was a rich
                                                                 merchant of Columbus, Ga.

- 1860 Muscogee Census: Dana Hungerford 70 CT and Mary E. 38 CT.

- 1850 Upson Co., GA Census: (In Hotel) D. Hungerford (m) 60 CT, Rachel 59 CT, James S. Parks 22 GA and Francis (f) 19 CT.

- Dana Hungerford, s/o John Hungerford and Sarah Bradley of Hawington, CT married Rachel Catlin born 1 June 1793 in CT, the d/o Abijah Catlin and Huldah Wiard.[92]

James Dana Parks   June 28, 1860   s/o J.S. & F. Parks (baby)

Lot 127, no name on wall

Frank King Johnson   July 2, 1852   Oct. 14, 1894
                            Columbus, Ga.   Columbus, Ga.

- 1880 Muscogee Census: Frank Johnson 28 GA GA GA, wife Fannie 21 AL AL AL and son Rockwell 2/12 GA.

- 1870 Muscogee Census: Frank Johnson 53 GA, Joanna 32 GA, Frank 17 GA, Edward 10 GA, Urqhart 10 GA, Joanna 3 GA and Clifford D. 1 GA.

James D. Worthy   Jan. 10, 1834   June 25, 1880

- 1870 Muscogee Census: James D. Worthy 36 Louisa V. 27 GA, Beatrice F. 11 GA AL, Nettie E. 8 AL, Martha Averett 33 GA and Charles L. Averett 11 GA

1 adult slab, n/m

Lot 128, no name on wall

Mary Bedell Thompson   July 28, 1850   July 7, 1936

-

Albert G. Bedell   Nov. 28, 1824   June 28, 1878

- 1870 Muscogee Census: Albert Beddell 45 GA, Eliza 38 GA and Mary 18 AL.

- 1860 Muscogee Census: Albert G. Beddell 37 GA, Eliza 29 GA and Mary 15 AL.

- 1850 Harris Co., GA Census: William C. Osborn 52 GA, Rhody 65 GA, Albert Beddell 28 GA, Lemuel Mobley 25 GA and Morris Raiford 25 GA.

- Rhoda Clark Smith was the w/o 1) Abner Bedell (d. 1814) and 2) Col William C. Osborn.

J. R. Bedell   Co. I, 36 Regt. C.S.A. 1861-65

4 adult slabs, n/m   1 baby slab, n/m

Lot 129, no name on wall

Mrs. F. S.   Jan. 25, 1845   Mar. 14, 1881   w/o C.T. Porter

- Talbot Co., GA Marriage Records show C. T. Porter married S. F. Love 29 Nov 1870.

- 1850 Talbot Co., GA Census: John H. Love 41 GA, Louisianna 31 GA , Eugene 10 GA and Francena GA.

- 1860 Talbot Co., GA Census: John H. Love 53 GA, Louisiana L. 42 GA, Eugene E. 19 GA, Francena 15 GA, Isaac Cheney guardian for John Callier and Isaac Cheney guard for Donaldson Huff.

- 1870 Talbot Co., GA Census: Isaac Cheney 58 GA, Matilda 65 GA, Louisianna Love 58 GA, Mittie (no last name listed) 25 GA, Isaac Thompson 15 GA and Isaac McCrory 15 GA.

Charles Thomas Porter   Nov. 13, 1837   Aug. 30, 1898

- 1880 Muscogee Census: Chars Porter 42 GA GA GA, wife Francesina 34 GA GA GA, son Jammie 3 GA, son Riley Rix 7 GA GA GA and mother Lou Love 62 GA GA GA.

- 1870 Talbot Co., GA Census (enumerated twice) Charles Porter 34 GA, Elizabeth 40 GA.

- 1860 Drew Co., AR Charles Porter 23 GA in HH of Eli W. Good.

- 1860 Talbot Co., GA Charles H. Porter 63 GA, Frances 57 GA, Francis Bivens (m) 15 GA and Elizabeth Cato 71 SC

- 1850 Talbot Co., GA Census: Charles Porter 53 GA, Martha 50 GA, Cicero 25 GA, Elizabeth 22? GA, Mariah 19 GA, Williamj 18 GA, Jerusha 16 GA and Charles 14 GA.

1 baby brick slab, n/m   1 adult brick slab, n/m

Lot 130, open lot

LeGrand S. Wright   Nov. 13, 1813   Oct. 12, 1867   53 yr 10 mo 29 dy

- Legrand S. Wright married Sarah L. Kimbrough 13 June 1843 in Muscogee Co., GA.

- 1860 Muscogee Census: L. S. Wright 46 GA, Sarah L. 39 GA, William K. 15 GA, Sarah S. 12 GA and Legrand S. 9 GA.

- 1850 Muscogee Census: Legrand S. Wright 36 GA, Sarah L. 29 GA, William K. 5 Ga and Sarah S. 2 GA.

1 adult brick slab

Lot 131, no name on wall

Wm. Candler Phelps   Oct. 19, 1863   Feb. 2, 1913

- Atlanta Constitution 3 Feb 1913: "Blind Poet is Dead, Interment in Columbus" William Candler Phelps, the blind poet died 11:30 o'clock last night at a private sanitasrium from concussion of the brain. Mr. Phelps was 50 years old and is survived by his father Col. William H. H. Phelps, two sons William Walter Phelps of New York and Wilbur Phelps of Atlanta, two sisters; Mrs. R. Speight and Mrs. Elena McBride of Atlanta.

Clinton   Nov. 13, 1856   Jan. 23, 1863   s/o A.H. & S.A. DeWitt

Wm. Henry Harrison   1839   1924   Capt. Lula Guards, Co. H,
Phelps   SR:bur.5/20/192   3rd Bat. Inf. Ga. Vol. C.S.A.
                                              5, 85 yrs old

- 1920 Fulton Co., GA Census: William H. H. Phelps 82 GA GA GA (wd) and SIL Robert L. Pate 52 GA GA GA (wd).

- 1910 Fulton Co., GA Census: William H. H. Phelps 71 GA GA GA (wd) and William C. Phelps 46 GA GA GA (wd).

- Col. W. H. H. Phelps gives a wonderful recollection of Columbus, his life and Civil War in the Atlanta Constitution of 20 June 1923. He tells that he married Lucy Elizabeth Briggs in the spring of 1862 and how they spent their honeymoon in the army.

- 1860 Muscogee Census: Henry C. Phelps 53 GA (physician), Wm H. H. 21 GA, Georgia 22 GA, and Levi 17 GA.

- 1850 Muscogee Census: Henry C. Phelps 43 GA, Mrs. Felicia H. 21 GA, Sarah A. 17 GA, Georgia C. 14 GA, W. Henry 12 GA and Levi D. 8 GA.

Lucy Lula Briggs   Mar. 1, 1812   May 2, 1891
                            Columbus   Atlanta, Ga.

1 baby brick slab, n/m   6 adult brick slabs, n/m

Sexton Records indicate are buried in this lot.

Robert L. Pate   *born 4/2/1866, bur. 12/4/1922*

- Robert Pate married Augusta D. Phelps 20 July 1891 in Troup Co., GA.

W. H. H. Pate   *bur. 3/10/1868, 2 mo.*

Bessie Pate   *born 9/25/1877, bur. 7/28/1915, 42.*

Miss Phelps   *bur. 5/17/1882, 17 yrs.*

Lot 132, open lot

No evidence of graves.

Lot 133, no name on wall

Margaret   Nov. 1, 1839   July 11, 1860   d/o B. & Mary McCormick

- 1860 Muscogee Census: Barney McCormick 54 Co. Mead Ireland, Mary 54 Co. Mead Ireland, Margaret 24 Co. Mead Ireland, Thomas 16 Co. Mead Ireland, John 13 Co. Mead Ireland, Rose 5 Co. Mead Ireland and Bridget 4 Co. Mead Ireland.

1 adult brick slab, n/m

Lot 134, open lot

Cecil Johnston   Jan. 14, 1899   July 22, 1928

- 1920 Muscogee Census: Boarding House – Cecil Johnson 19 (wd) GA GA GA.

John A. Murphy   May 8, 1884   Jan. 10, 1952

- John A. Murphy died in Russell Co., AL.

L.S. Sims   July 2, 1879   Dec. 9, 1880

3 adult slabs, n/m   Evidence of 4 graves, granite rocks & 1 sink

Lot 135, J.W. Martin on wall

No evidence of graves.

Sexton Records indicate buried in this lot.

J. W. Martin   *bur. 6/11/1901, 63 yrs.*

Lot 136, Abbott on wall

Harry L. Abbott   Oct. 11, 1862   Nov. 3, 1929

- 1920 Muscogee Census: Harry Abbott 58 GA Canada GA, wife Jennie Lee 47 GA GA Iowa, son Earle 24 GA, dau Jenie Lee 17 GA and Dau Mary Ann 19 GA.
- 1910 Muscogee Census: Harry L. Abbott 47 GA Canada GA, wife Jennie 39 GA GA England (m1-18; 4/3 children), son Harry E. 14 GA, dau Mary A. 10 GA, dau Jennie L. 7 GA, sister Mamie L. Webster 34 GA GA Eng, sister Nellie R. Webster 32 GA GA Eng and brother Lewis Abbott 43 GA Can GA.
- 1880 Muscogee Census: Mary Abbott 37 GA MD GA, son Harry 17 GA, son Louis 13 GA, dau Carrie 11 GA, son Joe 8 GA and boarders Edgar Johnson 24 GA GA GA and Lola 19 AL AL AL.
- 1870 Muscogee Census: Francis J. Abbott 47 Canada, Mary A. 27 GA, Frank G. 14 GA, Harry L. 8 GA, Louis J. 3 GA and Carrie G. 1 GA.

Jennie Lee West   Feb. 28, 1871   June 13, 1948   w/o H.L. Abbott

Martha Irene   Apr. 28, 1828   June 28, 1860   d/o H.P. & R.J. Garrison, w/o

F.J. Abbott

- 1860 Muscogee Census: Francis J. Abbot 39 Canada, Martha I.32 GA, D. M. Quitman (m) 7 GA and Frank Quitman 6 GA. (Note: this appears to be an error and these children are actually Don Quitman Abbott and Frank Garrison Abbott.)

- 1850 Muscogee Census: Mrs. Rachel Dutton 38 GA, Martha Garrison 22 GA, Henry Garrison 18 GA, Mary A. Dutton 7 GA and Mrs. Sarah Rees 59 GA.

- Henry Parks Garrison was born between 1800-1810 in SC and died in Muscogee Co., GA 4 Sept 1834. He married Rachael Jane Bosworth 10 Aug 1826 in Fayette Co., GA. After Henry died, Rachael married Thomas Walton Dutton before 1839.

Carrie G. Abbott	Apr. 27, 1869	June 26, 1948	
Louis J. Abbott	Dec. 22, 1866	Dec. 25, 1946	
Louise Pieree	Nov. 24, 1883	Jan. 1, 1931	w/o Louis J. Abbott
2 children's brick slabs, n/m		4 adult brick slabs, n/m	

Sexton Records indicate buried in this lot.

Charles Lewis Abbott	*bur. 8/3/1900, 7 ½ yrs.*
Abbott child	*11 yrs.*
Mrs. M. A. Abbott	*bur. 11/4/1901, 58 yrs.*

- Mary Antoinette Dutton was born 23 Mar 1843, the d/o Thomas Walton Dutton and Rachael Jane Bosworth. She married Francis J. Abbott 10 Dec 1861.

F. J. Abbott	*bur. 6/23/77, 50 yrs.*

- 1850 Muscogee Census: Francis J. Abott 29 Canada.

- Francis Judd Abbott married Martha Irene Garrison 14 Dec 1851.

Lot 137, no name on wall

Louis Edw. Lummus	Jan. 1, 1862	Dec. 12, 1910

- 1900 Muscogee Census: L. E. Lummus Jan 1861 NY MA NY, wife Josie Apr 1860 NY Ger NY (M-13; 3/3 children), son Julian Nov 1887 GA, son Hadley Dec 1889 GA and dau Eleanor Nov 1894.

- Born in Brooklyn, Queens Co., NY, the s/o Franklin Hadley Lummus (1824-1896) and Sarah A. Smith (1833-1912) who were married 21 Apr 1852 in Queens Co., NY.

Josephine Wendt Lummus	1860	1940	SR:bur.12/16/1940, 82 yrs.

- 1870 Union Co., NJ Census: Herman Wendt 58 Bermen, Eliza 38 NY, Thomas 31 NY, Eva 19 NY, Julia 13 NJ, Josephine 10 NJ and Herman 7 NJ

Lot 138, no name on wall

Iris Godfrey Ingram	Dec. 8, 1907	Jan. 4, 1956

Lot 139, Dowdell on wall

Rubie D. Holt   July 16, 1897   Jan. 26, 1973

Louis P. Dowdell, Sr.   Apr. 30, 1867   Feb. 21, 1942

- 1930 Muscogee Census: Lewis P. Dowdell 60 AL AL AL (m@30), wife Ruby W. 50 AL AL AL (M@22) and boarder Alice Daniel 81 GA GA GA (wd).

- 1920 Muscogee Census: Louis P. Dowdell 52 AL GA GA, wife Rubye 42 AL AL AL, dau Ruby Rae 23 GA and son Louis 22 GA

Ruby Rae Wilson   Apr. 3, 1876   Sept. 28, 1954   w/o Louis P. Dowdell, Sr.

- 1880 Union Springs, Bullock Co., AL Census: William C. Wilson 44 AL GA GA, wife Ordelia S. 42 GA GA GA, dau Roxanna 17 AL, son James 16 AL, son William 14 GA, dau Parmilla 12 AL, dau Genie 10 AL, son Walter 7 AL, dau Rubie 5 AL and Jeraldine 2 AL.

- Ruby Rae Wilson was born in Union Springs, AL. She married 14 Oct 1896 in Union Springs, AL Louis Pierce Dowdell (b. 30 April 1867 Tuskegee, AL the s/o Rev. Louis F. Dowdell and Arcadia Mitchell)   To this union was born 2 children; Ruby Rae Dowdell, who married Robert Nesbit Holt (s/o Benjamin J. and Hattie Holt) and Louise Pierce Dowdell born 16 Oct 1904.[93]

- William Cawthorn Wilson (born Columbia, AL and d. 1925 Union Springs, AL) married Ordelia Shine Battle 24 Feb 1859 in Union Springs, AL. She was the d/o William Whitehead Battle (1812 GA-1873 Bullock Co., AL) and his first wife, Permelia Caroline Westbrook (d/o Thomas Westbrook and Mary Shine). [94]

Delia Louis Dowdell   Dec. 31, 1904   Mar. 28, 1906

Lot 140, open lot

No evidence of graves.

Lot 141, open lot

No evidence of graves.

Lot 142, no name on wall

Robert P. Bellah   Apr. 15, 1846   Dec. 2, 1921

- 1920 Muscogee Census: Robert P. Bellah 73 GA GA GA, wife Sarah C. 67 GA GA SC and dau Lizzie B. 37 GA.

- 1900 Russell Co., AL Census: Robert P. Bellah Apr 1847 GA GA GA, wife Sarah Dec 1852 GA GA GA, dau Mary H. Mar 1895 GA, dau Elmira L. Oct 1878 GA, dau Lizzie H. Aug 1881 GA, dau Kate S. May 1884 GA and son Samuel O. July 1876 GA.

- 1880 Milton Co., GA Census: Robert P. Bellah 31 GA GA GA, wife Mary J. 28 GA GA

GA, dau Percy T. 6 AL, son Samuel O. 4 Al and dau Elmire L. 2 AL.

- Robert Pollock Bellah (s/o Rev. Samuel J. Bellah 1811-1889 Cobb Co., GA and Sarah Patterson 1819-1892 Cobb Co., GA) married 1) Mary Josephine James 18 Aug 1872 and 2) Sarah Bowden 12 Nov 1893.

Mary H. Bellah	Mar. 20, 1895	Oct. 9, 1910
Mrs. Sarah Catdonea Bellah	Dec. 18, 1852	Jan. 8, 1936

Hugh W. Barr	SR: born 11/5/1838	SR: bur. 3/4/1908	Co. A, 1 Bn., Ga. Vols., C.S.A.

- 1880 Muscogee Census: Hugh Barr 47 GA Scot GA, wife Ellen 37 GA GA GA, dau Eliza 15 AL, son John 12 AL and dau Nancy 8 GA.

- 1870 Bibb Co., GA Census: Hugh W. Barr 31 GA, Ellen A. 26 GA, Eliza J. 4 AL and John W. 9/12 GA.

- Hugh W. Barr married Ellen A. Bess 17 Dec 1864 in Bibb Co., GA.

2 children's brick slabs,
n/m

Lot 143, DeWolf on wall

Charlotte Elizabeth	Sept. 2, 1811 Plattsburg, N.Y.	Oct. 24, 1869	58 yrs.
Walter Stratten DeWolf	July 24, 1850 Montgomery, Ala.	Oct. 1, 1909 Atlanta, Ga.	

- 1880 Muscogee Census: Walter S. De Wolf 29 AL GA SC, wife Carrie V. 25 VA VA VA.

Kate Louise DeWolf	Dec. 12, 1892 Atlanta, Ga.	May 1, 1915 Atlanta, Ga.	d/o Walter S. & Carrie V. DeWolf
Carrie V. Porter	Aug. 26, 1855 Richmond, Va.	June 4, 1905 Chatham, Va.	w/o Walter S. DeWolf

- Obit: Atlanta Constitution 6 June 1905 – Mrs. W. S. DeWolf died in Chatham, VA yesterday. Mrs. DeWolf was Miss Carrie Porter, d/o Mr & Mrs. J. C. Porter of Columbus. Survived by her mother and 3 brothers; John Porter of Atlanta, Robert Porter of Birmingham and William Porter of Columbus. Besides her husband Col. Walter S. DeWolf, two daus. Mrs. Claud Miller of Columbus and Miss Kate DeWolf of Chatham survive her.

- 1870 Muscogee Census: Joseph C. Porter 41 VA, Annie E. 38 VA, Carrie 16 VA, John 11 TN, Robert 10 VA, Willie 7 GA and Beulla Daniel 24 VA.

Harriet Grace Nutting	Aug. 12, 1822 Columbia, S.C.	May 17, 1880 Chattahoochee Co., Ga.	w/o Thomas DeWolf
Ethel		May 12, 1881 Richmond, Va.	Foster d/o Walter S. & Carrie V. DeWolf, age 9 months.
Josephine Adalaide	May 15, 1824 Columbia, S.C.	May 17, 1880 Chattahoochee	w/o Thomas DeWolf

Co., Ga.

- 1850 Columbia, Richland Co., SC Census: John J. Walter 58 PA, Sarah A. 45 NC, William T. White 26 ME, John Madrey 18 SC and Josephine A. Nutting 23 SC.

| Thomas DeWolf | Jan. 1, 1812 Waynesboro, Ga. | Dec. 13, 1893 Columbus, Ga. | |

- 1880 Chattahoochee Co., GA Census: Thomas Dewolf 68 GA Fra -, son Silas W. 21 GA, son Gilbert P. 18 GA, SIL Josephine A. Collins 55 SC SC SC and visitor Margaret Affleck 69 Scot Scot Scot.

- 1870 Muscogee Census: Thos DeWolf 56 GA, Harriet 49 SC, Walter S. 20 GA, Silas W. 12 GA and Gilbert P. 10 GA.

- 1860 Chattahoochee Co., GA Census: Thos Dewoolf 45, Harriet 40, Thos. 13, Waton (sic) 10, Sarah 8, John Stewart 12 and Silas 1.

- On 30 July 1855 Thomas DeWolf established *The Daily Sun*, the first daily paper published in Columbus. He had previously owned interest in the *State Gazette* of Chambers Co., AL and had also been publisher of The *Dallas Gazette* at Cahaba. He was also connected with the *Montgomery Advertiser.*

- 1850 Montgomery Co., AL Census: Thos. DeWolf 38 GA, Harriet 29 SC, Thos. 4 AL and Walter 1/12 AL.

- Thomas Dewoolf (sic) married Harriett Nutting 31 Dec 1835 in Perry Co., AL.

- According to the History of Chattahoochee County, Thomas DeWolf came from Connecticut to first Selma, AL. It further states that after Harriet died, he married second, her sister Mrs. Collins who accompanied him to Atlanta in 1882-1883 and thirdly Miss Mamie Daniel.

Charles Abercrombie	Aug. 31, 1850	Jan. 3, 1860	s/o Thomas & Harriet DeWolf
Ida	Aug. 25, 1864	Sept. 5, 1864	d/o Thomas & Harriet DeWolf
Thomas Nutting	June 4, 1846	Sept. 9, 1860	s/o Thomas & Harriet DeWolf
Sarah Adaline	May 12, 1854	Dec. 4, 1863	d/o Thomas & Harriet DeWolf

Lot 144, J.G. O'Neal on wall

| John Gibbs O'Neal | May 10, 1858 | Dec. 1, 1909 | |

1 adult slab, n/m

Sexton's Records indicate buried in this lot:

| Sallie O'Neal | | *bur. 4/13/50, 92 yrs.* |

Lot 145, no name on wall

| Janie Bishop Johnson | Nov. 4, 1889 | Nov. 3, 1918 | w/o C.R. Johnson |

Clifford Ross Johnson	June 30, 1869	Apr. 30, 1929	
Lottie Moon	Nov. 17, 1878	Jan. 16, 1975	w/o Early Hurt Johnson
Early Hurt Johnson	Apr. 12, 1878	Sept. 6, 1947	s/o Joanna Lyon Day & Franklin Cosby Johnson
Mary A. Day		May 14, 1883 age 63 years	w/o E.H. Day

- 1850 Muscogee Census: Mrs. M. A. Day 30 NY, Frances L. 10 NY and E. Henry 8 GA.

Joanna Lyon Day	Apr. 2, 1838	July 8, 1905	w/o Franklin C. Johnson

- 1900 Muscogee Census: Johanna L. Johnson Apr 1838 NY NY NY(wd; 3/3 children), son Clifford R. June 1869 GA GA NY, son Louis M. May 1872 GA GA NY and son Early H. Apr 1878 GA GA NY.

- 1880 Muscogee Census: F. C. Johnston (sic) 63 GA GA GA, Mrs. J. L. 41 GA GA GA, son Henry W. 15 GA, dau Joannah E. 12 GA, son Clifford R. GA, son Louis M. 8 GA and son Early H. 2 GA.

- 1870 Muscogee Census: Frank Johnson 53 GA, Joanna 32 GA, Frank 17 GA, Edward 10, Urquhart 5 GA, Joanna 3 GA and Clifford 1 GA.

- 1860 Muscogee Census: Franklin C. Johnson 43 GA, Joanna L. 27 NY, Mary J. 15 GA, Francis (f) 8 GA and Edward H. 2/12/ GA.

- 1850 Muscogee Census: F. C. Johnson (m) 33 GA, R. R. (f) 33 CT, Mary Jane 5 GA and Martha A. 13.

- Franklin C. Johnson married Rebecca R. Foot 29 Mar 1843 in Muscogee Co., GA.

Inf. d/o R. Brice & Betty Carson	July 21, 1953 (only date)
1 adult brick slab, n/m	1 baby brick slab, n/m

Lot 146, no name on wall

Henry Bradford Walker	Apr. 6, 1855	Mar. 24, 1906	
Frances Ellen Corcoran	July 28, 1833	Sept. 10, 1909	
Thomas Quinn	1790	1861	

- 1850 Muscogee Census: Thomas Quin 60 VA, Dorah 27 GA, James L. 3 Muscogee Co. and Lunnia 2 Muscogee Co.

Mary Corcoran			b & d 1856, 1 month
James B. Corcoran	1833	1870	Father
1 adult brick slab, n/m			

Lot 147, open lot

1 baby obelisk, Malcolm	May 3, 1846	Dec. 9, 1846	Inf. s/o McArdle
3 adult brick slabs, n/m			

Lot 148, J.C Porter on wall

Annie E. Anderson	July 11, 1829 Richmond, Va.	Columbus, Ga.	Mother
J.C. Porter	July 5, 1828 Richmond, Va.	May 2, 1897 Columbus, Ga.	Father

- 1880 Muscogee Census: Josiah Porter 40 VA VA VA, wife Ann 45 VA VA VA, son Robert 19 GA, son William 19 GA and boarder Elizabeth Daniel 28 VA VA VA.

- 1870 Muscogee Census: Joseph C. Porter 41 VA, Annie E. 38 VA, Carrie 16 VA, John 11 TN, Robert 10 VA, Willie 7 GA and Beulla Daniel 24 VA.

- 1860 Henrico Co., VA Census: J. C. Porter 32 VA, Ann 30 VA, Caroline 7 VA, John 2 VA, Robert 2/12 VA, Jeremiah Porter 57 VA and Caroline Porter 57 VA.

- Jeremiah Porter married Caroline C. Spencer 22 Jan 1826 in Henrico Co., VA.

Mary Elizabeth Tune	July 8, 1905	June 30, 1963	d/o Charles J. & Sallie Griggs Tune
Charles James Tune	Jan. 27, 1872	July 28, 1927	
Sallie Outlar Griggs		Nov. 20, 1938	w/o Charles James Tune

2 baby brick slabs, n/m

Lot 149, no name on brick wall, partially fallen

Janie	Jan. 27, 1838	Oct. 11, 1852	d/o A. & S.A. Ferguson
Eddie Walton	May 20, 1850	July 14, 1857	Inf. s/o A. & S.A. Ferguson
Lt. Thomas Ferguson			Cols. Guards 1861-65
William Ferguson			Nelson's Rangers, C.S.A.
John Ferguson			Cols. Guards 1861-65

- 1860 Muscogee Census: Aaron Ferguson 68 NC, Sarah 48 NC, Ellen 15 GA, Virginia 13 GA, Sarah 12 GA, William 17 GA, Thomas 17 GA, and Aaron 9 GA.

- 1850 Muscogee Census: Aaron Ferguson 59 VA, Sarah A. 40 NC, John 17 NC, Jane 11 Muscogee Co., William 9 Muscogee Co., Thomas 7 Muscogee Co., Ellen 5 Muscogee Co., Virginia 3 Muscogee Co. and Sally 2 Muscogee Co.

1 adult brick mound, n/m   1 sink, baby

Sexton Records indicate buried in this lot:

Mrs. Fannie L. Ferguson   *d. Apr. 2, 1937*

Lot 150, open lot

No evidence of graves.

Lot 151, Mims-Brannon on wall

Louisa Augusta Mims	Mar. 16, 1817	July 28, 1865 Union Springs, Ala.	Consort of K.W. Griswold
Drury Mims	Jan. 16, 1783 S.C.	June 18, 1858 Eufaula, Ala.	

- Kelsey, Floyd & Parsons, Marriage & Death Notices from the South Western Baptist Newspaper, (Heritage Books 1995), P. 105. 7/1/1858. Departed this life, in the city of Eufaula, Ala., on the 18th, Deacon Drury Mims, aged 75 years, 5 months and 2 days. Father Mims was born in Edgefield District, S. C., January 16th, 1783. In 1830 he moved to Muscogee County, Ga., and to Russell County, Alabama in 1837, where he lived until January 1855. Having been bereft of his companion, he sold his property and dividing most of the proceeds thereof among his children, he selected the home of his daughter Julia Brannon as his future home.

- 1850 Russell Co., AL Census: Drury Mims 67 SC, Charlsey 62 VA, William 30 SC, Louisa 28 SC and Julia A. Fuller 17 GA.

- Deacon Drury Mims was the s/o Drury Mims (c1730-1818 Edgefield Dist., SC) and his second wife Lydia Jones (c1746-1821 Edgefield Dist., SC). Drury Mims Sr.'s will proved 13 January 1819 in Edgefield Dist., SC. Drury Mims, Sr. fought in the American Revolution. He was a private and in the Revolutionary War records, it is written that Drury, Sr. killed a Tory in defense of his own home and life. He was sentenced to hang and his second wife, Lydia Jones Mims, secured a reprieve by riding horseback to Charleston, S. C. and interviewing the Governor. Drury was granted a pardon. He received 2871/2 acres on bounty for his Revoluntionary services in Washington County, Ga., Sept. 22, 1784 but he never left Edgefield County, S. C.

Mrs. Charlsey Mims	Mar. 25, 1783	Oct. 8, 1854	SR: b. S.C.

- Recorded in Halifax County Virginia 26 June 1809. Halifax Deed Book 22, page 374: Power of Attorney. We Mary Ann Hawkins Mims and husband Britton Mims and Charlsey Mims and husband Drury Mims legatees of Charles Edwards decd, appoint Leonard Edwards of Granville County North Carolina our attorney to receive titles of Memucan Hunt executor of Edward Wade decd to a certain tract of land in the fork of the Dan and Stanton River on both sides of Difficult Creek and Halifax County Virginia agreeable to a decree of Halifax Court of May 1806 and to sell the said land...this 29 August 1807. witness: M. Mims, P. Cleary. Briton Mims, Mary Ann H. Mims, Drury Mims Jr.?, Charlsey Mims.

  Edgefield District South Carolina- before Davis Williams, one of the Justices, M. Mims swore to the signatures of Briton Mims & Mary Ann H. Mims his wife, Drury Mims Junr and Charlsey Mims his wife and also to Patrick Cleary as a witness. 31 August 1807 Richard Tutt Clerk of Court of Common Pleas for Edgefield District certified that Davis Williams was one of the Justices of the Peace for Edgefield District. 31 August 1807. Recorded in Halifax County Virginia 23 April 1810.

- Charlsey Edwards was the d/o Charles Edwards (c 1740- bef. 6/1809 Halifax Co., VA) and his second wife Leticia Martin who were married 30 Apr 1779 in Halifax Co., VA. Charley's sister Mary Ann Hawkins Edwards married Drury Mim's brother, Britton Mims. Leticia Martin (born 25 Sept 1747) was the d/o Capt. Abram Martin (1716-1773) and Elizabeth Marshall (1726-1797). Leticia was married previously to Edward Wade.

Henry Greene Brannon	Nov. 27, 1895	Oct. 26, 1974	g/g/grandson of Drury &

Charlsey Mims, WWI vet.

- 1900 Russell Co., AL Census: Cal? J. Brannan June 1862 AL AL AL, wife Ellen E. Jan 1869 AL AL AL (m-7; 3/3 children), dau Dovey Jan 1894, son Henry Feb 1896 AL and son Robert May 1898.

- 1850 Russell Co., AL Census: Thomas Branon 37 SC, Julia 34 SC, Thomas 15 GA, William 12 GA, Rodney 10 GA, Alexander 6 GA, Abner 4 GA, Julia 3 AL and James 2 GA.

Mattie Lou Bussey	Feb. 11, 1902 (only date)		w/o Henry Greene Brannon
Madge Norman Brannon	Mar. 16, 1931	May 13, 1990	d/o Henry Greene Brannon & Mattie Lou Bussey Brannon

Lot 152, J.W. Bostwick name plate, open lot

J.W. Tooke	Aug. 10, 1810	Dec. 28, 1851

2 children brick slabs, n/m

Lot 153, open lot

Bettie Hettie A	Oct. 23, 1854	July 13, 1859	d/o Thomas H. & Charlotte C. Burch
Editha L. Gray		Apr. 2, 1853 aged 45 years	w/o Patrick Gray

- 1850 Russell Co., AL Census: Editha Gray 42 GA, William 23 GA, Mary 22 GA, Martha 21 GA, Charlot 18 GA, Susan 16 GA, Randolph 13 GA, James 20 GA and William 2 AL.

W.T. Hall	Mar. 20, 1912

Lot 154, no name on wall

One slab:

Harriet A. Valentine	Sept. 1, 1817	Apr. 4, 1846	w/o Philo Hall Wildman
Gertrude Wildman	Mar. 16, 1846	May 14, 1846	
Julia Wildman	June 9, 1840	Aug. 29, 1841	
Clara Mary Wildman	July 19, 1842	Feb. 7, 1906	w/o Alfred I. Young
Thomas Valentine Preer	May 9, 1897	May 31, 1899	s/o G.T. & H.V. Preer

- 1860 Muscogee Census: Mrs. P. H. Wildman 39 GA, Ella Ingram 18 AL and Emma 16 AL.

- 1850 Muscogee Census: Philo Wildman 37 CT, Priscilla 35 Putnam Co. GA, Emma Ingram 14 Hancock Co., Ella 11 AL, Clara Wildman 8 Gwinnett Co., Valentine 6 Columbus and John Hurt 25 Putnam Co.

- Harriet A. Valentine married Dr. P. H. Wildman 26 Apr 1839 and left the following children: Julia, Clara who married Alfred Young of NY, Valentine and Gertrude. She was the d/o Harry Valentine (born 5 Oct 1786-7 Mar 1847 Brooklyn, NY) and Mary Mawney (d/o Dr. William Mawney and Elizabeth Clarke of Providence, RI).[95]

- 1900 Muscogee Census: Clara M. Young 57 GA GA GA (wd; 8/6 children), dau Augusta T. Preer Feb 1866 GA AL GA (wd; 3/3 children), son Alfred T. Mar 1891 GA, son Thomas S. Oct. 1892 GA, and Charles D. Feb 1895 GA.

- 1880 Muscogee Census: Alfred Young 42 AL NY GA, wife Clarara (sic) 38 GA CT NY, dau Elenener A. 14 NY, son William H. 12 NY, dau Claria Louise 9 NY, dau Harriet V. 4 GA and dau I Ellen Beall 1 GA.

- Alfred I. Young was the s/o William H. Young. He married Clara Wildman 1 May 1861 in Muscogee Co., GA.

Lot 155, Luckie & Porter 1921, on wall

William Foster		July 1857 age 6 months	Inf. s/o D.D. & E.O. Cox

- 1860 Muscogee Census: (In HH of L. M. Bigger, among others) D. D. Cox 40 GA, Mrs. Cox 25 GA, Infant (f) 2 GA, Lorrainia W. 8 GA and Madeline 6 GA.

Julia Ann Luckie		Feb. 8, 1851 age 10 years	
Nellie Clabourn	Jan. 13, 1897	June 30, 1901	d/o W.D. & Mrs. Porter
Emma J. Mote	1866	1912	SR:bur.12/21/1912, 46 years

- 1910 Muscogee Census: Emma Mote 45 GA GA GA and boarder Mattie Sellers 35 GA GA GA.

3 adult brick slabs, n/m   1 child's brick slab, n/m

One slab:

W.D. Porter	Oct. 5, 1863	Mar. 9, 1926	
Mollie S. Porter	July 27, 1865	Jan. 30, 1947	w/o W.D. Porter

- 1920 Muscogee Census: William D. Porter 50 GA VA VA, wife Mollie 50 GA Scot GA.

- 1910 Muscogee Census: William D. Porter 45 GA VA VA and wife Mollie 43 GA Scot GA (m-20 yrs).

- 1900 Muscogee Census: William T. Porter Mar 1874 GA VA VA, wife Mollie S. July 1873 GA Scot GA and dau Nellie Feb 1895.

Lot 156, no name on wall

Eddie	Aug. 9, 1872	Sept. 20, 1874	s/o E.J. & S.V. Morgan
Charles W.	July 6, 1882	Feb. 2, 1914	s/o J.L. & S.V. Wiggins
John T. Walker	Jan. 7, 1806	July 1, 1866	

- 1860 Muscogee Census: John T. Walker 55 GA, Melvina 34 GA, Sabrina 17 GA, Telitha 14 GA, Angerona (m) 13 GA and Mary A. 9 GA.

Melvina C. Walker	Nov. 22, 1827	Dec. 4, 1888	Erected by dght. Sabrina
John W. Burke	Oct. 28, 1873	July 15, 1913	
Ada Burke	July 17, 1871	Aug. 11, 1914	w/o D. Russell
Mariana Walker	Mar. 16, 1851	May 17, 1881	w/o W. Brooks
Talitha Walker	Mar. 1, 1846	June 7, 1915	w/o H. Burke

- 1880 Muscogee Census: Malvina Walker 54 GA GA GA, dau Tilitha Burk 34 GA GA GA, Filicia Morgan 44 GA GA GA, GS Marshall Burk 10 GA GA GA, GD Ada 8 GA, GS Jno.5 GA and ----- (m) GS 3 GA.

Mary T. Walters	June 29, 1900	Sept. 10, 1925	w/o Marshall M. Burke
Hilda Louise Jones		Feb. 16, 1952 age 45 years	

1 adult slab, n/m	2 baby brick slabs, n/m
2 adult graves outlined w/bricks	3 baby graves outlined w/bricks

Lot 157, no name on wall

Maggie Phillips	Apr. 12, 1887	July 2, 1951	w/o T.W. Burke
Tobe W. Burke	Nov. 21, 1877	Oct. 31, 1951	

Lot 158, no name on wall

Elizabeth Cook	Aug. 23, 1833	Jan. 24, 1900	w/o Major Hatch Cook

- Hatch Cook married Elizabeth Brown 26 Nov 1853 in Barbour Co., GA.

- 1860 Muscogee Census: Hatch Cook 32 MD (hotel keeper), Mrs T. L. 27 AL, John C. 6 AL, Celian H. 4 AL, Eula 2 AL and numerous others in the hotel.

- Major Hatch Cook of Georgia was killed at the Battle of White Oaks road in Virginia.

Joel T. Johnson	Feb. 27, 1827 Oglethorpe Co., Ga.	Nov. 29, 1884 Columbus, Ga.	

- 1880 Muscogee Census: Joel T. Johnston 53 GA GA GA, wife Jane 52 GA GA GA, dau Emma Granberry 26 GA, SIL Eugene Granberry 36 GA GA MA, dau Frances Johnston 24 GA, son W. Orlando 22 GA, DIL Hatchie 19 GA GA GA, son Charlie 19 GA, dau Alice 16 GA and dau Jodie 12 GA.

Jane Johnson	Mar. 28, 1828	Jan. 2, 1913	w/o Joel T. Johnson
Robert		May 11, 1880 1 yr 10 mo 5 days	Inf. s/o Eugene & Anna Granberry
Emma Dora Granberry	May 29, 1854	Oct. 4, 1881	w/o Eugene Granberry, d/o Joel T. & Jane Johnson
Alice Lee Johnson	Nov. 23, 1864	Jan. 23, 1882	d/o Joel T. & Jane Johnson

1 adult brick slab, n/m	1 child brick slab, n/m	3 baby brick slabs, n/m

Sexton Records indicate buried in this lot:

Eugene Granberry   *bur. 7/6/1887, 43 yrs*

- Eugene Granberry married Emma Dora Johnson 19 Sept 1877 in Harris Co., GA.

- 1870 Harris Co., GA Census: Mary B. Granberry 57 GA, Matthew R. 28 GA, Eugene 26 GA and Mary B. 24 GA.

- Eugene Granberry was the son of Rev. George Granberry (c1797 Pitt Co., NC-c1805 Harris Co., GA) and Mary B. Folsom. He was the editor of The Hamilton Journal.

Lot 159, fenced lot, no name

John Kyle   1814   Aug. 4, 1856   Father
                                                           age 42 years

- 1850 Muscogee Census: John Kyle 32 Ireland, Ann E. 23 GA, Lucy E. 6 AL and Sarah E. 3 AL.

Elizabeth Kyle Garrard   Oct. 27, 1828   Feb. 2, 1912   Mother

- 1860 Russell Co., AL: A. E. Kyle (f) 27 GA, L. E. (f) 14 AL, J. P. (m) 7 GA and J. M. (f) 4 GA.

- 1910 Muscogee Census: Lucy Norwood 60 GA Ire GA (wd; 0/0 children) and mother Elizabeth Garrard 82 GA NC VA (wd; 3//3 children).

- 1900 Muscogee Census: Lucy Norwood Feb 1845 AL Ire GA (wd), and mother Elizabeth Garrard Feb 1827 GA NC VA (wd; 3/3 children)

Dr. John Norwood   Aug. 5, 1836   June 28, 1897   Surgeon, C.S.A. 1861-65
                              Hillsboro, N.C.

- John Norwood married Lucy E. Kyle 18 Feb 1862 in Russell Co., AL.

Sallie   Child (unable to read)

Lucy E. Kyle   Feb. 14, 1845   June 15, 1923   w/o Dr. John Norwood

                    1 child's grave, marble stone at head & foot

Lot 160, open lot

No evidence of graves.

Lot 161, open lot

1 adult brick slab, n/m

Lot 162, open lot

Pensacola Musgrove   No dates.
                                                                    SR:bur.1/10/1930, 49

260

5 adult slabs, n/m   1 baby slab, n/m

Sexton Records indicate buried in this lot:

Emma S. Musgrove   *bur. 8/22/1926, 57 yrs.*

Mrs. A.F. Musgrove   *bur. 11/13/1887, 55 yrs.*

Susie Musgrove   *bur. 7/31/1934, 70 yrs.*

- 1880 Muscogee Census: Edward H. Musgrove 28 GA GA GA, mother Adeline F. 52 GA VA GA, sister Emma J. 22 GA, sister Susan B. 21 GA and sister Pensacola 18 GA.

- 1860 Muscogee Census: E. H. Musgrove 37 GA, Adeline F. 30 GA, Edw H. 9 GA, Emma S. 7 GA and Susan D. 2 GA.

- Edward H. Musgrove was born ca 1823 in Augusta, Richmond Co., GA. He married 1)Emma J. Thompson 11 July 1845 in Richmond Co., GA and 2) Adeline F. Burch 6 Nov 1850 in Autaga Co., AL.

Lot 163, open lot

1 adult brick slab, n/m   2 children brick slabs, n/m   1 adult sink

Sexton Records indicate buried in this lot:

Mrs. M. G. Cotton   *bur. 3/29/1882, 34 yrs.*

Lucy Mary Cotton   *bur. 7/30/1902, 8 yrs.*

W. G. Cotton   *bur. 2/20/1918, 78 yrs.*

- 1880 Muscogee Census: William Cotton 39 GA GA GA, wife Martha 32 GA GA GA, son Thomas L. 6 AL, son Parnelle 4 AL and brother John 20 AL GA GA.

Lot 164, Kendall on wall

Charlie Geo. Kendall   Dec. 8, 1869   Jan. 2, 1908

Mamie Jackson Kendall   Mar. 23, 1871   Oct. 18, 1912

Fannie Vardeman Kendall   Sept. 9, 1841   June 2, 1926

- 1860 Monroe Co., GA Census: Mary Vardeman 38 GA, Fannie 17 GA, Sam 15 GA, Albert 13 GA, Josephine (f) 11 GA, James 8 GA, George 6 GA and Leonard 3 GA.

- 1850 Harris Co., GA Census: B. B. Vardeman 30 GA, Mary 30 SC, Margaret Huey 60 SC, Frances A. Vardeman 9 GA, Samuel 7 GA, Joseph A. (m) 5 GA and Isabella 2 GA.

- Benjamin Vardeman married Mary Ann Huey 12 Dec 1840 in Harris Co., GA.

C.A. Kendall   Sept. 11, 1844   Jan. 26, 1909

- 1900 Muscogee Census: Charles A. Kendall Sept 1844 AL MA Scot, wife Fannie Sept 1844 GA GA SC (m-33; 4/4 children), son Charles G. Sept 1869 GA (m-3), dau Alice Miller Feb 1872 GA (m-1; 0/0 children), DIL Mamie Kendall Mar 1871 FL GA GA (m-3; 2/2 children), GD Elise May 1898 GA and GS Charles A. Apr 1900 GA.

- 1880 Macon, Bibb Co., GA Census: Chas. Kendall 35 AL MA Scot, wife Fannie 35 GA SC GA, son Charlie 10 GA, dau Alice 8 GA, dau Katie 6 GA, dau Lena 1 GA, BIL James Vardeman 23 GA GA SC, SIL Josephine 21 GA GA GA and nephew Eugene Farber 17

GA GA GA.

- 1870 Muscogee Census: Charles Kendle24 GA, Fannie 24 Ga and George 6/12/GA.

- 1860 Muscogee Census: Jane Kendall 54 Scotland, Selina 20 AL, Charles 16 AL and Martha Tucker 20 AL.

- 1850 Muscogee Census: Charles Kendall 40 MA, Jane 39 Scotland, Eliza Dudley 25 SC, Solina Kendall 10 AL, Charles H. 6 AL, Charles Crichton 26 Scotland, John McGalligan 25 PA and James Jamison 20 GA.

Augustus Eyman	July 3, 1856 3 months	Inf. s/o Charles & Jane Kendall

1 baby brick slab, n/m

Lot 165, open lot

2 adult sinks

Lot 166, Cooper on wall

One slab:

Ellen Heath Harris	Sept. 6, 1808	July 11, 1888	
Ann Elizabeth		1845	d/o E. A.? Billups & w/o Alexander H. Cooper . aged 19 yrs 6 mo 17 days
Harry Cooper	Dec. 4, 1853	July 10, 1933	
Alexander Hamilton Cooper	Jan. 20, 1820	Sept. 20, 1863 killed at Chickamuga	Capt Co. C., 46th Ga., C.S.A.
Eliza Harris Cooper	Nov. 2, 1830	June 8, 1905	
Alice Billups	Apr. 24, 1803	June 6, 1849	
Nell Cooper Frederick	Aug. 18, 1862	Dec. 27, 1945	
Francis Marion Frederick	Mar. 4, 1852	Nov. 28, 1911	

- 1880 Muscogee Census: Elizabeth Cooper 48 GA GA GA, son Harry 25 GA GA GA, soin Aleck 20 GA GA GAdau Nellie 17 GA GA GA and mother Ella H. Harris 71 GA GA GA.

- 1870 Muscogee Census: Ellen Harris 61 GA, Ellen 41 GA, Eliza Cooper 39 AL, Milton 21 GA, "Harrie" 16 GA, Alexander 10 GA and Ellen 7 GA.

- 1860 Muscogee Census: Capt. A. H. Cooper 44 GA, Eliza 29 AL, Milton 11 GA, Harry 6 GA, infant 1 (m) GA, Ellen H. Harris 52 GA and Ellen M. 31 GA.

- 1850 Muscogee Census: Alexander H. Cooper 30 Putnam Co., Elizabeth C. 20 AL, Martha 1 Muscogee GA, Ellen H. Harris 38 Greene Co. GA and Ellen M. Harris 21 GA.

- Alexander H. Cooper married 1) Ann E. Billups 10 Oct 1844 and 2) Eliza C. Harris 11 July 1848 in Muscogee Co., GA.

- 1910 Muscogee Census: Frank M. Frederick 53 GA SC GA, wife Nell C. 47 GA GA AL (m1-19; 0/0 children) and niece Heath Cooper 11 FL GA FL.

Ellen Maria Harris   July 15, 1828   June 20 1877

Lot 167, no name on wall

Eugenia Holmes   July 4, 1823   Feb. 27, 1908

Chester G. Holmes   July 18, 1814   Aug. 10, 1866

- 1860 Franklin Co., FL Census: C. G. Holmes 45 CT, Eugenia 35 GA and Charles R. 16? FL.

2 adult brick slabs, n/m

Sexton Records indicate buried in this lot:

Charles T. Holmes   *bur. 5/7/1909, 67 yrs.*

Lot 168, Bates on wall

Thomas Jefferson Bates   Mar. 18, 1836   Mar. 12, 1910

- 1900 Muscogee Census: Thomas J. Bates Mar 1836 GA MA SC, wife Louisa A. Sept 1837 AL VA AL (m-45; 6/4 children) and dau Martha Dec 1866 AL.

- 1880 Muscogee Census: T. J. Bates 44 GA GA GA, wife L. A. 44 AL AL ?, dau E. H. 27 AL, son T. W. 18 AL, son Geo C. 18 AL, dau M. B. 13 AL and dau C. B. 11 GA.

- 1870 Russell Co., AL Census: Thos J. Bates 34 GA, Netty 30 GA, Eugene (f) 10 AL, Thomas 9 AL, George 7 AL, Matty 5 AL and Lola 2 AL.

- 1860 Russell Co., AL Census: Thomas J. 24 GA, Louisa A. 22 AL, Eugenia 4 AL and Emma 1 AL.

- Thomas J. Bates married Louisa A. McGehee 9 Sept 1855 in Russell Co., AL.

- Capt. Thomas Jefferson Bates was the son of Asa Bates of Springfield, MA who came south during the Sminole War and settled in Columbus, GA. Asa's father was Eli Bates and grandfather was Edwin Bates, both of Massachusetts. [96]

Emma Antoinette Bates   Jan. 28, 1858   Dec. 11, 1862

Louisa Antoinette   Sept. 9, 1838   July 5, 1926   w/o T.J. Bates
McGehee

- 1910 Muscogee Census: Louisa A. Bates 72 AL GA AL (wd; 6/4 children) and dau Martha B. 42 AL GA AL.

- 1850 Russell Co., AL Census: Isaac McGehee 54 VA, Martha 36 GA, Elizabeth 14 AL, Antoinet 13 AL, Christopher 11 AL, Isabella 10 AL, Isaac M. 8 AL, Rodolphus 4 AL, Olivia 1 AL, John Cane 17 AL and Sarah Kennon 60 GA.

- Southern Christian Advocate 20 Oct 1875: Isaac McGehee, one of the old settlers of Columbus and Girard, died at Porter Springs, Lumpkin Co., Ga., Aug. 13, 1875. C. L. Pattillo

- Isaac McGehee (born VA), son of Jacob McGehee and Sarah Collier married Martha Harrison Kennon. [97] Martha Kennon was the d/o William Warner Kennon (1779-1850) and his wife Elizabeth Leverette. William W. Kennon was the 2nd son of William Kennon and Elizabeth Harrison.[98]

M.B.B. marker (adult)			SR:bur.3/31/1955, 88
Carrie Belle Cleburne Bates	Apr. 6, 1869	July 26, 1895	
Geo. Hall Smith, Jr.	Mar. 10, 1893	Jan. 18, 1951	
1 baby obelisk, unable to read			

Lot 169, Mullin on wall

Wm. Lafayette Mullin, M.D.	July 2, 1878	Sept. 8, 1925
Elizabeth F. Mullin	Feb. 15, 1886	Mar. 6, 1974

Lot 170, no name on wall

John Alrie Summerlin	Sept. 18, 1882	Jan. 31, 1957
Maye Watkins Summerlin	Feb. 12, 1886	July 5, 1966

Lot 171, open lot

Thomas Jefferson Shivers	June 30, 1810	Dec. 15, 1876

- 1870 Muscogee Census: Thomas J. Shivers 60 GA, Sarah A. 59 GA, Thomas B. 18 GA and Sarah E. 22 GA.

- 1850 Muscogee Co. Census: Thos J. Shivers 40 Hancock Co., Sarah H. 40 Greene Co., GA, Robert M. 12 Muscogee, Charles A. 10 Muscogee, Mary C. 9 Muscogee, Lucretia A. 7 Muscogee, Mary E. 5 Muscogee, John Isham 30 VT Teacher. Benjamin K. Hurt 11 AL and William Hurt 8 GA.

- Thomas J. Shivers married Sarah Ann Martin 25 Feb 1836 in Greene Co., GA.

Sarah Eugenia Shivers	1853	1874	d/o Thomas J. Shivers, SR:bur.8/14/1874, 21 yrs.
Robert Martin	Sept. 28, 1838	Nov. 24, 1851	s/o Thos. J. & Sarah Ann Shivers
C.A. Shivers			Cols. Guards 1861-65 SR: bur.10/21/1876

Sexton Records buried in this lot:

T.R. Shivers	*bur. 10/10/1889, 47 yrs.*

Lot 172, open lot

Mrs. Ann Eliza	Aug. 20, 187? age 80 yrs.	w/o T. J. Stevens, d/o David & Martha Coller? of Richmond Co., Ga.

1 adult grave marked w/granite stone at head

Lot 173, open lot

Katie Belle Whithurst	Oct. 1, 1894	Feb. 12, 1966	w/o Percy L. Munford

- 1900 Russell Co., AL Census: Jens T, Whithorst Sept 1866 AL AL Al, wife Ada Feb 1872 AL AL AL, dau Winnie L. Mar 1890 AL, dau Etta M. Mar 1892 AL, dau Katie B. Oct 1894 AL, dau Rube A. Dec 1897 AL and son Earl S. Sept 1899 AL.

Ada Modell Whithurst	1902	1921	SR:born 5/6/1902 SR:bur. 8/15/1921, 19
Ruby Whithurst	Dec. 20, 1898	May 23, 1988	
Bartley Whithurst	Oct. 22, 1793	June 11, 1856	s/o Laufer & Unity Whithurst

- 1850 Russell Co., AL Census: Bartley Whithurst 57 GA, Sarah 57 GA, Washington B. 26 GA, Francis M. (m) 24 GA, Osburn M. 18 GA, Georgia A. 13 GAand Augustus 18 GA.

1 baby slab w/marker, no dates or name

Lot 174, open lot

Maudant H. Bozeman	Oct. 9, 1880	Apr. 30, 1930	
Annie Lee Bozeman	Apr. 18, 1881	Sept. 25, 1935	
Annie Lucille Austin	Aug. 13, 1900	May 3, 1971	
W.V. Bozeman	Sept. 3, 1844 Muscogee Co., Ga.	? 24, 1904 Columbus, Ga.	C.S.A. (unable to read)

- 1900 Muscogee Census: W. V. Bozeman Mar 1844 GA NC GA and wife Mary E. May 1851 GA England G (m-35; 8/4 children).

- 1880 Muscogee Census: Van Bozeman 34 GA GA GA, wife Mary E. 27 GA GA GA, dau Florence 9 GA, dau Blanchard 7 GA, son Lee V. 5 GAand son Mordie 3 GA.

- 1870 Muscogee Census: William Agt. Bozeman 26 GA, Mary 17 GA, Florence 9/12 GA and John Wynn 15 GA.

- 1860 Muscogee Census: Wm A. Bozeman 51 NC, Mary E. 44? GA, Mary A. 24 GA, Jane A. 22 GA, John W. 21 GA, Sarah A. 18 GA, Ann V. 16 GA, William V. 14 GA, Martha A. 12 GA, Caroline 9 GA, James F. 7 GA, Georgia S. 4 GA and Pinkney B, 2 GA.

Leonard Hobbs	July 2, 1892	Feb. 1, 1896

Mary D. Clarke	Nov. 1, 1823	May 13, 1857	SR: bur 16 May 1857 age 34
Michael A. (sic) Clarke	Apr. 5, 1798	Sept. 25, 1858	SR: born London, England.

- 1840 Muscogee Census: Michael N. Clarke: 1 m 40-50, 1m 20-30, 1m 10-15, 2 m under 5, 1 f 50-60, 1 f 20-30, 1 f 15-20, 1 f 10-15 and 1 f under 5.

- 1850 Muscogee Census: M. N. Clark 53 England, Mrs. H. A. 36 GA, Jack D. 17 GA, Martha 13 GA, William 11 GA, Sarah I. 9 GA and Frederick T. 3 GA.

- Michael N. Clark and Miss Pamelia Hale were married 25 August 1832. *(The Columbus Enquirer.)*

- Michael N. Clarke married Milissi Hinton 17 Mar 1825 in Clarke Co., GA. *(Clark Co., GA Court of Ordinary Records.)*

Wm. Clark Bozeman	Oct. 10, 1906	Oct. 9, 1953

Sexton Records indicate buried in this lot:

Bessie Bozeman	*bur. 1/9/1896, 10 yrs.*
inf./o M.H. Bozeman	*bur.10/27/1918, s/b*

Lot 175, open lot

Edna E. Threlkeld	Mar. 7, 1867	May 15, 1920

- 1920 Muscogee Census: John Threlkeld 56 GA GA GA (wd) and sister Edna E. 52 GA GA GA.

- 1900 Muscogee Census: Nancy Threlkeld July 1834 GA GA GA (wd), son John W. Dec 1864 GA, dau Edna E. Mar 1872 GA, son William P.Oct 1875 GA and dau Jessie H. Oct. 1877 GA.

- 1870 Muscogee Census: John Threlkeld 39 GA, Delphini 36 GA, Mary 17 GA, Clara 13 GA, Cora 10 GA, Willis 6 GA, Edna 3 GA and Pope 7/12 GA.

- John Wiley Threlkeld, s/o John Willis Threlkeld (b. c1805-) and Louise Pope married Nancy Delphina Barden the d/o William Barden.

Fredonia V. Barden	Sept. 23, 1838	Apr. 25, 1887

- 1880 Muscogee Census: Wm S. Kennedy 23 GA Ire GA, wife Mary B. 43 GA GA GA, sister Fredonia Barden 42 GA GA GA, sister Eoleata Barden 39 GA GA GA, niece Eliza J. 19 GA GA PA, nephew Evans 10 GA GA PA and nephew Harry 6 GA GA PA.

- 1870 Muscogee Census: John W. Barden 41 GA, Helen R. 34 PA, Eliza J. 8 GA and Evans 8/12 GA.

- 1870 Muscogee Census: Fredonia Barden 30 GA is listed as Housekeeper in home of Frank Wilkins.

- 1860 Muscogee Census: Wm Y. Barden 57 GA, Mary A. 28 GA, Fredonia 21 GA, Eolita 19 GA and Virgelia (f) 17 GA.

- 1850 Muscogee Census: William Y. Barden 44 GA, John W. 21 GA, Mary A. 18 GA, Delphena 16 GA, Fredonia V. 11 GA, E. Oleatha 9 GA, V. Eliza 7 GA, A. G. Barden 47 GA and Martha 44 GA.

- Alfred G. Barden married Martha Harris 29 Sept 1825 in Columbia Co., GA.

4 children brick slabs, n/m

Lot 176, open lot

Ralph F. Williams	Oct. 15, 1898	Oct. 17, 1928
Kate Williams	Sept. 12, 1886	Dec. 21, 1934
Mary Osie Williams	May 25, 1903	Oct. 4, 1953
Charles W. Williams	Sept. 10, 1849	Dec. 6, 1919

- 1910 Muscogee Census: Charles W. Williams 62 GA GA GA, wife Ella V. 49 GA NC NC (M-33; 10/6 children), dau Marna L. 21 GA, son Albert C. 19 GA, dau Flo M. 14 AL, son Andrew R. 10 AL, son Frank R. 9 AL, SIL C___W. Corley 24 GA GA GA and dau Catherine B. 23 GA (m-3; 1/0 children)

- 1900 Lee Co., AL Census: Charles W. Williams Sept 1850 AL GA GA, Wife Ella V. Sept 1861 AL GA GA (M-28; 5/5 children), dau Katie Sept 1886 AL, son Warner L. Mar 1888, son Albert Apr 1890 AL, dau Ida Mae Aug 1894 AL and son Ralph Oct 1898 AL.

Ella V. Williams	Sept. 6, 1861	June 21, 1946
Charles Albert Williams	Mar. 9, 1891	Sept. 25, 1958

Lot 177, fenced lot, no name

Inf.		Nov. 25, 1862	d/o Peyton H. & Julia T. Colquitt
Peyton H. Colquitt	Campbell Co., Ga.	Sept. 21, 1863 near Ringgold, Ga. in battle of Chickamuga	Age 31 yrs 11 mo 14 dy

- 1850 Orange Co., NY Census: at US Military Academy, West Point – Peyton H. Colquitt 18 GA.

- Gen. Peyton H. Colquitt,, born 7 Oct 1832, was killed in the battle of Chickamauga. A monument commemorating his bravery and heroism has been erected by the Government on the spot where he died. He was the s/o Walter Terry Colquitt (1799-1855) and his first wife, Nancy Hill Lane (d. 1840, the d/o Joseph Lane & Elizabeth Hill.). Peyton married Julia Flournoy Hurt 24 Oct 1861 in Muscogee Co.

Julia Flournoy Jordan	June 13, 1842	Dec. 30, 1891	Only child of Joel Early & Fannie Hurt

- Atlanta Constitution 6 July 1890. The Wives of Some Georgians. No American beauty has ever received more adulation in foreign court circles than the wife of Mr. Lee Jordan of Albany. Mrs. Jordan was Miss Julia Hurt. She first married Col. Peyton H. Colquitt , the handsome and brilliant and and brave soldier who was killed at the Battle of Chickamauga. After her marriage to Mr. Jordan they lived abroad for several years, and in Paris she was feted by the Emporer Napolean who pronounced her the most handsome woman that he had ever seen…Mr & Mrs Jordan have a winter home near Albany, a summer home in Macon and are building an elegant mansion in Atlanta.

Frances Flournoy	Aug. 21, 1821 Putnam Co., Ga.	Mar. 20, 1899 Columbus, Ga.	w/o Joel Early Hurt

- Obit: Francis "Fannie" Flournoy was born in Eatonton, daughter of Josiah amd Martha

D. Flournoy, married Joel Early Hurt in Eatonton, Sisters Mrs. Caroline Bass of Rome, GA; Mrs. Lizzie Brecham of Oxford, GA; and Mrs. Martha Adams of Columbus, GA.

Frances Hurt Adams   Dec. 5, 1940

Joel Early Hurt   Jan. 1, 1821   May 19, 1865
Putnam Co., Ga.

- 1860 Muscogee Co. Census: Joel E. Hurt 40 GA, Francis (sic) 38 GA and Julia 17 GA.

- 1850 Muscogee Co. Census: Joel E. Hurt 29 Putnam, Frances 27 Putnam, Julia 8 Putnam, Rebecca 12 Hancock and Louisa 6 -?.

- s/o Joel Hurt and Martha Herndon. He married Frances Flournoy 28 Jan 1841 in Putnam Co., GA.

Henry Hurt   Apr. 11, 1857   Nov. 5, 1901

Geo. Troup Hurt   Oct. 8, 1825   Dec. 11, 1901

- Atlanta Constitution 12 Dec 1901. George T. Hurt Dead. George Troup Hurt died at the home of his son-in-law F. W. Akers yesterday. He was 77 years old and a long time resident of this city. He is survived by two daughters and one son; Mrs. Frank Akers of Atlanta, Mrs. Judge Lawton Miller of Macon and Dr. J. W. Hurt of Atlanta.

- s/o Joel Hurt and Martha Herndon.

Nancy J. Flewellen	Aug. 23, 1865	Age 33 yrs 11 mo 27 dy
Edgar Flewellen Hurt	Apr. ?, 1861	One slab (very hard to read).

- Nancy J. Flewellen was born 27 Aug 1831, the d/o Dr. Abner H. Flewellen (1800-1849) and his first wife, Nancy Jones (1802-1832).

Sarah, inf.   Oct. 12, 1853   Oct. 20, 1853   d/o A.F. & A.E. Hurt

- d/o Augustus F. Hurt (1830-1921, s/o Joel Hurt and Martha Herndon) and Ann Eliza Freeman (1831-1903, d/o James & Sarah Freeman).

John Franklin, inf.   Apr. 26, 1858   June 24, 1858   s/o J.W. & S.M. Hurt

Martha   Nov. 2, 1789   July 3, 1862   w/o Joel Hurt, d/o Reubin Herndon

Joel Hurt   Mar. 9, 1783   Jan. 4, 1843   Age 60 yrs. (one slab)

- Joel Hurt was the s/o William Hurt (1756-1812, s/o Joel & Hannah Hurt) and his first wife, Priscilla Yancey (c1757-1790, the d/o Jeconias Yancey and Hannah Kimbrough).

Annie   Sept. 20, 1857   June 10, 1864   d/o Joseph G. & Maria L. Blount

- 1860 Cherokee Co., AL Census: Joseph G. Blount 27 GA, Maria L. 23 GA and Anna F. 2GA.

1 adult brick slab, n/m

Lot 178, no name on wall

Andrew Wesley Hill   1860   1901   SR:bur.8/4/1901, 40

- 1900 Muscogee Census: Andrew W. Hill June 1860 GA GA GA, wife Emma Sept 1860 AL AL SC (m-15; 8/6 children), dau Maud July 1884 GA, son Velma Dec 1897 GA, dau Carrie Jan 1890 GA, dau Nellie Jan 1893 GA, son Hoyle July 1895 GAand dau Nora

Mar 1897 GA.

- Andrew W. Hill married Emma A. Whatley 24 Dec 1879 in Troup Co., GA.

Emma Angeline Hill	1861	1918	SR:born 9/6/1861
			SR:bur. 10/26/1918, 57

Andrew Wesley Hill, Jr.	July 6, 1901	Dec. 7, 1965
Nellie Hill Carter	Jan. 1, 1893	Dec. 7, 1965
Mary Angeline Dolan	b&d May 8, 1927	

Sexton Records indicate buried in this lot:

Albert S. Hill	*bur. 7/9/1887, 14 mo.*
V.D. Hill	*bur. 3/31/1907, 19 yrs.*

Lot 179, Attaway on wall

Sarah Attaway	Sept. 18, 1800	Dec. 2, 1882

- 1880 Muscogee Census: E. C. (f) Attaway 52 GA GA GA, mother Sarah Attaway 80 GA GA GA (wd), sister J. M. 54 GA GA GA. brother C. M. 43 GA GA GA and SIL Fannie Graves 45 (B) GA GA GA

- 1870 Muscogee Census: Charles Barrow 41 GA, Jane Attaway 45 AL, and Caroline Attaway 42 SC.

- 1870 Baldwin Co., GA Census: Sarah Attaway 70 NC, Sarah 35 GA and Emma 14 GA.

- 1860 Baldwin Co., GA Census: Isaac Attaway 65 SC, Sarah 50 TN, Chesley W. 26 GA, Sarah 24 GA and Emma 4 GA.

- 1850 Baldwin Co., GA Census: Isaac Attaway 55 GA, Sarah 50 GA, Chesley 14 GA, Jane 25 GA and Caroline 22 GA.

- Sarah Attaway was born in Rutherford Co., NC, the d/o Edward and Sarah Reeves. Her date and place of marriage is not currently known. They were in Hall Co., GA in 1830. In 1840 they were residing in Hall County Georgia District 545. Sarah shows as head of household. Isaac was possibly on a trip to Lafayette Louisiana to settle a piece of property left to her by her brother Joseph. The land was purchased by her brother Edmond Reeves. [99]

  1870 Mortality Index page 6 a line 26 Isaac Attaway Sept 1869, Kidney Affection, Retired Gambler.

Caroline E. Attaway	Dec. 1, 1827	Sept. 14, 1883
Chesley M. Attaway	July 4, 1833	Aug. 14, 1883

- The Atlanta Consitution 15 Aug 1883.
  Columbus Georgia, Special. Columbus August 14. While fishing in the river opposite No 1 rock at the foot of St Clair Street early this morning C.M. Attaway fell forward in an epiliptic(sic) fit. He fell forward in a bowl of water in the rock and no help being at hand he was drowned in little more than a gallon of water. When discovered he was dead.

Mary Jane Attaway	Nov. 10, 1824	Aug. 14, 1887

Lot 180, no name on wall

Melissa A. Sparks	Feb. 7, 1843	Apr. 7, 1884	w/o Dr. E.B. Schley

- 1860 Talbot Co., GA Census: McCurdy Sparks 45 GA, Penelope T. 47 GA, Melissa 17 GA, Susan P. 15 GA and McCurdy Jr. 7 GA.

- McCurdy Sparks married Penelope Milner 19 Nov 1835 in Jones Co., GA.

- Melissa Sparks married Edward B. Schley 9 Jan 1866.[100]

Louis Hamlin	Feb. 26, 1888	June 25, 1888	Inf. s/o J.H. & Pet. H. Whittlesey
Emily Ann Schley Whittlesey	1825	1883	SR:bur.10/19/1883, 58 yrs.
Jaberis Hamlin Whittlesey	1818	1868	SR:bur.10/26/1868

Dr. City Physician |

- 1860 Marion Co., GA Census: Jabez H. Whittlesey 42 CT, Emily A. 35 GA, Frances S. 10 GA, Hamlin 6 GA, Sarah 5 GA, Anna M. 1 GA, Edward B. Schley 22 GA and Philip T. Schley 19 GA.

Philip Thomas Schley	1798	1862	

- 1860 Chatham Co., GA Census: Philip T. Schley 60 Jefferson Co., GA and George 14 Muscogee Co., GA.

- 1850 Muscogee Census: Philip T. Schley 57 GA, Frances V. 42 GA, Anna M. 20 GA, Frances 18 GA, Rebecca J. 17 GA, Edward B. 12 GA, Philip T. 9 GA and George 3 GA.

- Phillip T. Schley married Frances V. L. Brooking 8 July 1824 in Hancock Co., GA. He was born in Maryland. His father was John Jacob. Schley a native of Germany.[101] Another source states that John Jacob Schley was the son of John Thomas Schley (1712-1780) who was the emigrant ancestor.[102]

Francis Vivian Brooking Schley	1808	1852	SR:d. June 19, 1852, 44
Rebecca Jackson Schley Whittlesey	1833	1870	

- Rebecca J. Schley married Joseph P. Whittlesey 27 Mar 1853 in Muscogee Co.

Wm. Henry Whittlesey			No dates (baby).
Maggie Lou		d. Mar. 13, 1896 3 yr 3 mo 15 dy	d/o F.P. & M.A. Whittlesey
Cornelius		d. July 9, 1852 7 mo 20 days	s/o Jabez H. & Emily A. Whittlesey
Frances Schley Ford	Mar. 28, 1850	Apr. 7, 1942	w/o Leroy Sutherland Ford
Joseph Whittlesey	1829	1862	

- 1860 Harris Co., GA Census: Joseph Whittlesey 30 CT, R. J. (f) 26 GA, F. L. (f) 6 GA, J. P. (m) 4 GA, E. S. (m) 2 GA and ?. E. 2 (f) 2/12 GA.

Lot 181, no name on wall

Maj. Dozier Thornton   Oct. 24, 1801   June 10, 1860

- 1860 Cherokee Co., AL Census: Dozier Thornton 58 GA and Ann C. 56 SC.

- 1850 Muscogee Census: Dozier Thornton 49 Elbert Co., GA, Ann 47 Elbert Co., GA and Rett L. 11 Columbus, GA.

- s/o Joseph Thornton (1777-1848, the s/o Rev. Dozier Thornton c1755-1843 and his first wife Lucinda Elizabeth Hill) and Elizabeth Allen (1779-1845, the d/o Nathaniel Allen c1750-1812 and Permelia Hudson b. c1758).

Ann Caroline Early   Jan. 26, 1861   w/o Maj. Dozier Thornton
                                       age 60

Emma L. Kyle   Mar. 27, 1864   Oct. 2, 1873
                             Columbus, Ga.   Gadsden, Ala.

- 1870 Gadsden, Etowah Co., AL Census: R. B. Kyle 44 NC, Mary V. 34 GA, Mary A. 15 AL, Nina 11 GA, Emma L. 6 GA, Stonewall 4 AL and Joseph 2 AL.

- 1860 Cherokee Co., AL Census: Robt B. 34 NC, Mary V. 26 GA, Benj. A 12 LA, Mary A. 5 Al, Jennie J. 2 AL and Cornelia A. 1 AL.

- Robert Benjamin Kyle married Mary A. Thornton, d/o Dozier Thornton on 5 Dec 1848 in Muscogee Co. He then married Mary V. Nuckolls, d/o Nathaniel Nuckolls and Louisiana Hawkins Thornton (sister of Maj. Dozier Thornton) on 2 Oct 1856 in Muscogee Co.

Eva Theresa Kyle   Apr. 18, 1869   Oct. 18, 1869
                            Gadsden, Ala.   6 months

James Nat Kyle   Dec. 15, 1860   Sept. 24, 1864
                                      3 yr 9 mo 9 d

Roberta E. Kyle   July 5, 1862   Aug. 2, 1863
                                      12 mo 28 d

Jennie J. Kyle   Aug. 2, 1857   Dec. 23, 1861
                                      4 yr 4 mo

Mary Allen   Dec. 6, 1829   Mar. 12, 1855   w/o Robert B. Kyle

Robert Dozier   Nov. 7, 1855   s/o Robert A. & Mary A. Kyle
                                      9 mo 11 d

Virginia Foster   Mar. 9, 1876   Feb. 7, 1928   w/o William W. Hunt

William W. Hunt   Feb. 19, 1872   Dec. 18, 1946

- 1930 Muscogee Census: William W. Hunt 58 GA GA GA (wd) and son Alek K. Hunt 10 GA GA AL.

- Virginia Foster was the d/o Mary A. Kyle (c1855-1892) and Marcellus L. Foster (1850-1933).

Lot 182, open lot

John W. Howell   May 9, 1849   Dec. 3, 1882

Columbus, Ga.

- 1870 Muscogee Census: Jordan Howell 46 NC, Elizabeth 43 GA, John W. 21 GA, Charles J. 19 GA, Lizzie 17 GA, Lucy 7 GA, Lula 13 GA, Lawrence 3 GA and Jose 1 GA.

- 1860 Muscogee Census: Jordan L. Howell 35 NC, Elizabeth 32 GA, Edward W. 12 GA, John W. 11 GA, Charles J. 9 GA, Elizabeth J. 6 GA, Lula 3 GA, Amenia 1 GA and Charles E. Johnson 42 PA.

- 1850 Muscogee Census: Jordan L. Howell 26 NC, Mrs. E. 22 GA, Edward 2 GA, John W. 1 GA and Mrs. M. H. Robinson 78 England.

- Jordan L. Howell married Elizabeth S. Johnson 24 Nov 1846 in Muscogee Co.

1 child grave, marked w/ granite at head & foot.

Lot 183, no name on wall

Newell K. Bowden	Nov. 26, 1876	Sept. 15, 1921	
Carrie Love Hamer	July 18, 1874	May 4, 1909	w/o N.K. Bowden
Sarah Lula Hamer	Jan. 15, 1872	Nov. 8, 1908	w/o Toombs Ellison
Susie Lee Hamer	Jan. 26, 1880	Oct. 21, 1913	w/o E.B. King
Frances Parker Hamer	Apr. 6, 1851	Feb. 18, 1920	
George W. Hamer	May 11, 1848	June 6, 1923	

- 1920 Muscogee Census: George W. Hamer 71 GA SC GA, wife Fannie 68 GA GA GA, son Thomas Z. 49 GA, son Gordon 31 GA, dau Eva 27 GA, SIL B. Forest Johnson 22 GA GA GA and dau Frances 22 GA.

- 1900 Muscogee Census: G. W. Hamer May 1849 GA SC GA, wife Fannie Apr 1852 GA GA GA (M-30; 8/8 children), dau Love July 1877 GA, son T. J. Apr 1878 GA, dau Susie Jan 1881, son Stanford Aug 1884 GA, son Gorden Apr 1887 GA, dau Eva June 1890 GA and dau Fannie Jan 1894 GA.

- 1880 Muscogee Census: George Hamer 33 GA GA GA, wife Fannie 31 GA AG GA, dau Lula 9 GA, dau Lou 6 GA, son Thomas 4 GA and dau Susie 5/12 GA.

- 1870 Muscogee Census: George Hamer 22 GA, Mary 58 GA, Charles 18 GA, Alonzo 17 GA and Elizabeth 12 GA.

- 1850 Harris Co., GA Census: John Hamer 34 SC, Mary 35 GA, Thomas 18 GA, Martha A. 15 GA, Nancy 14 GA, Caroline 11 GA, William 8 GA, Colen 6 GA, Henry 4 GA and George W. 2 GA.

- George W. Hamer married Frances M. Parker 11 Dec 1870 in Muscogee Co.

Lot 184, no name on wall

Alvira Virginia	Jan. 26, 1826	Feb. 6, 1860	w/o J.D. Williford
			d/o Martin & Matilda Brooks

- 1850 Muscogee Census: James D. Williford 27 GA, Mrs. A. V. 23 GA, Adona 5 GA,

Amoret 3 GA, infant (m) 1/12 GA and Josephine M. Brooks 17 FL.

Matthew	May 1852 3 y 2 wks 5 d	s/o A.V. Williford
Amoret Williford	Dec. 3, 1936 (only date)	SR: 90 years old

- 1870 Tallapoosa Co., AL Census: James Williford 46 GA, Amoret 18 GA, Melodia 16 GA and James 14 GA.

- Atlanta Constitution 18 Dec 1900. J. D. Williford Tuscaloosa, AL. Columbus, GA Dec. 17th Special. J. D. Williford, formerly of this city died at Tuscaloosa, AL Friday and buried yesterday at Union Springs. He was a brother of Mrs. T. G. Coleman and Miss Amoret Williford of Columbus.

- Mrs. B. F, Coleman was a sister to two well-remembered teachers, Miss Josephine Brooks and Miss Amoret Williford.[103]

2 adult brick slabs, n/m

Sexton Records indicate buried in this lot:

Ladina Williford	*bur. 11/10/1875, 22yrs.*
J.D. Williford	*bur. 12/6/1884*

Lot 185, open lot

Mary Ella Godfrey	June 8, 1861	June 12, 1941

Lot 186, Perry on wall

James B. Shores	Feb. 24, 1872	Mar. 31, 1951	
Emma Hannah	July 10, 1875		w/o J.B. Shores
Lillian Shores Killan	Feb. 20, 1899	July 5, 1979	
Karl Duport Perry	May 18, 1893	Jan. 11, 1970	
Myrtie Shores Perry	Nov. 1, 1894	Sept. 14, 1970	

Lot 187, Schaffer-McKeen on wall

William H. Schaffer	1900	1979	SR:bur. 9/18/1979
Margaret B. Schaffer	1900	1985	SR:born 1/31/1900
			SR:bur. 3/1/1985, 85 yrs.

- Margaret Bryan Bullock was the d/o Osborn Cody Bullock (1852-1929) and Minnie Drane (1857-1937). She married 1) William Cloyd McKee (s/o Lee J. Bourke McKee and Florence Belle Mahone) on 2 Nov 1921 and 2) William H. Schaffer.

William Cloyd McKee	Dec. 18, 1895	Nov. 4, 1937

Lot 188, no name on wall

John Neal Griggs			Age 9 months
Mary Louise Griggs		d. Mar. 23, 1940	d/o Wm. M. Griggs & Eliz. Henry Griggs
Elizabeth Britt	Aug. 25, 1831	Jan. 19, 1893	d/o Col. Benj. & Ann M. Henry
			w/o Wm. M. Griggs
Wm. Maxwell	Aug. 6, 1832	Oct. 24, 1896	s/o Wm. & Louise C. Maxwell Griggs
Elizabeth Henry Griggs		d. Apr. 23, 1947	d/o Wm. M. Griggs & Eliz Henry Griggs
Lila H. Griggs		d. Dec. 28, 1928	d/o Wm. M. & Eliz Henry Griggs

- William Maxwell Griggs, s/o Judge William & Louise C. Griggs, was born 8/6/1832; married Elizabeth Henry. He died 10/23/1897. She died 6/19/1893. Their children: Mary Louise, Tallulah Haseltine (sic), James Fenemore C., Ann Eliza (sic), Elizabeth Britt, Lillie Howard, Cordelia Hill and Sarah Outlaw Griggs. Mary Persiana Griggs (born 4 Jan 1834, sister to William Maxwell Griggs, married John H. Neal 20 May 1852.[104]

1 adult brick slab, n/m   1 baby brick slab, n/m

Lot 189, no name on wall

Sarah Elizabeth Woomack	Nov. 26, 1840	Aug. 1872
Robert A. Outler	Aug. 30, 1848	Mar. 29, 1905

- 1900 Lee Co., AL Census: Robert A. Outler Aug 1848 GA GA VA and wife Elizabeth Aug 1847 GA GA GA (m-28; 1/1 children).

- 1880 Muscogee Census: Robert Outer 31 GA GA GA, wife Elizabeth 30 GA SC SC, dau Mary 7 AL and dau Pearl 3 AL.

- 1870 Muscogee Census: Mary Ohtter 50 SC, Louisa 23 GA, Robert 21 GA, Demarius Phillips 19 GA and Sarah Pready 24 GA.

Elizabeth Lamb Outler	SR:bur.1/19/192 7, 77 yrs.	No dates, w/o Robert A. Outler
Acie		Age 7
David		Age 3, s/o Sarah Eliz. Woomack

Lot 190, fenced lot, no name

Mrs. J. Anne Venning		Mar. 12, 1859	Consort of Nicholas

Mary C. Fishburne		July 19, 1915	w/o John Riggs Hull

- 1860 Muscogee Census: John R. Hull 40 NY, Mary C. 26 LA, Herbert L. 5 AL, Anna A. 3 GA, Jennie E. Briggs 14 MO, Anna L. 17 MO, E. B. (m) 21 MO, Susan 16 MO, Charles Mygatt 50 NY, Bill Measels 40 GA, Wm Marinian 20 Al and unreadable male.

- John Riggs Hull was the s/o Col. Elias Hull (1786 Bethlehem, CT-1865 Columbus, GA) and Anna Riggs of Lyons, NY. He married Mary C. Fishburne about 1852 and died 1870. Mary Fishburne was the d/o Gen. Benjamin Fishburne of Charleston, SC. Children: Herbert L. Hull married 1881 Sarah J. Benning, Anna Augusta m. 1893 Herbert Mason, John M. Hull d. 1865, Edmund E. married Margaret Reiley, Walter Bacon married 1886 Rhoda E. Hubert and Elliot Clay Hull.[105]

Walter Bacon Hull	Jan. 12, 1863	Oct. 3, 1922	s/o Mary Clay Fishburne & John Riggs Hull
Ruth Rhoda Hull Arechavala Lummus	Oct. 8, 1892	July 24, 1966	w/o Kenneth Oscoe Lummus
Herbert Ladson Hull	Aug. 27, 1854	Jan. 12, 1929	s/o Mary Clay Fishburne & John Riggs Hull
Herbert Ladson Hull	Mar. 14, 1882	Mar. 29, 1975	s/o Herbert Ladson Hull & Sallie Benning, g/son of Gen. Henry Lewis Benning
Benning Hull	June 2, 1884	Feb. 7, 1968	s/o Herbert Ladson Hull & Sallie Benning, g/son of Gen. Henry Lewis Benning

Lot 191, fenced lot, no name

Rev. Josiah Evans	1788	Dec. 17, 1856

- 1850 Russell Co., AL Census: Josiah Evans 62 GA, Denson (f) 40 GA, Caroline 16 GA, Josiah 14 GA, Camden 12 GA, Julia 9 GA, Adaline 9 GA, Ann 3 GA and Georgia 1 AL.

- 1860 Russell Co., AL Census: Susan O. Evans 49 GA, Caroline E. Guerry 27 GA, Josiah Evans 23 GA, Julia K. Evans 18 GA, Adaline Evans 14 GA, Hannah P. Evans 12 GA and Georgia T. Evans 12 AL.

- Josiah Evans married Mary Denson 15 Jan 1818 in Madison Co., AL. He married Susan D. Garvin 5 May 1832 in Camden Co., GA.

My Julia	Aug. 26, 1812	Oct. 30, 1878

1 adult brick slab, n/m   2 children brick slabs, n/m

Lot 192, E.W. Buchanan on wall

Hugh Buchanan	No dates. SR:bur.6/22/1925, 49 yrs.

- WWI Draft Registration: Hugh Oscar Buchanan born 9 Mar 1876, wife Rosa Lee Buchanan.

- 1910 Muscogee Census: Hugh O. Buchannan 36 GA GA GA, wife Rosa L. 29 GA GA GA (m-8; 0/0 children) MIL Emlie Hagler 64 GA GA GA(wd; 4/3 children).

Lot 193, Farr on wall

| J. H. C. Farr | Mar. 30, 1842 | July 29, 1913 | A veteran. |

- Civil War Records: John Henry Clay Farr enlisted as a Private on 22 February 1862. Enlisted in Company G, 20th Infantry Regiment Georgia on 22 February 1862. Wounded on 19 September 1863 at Chickamauga, GA. Wounded on 06 May 1864 at Wilderness, VA. Surrendered Company G, 20th Infantry Regiment Georgia on 09 April 1865 in Appomattox Court House, VA. He received a Distinguished Service award.

- Born in Harris Co., GA, the s/o Tilman Farr (1809-1888) and Mary Armstrong (1811-1890). He married Celesta Amanda Jones 17 Jan 1881 in Chattahoochee Co., GA, the d/o Willis and Mary Florence Jones. They had 4 ch.: Mary Pearl, Ethel, Lula Belle, Tilman Jones.[106]

| Celestina C. Jones | Sept. 18, 1851 | Nov. 3, 1913 | w/o J.H.C. Farr |

Lot 194, Davidson on wall

| J. W. T. Davidson | 1860 | 1886 | |

Lot 195, open lot

| Barbara Ann Chadrick | Jan. 8, 1833 | Nov. 25, 1856 | w/o John McGovern |

Lot 196, open lot

Annie J. Brady	1869	1920	SR:bur.2/10/1920
A.B. Zeigler	1877	1922	
John Brady	Killabeye Co., Danegal, Ireland	Dec. 25, 1887 Columbus, Ga.	

- 1880 Muscogee Census: Wm Bynes 26 NJ NJ NJ, wife Mary 23 GA Ire Ire, son Wm 2 GA, dau Susie 6/12 GA, FIL John Brady 60 Ire Ire Ire, dau Nellie Brady 10 GA, dau Bridget Brady 8 GA and dau Julia Brady 6 GA.

3 adult brick slabs, n/m

Sexton Records indicate buried in this lot:

| *Hattie F. Brady* | | | *bur. 12/14/1922, 55 yrs.* |
| *Briget Brady* | | | *bur. 4/25/1898, 63 yrs.* |

Lot 197, no name on wall

| Racheal Bennett | Feb. 26, 1793 Scriven Co., Ga. | Feb. 19, 1885 Columbus, Ga. | d/o Benj. & Susannah Dayle |

- 1880 Muscogee Census: Rachel Bennett 86 GA GA GA.

- 1870 Muscogee Census: Rachael Bennett 76 GA.

- Benjamin Daly married Susannah Garnet6 Jan 1774 in Effingham Co., GA.

Elvira Caroline	June 18, 1808	Oct. 17, 1857	w/o Elisha Bowen, M.D.

- 1950 Muscogee Census: Elisha Bowen 30 VT, Elvira 40 Scriven, Eliza Bird 12 Cols GA and Elvira C. Bowen 2 Cols GA.

- Elvira C. Daly married Robert Bevill 8 Oct 1835 in Screven Co., GA. Elisha Bowen married Alvira C. Bevill 17 Jan 1844 in Muscogee Co., GA. Robert Benjamin Bevill married 1)Frances Williams 8 Oct. 1829. He was the s/o Claiborn Bevill (1781-1852) and Susannah Daly (b. c1784) who were married 15 May 1802 at Jerusalem Luthern Church in Ebenezer, GA. This Suzanna Daly was also a d/o Benjamin Daly (born c1750 SC) and Susannah Garnet. (Note: for people researching this line, check Ebenezer Church records.)

- Elisha Chandler Bowen was born 22 April 1820 in Reading, VT, the s/o Elisha Bowen (1779 CT-1853 VT and Frances Chandler Morris 1787 MA-1863 VT who were married 20 Oct 1806 in Hampden Co., MA.[107]

Elvira	May 26, 1847	Sept. 13, 1863	d/o E.C. & Elvira A. Bowen
Eliz. D.	Mar. 1832	Oct. 4, 1837? (unable to read)	d/o ? (unable to read)

Lot 198, open lot

Mary Murray	Tuarn Co., Galway, Ireland	Sept. 4, 1859 Columbus, Ga.	w/o John McGoff
Stephen McLaughin		Mar. 28, 1882 64 yrs.	A native of Galway, Ireland

- 1880 Muscogee Census: S. Mclaughlin 60 Ireland, Ireland, Ireland.

- 1870 Muscogee Census: S. Mcloughlin 50 Ireland

Lot 199, Reinschmidt on wall

Maggie Dodd	Aug. 4, 1866	Dec. 8, 1899	w/o Dan Y Reinschmidt
Rose Ellen Dodd	Nov. 21, 1858	May 8, 1939	w/o Abraham Skotzky

- 1930 Muscogee Census: Rosa L. Skotzky 69 GA GA NY (wd), dau Louise Anderson 34 GA GA GA (wd), GD Margurite 9 GA GA GA and son John D. Skotzky 25 GA GA GA.

- 1920 Muscogee Census: Rosa Skitzky 59 GA Germany GA (wd), son Louis 38 GA Ger GA, son Arthur 29 GA, son Albert 24 GAson Phillip 20 GA, dau Annie 31 GA, dau Louise 26 GA, dau Margarette 23 GA, son John 14 GA, DIL Myrtle 31 GA GA GA and DIL Bertha 25 SC VA VA.

John D. Reinschmidt	Dec. 2, 1899	Nov. 14, 1900	w/o Dan J. & Maggie Reinschmidt
Philip L. Skotzky	Jan. 18, 1900	Jan. 25, 1927	

1 adult grave, stones at head and foot   3 adult brick slabs, n/m

Lot 200, no name on wall

B.L. Johnson	Jan. 30, 1849	Nov. 15, 1900	

- 1870 Bullock Co., AL Census in HH of Paschal Baker, Berry Johnson 21 GA.
- 1850 Coweta Co., GA Census: Wm P. Johnson 18 SC, Sophiah 19 GA and Berry L. 1 GA.

Lillian Zula Smith	July 4, 1866	Jan. 15, 1949	w/o Berry L. Johnson

- 1880 Bullock Co., AL Census: William Smith 60 NC NC NC, wife Sarah 46 GA NC GA, son Joseph 22 AL, son Price 18 AL, son John 15 AL, dau Zula 13 AL, dau Tempy 11 AL, son Wesley 9 AL, dau Sarah 5 AL and son Walter 2 AL.

Wm. L. Johnson	1889	1959	SR:bur.12/19/1959, 70 yrs.
Wm. L. Johnson, Jr.	1919	1972	SR:bur.4/22/1972, 52 yrs.

Lot 201, Clark on wall

James J. Clark	Aug. 4, 1862	Oct. 7, 1885	
Lucy Clark	Dec. 12, 1876	Mar. 23, 1958	w/o C.N. Overby
C.N. Overby	1872	1929	SR:bur.1/18/1929, 56 yrs.
Geo	Apr. 15, 1900	May 24, 1901	Inf. s/o C.N. & L. Overby
Edward R. Clark	1867	1945	SR:bur.1/9/1945
Geo. R. Clark	Mar. 24, 1836	May 10, 1913	

- 1900 Muscogee Census: Geo R. Clark Mar 1836 GA GA GA, wife Rhoda A. June 1839 AL GA GA (m-39; 10/9 children), son Edward R. Apr 1867 GA, dau Lilliam Mar 1869 GA, dau Mary B. July 1873 GA, dau Annie Oct 1878 and son Fletcher July 1882.
- 1880 Muscogee Census: Geo R. Clark 41 GA GA GA, Mrs. Rhoda 41, son Jas. J. 18, son Benj L. 16 GA, dau Miss Emma 13 GA, son Edd 12 GA, dau Lillian 11 GA, son Jno 9 GAdau Lucy 4 and Annie 2.
- 1860 Muscogee Census: George Clark 24 GA and Peyton Johnson 20 GA.
- 1850 Muscogee Census: Benjamin W. Clark 41 VA, Sarah A. 21 Putnam GA, Ann E. Upson GA, Mary P. 14 Upson GA, Geo R. 13 Upson GA, Benjamin A. 11 Upson GA, Thomas S. 9 Upson GA and Sarah D.? 2 Muscogee GA.
- George R. Clark married Rhoda A. Odom 5 June 1861 in Muscogee Co., GA.

Emma Clark	June 4, 1866	Feb. 12, 1951	w/o Philip Sapp
Rhoda A. Clark	June 19, 1839	Oct. 16, 1901	

- 1860 Muscogee Census: Andrew J. Odom 39 GA, Ann E. 29 GA, Fanny E. 10 GA, Rhoda 24 GA and Emily G. AL.
- 1850 Muscogee Census: Jackson Odum (sic) 28 Washington, Ann 26 Green GA, Julius W. 2 AL, Frances E. 10/12 Muscogee Co., Rhoda 11 Muscogee Co. and Daniel Odum

21 Muscogee.

1 adult brick slab, n/m

Lot 202, no name on wall

2 adult brick slabs, n/m

Lot 203, open lot

James F. Lynah	Sept. 9, 1865 10 yrs. 5 m 16 d	
Gracy H.	Sept. 18, 1857 36 yrs.	w/o James Lynah

- 1860 Muscogee Census: James Lynah 46 Ireland and James P. 5 NY.
- 1850 Muscogee Census: James Lynah 35 Ireland.

Lot 204, open lot

John Robby	Ireland	Mar. 1874	C.S.A. SR:bur.3/23/1874, 50 yrs.

- 1870 Muscogee Census: John Robb 40 Ireland (day Laborer in HH of Joseph Kyle).

1 adult grave, marked w/granite stone

Lot 205, open lot

Headstone toppled, unable to read.

Lot 206, no name on wall

Frank Hudson	Aug. 29, 1862	Mar. 6, 1901
W. F. Hudson	Dec. 3, 1840	May 20, 1906

- 1900 Muscogee Census: Wm F. Hudson Dec 1840 GA GA NC, wife Eliza J. Dec 1840 GA GA SC m-40; 11/6 children), dau Sarah A. June 1876 GA, dau Willie A. Sept 1879, dau Elizabeth M. Barber Nov 1881 AL (m-2), son Jas T. Hudson Apr 1886 GA, GrS Clifford E. Steadman Nov 1890 GA SC GA and GrD Buhler E. Steadman Apr 1893 GA SC GA.

- 1880 Russell Co., AL Census: William Hudson 36 GA – NC, wife Eliza 34 GA GA SC, son Frank C. 17 GA, dau Beulah 13 GA, dau Eugenia 11 GA, dau Sallie 6 GA, dau Mary Lu 4 GA and dau Willie 2 GA.

- 1870 Muscogee Census: William F. Hudson 29 GA, Eliza J. 23 GA, Franklin 8 GA and

Beaulah 3 GA.

Beulah Steadaman	Aug. 9, 1866	1899	SR:bur.7/13/1899
Mary Dixon	Nov. 9, 1875	1898	SR:bur.3/28/1898, 22
Linda S. Watley	Sept. 19, 1948	Sept. 26, 1948	
Eliza Hudson	1846	1917	

Sexton Records indicate buried in this lot:

Mary J. Hudson   *bur. 9/13/1897, 84 yrs.*

INDEX

SOURCES

---

[1] Memoirs of Georgia,, Vol. 2, (The Southern Historical Society, Atlanta, GA 1895), 33-34.

[2] Harris Co., GA Marriage Records.

[3] Wilkes Co., GA Marriage Records.

4 Muscogee Co., GA WB A P. 94-96.

5 Boykin Bible. In possession of Mrs. Thomas Whitner, Atlanta, Ga. On the fly leaf is inscribed, "To sister Emily from Sam and Laura, April 16, 1861."

6 Muscogee Co., GA Marriage Records.

[7] Talcott, Alvan and Ricker, Jacquelyn., Families of Early Guilford, CT, Vol. 1, Bowen and Bradley Families, (Genealogical Publishing Company; Reprint edition, October 1997) 140.

[8] Muscogee Co., GA Marriage Records.

[9] Worsley, Etta Blanchard, Columbus on the Chattahoochee, (Columbus Office Supply, Columbus, GA, 1951) 561.

[10] Macon Co., AL Marriage Records.

[11] Sumter Co., AL Marriage Records.

[12] Laurens Co., SC Will Book E:530.

[13] Holcomb,Brent H., Southern Christian Advocate Death and Obituary Notices, 1867-1878., (Columbia, SC 1993), SCMAR, http://www.ancestry.com.

[14] Nottingham, Carolyn Walker, History of Upson County, Georgia, (Macon, Ga.: Press of J.W. Burke Co. 1930) 894-896.

[15] Yelverton, Lois, The Battle Book, a genealogy of the Battle family in America, (Paragon Press, Montgomery, AL, 1930) 636.

[16] Atlanta Constitution, Atlanta, GA, 18 Dec 1884.

[17] Putnam Co., GA Marriage Records.

[18] Rogers, N. K., 386-387.

[19] Erath, Clara Ellison, Descendants of John and Robert Ellison, Fairfield County, South Carolina, (Houston, Texas, 1972).

[20] Holcomb, Brent, Marriage and Death Notices from the Charleston Observer 1827-1845. (Greenville, S.C.: A Press, 1980) http://www.ancestry.com.

[21]Rogers, N. K., 396-397.

[22] Hartz, Fred R. and Emilie K., Genealogical Abstracts from the Georgia Journal, Vol 3. 1824-1828 (Vidalia, Ga. : Gwendolyn Press, 1994) 356.

[23] Sherwood, Adiel, A Gazetteer of Georgia, (P. Force, Washington City, 1837), 310-311.

[24] GA Death Index, http://www.ancestry.com.

[25] Barfield, Louise Calhoun, History of Harris Co., GA, (Cherith Creek Designs, 1963) 380.

[26] Rivest Marriage Index, FHL film #0933161.

[27] Worsley, 559.

[28] Telfair, Nancy, A History of Columbus, Georgia : 1828-1928,(Columbus, Ga.: Historical Pub. Co., ca 1929), 531.

[29] Worsley, 150.

[30] GA Death Index, http://www.ancestry.com.

[31] Phelps, Oliver Seymour and Servin, Andrew T., The Phelps Family of America and their English Ancestors, (Pittsfield, Mass., Eagle Publishing Company, 1899) 825.

[32] Talcott and Ricker, Vol. II, Meigs Family, 816-817.

[33] Records of Arlington National Cemetery, http://www.ancestry.com.

[34] Washington, DC Marriage Records.

[35] Newton Co., GA Marriage Records.

36 Chattahoochee Co., GA Marriage Records.

37 Holcomb, Brent H., Marriage Notices from The Southern Christian Advocate, 1867-1878, http://www.ancestry.com.

[38] Ibid.

[39] Hancock Co., GA Marriage Records.

[40] Holcomb, Marriage Notices from The Southern Christian Advocate, 1867-1878.

[41] Telfair, 501.

[42] Rhode Island Birth Index (http://www.ancestry.com)

[43] Fothergill, Augusta B., Peter Jones and Richard Jones Genealogies,(Richmond, VA, Old Dominion Press, Inc., 1924) 64.

[44] Worsley, 451.

[45] Oglethorpe Co., GA Marriage Licenses.

[46] DAR Records Page: Vol 99; #98109, Mrs. Lucy Vaughan Stockard White; Page: Vol. 34, #33607, Mrs. Thomas Erskine Young White.

[47] Pomeroy, Albert A., History and Genealogy of the Pomeroy Family, Vol 2, (Privately Published) 388.

[48] Biographical Directory of the United States Congress, http://bioguide.congress.gov/biosearch/biosearch.asp

[49] Albany Sunday Herald March 26 1961 or April 9 1961-Doughtery, Baker Civil War Companies Listed.

[50] Personal communication, Sarah Sharpless, Pine Mt. GA; performs a one-name sturdy of Kimbroughs of the Southeastern U.S.

[51] Telfair, 459.

[52] Pease, Rev. David; Descendants of John Pease, (Samuel Bowles & Co., 1869).

[53] Boddie, J. Bennett and Mrs. John Bennett, Historical Southern Families, Vol. XIX, Pitts of Georgia and Alabama, (1975, Reprint. Clearfield Co., Inc., Baltimore, MD. 1995) 167.

[54] Ware, Louise, Dictionary of American Biography (New York: Charles Scribner's Sons, 1958) 23: 520-521.

[55] Campbell, Jesse H., Georgia Baptists, (Macon, Ga., J.W. Burke & Co., 1874) 420.

[56] Hoxie, Leslie Ray, The Hoxie Family-Three Centuries in America, Ukiah, OR, 1950.

[57] The Columbus Enquirer.

[58] Ancestry.com. U.S. Army Historical Register, 1789-1903, Vol. 2 [database online]. Orem, UT: Ancestry.com, 1997. Original data: Heitman, Francis B. Historical Register and Dictionary of the United States Army, 1789-1903, Volume 2, Washington, D.C.: U.S. Government Printing Office, 1903.

[59] Barfield, 470.

[60] Harden, William, A History of Savannah and South Georgia, (Chicago. Lewis Pub. Co. 1913), Vol 2:918.

[61] Muscogee Co., GA Marriage Bond.

[62] Stiles, Henry R., History of Ancient Windsor CT, Vol. II (New Hampshire Publishing Co. Somersworth, 1976) 773.

[63] Newton, Rev. Ephraim H., The History of the Town of Marlborough, Wyndham County Vermont, (VT Historical Soc. 1930) 209-212.

[64] Barfield, 472.

[65] Rev War Pension r 4822 Appl. Dtd 11/18/1845 of John Germany Heard age 81 on 11/12th last from Walton Co. GA.

[66] Hardy, Stella Pickett, Colonial Families of the Southern States of America, (Baltimore, MD: Southern Book Co., 1958)160.

[67] Bardwell, Robert, Descendants' American Ancestry Association, (Bardwell/Boardwell Descendants, self published).

[68] Harris Co., GA Marriage Records.

[69] Biographical Souvenir of the States of Georgia and Florida, (Chicago, IL: F.A. Battey & Company, 1889) 495.

[70] Manuscripts Department Library of the University of North Carolina at Chapel Hill: Southern Historical Collection, #532 Murdock and Wright Family Papers.

[71] Rocker, Willard R., Marriages and Obituaries from the Macon Messenger 1818-1865, (Easley, S.C.: Southern Historical Press, 1988) 479.

[72] Johnson, Forrest C., A History of LaGrange, GA 1828-1900, (Family Tree, LaGrange, GA, 1987).

[73] Worsley, 66.

[74] Worsley, 134.

[75] Muscogee Co. Genealogical Society, Muscogiana, Vol. 1, No. 1.

[76] Walker, Annie Kendrick, Old Shorter houses and gardens, (New York. T.A. Wright. 1911)53-55.

[77] Wilson, Nancy www.kudzufamilies.org, McDougald & Dixon Families and private correspondence.

[78] ibid.

[79] ibid

[80] ibid

[81] Griggs, Walter S., Genealogy of the Griggs family,(Pompton Lakes, N.J.: Biblio. Co., 1926) 103.

[82] Kelsey, Floyd & Parsons, Marriage & Death Notices from the South Western Baptist Newspaper, (Heritage Books 1995),105.

[83] Worsley, 373.

[84] Barfield, 645.

[85] Muscogee Co., GA Marriage Records.

[86] Moore, John Trotwood & Foster, Austin P. , Tennessee, The Volunteer State, 1769-1923, Vol. 4, (Chicago: S. J. Clarke Publishing Co., 1923) 619.

[87] Georgia State Archives, Muscogee Co., GA Pension Records.

[88] Goodspeed's "History of East Tennessee" 1887.

[89] Franklin, Sarah B., Genealogical Record of the Banks Family, 3rd ed., (Heritage Papers, Danielsville, GA 1972) 86.

[90] Buster W. Wright, Abstracts of Marriages Reported in the Columbus (Georgia) Enquirer, 1832-1852.

[91] Franklin, 61.

[92] Hinman, Royal R., Connecticut Puritan Settlers, (Press of Case, Tiffany and Company. Hartford. 1852) 506.

[93] Battle, Herbert Bemerton PhD, The Battle Book, A Genealogy of the Battle Family in America, (The Paragon Press, Montgomery, AL 1930) 209-210.

[94] ibid

[95] Valentine, T. W., The Valentines in America 1644-1874, (Clark and Maynard Publishers, 1874) 157.

[96] Memoirs of Georgia, Vol. 2, (The Southern Historical Society, Atlanta, GA 1895), 607.

[97] Frost, Earl C.and May (Miller), DeJarnette & Allied Families in America (1699-1954); (Pacific Coast Printers, Redwood City, CA, 1954).

[98] Cherry, Rev. F. L., History of Opelika and Her Agricultural Tributary Territory Embracing More Particularly Lee and Russell Counties from the Earliest Settlement to the Present Time, (Opelika, AL, 1996).

[99] Personal communication. Sharon Warnock, El Centro, CA. E-mail: erollins10241@aol.com .

[100] Biographical Souvenir of Georgia and Florida, (F.A. Battey & Co. 1889), 728.

[101] ibid.

[102] Worsley, 113.

[103] Worsley, 336.

[104] Griggs, Walter S., Genealogy of the Griggs Family, (Pompton Lakes, N.J.: Biblio. Co.,1926), 92, 103.

[105] Weygant, Col. Charles H., The Hull Family in America, (The Hull Family Association, 1913) 547.

[106] Rogers, N. K., 328.

[107] Bowen, Daniel, Family of Griffith Bowen, Gentlemen, Welsh Puritan Immigrant, Boston Mass., 1638-9, Especially the Branch of Esquire Sila, (unknown 1893), FHL US/CAN 896877.